T0369550

PASSING

THROUGH

BOOK II

 Passing Through The Mist
into the Future

DAVID L. MARSHALL

Order this book online at www.trafford.com
or email orders@trafford.com

Most Trafford titles are also available at major online book retailers.

© Copyright 2012 David L. Marshall.
All rights reserved. No part of this publication may be reproduced, stored in a
retrieval system, or transmitted, in any form or by any means, electronic, mechanical,
photocopying, recording, or otherwise, without the written prior permission of the author.

Printed in the United States of America.

ISBN: 978-1-4269-8195-1 (sc)
ISBN: 978-1-4669-0398-2 (e)

Library of Congress Control Number: 2011960622

Trafford rev. 01/12/2012

 www.trafford.com

North America & international
toll-free: 1 888 232 4444 (USA & Canada)
phone: 250 383 6864 ♦ fax: 812 355 4082

Acknowledgment

ABOUT THE FIRST OF THE beginning of my pass life, the life that I have live that is not a pretty picture, and the things that I did in my pass life, that was not right but what you about to read about, I hope what you read about my pass life, you take what I had did in my pass, and take the bad things and don't do that for yourself in your life, and the good things that you read about, you take that and build on that and make it better.

You see God is good, he gave you 5 sense to use to think, about things that you are about to do, if you are not sure take it to God and Jesus, God only gave you one life to live, think about it, like teeth he gave you two sets, after the second set and you don't take care of them, the third set you have to pay for them, if you want them, like the life that he gave to you, take care of that one no more after that, you know about.

Life is a gift from God from him to you, that life God gave to you he put you here, you will stay until he get ready to bring you back to him, the body of the feeling will make you sick sometime, and sometime you will feel find, when you are not feeling find you find a doctor, all the doctor can do for you is prolong the feeling, in life that mite you feel good, sometime the doctors cant, but the one I know who can heal all pain of things, all kind of Illness you can have, the one I know is my father God.

Man a doctor, is only an instrument, tool or implement for scientific purposes, I hope you know that if you keep, God and Jesus in your life he will see you through, while you are passing Through.

My Grandmother after she had to raise me, she showed me everything about, what she know about the life of hers, she pass it on to me, how to use and take the same thing that, I was made from the earth to keep me living, she showed me how to tilt the earth, plant a seed that it might grow, raise my own food.

My Grandmother she, showed me how to respect the elders and others around me, also everything about life form, to only kill if for food of what you need, that any other kill is a waste, and a mind the heart is something that you should not waste, if you waste that you can't get it back, don't take something that you can't give it back, that is life, we was poor, had nothing but our self, and God and Jesus.

After my Grandmother pass on, I had to go and stay with my mother, I had always call my Grandmother my mother, she had always call my mother (sister), it took me a while, for me to get used to, call my real mother, mother because I was raise by my Grandmother, and she was the only mother I knew, but my Grandmother she taught me respect.

After I had to stay with my mother, stepfather, (I call him father) and my brothers, ARTHER (jay boy) and ZEBEDEE BRY, my other brother Hubert and my sister Willie Mae, they stayed with their other Grandmother, from their father, my brothers that I live with, we had to go into the woods or go to where daddy work, and bring wood to the house to, keep warm from the cold or for cooking, and the drinking water we had a pump, now if we didn't save some water on the side to, precise the pump we could not get any drinking water, what we had to do was go to the ditch, behind the house through the corn field, into the woods and get some water from the ditch, and come back to the house with the water, to precise the pump for drinking water, or for washing cloths etc. in my pass I had it hard, (kids today, could not make it, in my pass time)

But also with my Grandmother, before she, pass on it was the same thing hard times, that is what it was when I was passing through, but it was the grace of God and Jesus, that I am here now to have the opportunity, to tell you about it.

Now it was time for school, after I got older to go to school, my sister Willie Mae she would walk me to school, she was in school also, after school was out she would wait on me, and I would walk back home with her, then she would walk home to where she live, she didn't live with our mother.

After I got older to go to school by myself, and pass on into other grades to be a big boy, I did things that, I wanted to do and didn't want to do, at that time I thought that, it was cool with me to think that I knew something, (later I was wrong) I start playing hooker from school, (to this day it was on me, to see that it was wrong) I have always had a way

David L. Marshall

with my teachers, I had them believing that I was a good boy, the things that I would do for them, like helping them when they needed help, I could not do anything wrong in their eye site, when I was there, I was a little devil that was why my mother she, would whip me all the time, she said that she was beating the devil out from me.

The way I did while I was playing hooker, some of my school partner and I, would leave home going to school, get into the crowd walking playing talking then we, get to by the wooded area we would duck into, the woods where no one could find us, unless we wanted them to find us, we would see those bootleggers guys, hide their whiskey and leave, we would go and get the whiskey, and take it to where we hide out playing hooker, for later then when school was out, we get back into the crowd and come back home, like everything was ok, I would do my work that my mom and dad, had me to do after that, my partner and I would play ball, after playing ball it was time for bed, for school the next day, if we went that day.

Now one day we was playing hooker, just fooling around we wrote notes about the principal, Mr. Fisher, and put them out on the side of the road, we knew that the principal he had to go, down town to do the school business, and come back to school he would see the notes, but the next day boy he did find those notes, he call me into his office only me, he had all those notes on his desk, he said that he knew that it was me who did that, and he wanted to know, who else was with me putting those notes on the road, I could not tell him that, I was not rat and I took that on myself. Now after I didn't rat on my partners, the principal gave me 5 days suspension from school, and to bring my mother back with me, after the 5 days suspension for putting those signs up on him, now I was so worry that my mom and dad they was, going to find this out about my 5 days suspension, in those days the teacher would give a visit to your folks, and let them know what was going on with you, every day after I would do the same thing that, I use to do while playing hooker, sometime by myself and sometime not.

On the 5th day of my suspension I went on the school yard I, had my rifle with me because I was going hunting after I, saw the principal so one of my teacher said that I, could see the principal but I, had to leave that rifle with him, I did that, after I got to the principal office he ask me where was my mother, I told him that my mother she don't know what happen, that I have grown up and I could take care of my own business, he said have a seat, I did that and he talk to me, he told me something that change my whole life style, about being a man.

He told me that to be a man I, had to do and own up to my responsibility because, everyone that put his pants on don't mean that he was a man that, father on in life I will have responsibility as it be a wife, kids or what every come into my life, it will be your responsibility to bear no one else, now I know that he was right, and he knew that I heard him because the way I was looking, he told me that on Monday morning he, wanted to see me in class, now go on and think about what he had said, I was going to leave out from his office, I look back at him and said thanks, he smile then I left and went back outside, everyone out there look at me and ask what happen, I took my rifle and said that, I will be at school on Monday morning then I, went into the woods hunting squirrel.

David L. Marshall

When Booker T. Washington high school got a football team, I tried out for the team and made it, with in those three years I played football, we only loss 3 games those was from Atmore Alabama, and we only loss those 3 games with a field gold, with in that time I never played hooker again, then I start going with my first wife, Barbara Jean Mallard, I loved her so much I would save my money, to get her a ring to put on her finger I did that, one day my buddy Billy STALLWORTH came to my class room, and told me that Barbara Jean was in the Library, with Johnnie white and he had on the ring that I had brought Barbara Jean on his finger.

That was when I got up, and left out from my class room going to the Library, after I got there I walk over to where they was, then I grab Johnnie white hand and took my ring, off his finger that was when the fight was on it was bad, it was so bad until they had to close down the school, that day I shut it down because, I was mad as hell.

Now after that my mother I do believe, that she had found out that I, was going with a white woman the Avon lady, she knew that I would never own up to it, and in that years of time I, didn't want those white peoples Missing with my family, in Alabama so I got in touch with my real father in Chicago, Ill. And left Brewton, Alabama before Gradation and, went to Chicago in 1959.

After I got to Chicago, I meet my others Brother and my Sister on my father side, and sometime later I left Chicago, and went back to Brewton, Alabama, then I started working with a swimming pool Company, and then that was when Barbara Jean and I got marry, after we had finish with those two pools, the Company had one more down in Florida to build, they wanted me to go with them, I had to talk to my wife about that, I did but Barbara Jean she didn't want me to go, she wanted to go to Chicago.

So I took my wife, she and I went back to Chicago that was when Barbara contacts her father; his name was David STALLWORTH he lives in Maywood Ill. He came and got Barbara and I, and took us to Maywood Ill. That was when I meet Barbara other sisters and brothers.

We was in Maywood about 2 weeks, I found myself a job working where Barbara Jean father work, there was when I meet Barbara two Aunts and a uncle, they work there also, now I was working to save money, to get apartment for my wife and myself, just in case we start a family I loved my wife, and I had all the respect for her until, one night she and I was in bed, and her father knock on the door for her, to come down stair he need to talk to her, she went in a little while she came back and, start packing a bag I didn't say anything but look, she didn't say anything but take the bags and left out the room, later on I found out that, her father brother live in Peoria Ill. His wife was going to have a baby, and needed Barbara Jean to go and help, until the baby come, no one ask me was it ok like I, didn't have anything to say or it was not my business, come on I am her husband, that was when I said forget it, under someone else roof what can you say, but find and get your own roof, then you can control that.

That morning I went to work I didn't say anything to Barbara father, if I did I would have lost my job that I need, but all that day I was thinking, that what she had did not respecting me as her husband, that she left now it was my time to move on, that Saturday her father wife ask me, did anyone talk to me about Barbara Jean going to Peoria, I said no but now it is over with Barbara and I, Louise said that her and her father was wrong about that, I said don't worry when she get back I will be going.

Later on I saw two peoples sitting on their porch talking a man and a woman, I was going to take a bus going back to Chicago, with my bags in my hand they stop me, they live across the alley from Barbara father house, I talk to them they gave me a room because, it was close to my job, then going back to Chicago, they was good people names Mattie and Otis, that night I meet a woman name Mary a friend of Mattie and Otis, that showed me that, because Barbara Jean did what she did, one woman don't stop anything there are, more women out there for me.

My first kiss from Mary, it took my mind off Barbara Jean, and with Mary and that kiss and that smile, took and move inside of my heart even that she was marry, but at that time it was ok she and I, still had fun until after 4 month, she decided to go and try getting back together, with her husband he left her and move to Maryland, they had one son name Dewayne, that needed his father as every son do, that was ok but it hurt me very bad, after she left but life have to go on.

After that Barbara Jean and I, had one son David Jr. Barbara and I tried to overcome, what she had did to me, she and I was in and out of love together, then our second son John Marshall was born, I tried all that I could to be a husband to her, but it seem that it was not going to work, if it was not her it was me looking or with someone else, one of us was not right, because the first I wanted only her but, she push herself out from my heart, into the world of other women with love and sex, now I was after that like a drug addict, but I was a sex addict I wanted them all that I could get.

Now in my pass life time I had 6 wife at that time and divorces, not talking about those women that I shack up with, and been into and out of their or my bed having sex, until sometime in my life I saw the light, the light that brought me out from the darkens, into the light that the things that I am doing now was not right, the sky was blacken so dark with no light in site, until I ask to see my father that I came from not, the daddy that have taken care of me that I can see, I saw the darken parted, then a star appear become visible before me, it was so bright and beautiful it brought tears from my eyes, tears and blood change my life, from my pass into my future.

Now after I saw the star, I still didn't lay down and die because life still have to go on but, live it in another way for the good ways, with those 5 senses that God gave to you to use, but use them wisely and live your own life, be yourself and help other that need help, if you can while doing that put, God and Jesus first.

After I was trying to go and walk on the path, that my father had put me on for myself, going to work trying to help someone that needed it, and going home minding my own business, having fun and respecting what I was doing, until one night my play sister God bless her, she and I was and still close her name is Bobby Jean, she call me on the phone late on a Saturday morning to see if, I was sleep, I told her not what was up, she and I was talking she brought up about her cousin.

That she was looking for herself a good man, (I didn't say anything) and that she live in Vegas, I ask where was she at now in Chicago, Bobby said no that she was still in Vegas.

That was when I said to Bobby, if she had a good man what and how would she treat him, that was when her cousin she spoke up, we was on the phone with a 3 way call, and said that she know how to treat a good man, we all went on and on talking I started liking what, she was saying later on we all hung up, I was hook.

After that night she and I would call or one way or the other, we would hear from each other every day, my heart was full of love, now I work from 11: am to 7: pm 5 days a week sometime more, every night I would write a letter to her, or sometime she would call me at work, and in the morning after I get off work I would call her, before she went to work just to say good morning.

Later on I sent a picture of mind to her, and after that she sent a picture of her to me, that was the first time she and I saw what we look like, I was so proud of her, I showed her picture to everyone I saw, I was so proud of talking to peoples about her, and how find she was, later on she and I was talking, I said that if I sent a ticket to her would she come, to Chicago and spend a couples with me, she said yes she would, that was what I did after she got the money from me, she came for a couples of days with me, I was a happy man with those few days, then she had to go back to Vegas, I was still happy after.

After two or three visit she and I got marry, when I got marry to my 7th wife, I thought that I had the world around me, I had it all, because at one time I had said that I would never, get marry again, that I had did it 6th times it didn't work for me, some always say don't say never, now I have did it 7th times it might be lucky to me, until I left Chicago going to Vegas I was a proud man.

After I got to Vegas and got off the plane, my 7th wife she was there to greet me, with her cousin to pick me up to take me to where, she and I was going to live, before we got there she showed me a place, on Martin Luther King Blvd. And Lake Mead, that she don't never want to see me in there, I didn't ask why because I was looking to where, I was at that one day I have to learn my way around Vegas.

After about a week in Vegas, I was looking for myself a job o yes a job, the first one that I found, it was not me but a man have to do something, that he don't want to do in order to make it, until he get something that he want or need, I work on that stinking job until, I made the money to get my Sheriff card to work on a good job, after that I work in security at the casinos etc.

Later on with my 7th wife, I saw something about her that I didn't like, and that I was not Satisfy with, but now that I was a long ways from home, I now have to be careful and find my way around, that now I am here, one Sunday morning one of my 7th wife girlfriend, she pick me up I went to Church with her, I got up in Church and gave my testimony, that I was here from Chicago, because I am here along but not along that I have, God and Jesus with me, I am in between both of them, they are holding my hand.

After I was trying to find my way around Vegas, I found that I had made a big Mistake again, in my life every time and that was a very little time, she and I was out going to a store, or at one of her sister house, it didn't matter where she and I was at she, have been here in Vegas a long time, she know peoples and when I was in the present, while she saw one of them and was talking, she would never say that this is her husband David Marshall, she would not induce me to her friends, no matter as it be a woman or man, I start thinking that there was something wrong with me.

Was she a shame, I said to myself that if Heaven and hell was here on earth that, I am now in hell the way this woman think that, she are trying to treat me no way.

And if that she think that she can treat me anyway she want to treat me, she was Mistake and she don't understand about her opinion of that, she was making one of her biggest Mistake, that she don't know what she had on her hand, someone to be good to her and treat her like a lady, if that was what she wanted in her life, as what she had ask for before she and I got marry, Mistreat me I don't think so.

Within the time that my 7th wife and I got marry, I had to move out from her three times, she had a pet pee about if she could not have her own way, she would say get out, get out of her house, I would move out and get myself apartment, after she get her sense back she want me back, later on there I was going back with her until, about three weeks everything was going good, she start doing the same thing again before, I leave again some others would say to me, why don't you give her another chance, she need you just give her one more chance, and if she do the same thing again, don't go back to her, I said ok if she do the same thing again, don't say anything to me, if you do we will end our friendship, there I go right back later on she do the same thing, I move out again and made up in my own mind, that was enough.

Now I made up my mind that every road, have to end someday or somewhere this was the day, and time to take another road to go on, I took it to pass through for my life, at that time I meet and found my cousin Joyce and her husband Robert Thomas, he had went with me and found myself apartment, at Loma Vista 1200 west Cheyenne, rent was $650.00 a month for one bed room, I was a happy man on that second flood.

After I was in my apartment, I was still working in Security at Rhodes Ranch, (the ranch beside the road) my niece from Chicago, my cousin and her husband, my niece man friend they would come by and sit and talk to me, having dinner with another neighbor lady friend of mind name Coco, you see I am a friendly guy love peoples, that love them self, one Super bowl Sunday, that Friday a lady and a guy that live under me, where I live, I saw her and invited both of them to come up, to my apartment that I was cooking dinner, and with my family and friends was watching the game, they was welcome to come up, she said ok that she would let him know, that was find.

That night before I went to work, there was a knock on my door I went and answer it was him, the guy down stair the words he said to me, I was stun he thought that I wanted his woman, the way he decline my invitation to have some fun, he left I close my door back it was almost time, for me to go work after I got to work I was telling, a fellow worker about the attitude of the guy under me, where I live, they said Captain you can't be nice and friendly to some peoples, I said now how don't I know it.

After I had my small stroke and was doing find my, Chief of security and the others security, they set me up, they had to use a black woman other then, a white woman because she tried, that didn't work I was use to white women, I lost my job about a lie that black woman told about me, that was right at Christmas time the next June I was to be 62 years old, the Chief he always thought that I wanted his job, no way.

Now it was almost the time for me to renew my new lease, for my apartment it was so good that I don't Misuse my money, anymore I had money to keep me until I found another job, so I started drawing my un employment until it was over with, I also had start writing on my first book passing through number one, I also went and got my Social security started, I was 62 then, then it was time for my new lease to be sign, my cousin Joyce she had told me before, to go over to Frank Jr. place that he have apartments for 55 years older, and get an apartment and save some of that rent money.

Then she said that I wanted to stay young for them women, I said no, it was not like that, she said ok then think about what she had said, I said ok.

After I had went and sign my new lease and went back to my apartment, and had taken off my shoes, and sit down to put something into my computer, look like something

came into my mind and told me, get up, put on my shoes
and go back to the office, and let them tear up that lease,
and go and do what your cousin Joyce told you, what to
do, I did that, I went back to the office of Loma Vista
apartment, you see I was not satisfy of what, they wanted
me (us,) to pay now for rent, they went up from us to pay
for rent $650.00 to $700.00 a month, because now we had
to pay for garbage, sewers and water, so I talk to Janice the
property manager, after talking to her she tear up the lease,
and said David you are one of our best tenant here, and that
she didn't want to lose me, I said thanks Janice but this is
too much but, I will come and see her time to time, she hug
me and said thinks that she would love that, then I left to
take care of my business.

That was when I went to Louise Shell Senior apartment, at
2101 N. Martin Luther King Blvd. And got and fill out an
appreciation and did all the things necessary, to be done to
get my apartment that was March the 30th 2004, I got my
apartment key to move in April 01-2004, my lady friend
Coco gave me a hand, Janice Loma Vista manager hug me
to say David, sorry you are leaving but take care of yourself,
I said that I will.

After I got my key, I meet Larissa she was the manager of
Louise Shell Apartment, and I got my things and myself
straighten out, for later on to find out that Larissa she, was
my daughter, I would sit and hear and see the peoples that
live here, and take it all in strived something I found, was
some was good and some was not to good, but sometime a
still tongue will hold the peace sit and listen.

Now I would help cook breakfast in the morning time, in the lobby when they wanted to have an outing with the tenant, to come together, then I would cook out on the grill use my own money, to feed someone that I thought would appreciate it, because I made a promise to my God and Jesus, to try and help those that needed me.

Then I meet this lady name Mary that move in here, there was something about Mary that I like, what I saw was sweetness, kindness and I thought that she would be fun to be with, that is why I started going with her, after Mary and I start being with each other, the other women that live in here, they didn't like that, because they could not get with me in bed, they gave Mary and I a big problem, telling lies about me to her about what they didn't know about, me going to bed with another woman, because I didn't go to bed with one woman, she put human feces on my porch.

And one night Mary she was at my apartment with me, the next day she call me to ask me, did I have a woman living with me, lies things like that, until Mary found out she had cancer, and she told me about it I told her, with the love that I have for her, that she and I can beat that, I did any and everything that I could for her, until she went to the hospital, for her last time she didn't want me to see her, she shut me out of her life, from coming to the hospital to see her.

The last time I saw Mary was, when her daughter brought her by to see me, before she was going back to her hometown, I ask her daughter to keep in touch with me, so I could see how Mary was doing. Her daughter said to me that she would do that, Mary had a smile on her face then, now when I found out that Mary had pass on, I was so sadden, I found out from her daughter, when the funeral was then I sent the poetry she loved, to her daughter to read at the funeral for Mary, passing through.

After Mary had pass on I didn't mess around with another woman that, live in the complex, but they still gave me hell trying to get in bed with me, if I did that they would shut me down, if I talk to another woman, they would say stay out of her man face, I can't have that because I treat them all the same, without going to bed with them.

After I had finish book number one of passing through, I ran for the president of the tenant council, and won I could not get a full slate to work with me, all I had to work with me was three trustee, no one else wanted to be bother with me, but we did the best job of any, we had a cook out three times a month to raise money, to put up two canopy to have some shade over, the peoples head while they was sitting out in the sitting area.

It get hot here in Vegas, the more I tried to do for the tenant, the more some they didn't appreciate it or me, even after I taken my own money to help or make them happy, the thing about it, I knew the ones that tried to put a fork in me, until I was done cook they falsify my accountability for my goodness, but to God and Jesus I gave my word.

We was without a manager at the complex for a while, I was so tried, of the tenants thinking that I was the manger also, they would come to me about things, that I could not do anything about it, I sent out a letter to the whole board director, that was over the complex now, they had two

David L. Marshall

others that was low on the totem-poll, I would go to them with the problem they would reply to me, they was not a manger, we needed someone here to answer the question that we had.

After about a week I guess, I saw this find lady walking around with one of the, one on the low totem—poll, walking around with that find lady for 4 days, now I was the president of the tenant council, look like one of them would have said David Marshall, this is your new manger inter duce me to her, as the manger and to me to her as the president of the tenant council, that would have been the right thing to do, they was so dumb.

Now I had to find out for myself, how, let me explain about the coordinate that work at the complex, we have a monthly calendar they send out for the tenant, about the things that is going on in the complex, we had one lady that was going on vacation, we was having a dinner for her before she left, for that day I ask the coordinate to put on that date, we are coming together, she put on coming out, she thought she was smart or she was so dumb, she don't know the meaning of coming out.

You see I have been out every sense I was 11 years old, on that day it was when I meet the new manager, I had to go into her office to induce myself to her, now after meeting the new manager, I got a messenger from the above, I resign from the tenant council for my own reason.

Now in my heart and mind I to myself, she was going to need some protection, I knew what she was in for, this was for me not for her, I was just like a tree planted by the water, the felling with in my heart kept on growing and growing, now the way I have been treated in my pass life, and the way I have heard and seen how others men and women been treated, I was going to close to the edge of a cliff, I can fall, I can't let that happen to me again, and for another reason is that the way, I saw how those women did to Mary, when she was living and she and I was together, keep on reading into my book passing through, one and two I can't take another woman through that, with me, it would not be right I had a un rightness life, in my pass this is my testimony of my life.

That Chapter 1

Passing Through Book-2
By
David L. Marshall
10-10-05

NOW MARY AND I WERE going through something that we should not have to go through, peoples should mind their own business, and let others alone.

Now I would sit and talk to those old ladies on the outside, now Mary she live in building two, she can walk in the front of her floor, and see everything that I was doing, she knew that I was not doing anything, about going to bed with one of those women's, all I was trying to do was be a friend to someone.

But the harder I tried to do that and try to please Mary to, that was a job I think it was Miss Queen, she said that to do a job for God and Jesus, it was hard to do all you have to do is trust in them, and they will see you through.

Now this is the reason I sit out with those old peoples, I need their wisdom to put with mind, because all we are doing are Passing Through this land.

Sometime Mary and I, we was so loving laughing and talking with each other, I was happy but when I had to listen to her she said, I was trying to write a book and be outside, to air out my mind that was all I was looking for, a break.

There was another woman living here the one who, my daughter Larissa had said sit down boy, down boy to me before, her name is Gladies, now I can deal with anything or someone, because I have God and Jesus in my life, now Gladies she was so sure that she was going to take me to bed, and I was determinate that it want happen, I would say around her with others on the outside, that I don't go to bed with anything or person, I cant.

Now there was not only Gladies who was flirting with me," I saw it," some would sit beside me and rub my arm, I would always say don't do that, your mate might see that and he and I would be at each other throat, she said that he flirt, I said that don't make me do it.

Now when I see Mary, I will hear this again but they will put their own words to it, when they get around Mary, to see what she are going to do, but I get hell, from Mary because she don't hang out.

Now, my problems with trying to just be a friend to these women's, just begin there was another woman living here, I want call no name she came to my apartment one night, we was talking she did all she could do, to get me in bed with her, she went as far to say to me," what if she get naked, and get in my bed," I told her if anything or anyone get into my bed naked, I have the right to roll over on whatever in my bed, she said that I was a hard man, she didn't have a clue why I didn't go to bed with her, you see in all womanize mind man was a dog, some friends of mind had already told me, about that woman now who are the dog.

After she could not get me in bed with her, I had a problems with my computer," I was telling her about it," she said that she could fix that," I turn the computer on," she said not now later that she would call me tomorrow, and that she would come to my apartment and fix that problem," I said OK," on her way to leave my apartment, she look down at me and said," could she feel it," I said no I would talk to her tomorrow, as she leaving she said David Marshall you are a hard man.

Now Mary she had to go to work, after Rose left my apartment Mary she call me and said what are you doing, I said that Rose from building two she just left, she was seen could she fix my computer, so I could keep on writing in my book," what up," Mary said nothing that it was her Friday, and what was I going to do in the morning after she get off work, I said nothing that I belong to her, she said that she bet see me in the morning," I said OK love her," she said that she love me also, we hung up I tried to fix my computer but I didn't know how.

Later on I went on the outside to see who was out there, there was Grace, Miss Blackwell, Queen, Mr. and Miss Brown, Gladies and Rose my neighbor, we all was talking and having fun, Mrs. Brown said David are you ready to cook next week," I said yes I am ready," Mr. Brown said David is like Freddie, he is always ready, I said as long as peoples are having fun I am ready for that.

Then Mary that live on the first floor on building two, who is one of those who like to rub on me," I said here come Mary," then Miss Queen said David you better watch yourself," I said why I am not Missing with anybody," Queen said with a soft laugh," that I know what she was talking about.

That was when Gladies said, that while I was cooking she was going to keep me Company, she laid her head on my shoulder and said, can she watch me cook, Queen she look at me and said hum, I said OK that she could keep me Company, while I cook.

Then my girlfriend Joe she came out side, and spoke to everybody, then she said to me that she started to call me," I said why didn't she," she said that I would not have been home, that I was on the outside, I ask what did she want, she said that she only wanted to talk," Gladies she was all over me," I did her the same as I do Mary on the first floor," she try to rub and sit on my lap, I always move over.

Now Joe, she love Miss Queen she would always say, when she didn't see her, where is Queen have anybody seen her and Miss Blackwell, someone would say she was coming out, or they didn't see her one way or the other.

Joe she was combing Queen-hair, "Joe she said, here come Mary," Gladies said so they was not married, I said," no matter I was going to respect her, Mary.

It was now getting kind of late, Queen said that she was going to go home, and go to bed she was slow getting up, I said to her take her time, then everybody else started to leave, Miss Blackwell she live in the same building, with Miss Queen they are neighbor, I would stand and watch them, until they got into their building, then I would leave if Rose was out there, she and I would leave together, we live in the same building she is my neighbor.

That morning Mary she had got off work, she was at home she call me and said, that she was coming to my apartment, I said OK, then she said be at the door to let her in, I said that I would be there to open the door.

When she came in she look at me," and she said good morning," I put my arms around her and I kiss her, and I said good morning she was in smile and said hum, I ask what was that for," she said with that smile," that she don't know, I said that I know.

We got into my apartment, Mary said to me," turn that computer off," that she was going to be the only Company that I need, I turn the computer off, Mary she was on the couch, I then sit by her and kiss her, then I said what was on her mind, she said you don't know, Now I am no fool I knew what she wanted, and I gave it to her all of it.

Now after making love," I call it fighting," Mary she still had a smile on her face, I look over to her and said," that she should smile like this all the time," she said why," I said because she has a dam good man, she said yes, with all the others ladies, I ask why did she say that?" she said all those old ladies, I said hold it she have to get old one day, then I said those old ladies are friends of mind, they don't get this that I just gave her! She got up and got dress and she look at me, kiss me and said, talk to you later on then she left, I went back to working on my book one.

At the time we had to do the cook out, everybody who came into the complex, the barbecue smoke smell so good, the music was sounding so good and Gladies she was putting on a floor show.

 peoples coming and going out, they was telling me how good it was smelling outside, and what time the food was going to be ready, I would tell them," and some would slow down, to see Gladies dancing," they would say," nice floor show," I would smile and say someone have to keep me Company.

Sometime I had to go across the street, going to the lobby to check and see if the others, that was cooking food," was OK also," now I didn't have to do all the cooking, there was Toni, Mary Helen, Mr. and Miss Lee, he was sitting in the lobby, after I got in the lobby, Mr. Lee he said," David man you got a floor show, on the outside with you," I laugh and said yes," now Miss Lee I saw she was having a ball, then I ask Mr. Lee how was he doing, he said that he was doing OK, then I went to the kitchen to check and say hi, and see was everything's was all right, the lades said they was OK in the kitchen, they said because Gladies was dancing for me, they was looking, one ask what kind of dance was that was," I laugh and said," that I didn't know it look like a peacock, sworn that I don't know, then I went back to my cooking and enjoy my floor show.

After I had cooking all the meat, and took it into the lobby, and the rest of the food was ready to be serve, after cooking

I didn't want anything to eat, Toni, Kopoe, Miss Lee, Miss Blackwell and Miss Brown, and some of the others tenant like Mary Ann, they serve the food.

That was when I got to know Larrissa husband, Greg, he was at the cook out that day, I don't have to say about Mr. Stewart, he was going to be there and Larrissa kids was there.

While everybody was getting there food, I sit in the lobby and watch them having fun, there was another man that was sitting on a stool, to me it seem that he was drunk, Lorries saw him with his head down, she ask him," she call his name Mr. Childless," was he all right, he look at Larrissa and said he was OK, Lorries look at me as to say what did I think, I said that he was drunk.

Later Mr. Brown he came up to me, and said David that was some good barbecue, and that sauce man it was so good.

Then Mr. Brown said David he saw that I was proud, that I was sitting on my throne patting my own back, I said as long as you all enjoyed the food, was enough of pat on my back, yes I was so proud.

After the cook out was over, I went home I was beat then I call Mary, she ask me how was the cook out, I ask why didn't she come, Mary said that she didn't want to be around some of those peoples, because they don't like me and she don't want to be around them, I said that I don't care about what peoples think about me, it was about what I think about them, because they have a problem not me, Mary said that after work in the morning, she was coming by my house.

Now in my house I sit and think and talk to my God and Jesus, now after I had went to my hometown that fourth of July, my daughter Jackie and I was on bad turn, we was not talking and when I see, other peoples with their family members, how happy they are I was unhappy," why," because I guess that I didn't have mind with me, or with them.

Now my sons David Jr. and Johnnie Marshall, I was with them most of the time, we knew something's about us, but Jackie when she was a baby, her mother took Jackie away from me and they went back to Brewton, Alabama, and I was not there to hear her say daddy, make her first step, hold her when she cried and say that it was going to be all right, I Missed that I guess that was why she treat me as she do.

Now my sons, when John used to drink my beer, when I would put it down, and I would catch him and open one for him to drink, now David Jr., he was more like me, sometimes quite, whenever there was something on his mind he was easy going. I Miss now my kids grown up, I had to be on the move in order, to have something for the mothers to help raised them, I was trying to make money, but money was not only thing to raise a family, you have to give love also, but I did what I could for my kids, and I still love them living or dead, after all I am there father they are not mind.

Now Kopoe she had already ask me not to pour water, on the fire to let it burn out in the morning I would, take the girl back to the storage room for the next time," now yes I talk to God and Jesus," there is where I get my answer from, wisdom and my trust.

That morning I got up, got dress and went and took Kopoe girl back to where it was, then I saw her, I said that I had taken her girl back, she said OK my brother then she saw Glen, Kopoe said watch this, she ask Glen how was the cake, Glen said," woman you know you are not right," Glen told Kopoe that he gave her a half dozen of brown eggs, and a pound of pure butter came from the base, and that Kopoe didn't use what he had gave her.

Now they are neighbor, and when we know each other neighbor or not, we talk shit joke at each other, but you better be able to take what you put out, don't get mad now because who care, if you are going to get mad when someone say something back, after you had said what you said, stay out of others conversation.

After I had my laugh for the morning, I saw Mary coming home from work, Kopoe and Glen said good morning to Mary, she said good morning to them, then she look at me with that smile, she said hi David," I said why was I the last to be spoke to," she said later David," Mary went to her apartment.

Now this was on a Saturday morning, Mary she came to my apartment I knew what she wanted, it had been three day that she haven had what she needed, so we lock up with each other and made each other happy, Mary she got dress and I did to, then we left out from my apartment and went on the outside, Mary said that she was going to go and get her some sleep, I said OK that I would call her later, she said see you later.

After the office open Larissa went to work, she ask me did anything I had to do now, I said no what was up, she said that," Miss Grand her boss wanted her to go and pick up a TV, and bring it on eleven street and will I go with her," I said yes when? She said in about an hour, I said OK.

When it was time to go and get the TV, Larissa and I went and got the TV and took it on eleven street, I took it in side," man I saw this lady I smile and spoke to her," this guy he took the TV from me and took it where ever, I was looking at that lady on the sly, when Larissa and I left to leave, I said who was that lady that she was talking to, she said that was her boss Miss Grand and no, that was the first time I had seen Miss Grand.

When we came back to our complex, Larissa she went into the lobby, I went back to where I park my truck, by where I live and went into my apartment, I check on my massages on my machine, one was from a friend of mind Kevin Banks, he is an ex-boxer from the Olympic, he wanted me to call him.

So I call him, he said that he was off on Monday, and he wanted to come by and talk about, old times and catch up on others things, would I be at home. I said that I would be home what time, he said about ten am, I said OK see you then, I, gave Kevin my address how to get here, at me apartment.

After a little while, my friend Coco called she and I was talking about what was in her life, and I was talking about what was in my life also, we talked because some talk help one of us keep up with each other.

That night we all was sitting in the sitting area, someone start talking about how some Grandkids, how good they were with their Grandparent, how they take time for them, and come and see them.

That was when my memory open up," I said that it was a shame," how your kids and some Grandkids, treat their elders, and some have all the respect for their elders, those I can take off my hat to them, God bless those and the others also.

Because how minds treat me, like I don't excise they will cut me out, or cut me away until they need or want something, on happy new year no call, matter fact no holiday call no cards, no birthday call or cards, the only way I will see minds is, when I go to see them, sometimes I don't even see them then, minds don't have time for me they want even call me, they don't have time for me, so I could have kept my money that I spend, going to see them because sometime I don't even see minds then, what is the use.

Then I said that was OK, every day in your or my life is a learning process, I am glad that God and Jesus are with me, I have with them all I need.

Then Miss Blackwell said yes, that it was wrong how some kids treat their parent, I said that Miss Blackwell she was right, kids today don't have no sympathy or respect for others.

That Monday Kevin he came to visit me, we sit talk and had some food to eat, we was talking about when we was working at Lucky, and they was working on the outside with another security company, and I was working for world wide security, I let Kevin read what I had did in my book, when he had got ready to leave he was going to the Gym, he train kids to box, I said that I would take Kevin to the Gym, we was on our way out from my complex, I saw Kopoe and Killer, another ex-boxer, they was standing on the outside by Kopoe's porch talking, I wave then I ask Kevin, have he ever seen that guy standing there by the porch," he look and said no," I said that he use to box, they call him killer, I took Kevin to the Gym and I came back home.

Now in the world of make believe, peoples always sit and talk about, what they have did in the pass life," just talk" they are trying to make themselves look good, in another eyes, me I am writing about mind, what are you doing just talking.

Just before Larissa arm started bothering her, it was just before we had a reduce in rent, first I was paying $420.00 a month, the managers had to refund some money back to the tenants, Larissa she had a envelop in her hand," she gave it to me," now I didn't think about it we all in the lobby was talking, I said to myself it was from the rebate rent, it was reduce to $395.00 a month, look like something came to me and said open that letter," so I did," when I read it I said to myself," what is this," then I hand it to Larissa and said read this, she read it and said dad, she look like she want you to take care of her," hum," I left and went back to my apartment.

Later on I was going to call Mary, and ask her what have I did to her, for her not to trust me I said no, I want call her now she have to go to work, that I would call her in the morning after she get off work.

That evening about six o clock, we all was sitting outside talking, Mary that live on the first floor in building two, and Gladies they was a pest, they don't know how to quit trying to get in bed with me, Miss Queen she said again," David you better watch yourself," I said you are right Miss Queen," but they don't have anything coming.

Because when something bothering me, and I get home I talk to my God and Jesus about it, sometime we have a go around talking about it, but you know who win, sometime it bring tears from my eyes, because God and Jesus is good and want lead you astray, and I have to follow that, Gladies said what was that?" I said that she don't want to know.

Now Gladies, she just keep on and on about what was that, I was talking about that I was single, until I got restful that was when I said," that I could not go to bed with her, because I didn't want to go through the gates of hell," now she wanted to know, where was the gates of hell? I told her it was between her legs, now she didn't like that but I didn't care.

Now the other side of God creation came out, it don't care about what she want from me, it was what I wanted, that was to leave me along, I found out that Gladies was a she devil.

Now every time I would see my lady Mary, she knew everything that went on outside, I said to myself," how in the hell," Mary know what going on out there, like she was out there! Until one day my neighbor Rose and I was in the sitting area talking, about how Mary know everything I do out here, Rose said that she had tried to tell me before, that

Mary can see from the second floor, over the lobby in to the sitting area.

Then she said take a look and tell her what I saw, I look up over the lobby on the second floor, and I said you are right Rose, she can see everything going on, that is why I keep it clean out here, Rose said you better then she laugh.

You know it is hard to write about your," mind pass life," all of that is like something's was o OK, and the rest is trash or something, that in my mind I put in storage, to see if I can do better in the future, it is hard to untangle it in order to fix it, I will do my best.

That is why I am on my computer, trying to get my pass almost like I had live it, every time I thought that I had it right it was not, I had to delete all of that work and started it over again, you can't only write what was behind you, day back in the day you have live that time, you better tell the truth about what you write, you never know who might read it.

What you write about is what you see or what you know, or think that you know or hear be very careful.

That is when Mary come to my apartment, or call me on the phone I am on the computer, she get mad but I can't help that, writing about my pass relieve me from my conscious, about what I have done while I was growing up, you never grow up in the heart of God and Jesus.

Now Larissa she said that her arm, was not getting any better, and she had to see a doctor to find out what was wrong, I knew that her husband Greg he work knights, but she as my daughter knew that I would be there for her.

Now Miss Grand she sent another lady over as the manager, to where I live, they induce me to her as Glenda, Larissa said that Glenda she also work as manager, at the complex next door, I said o yes then Larissa said dad she was hunger, I said what did she want to eat," she said I don't know! I said OK we will go to the wildfire, then Mr. Stewart the maintain man came to the office, I said hay Mr. Stewart we are going to lunch, you want to join us, he said sure so we all went to lunch, Glenda so as I see her, she is a nice lady.

One day Larissa she had a doctor appointment in Henderson, now her arm was hurting and she could not go to the doctor by herself," because her arm she could not drive," I took her in my truck, she is my daughter life go on we got there, and went to the doctor office," while I was waiting for Larissa," there was a fish tank in the office with a fish in it, I could not take my eyes off that tank.

That fish it had teeth like a person I have never seen that, well there is a lots things you, I haven't seen after Larissa had seen the doctor, and came back to where I was," I ask Larissa what kind of fish is that, she told me but at this moment now I forgot, so we came back from Henderson back to where I live.

When I got to my apartment I check my message Mary had call, I call her back she ask me how was Larissa, I said she was going to be all right, Mary said yes she will after she get away from her problems, I said yes you are right one day she will get away, and she would be OK.

Then Mary she said what are you doing tomorrow?" I said not anything what wrong," she said that she had to pick up a couch that she wanted, I said OK call me when she get off work, she said OK that she love me, I said that I love her to also.

That evening later on I went on the outside to get some air, it was the same as the others times when I see Gladies, I have to tell her the same thing no. Just be friends can't we do that without going to bed together, she said that she can't give David Marshall her pussy, I said look at herself now and hear herself, that is why I don't go to bed with her, and nobody else who can't keep their mouth close, I said that I have to go now and work on my book, I said good night to all and went home, and had a talk with God and Jesus to show me the way.

One day I was going to the mail box to check on my mail, Larissa and I was standing in the lobby talking, how was she doing OK," she was doing OK," we start talking about Mary, how she don't trust me that I can't see how she don't, that was when I said that," I was going to ask Mary to marry me, Larissa said hum, you love Mary don't you, I said yes that I do.

That morning I saw Mary, my mind was all made up to ask Mary to marry me, we was sitting on my couch talking about things at her job, I said well honey that come with the work force, that was when I ask Mary to marry me," she just look at me and look at me, then she said that she had to go home, and fix her some breakfast, I said don't she want go to wildfire and have breakfast, she said that she was going home and that was what she did.

One day another lady that live in here, she was trying to get me in to her apartment, now I am a man and I know that I am a good one to, but I don't talk about it, I try and show you how I am, to make that termination for yourself, this lady she told me one morning that I was afraid of her, the lobby was at mail time, I look at her in front of everyone in the lobby, that she was wrong that I was not afraid of her," I was afraid of myself, and left it along. (I don't want her to die under me.)

She, want to hug and feel, when I put her water up on her water fountain, I don't mess around, you see what I have to go through.

Later one day Larissa she got sick again, she call me about four o clock, that she needed to go to the hospital, I said that I was on my way, when I got to her we went to the hospital in Summerlin, I stayed with her until Greg and Marcia came, she had to call her husband to let him know, where she was, that was the only way I would leave her, when I got back home, everyone who saw me ask about how was Larissa, I said that she will be OK, I could not say anything about her arm, that was for her to say if they saw her.

When Larissa arm was not getting any better she went on medical leave, I told her that if she needed me call me anytime, I will be there, now Glenda she was still the manager in the complex, and still next door also until Linda came here for manager.

Now I saw Mary, she ask me how was Larissa?" I said that she was going to be all right, that she was OK," then I look at Mary and said how was she doing," Mary said she was OK," then she said that, what was wrong with Larissa was stress, that she don't have any help, she was in a tough of war, and the ones on the other end are pulling hard against her, I said yes I know but there was anything, I can do about it," only Larissa can fix that," Mary said that, Larissa is a lucky daughter to have you, I said that I know and it was lucky for me to have her, Mary. All Mary would do was look at me and say hum, talk to you later then she just walk away, she still want say that she would marry me.

One morning I went to get my mail, when I got in to the lobby the peoples in there I speak to all, and then my eyes lit up to this lady I saw," I said dam," now Killer and Glen was in the lobby also, I ask Killer who was that lady?" Killer said that her name is Linda," I said o yes Linda nice, I got my mail and went to the sitting area, then later Glen and Killer came out we all was talking, then Mr. Stewart he walk up and said man, did you all meet Linda! I said o yes is she marry, Stewart said that he did not know, Glen said that she had an old man, Killer said she sure do, I said he is a lucky man.

Now when I did meet Linda for myself, I found out that Linda was a very good person, and she do not meet no strangers "she to me," is beautiful she bring life to other that she was around, now if I spend my money for you, I must love you, no matter as it was woman or man.

One day we all was sitting out talking, Stewart, Linda, Miss Blackwell, Queen, Rose and I, Mr. Stewart said something, now I can't say. But, Linda she heard what Stewart had said.

Linda she responded to what Stewart had said," man she had the words," that was when I from my conclusion that she was no one fool, that was when I said, that she can handle herself, I said to Mr. Stewart, if it was me I would curve that you can't win, that lady she have a razor in her mouth, because I feel that sharp edge myself, and she was not talking to me, Stewart he lean back holding on to the table, and just laugh, Linda said now, that she was going back to her office, as she was leaving a vehicle pull up, this guy got out and took Linda hand, as they was walking back to her office, Glen said he look like a teenager, I said who was he I thought he was her son, Killer said no way that is her old man, I said in my mind leave that along now, she has a husband and a man don't cross another man.

That was when I went into the lobby, that was when I meet Linda old man, she induce me to him as Chris, I said to Chris that it was good to meet him, he said, likewise.

Now that thanksgiving we was having another cook out, it was a barbecue and it was not too hot," but it was hot," in Vegas it get hot, and I was on the girl it is hot also, I was cooking some ribs that Glen and I went and got to cook also.

Now another well I can say, a friend of mind I will not say his name," why" because it was not to good what they did," it shock me," they had some meat that they was going to put on the girl, and we all will have a good time, now when it was time to put their meat on the girl," I went to get it," they had change their mind," that they was not going to put their meat on the girl, they was going to save it for their family.

Now I didn't say another word, I went back to work with the girl shaking my head, now after some of the meat was done, I gave some a taste test then I took the other to the lobby, for the food to be serve.

You know peoples are a trip, some peoples would fix plates and take them home, for to eat later then they come back for more, now I see this and I was going to see, if any one else was going to stop this," I call this stealing food," one lady came up to me and told me what she saw, that they was fixing plates and taking them home," I said to her," why don't you all say something to them, that I had cook so tell them no carry out.

Then something came to me, that I better fix Glen a plate and save it for him, otherwise these peoples was going to take all this food home, then I saw some that don't even live in here, they was fixing plates and taking then home, because it was free.

So I fix two plates for Glen and put them up," to my surprise," one guy said that it was my fault, why they was taking those ribs, I said what was he talking about, he said to me if I had never gave a taste test, of those ribs that they was so good, now my cousin Joyce she was here also, some one must had said that the barbecue sauce, was so good would I show them how to make it, Joyce call me over to the table where she was, and said that the barbecue sauce was so good, would I show her how to make it, Joyce said that she told them that you would not do that, I said no way my dad show me how, to make it and I can't give it out, sorry then I smile and walk away, that someone else had call me.

It was Miss Russell, she said David did you see," she call the name of the peoples who was taking food home," I will not tell you who it was, Russell said they was fixing plates, and taking them home with them that is stealing, why do they steal when they can eat all they want, and if any food was left over after everybody eat, they could take it, don't steal from others why.

That was when I said, if they take five plates and take them home, and there is only two live in the apartment, there was three that could not get one, no I am talking about five other could have had one, because the stealer came back and fix some more and ate, in the lobby with everybody else did.

Now I know Miss Russell was not a liar, because I saw it with my own eyes, the man he was taking some soda, I saw him taking six can, I said that the soda was to be poured up in cups, don't take the whole can someone else might want some, he put the soda back and said sorry man, that was the end of that, I had to check him no one else would do it.

Now here I am trying to help some people, and the others is trying to hurt me in the process, peoples will never change from the way they are, no matter as it be for the good, or the bad I am the first one, I have pass on from the bad to try and be good, I had them both before now I had to leave the bad things along, I am a believer of you can change from the bad to good, now you must watch yourself, some peoples can make the good go bad.

Now where as I am good or bad if it was good, I am trying to help you, if I am bad then you better watch yourself, I will explain to my father and my big brother Jesus, what you have did why I change, and let them take care of that problems, I am just passing Through.

Now I might act like I am a fool, the way I let peoples treat me, because why should I be better than Jesus, the way peoples treated him, he was trying to help them what did they do to him, they threw stones at him as he was passing Through, now he has pass once before, and you didn't want him and appreciate him, God said to Jesus go back forth and save his creation, Jesus is back reconcile and come together.

Now I am no one fool I have a good heart, check into your and see what was in there, I see the out-side of your heart, show the world what is inside, while you are stealing food and someone else, mite can't get a plate now where are your heart, now I said that I was not going to cook, and try to make others happy and they don't appreciate it, no more.

Now I am writing a book about my life, I have plenty work to do for myself, now what I do with my time now is work on my book, every chance I think about what I had did in my pass, I write it down on my track sheet, to not forget and put it on the right path, sometime my truck have me busy, so I write it down to put in the computer later.

And I can't forget the promise I gave to some of the tenant, that at the first of the year, I would run for the President of the tenant council, I will keep that promise.

Now Christmas is coming," I don't swap present," if you give me one don't be looking for one, there are plenty others days in the year, that you might need me to help you with anything, this is what God and Jesus want me to be.

As I said in Passing Through book one, about Christmas was for the baby, baby Jesus so how can you aspect a birthday present that was not your birthday.

Now Annie she had said, that she would edit my book," I ask her what was the charge for each page," she said she charge a dollar a page, but if I buy the paper and the ink, that she would charge me fifth cent a page, I said OK that I need her to take the book pages off my computer, and put it on a disk," I said that I would call her," she gave me her phone number.

When I saw Mary I ask her how was she doing, she said that she was OK, I ask her to breakfast, she said that she didn't want to go, I said that every time I ask her to breakfast, or go to another place, other than the bedroom you say no, she said that she love that one," but she don't be hunger," I said OK, that I want ask anymore.

Now one day we had a Christmas present drawing, it was at the party we bring our present and exchange them, Miss Blackwell she pull my name, I had drew Norma Cottrell Cotter, now I didn't know who Cotter was, I ask some peoples who was she and I thought, that I knew most peoples that live in this complex, some I know by seeing them, the other by their name.

Now I had ask Rose, Blackwell, Miss Russell, and Miss Queen until I saw Mr. Stewart," I ask him," he said Miss Cotter he start thinking, then he said that she live at he gave me the apartment number, I said that I don't think that I know her, but I had pull her name in the Christmas present drawing.

One day I was in the lobby, we all was talking a lady needed my help, she said that her garbage disposal was not working, I went with her to her apartment to check out the disposal, when I saw the number on her apartment," I ask her was she Miss Cotter," she said yes it is why?" I said with a smile, that it was not anything wrong," she look at me and said o no, then she open the door and we went to the kitchen, to see what was wrong with the disposal, she had put lots of asparagus into the disposal, I took my hands and pull the asparagus out, and put them in the garbage can, I showed her and I told her how I do my garbage, the bigger piece put it in the garbage can, then she thank me I left.

On the day of the Christmas party, we all Toni, Miss Brown, Miss Blackwell, Gladies, Miss Russell, Miss Elizabeth, Miss Mary Helen, Mary Ann and I we all was cooking, talking and having a good time, Miss Frizzier she live down the hall from me, she came to the lobby and saw me," she said David how are you, that she had knock on my door and here you are, she had some present in a bag for some others, Miss Frizzier said David you are cooking! That she was going to get her mail and go back home, I said why don't she stay and have dinner with us, she said that she haven't been to long left work, that she was tried. She had gave me a coffee mug for Christmas, I ask did she want me to bring her something, she said no David that she was going to sleep.

Miss Blackwell she make money shirts, she gave me one for Christmas, we gave out the present then we got ready to eat, I gave Miss Cottrel a servant set for her present, Miss Cottrel and a friend of hers name Miss Davis, and I was sitting at a table together eating and talking, I had someone take a picture of the three of us, I had taken pictures of the others some was with me, we all was having a good time.

There is another lady live in here, name is Miss Dorothy Ghoston, she is a sweetheart she call me sometime we talk, about what was around us and how things, how deference things that we see and hear, that was wrong or right.

One day Miss Dorothy she call me, that she needed me to move something's for her, and her daughter, I said that I would when she got ready, she said OK how about Saturday, I said that I was ready about ten Am., she said that her daughter was be here also, I said OK.

That Saturday I meet one of her daughter, the far as I see she was all right with me, when I see her or them we talk, I didn't want to get so close to them," why," because I know me and I am with Mary, I can't do Mary wrong, but I did look at Miss Dorothy daughter, I had to say something in order to curve my mind and thinking, I told her," she was riding with me in my truck, moving a refrigerator," we was talking about marry peoples, that I would never get marry again, she said that she think the same as she did also.

That was when I said that marriage, was for the only way to loosed a friend or friends," she ask me," why did I say that, I told her that, I don't meet no strange, some I get to be just a friend, some we take it to another level, go out have fun and at home we have fun also, we enjoy each other smiling, when we see each other it bring joy, now when one or the other want more, and start talking about marriage," I been there before, seven times," she look at me and she said, that she heard wrong seven time, I said yes seven times, the way to run away a friend from your life, loose your friend ship from what you have built together, all you have to do is get marry, with a woman or a man soon or later, they will be at one or the other throat.

That was when an old man had told me a long time ago, that you can love another to death, as though they think that they can eat each other up," marry one, or the other," later on you might wish that you had eat them up, Miss Dorothy daughter said you might be right, that she will never go that away again," I said, if it was not broken why fix it.

Now I didn't get a Christmas present for Mary, because if she needed anything that she didn't have, she could get it from me, she was cheap, (smile).

At that time I was thinking about putting Passing Through on T. shirts, Joyce she call me on the twenty forth of December 04, was I going to do anything on that night, I said no that I had not planned anything, she said that Ross she was having a little thing going on, and if I wanted to come I was welcome, I said OK that I would be there, I keep my promise.

When it was time to go, I had already took my shower smelling kind of good, got dress and went to Ross house, I took her and Joyce a two liter bottle of wine," that I made," I make my own wine because, I make it the way my Grandmother showed me.

When I got to Ross house, I was looking for her address there was some others peoples, they was parking their vehicle, they got out of their vehicle I ask them for the address, I was looking for when I said Ross and Joyce name, the man he said that, they was going to the same place follow them.

When we got inside Ross she made me welcome, and hug me and said welcome come on in, I thank her and gave her the two liters of wine, for herself and Joyce.

Now Ross, she is a find lady and far as I know, she will be some man a nice lady, I said in my mind forget it David, Ross she is a friend of my cousin down boy.

Now Joyce she had made it to Ross house, I hug her and said merry Christmas, she said merry Christmas to me also, then she said that she had something in her vehicle for me, she and I went to our vehicle she had a Christmas present for me, I put it in my truck we went back inside of Ross house, Joyce she knew that right now, I can't afford to buy a present right now.

Then we started playing cards, that was when she induce me to Tony, one of the peoples came in with me, we was playing bid whisk Joyce she was my partner, that took me way back to Maywood, Ill, we was having a good time, I ask Ross how was the wine, I was under the weather and I was not drinking, Joyce said it is OK," look at Ross," then Tony he started to drink some of the wine, he ask me what kind of wine I call it, that was when I said Mississippi mud.

Then it was time for Tony to play a card on the table, he slap the card on the table and said, anybody need some T.

shirts made, then Joyce said o yes Tony make T. shirts, Joyce she wrote the phone number for Tony, and he put the price on it about the prices of each shirts.

That was when I took a look at the prices and said, that I will call him we can do business, Ross with her find self, she had the pretty smile on her face, and when I saw the love of her family, the way she took time and played with her daughter, and kids she is amazing.

After the party was over I got ready to leave, Ross she said thanks for coming I hug her, and said that I had fun then I said to Tony, that I will call him, he said OK then Joyce said that, she was leaving that she had to get home, Michael was there along, when I got home and said thank Farther for a fun night, and I made it home safe.

That morning I got up and had something to do, I got dress and went out to my truck what a surprise, someone had shot the driver side window out of my truck, it look as to be a B,B, gun or a pellet gun, I said a son of a bitch look at this shit, then I look on the back side of our complex, there is apartment that look over into our, on the second floor I said that I will bet that, somebody a grown up or a kid did that, now I have to spend some money that I don't have, I need money to get my book out, I said well that is what it is, God and Jesus will be with me.

That Sunday morning I got up and took my friend Popeye, to the grocery store I take him every Sunday morning, I have been doing that ever since I had my truck, he said dam man what happen, I said that happen last night, after I came home after the party I went to, I had fun but if I could find out who broken my window, I could have some fun with them, we got to the store Popeye got what he needed, we played some poker on the machine, lost our money and left I took Popeye home, then I went back home mad as hell.

One day Larissa called me it was after Christmas, that she had a cell phone for me, that she can't keep up with me that because, I need one also. I said OK that I would come and get it on that Tuesday, about two PM. Larissa said OK, I asked her how was Greg and the kids doing, she said they was OK, I said OK see her on Tuesday about two PM.(I don't like cell phone.)

That was when I contact Annie about editing my book, we talk about how much it was going to cost," for each page," she said that she charge a dollar a page, but if I buy the ink and the paper, she would charge fifth cent a page, I said OK that she would have to take the pages off my computer, and put them on a disk when she get ready, that when she finish editing them, I would reread them and if it was OK, I would pay her for them then.

She said OK then she said that she had some finance problems," who don't," I said that I would pay for fifth pages first that was twenty five dollars, and that I would give her twenty five a month, until the book was finish edited, that was our agreement.

Now I need to get my window fix in my truck, I was talking to little Joe about getting a window," Joe is the brother of Mary Helen," he told me about on Lose road going from Lake mead, that a junk yard was there where his brother Earnest, go and get use tires that he bet that I will find a window there, that he would go with me when I got ready, I said OK thank.

Now, I don't have too much money to do what I want to do, but I need my truck window fix it look bad, so that next morning I found Joe, he went with me to find the window, I found it they was coming out to my complex to fix the window, I gave them how to get to me then Joe and I came back home.

Later Mary she call," she knew that the window was broken," she ask me has the peoples came to fix the window, I said no not yet but he call and said that he was on the way, Mary said OK that she would see me later, I said OK that I was waiting on these peoples to come. There was about eight PM. the guy call that he was at the gate," so I told him how to get to my truck," then I open the gate and let him in, I went on the outside with him while he work on my truck, after about an hour he finish and I paid him he left.

Before Mary she was getting ready to go to work, she call me that she was leaving going to work, I said OK don't work too hard, that I got the window fix now, she said all right he came and that she would talk to me in the morning, I said OK that I love her, she said likewise.

That morning Mary she came home after work, she went home and call me, I ask her did she have to work on New Year eve, she said yes that it was a double time and half day, she didn't want to let that get away, I said OK that I would spend my New Year eve," by myself," she said you can live with that, that she was coming over to my apartment, I said OK I would be at the door to let her in.

Mary came I was at the security door for her, we got to my apartment she and I was at home, to do what every we want to do.

That December thirty one 04, New Year eve I was all along, but I was not along I am never along, I had God and Jesus.

Mary she did not call me at twelve midnight to say happy New Year's, I would keep looking at the phone, I was watching the celebration on TV," feeling bad," I said Mary she was not going to call, that was when I said, that I bet it was because at Christmas I didn't give her a present, and she had gave me one, that she was mad.

Then I thought about what Mr. Stewart had said before, that he had told Mary that Christmas was coming, and don't be cheap about the present she was giving," we are not cheap," I said she told me.

There was times she would ask me about my clothing size, Mary she did already told me that what Mr. Stewart had said, but I don't swap Christmas present," it is baby Jesus birthday," but her birthday are coming, I had to make it up to Mary, that I said was the reason Mary didn't call me, and say happy New Year to me.

For Christmas Mary she had given me a jump suite, it is black with gray and gold I love it, when I saw Mary, she ask me did I like the present and did it fit, I said yes I love it and it do fit, I ask her was she going home now?" she said yes," I said that I was going home and that I will be there.

After I got home I put the present on, and went so that Mary could see me, in what she had gave me she start smiling, and said it do fit and do I like it," I said I love it," she said and you look good in it, then she look at me as she was mean or want to say, for the other women's also, then she said you think you are bad don't you!, I kiss her and got ready to leave her apartment, I went out the door, and was walking down the hall to the elevator I looked back, Mary she was still looking at me smiling, then she said you know you are looking good," I said to myself if she didn't have to go to work, I could make her feel good," I said then that she make me look good, I got on the elevator and left, I said at her birthday I got to make it up to her.

One day I meet a guy we was talking, he had just got to Vegas he ask me a question, he ask why do peoples say that in Las Vegas, it is sin city. I stated that I don't know but you have to be strong, to live in Vegas.

He said to me, why! I said plenty money is in Vegas, I said if you can survive the drugs and the gambling, you can gambler just don't get hook on it, without those two things you can make it in Vegas, you can overlook the prostitute and gold digger, pay for the milk and go on.

While I am writing my book, I have lots on my mind and I love doing for someone, when they appreciate what I do for them, I don't have a problem doing for peoples.

But there are some who don't appreciate it because they don't appreciate themselves, I start thinking about how I love to cook, I said that I was going to cook a dinner at home, and invite some others like Mr. Jenson, Marlin, Rose, Toni,

Mary Helen, Blackwell, I call my friend Coco to bring her daughters, I invited others like Mr. Stewart to come if they wanted to, on that day Jenson came he could not stay, he fix a plate for himself and his wife, Marlin she is a sweetheart, she host for me she also know my friend Coco, she and I move Marlin from her house to where I live.

We all was having a good time, when everyone had left my sweetheart, Mary, came she said where are the others? I said they have left but now you are here, Mary said have you eating, I said yes but then I kiss her, and said that I will have my sweets after she have eating, then I will have my fun, and we did.

Now I was close to finish my book, and now I had made a promise to Toni and some of the tenant, that I will run for the president of the tenant council, when it was time to change office, now I have not finish the book but I have to make good on my promise, I really don't have the time but I have to run now.

After the others they didn't want black peoples, to have potato salad, potato pies etc. had said that it was wrong peoples pay their money, why can't they eat what they want to eat, especially on thanksgiving day, that is what black peoples eat on holiday, or anytime they want that was why I said, that I will run to try make these peoples happy.

One day Toni and I was talking about the election, and how the only way that I will run, I want to have a paper ballot and let the tenant check the names, who they want to vote for, Toni and I decide to do it that away.

Now the way I wanted to do the election that away, in the pass when I was a child," all we had to do was shack hands," and that was better than any agreement on paper, now you better have it on paper, peoples now will put you in the mud, all in your face.

Mary one day, she asked me why don't I celebrate Christmas, I said that I celebrate Christmas, I don't swap present, that was when I ask Mary question, I ask her what day was it that Jesus was born, she said December the twenty fifth," I said that was what they said it was, they don't know, Mary said it is on the calendar, I ask her who put it on the calendar," man," he don't know only God and Jesus know.

God put us here just for a little while, he put his creations here to learn, to learn to love, to be respectful for others and his earth, to this day I try to love, respect other sometime I get the short stick etc., Mary she said to me, now you said that Christmas, was not on December the twenty fifth, what day was it, I said now I didn't say that, Christmas was not on December the twenty fifth, I ask can anybody, tell me what day Jesus was born, she said no can you, I said no but I am still learning, and that I have a good teacher, the same teacher Jesus have, name is God my Father.

One day Mr. Stewart ask me, would I take him to the home depot, that he had to get something's for the complex," Stewart is the maintenance man," I said OK that I would take him when he got ready, Stewart he was eating behind the kitchen off the lobby, he said after he finish eating.

After I finish talking to Stewart, there was John and Jenson sitting at the table, Jenson he ask me could he talk to me," I said sure," he and I walk over to the couch to talk, he ask me what have he did to me that I don't like him," now I don't dislike anyone," what he ask me he took me for a surprise, I told him where as I like him or not, who give him the right to tell peoples, what they could eat or not, who gave him the right was he paying for everything, they paid their money, he put his hand into his pocket, I had my eyes on him, I told him when he pull his hand out of his pocket, it better be empty.

Because I am getting ready to tear his ass up, he pull his hand out of his pocket empty, there was another tenant that live in here, what is his name I don't care I saw him before, with his rusty feet. he is the kind like to brag about, his million dollars and his ranch in Arizona with his trailer on it, and that I found out he said, that he had a law suit about the complex, if he had a piss pot to pee in, he could not throw it out, that was the kind of man he was," I got dead on his ass," I told him as long as he and I live in here, don't he never, I ask him do he hear me, don't he never get into my confrontation," then I saw Mary," when I am with another he better walk on, if it was not his business, and that I mean that.

Jenson he took his creeper ass with his walking cane, and went and sit his ass down because, he is white he can say or do anything to a black person, not this one I went and got my truck, and came back to take Stewart to the home depot," I always thought Jenson was prejudice," if I am wrong I apologize.

Stewart and I went to the home depot, Stewart said that I had put that liar," Jenson," in his place, I said peoples should mind their own business, and leave others along, Stewart said now he know, Stewart and I got to the home depot, and we got what we came for and cane back to the complex, after Stewart and I finish putting things up we got, I was going out from the lobby door, I saw that guy that I had put in his place from my business, he was sitting in his vehicle he was motion to me, that he want to talk, the man I am I walk over to him," and ask him what he want," he wanted to shake my hand, I don't want to shake his hand not the devil, he said that I was right getting on that white man, they think they are better than we are, I listen to him for a minute I said it don't matter, what color you are if anybody, cross me the wrong way I will let you know, where as you like it or not I will speak my mind, he said you are right you told him, I said OK man then I walk away and was going home," to myself I said and you to," then I went home.

After I got home I had on my mind the promise I had made, about the election for president of the tenant council, and Mary how was she thinking after she saw me, getting on Jenson and that rusted foot man, I didn't want Mary to see my other side of me.

That was when I turn to my father," God and Jesus," I don't pray to my father I talk to him and Jesus man to man, My father don't want you to beg to him for what you want, talk to him.

Now I sit and talk to them about, what was in front of me, but what was in front of me was not promise to me, but I can think about what I want, and I talk to my Lord about what I want to try to do, I want to be the best about what God and Jesus, want me to be.

After I talk to my Lord and explain, all I have to do is sit or stand still, he will show me the way to go, sometime it make me mad it bring tears from my eyes," tears and blood," about how some peoples are," now me," at my age I don't know how long God, was going to let me stay here I want to have some fun, I want to do something in my life, maybe someone else one two or three of them, want the same as I do I said that I will split my time, from writing in my book and doing something for someone else also, that is what God and Jesus want, me to make someone else happy and help somebody who need it, I thank my Father and Jesus to give me the strength, to be able to do that, I will give what my Father and Jesus, pass on to me that is love.

That was when I started thinking about my daughter Larissa, and her husband Greg they was cooking out, and she ask me to come and bring Mr. Stewart, I said that I would come and let Stewart know, if he wanted to go that he would be with me, I ask Larissa what did she need me to bring, she said not anything but you all, I said OK that I would see her then.

That day Stewart and I was going over to my daughter house, Stewart ask me what was he and I was bringing, I said that I had already ask her that, she said not anything we got to the complex, where Larissa and Greg live we went in, I went to where they live and park, Stewart and I went into the house and spoke to everybody, we all was talking having fun then we eat, and there was a football game on TV. And my granddaughter and grandson, they was at home we all was together, watching the game laughing having fun, until the game was over, Stewart was getting ready to leave, we gave our thanks for having us over, that we had a good time and we will talk again, soon.

Now I am human breathing, and I can bleed because I am a human, and I have felling also I get lonely to, now I have two grandsons from my daughter Jackie, in Alabama one birthday is on January the first, the other one is January the tenth, now after that fourth of July, they don't want to talk to me, so I will go on with my life one day my daughter, will wake up and see that her Father, do love her and will never Mistreat her in anyway, but I thank God and Jesus that they are with me, now I have lots on my mind.

One day I was talking to my sister Delouse, I told her what had happen in Alabama on that fourth of July, I also told her that Jackie she was not, my mother nor my Father, but I am her father and that if it was not for her, my stepfather and my brother, I could have stayed in Vegas, I thought about all of my pass, and the future.

Hum, my sister Delouse had said that Jackie had call her, and said that she better talk to her brother, that was when I told my sister, and my niece Becky what happen in Alabama," I did that because," if I hear it from anybody else from the family, another way there will be two that know the truth.

Now my son Johnnie Marshall, I don't know about him, I have not talk to him every sense, I talk to him when he was in Alabama, with Barbara Jean his mother was in Brewton that was just before July the fourth 04, I call and leave massages for him to call me, he want call I guess he don't get the massage, or he just don't want to talk to me," but that is OK," now I only saw his son little Johnnie but twice, the last time I saw him was, his dad and mother Len, they and I took him to get him some shoes, I gave him some money that was the last time.

Now Johnnie he also have a daughter, he said to me before that his daughter name was Brittany, she use to live in Chicago but now, her mother move to Mississippi, the last time I was in Chicago, Johnnie he had Brittany on the phone, he let me talk to her I told her, to get my phone number and address and get in touch with me, she said OK that she would I gave the phone, back to John after he finish talking to my granddaughter, I also told him to give my number and address, so that Brittany can keep in touch with me, John said that he would.

Now Barbara Jean, my son mother I don't know about her also," hum," she said to me David, that she started to let me stay with her, other than a hotel but she would had to watch me, I said that was OK that she didn't have to watch me," watch herself," that was when Barbara daughter said, that she would be looking also, I said that no body have to watch me I had her mother, before she was being thought about, way long.

That was when Barbara Jean said to me, come on that she wanted to show me her house, I said OK we went on the outside she was shown me, and telling me how her husband treated her," my memory open up to the pass," she took me inside to the basement and the rest of her house, so my Father I came to you and Jesus, for guidance about what I am going to do, I can't do it by myself I need you Jesus to carry me on, so I now will go to sleep after talking to you.

Now I can sleep, because God and Jesus will give me the answer. That morning after I woke up from that night, and gave my Testimony about what was on my mind, kind of made me lonely about my family, kids and friends and what was in my future, I started to call Mary but I said later on I would call her.

That same day I saw Mary, she did not say anything about that argument, about I had to get on somebody and she saw it, and I did not remind her also, we was just talking and injuring ourselves, as we do when we see each other, that was when Mary ask me about the election? I explained what Toni and I had decided to do.

On January eight it was Miss Russell birthday, and my girl Linda the manager of the complex, her birthday also, it was on the fifteenth now I love to cook, and save money also I was going to take Miss Russell, and take her to dinner now it was so close to the fifteenth, I said to take one to dinner it was going to be expense, if I took two of them to dinner, it would be cheaper. That was when I said, that I could go to the store and get something's to cook at home, that I could invite some else of the others that live in the complex to join in with Miss Russell, and Linda birthday celebration.

Now I meet Linda daughter, she is like her mom as I see, she loving and friendly, I explain to her what I was planning to do, for Russell and Linda birthday and that I would love, to have her and her sister to be here, she said OK.

So what I did was find out what they like to eat, Miss Russell she said just anything that I wanted to cook, was OK with her. Linda said whatever I cook for her, she bet that it will be good, that open the door from my heart, and I let all that love I had in me, I let it out.

Now Toni she had made the ballot, Kopoe, Toni sister she made the ballot box, to put the ballot in, the last day to cast the vote for the tenant candidate, they seek for office was January the tenth, was the last day to vote.

Now on the last day to vote, the ballot was counted on the eleventh day, on that same day I gave Annie twenty five dollars, she are Editing my book Passing Through. after the ballots was counted, by Toni and Miss Brown the result of the count from the Election was, David L. Marshall—President, no one ran for vice President, no one ran for Secretary, David Montoya—Treasure, no one ran for finance Secretary, Elizabeth Johnson—Trusties, Grace Tallinn—Trusties and Miss Russell—she is the guide

On January the fourteenth, I had went and got the food that I was going to fix, I got a brisket of beef some celery, I season the beef just right, "before I start cooking, I bring Jesus and God in to it with me," then I took foil and seal it and put it in to the oven, for three hours on three hundred degree and let it start cooking.

When it was time I took my celery and I chopped it up, and put it in the pan with the beef, I put it even with equal amount around the beef, then I put it back in the oven for about two more hours, then I would take it out, so I went back working on my book.

Chapter 2

Now I HAD ALMOST THROUGH cooking what I was going to do, Miss Mary Helen, she said that she was going to help me, and cook a dish.

On the next day we was going to have the birthday dinner, about eleven O clock I had Finnish cooking, I had beef, corn bread and black eyes peas, I also made a sweet potato Poona, then I took the food to the lobby and put it on the table.

A little while Miss Mary Helen she came with her dish, she had cook a pot of Collar greens, now we was waiting on Miss Russell, and Linda daughter to get there, the peoples that was here already was Mr. Stewart, Toni, Mary Helen, and Linda she was at work here and her friend Chris, he was there also, you know I was there.

We was waiting on Miss Russell, and Linda daughter it was now about one o clock, Stewart said that it was their lunch time let's eat, they will be here later so Linda she came out from her office, I said to Linda with a hug happy birthday, we started to eating Linda she said, David this meat is so tender how did I do it, then she said that I had to cook one for her like this, that she was going to buy the meat.

Then Mr. Stewart, Toni, Linda, Chris, Mary Helen and I was having a good time, Stewart said to Miss Mary Helen, those greens are so good, she could have cook more of them, Mary Helen replied O yes you like them," with a smile," Toni and Stewart both said O yes they was good, I said yes Miss Mary Helen you put your foot in those greens, then Mary Helen said to me that I cook like a woman also, I said that my grandmother and my mother left that for me, after everything was almost over Miss Russell she came, Stewart said you are late it is almost over, Russell she said that is OK she had other things to do, that she would eat the rest.

Then Chris said to me David, man you sure cooked that meat it is so tender, I said thank that Linda said that she wanted me to fix one for her one day, I told her to let me know, now it was time to clean up things in the lobby, and let peoples get back to work, Mary Helen she ask me why didn't my Mary come to dinner, I said that she had to go and have a meeting, at the hotel where she work, then Linda said to me David thank you and Miss Mary Helen, I said don't mention it, we all should show some love to each other.

After I got home my lady Mary, she call she ask me how was the birthday dinner, I said it was good, she ask was any food left, I said that there was some left, and if it was not enough that I would fix her some more, she said that she was on her way, this was her day off.

About a half hour Mary she came to my apartment, I let her in with those bed room eyes, and her smile it did something to me," what," you know what I am talking about, how a man get when he see or have a woman, that look so good that he can eat her up.

David L. Marshall

That is a hard time feeling for a man, I don't know about a woman but a man, Mary she and I got in side of my apartment, she said that she was not going to stay all night, I said that she can stay as long as she wanted, Mary she fix her some food to eat now, and to take her some home with her.

She sit down with me and she was eating, I was looking at my computer, Mary she said that is a no that she is here now, and that she was my woman and not that computer, that she wanted my time until she got ready to leave, after she finish eating she took my hand and said, come on make her happy.

We went into the bed room now Mary, she know what I can do in that bed room, and I know that she loved it, because a man know what his woman want, if he don't do it, some other will.

Now I try to keep myself in some kind of shape, external and internal and I was as young as I, was when I was younger hard as a bone, Mary and I have a good time with each other, other than when some other woman have to put a blame, that I have so many women's to Mary, she pour all of that, so call blame on me it is hard on me.

After the lover affair faction was over, and I had tender rise my meat and she and I, was just laying on bed and talking, she got ready to go she got dress, she took her food and said to me, you are good then she walk away, after she had left I said to myself that I know that, I am so good because I don't play fair.

Now I like to pay my bills on time, my rent, utility and my insurances that come out from the bank, and all three are due around the sixteenth of the month, the utility is paid when it come to me, my truck is paid for.

Now every morning I get up have breakfast after I clean up, and do something in my computer, and when it time for the mail man to run, I go to the lobby after it open we all sit around talking, waiting on the mail if it was late.

Now Toni she have coffee made on the days she work, and sometimes she have some pastry, we have coffee and eat sweets and have a good time, until we leave and go on with our own ways, and do what we have to do for our own self.

On January the twenty first of five, I had my first meeting as the tenant council president, I did not have a regular meeting, I explain to the council members that, right now I do not have anything to report I have just got here, what I want to do this meeting is get to know each other, and that every-one here have a voice, and don't never forget that, then I ask who wanted to have the floor first, to just open up and talk about what was on their mind.

The floor was Quiet, I gave them the opportunity to speech, and get it out now so that, I would have something to go on, about what was on their mind about thinking, about what they wanted to do, about their happiness after all, we are all over fifth five years older, and some might not make it over fifth five, so why not have some fun now, I laid my heart out for them.

No one open their mouth," I said to myself OK," that I will start with myself first and let them know, who I am and what I wanted to do for them, but I can't do it by myself and Miss Elizabeth, Miss Russell, Grace or Mr. Monty, can do it for you after all it will take all of you.

We need the members also to stand by us, I said that most of you all know me, but this is the ones who don't know me, that my name is David L. Marshall and I am writing a book, about my life but I will be with you all, if you needed me all they have to do was call me, that I was going to put my phone number, on the board out in the lobby for you all, if someone needed me for anything but, not for things that I can't do anything about, for that you must go into the manager office.

Then I explain that I will do anything for them but one that is taken a life from someone else, I will not take anything that I can't give back, that is life.

And I do not want to go to bed with every woman I see, nor with those who want me to go with them, but I will love you as a friend not as your lover.

That I will help them if they wanted or needed me, and that I do not like to hear someone say, that they was hunger that God and Jesus that is in me, I have to feed you.

After I had laid out my heart to the members, I talk and I ask was anyone else wanted to speech, no one else had anything to say, I gave the floor to Miss Elizabeth she talk, then Miss Russell and Monty they talk, but Grace she was not at the meeting but we still had the meeting, but seem no one else had anything to say.

After about an hour I said that, if not anybody do not have anything else say, I need a motion from the floor to join the meeting, there was a first motion to a join the meeting, then there was a second, I said that there was a first and a second, to a join the meeting and all in favor say yes, there was all yes, and no others said no, that the yes have it and that the meeting was over.

Some had something's to say after the meeting that was David it was a good meeting, I said thank you we had some refreshment after the meeting, I had some then I went home.

After I got home I started to call Mary, but I didn't call her she work nights and I know how that is, I been there.

Now there was another lady, a white lady her name is Carmilla, I would see her there was something about her, one was the way she walk, and wink her eye when I saw her that did something to me, but I don't want to be no dog, because I have one woman that was enough, but I am a man I can look.

Now peoples they know how they want to live their life, the way that suit themselves it don't bother me, but what do bother me is, when someone try to tell me how to live mind, now God and Jesus only gave me one life to live, how can you live two yours and mind.

Now after God had only gave me one life, I am going to live that one that is mind not yours, that is not my life to live you have to live your own.

Now every day in and out in my life, all I was doing was, getting up in the morning and talking to my God and Jesus, for given me this day that was not promise to me, thank for my health and strength, and the air that he provided to me to breath, my eyes to see, my ears to hear, my legs to walk, my hand to feel and my mouth to speak, also give his others creation, the same God and Jesus had given me, I have something to be thankful for, thank you my lord also for given me something to write about.

And at that time for the mail man to run, I go to the lobby and get my mail, then I will sit and talk to others to see how they are doing, now everyone that live in here, are older than fifth five and some have some health problems, I feel good to see them walking around talking, all I can say is that God and Jesus is good.

Some say that after a woman reaches twenty-one years old, they are now in the same category as I am in, that is getting older now.

So now I don't say old, that is for cloths I am getting season, I have come through all kind of weather, now with that seasonal that God and Jesus put on me, don't you want some, that is love God pour on me.

So now I am proud of my God and Jesus to let me get older, it was hard for me to get to where I am to this day, tomorrow is not promise.

Now I know that I am bless, and all I want to do is this, show you how bless I am, maybe you will show me yours.

Then one day we was sitting on the outside, my girl Linda she was on her break, she was on her cell phone I overheard her said that, she was trying to get another job I said to myself, o no as soon I get use to Linda now she is trying to move on, and every time we have a manager that is good and nice, they don't stay now Linda, I like and love Linda because being Linda, I like that not only Linda but any others also.

After Linda left, there was things going on in the complex, I did not like but I was only one, and I don't own anything in this complex but myself, and I do not own myself, I have to report and answer to God and Jesus, now they gave me a job to do, can I handle it yes with the blessing of my lord, I will take it one day a time.

Now on February the second, I found out that Mary birthday was coming, and I did not had given Mary a birthday present, so I had to see what I was going to get for her, I had to get two, then I said no there was Valentine's day coming also, so I had to get three present it was so closer to Valentine's day, I had to get for Christmas, birthday and Valentine's day.

After I found out about Mary birthday, I ask one of her friend name is Jean, I explain to Jean that I was going to cook a dinner, for Mary birthday day, and that I would love it if Jean and Frank would be there, and I ask Jean could she get Mary to my apartment, at noon without Mary knowing about the dinner, Jean said no problem that she would have

Mary there, I said ok thanks then I went to the store, and got what I was going to cook.

Now I had told Rose, Miss Blackwell, Mary Helen, Joe, Stewart, Toni, Marlin, and I call my girl-friend Coco, yes my girlfriend," she is a girl and I am a boy, and we are friends," to bring my nieces, that is her daughters, I call my cousin Joyce also to come.

Now I ask Joyce, would it be ok if I could go and pick up Michael, and take him with me to get a present for Mary, Joyce said sure that would be ok.

So later on I call Michael, and said that I was coming and pick him up, that I had already talk to his mom, I had to get a birthday present and if he wanted to ride with me, Michael said yes cousin David that he would be ready, I said ok see him with in a half hour.

After I got ready and left home, I went and pick up my cousin Michael, he and I went shopping, Michael he had some things that he wanted also, I look and saw some gold chains, I said Michael what do you think about a gold chain, he said yes cousin David your lady would love that, then he said what about the other two days, I look and saw a watch I got that, then I saw some diamond ear rings, I also got a pair of diamond ear rings.

After Michael and I got back, he said that he love those present that I had got for my lady, I said thank, he said that those ear rings was a bonafide, open-air fire to express joy.

At that time the phone ring, it was Joyce, Michael told her what I had got for my lady, he hand me the phone, I was talking to Joyce, she said that I could have gave her those diamond ear rings, I said that I had already got it for Mary now, but otherwise that I would give them to her, she said ok, I told Michael that I was going to go now, and thanks again.

After I got back home I started cooking for Mary birthday, after I had did what I was going to do that night, I put everything up that was when I saw Mary, now I love Mary and she is no child, I said why do I have to hold her present, so I said that I had something for her, she said ok and that she had something for me also, I smile and gave her those present.

Mary, her face lit up with her smile, she said that she love all of her present, then she kiss me and gave me her valentine card, I open it and read it was so beautiful, on the front it read, I'm so glad I found you.—On the inside read, if I had my life to live over again, next time I'd find you sooner so I could love you longer. happy Valentine's day, love Mary.

That was when I smile and I kissed Mary, and said thanks that I will always keep this in my heart, I saw the light that I had seen before, that was love, when Martin Luther King said, that he had been to the mountain top, and his eyes had seen the glory.

Now that night I saw the light, through the darkness over the mountain top, I found love, and now I take pride, of renown, honorable fame, from my heavenly blessing door, when I saw that light through the darkness.

Mary she look at the smile on my face, I had went into my heart, she said David are you alright, I said o yes I was thinking back about some things then I took her into my arms and I kiss her, that was what took Mary and I into the bed room.

The day of Mary birthday dinner, Jean she came with Mary, when they got into my apartment, every one that was there said happy birthday Mary, she was surprise, she could not say a word all Mary could do was smile.

After Mary and Jean had come, we all started to eating our dinner and talking, I just look and smile to Mary, Jean she saw that I love Mary, then I said to Mary that I love her, she seam as she was not feeling to good, I told her that I love her, to perk her up but I do love her.

That was when Jean said, that Mary didn't feel too good. I ask Mary what was wrong was it anything that I can help, she stated that it was her stomach, I said if it don't get any better, she should see a doctor, and if anything that I can help her, she know that I will be there for her, when I got sick and got stop up she Mary, went and got something to help me, and I love her for that and many others ways.

Now my friend Coco came, and her daughter Peaches and her granddaughter Miss Molly, we all was having fun, now I had already been told by Coco, that Molly she didn't like chocolate, now Peaches she was just having fun, she put some chocolate into Molly mouth, you should have seen that expression on that baby face, I said to Coco did you see that, now that was the time I should had my camera ready, I could have got a good picture of that, I said to Peaches that Molly she was going to get her, Coco said and you know that.

After the dinner party was over, and every one had left, I put up the rest of the food into the refrigerator, and I clean up the kitchen then I sit down and relax.

Later on Mary she came back to my apartment, and said that she love her Christmas, birthday and Valentine present, then she smile and said, that I had one more present to give to her, now I am no fool I knew what it was, I gave her what was hers.

Now there was a no other lady that live in the complex a white lady, her name is Camilla, every time I saw her she had a smile, she was a sweet lady and every time she saw me, she would say hi David how was I doing, we talk and she started to coming out, and sit and talk to me and the others that live here also, not only to me.

Now I had all the respect for her, and I show mind to her, one night we all was sitting out talking, Camilla she had a man that live with her, now I always look and I am always thinking, I saw Camilla old man going out from the exit gate, I smile someone said David what do you see you are just smiling.

That was when I said it was not anything, I kept looking at Camilla old man vehicle, he turn around and came back through the enter gate, then he park in front of the lobby and sit there for a little while, then he back out and went out from the exit gate and left.

David L. Marshall

That was when I said to myself what was that, Miss Queenie said David what was on my mind, I said that it was not anything, after a little while Gladies she came out side, I said that it was time for me to leave and go home, I didn't want to hear Gladies begging, for something that I was not going to give her, and Camilla she didn't come out side, I said to myself ok that was what I saw, about Camilla old man, he had a problems with his woman, sitting out with those tenants, and I was sitting out there also, and I am black also.

So after I was going to leave some of the others, I was sitting out they said that they was leaving, because while I was out there they felt safe.

Now on Valentine's day, Mary and I was just sitting around my apartment, she came to me because, she didn't want no other woman saying that David Marshall, Mary they saw me coming out from some woman apartment she was with me, she had me all for herself.

Now on that Saturday morning, Mary she had come home from work, she call me on her cell phone, she said that Camilla, the man that live with her needed Mary, to call nine one for him, because he could not hardly breath, and he had chest pain. I said you call nine one, didn't she, she said yes she did. I said ok that I was one my way where was she at, she said that she was at the dumper by my building, I went there where Mary was, I saw Camilla old man lying on the ground, and his vehicle door was open, Mary and I was watching him we could not help him, because the paramedic was coming.

Mary she said to me, that the man he was getting dark, I said that was not a good sign he won't make it, then the paramedic they came and start working on the man, they work on him then they stop, and started putting their things up, I said to Mary that he was dead, I ask one of the paramedic after I let her know who I was, that they could not save him, she said no they could not save him in a low tone.

No I tried to find someone, who knew how to get in touch with Camilla at her job, no one knew, I said to Mary that when she came home, I would tell Camilla what happen. Now peoples they don't realize how they spread the extent, about things that they don't know. They spread that the man was dead, I explain that they don't know that. That they was not a doctor, and that only a doctor know that, Mary and I we did not say to them what, the paramedic said to us now how do they know.

After Camilla came home I saw her in the lobby, I ask her how was she doing, she said hi David that she was ok, other than she had a hard day at work, I said Camilla sit down that I had some bad news for her, she no David what was it, I explain to her what had happen, she almost fell down I put her in my arms, and I told her if anything else she needed to know, that she might talk to Mary, that she was the one who call me, I explain to her who Mary was and what apartment she live at, she said thank to me and she left, someone else was in the lobby she said me, David you handled that very well, I said thank you then I went to my apartment.

Now Gladies she was so process trying to get me into bed, she did not have the sense enough to stop trying, I was so relieved that she had stop trying, until she started back doing the same thing again, what a head ache.

One Sunday morning I was sitting on the outside, just smoking a cigarettes and minding my own business, Gladies she came out side and sit and she started her thing, she ask me why don't I want to go to bed with her.

That was when I tried to explain why not, that there was a deference between love and sex, but they both go together but there are some deference, Gladies she wanted to know what was it, I said that my Grandmother and my mother was a lady, I loved them but I cannot have sex with them," well I only speak for myself," I said that I can love you because you are a woman, but I only have one now I have sex with.

That was not good enough, Gladies she tried to sit on my lap, I push her away and said don't do that," she ask why not?" I said that Mary she can look out from the floor, where she live and see everything I was doing, Gladies she said so what you are not marry to her, I explain to her that I might not be marry to Mary, but I will respect her.

Gladies she kept on I got up and left and went home, when I got to my apartment I made a phone call, while I was on the phone talking, I look out on my porch I had some boxes out there, I kept looking at a bag on the boxes, I said to myself who put a bag on my porch, without letting me know who put it there, I told the person who I was talking to, that I would call them back I hung up the phone, to see what was in that bag.

When I look at that bag it was tied up, I pick it up it was warm and soft, I said O no she didn't, I went to the lobby before I got there I saw Gladies, I ask Gladies did she put a bag on my porch, she said yes that she did, put some shit on my porch because I want go to bed with her, I smell blood in my head, I said David be cool you have change now, so I went and found Mr. Stewart.

When I saw Stewart he was coming from his apartment, I said that I need him to come out here with me, that Gladies she put some shit on my porch, and if I talk to her without you with me, I will kill that bitch.

So Stewart and I went on the outside in front of the lobby, there was Gladies standing there, I said to her why did she put that shit on my porch, she said that she did it because I want go to bed with her, then she lost her mind she went back into the building, and she was talking loud, and she was trying to get into others peoples apartment, Stewart he look at me, I said to Gladies that she had lost the best friend, that she could had.

She got so loud until peoples came out from their apartment, she was going crazy trying to open others apartment, she open the apartment from one twenty five, I saw that the lady was afraid I said to Stewart, that I was going to call the police.

So I call metro police, and explain to them what was wrong, that there was a crazy woman and that we need them, so the switchboard said that they were sending a car.

So I went to the enter gate to wait for the police to let them in, now Gladies she knew that I was not playing, she tried to

tell me that she was sorry please forgive her, I had nothing
to say to her then the police came, I open the gate for him
as soon the police came through the gate, Gladies she said
to the police, that I had hit her, I shook my head.

Stewart and I was standing on the side walk, then Gladies
she started in on the police, she was asking him that I David
Marshall, don't want to go to bed with her, why don't he the
police go with her with his find ass, the police said no way,
then Gladies said to the police that she would take his gun,
and shoot him, the police said to Gladies no mam don't do
that, Stewart look at me and said, the police he was as crazy
as Gladies was, I said you are right.

Then the police made a call for Ambulance, to come and
pick up Gladies, she was in a bad way, so the Ambulance
came, Gladies she started in on the Ambulance driver,
Gladies she tried to open the back of the Ambulance, the
driver said to the other guy that was with him, take that
crazy bitch out from the Ambulance, they ask Stewart and
I was she on medication, I said that I don't know but I do
know that she was crazy, Stewart told them what he knew.

So later on they took Gladies away from the complex, then
I found out that Gladies had said, that she was going to
turn on the gas, from her stove and blow up the building,
I said ok she is danger she don't need to be here, she could
kill others peoples.

Now on the monthly meeting of February, was the real
meeting the first one was to show the tenants, exactly what
and who I was, if they like, love or don't like me that is ok,

that I love them, the ones who say that I am wrong, they don't realize who I am.

Now if they don't know me, that is their own problems they are slow, they will catch up if it was not too late, after all I," we are only passing through," you only pass this way once, don't blow that time you have, try loving someone.

The meeting started at five p.m. the President open the meeting, the council in control, David Marshall President, David Montoya treasure, Elizabeth, trusties, Grace Taplin, trusties, Miss Russell the guide, she was also leading in pray.

Now I can't bore you about the meeting, they keep their mouth closed, until the meeting is over, then everyone has something to say.

Now I had explain in the meeting about the money from the month dues, that after I get the money from David Montoya, I with Miss Elizabeth and Miss Russell, we will put it in the bank because, that is where it should be.

Now before we left the lobby, Stewart came to lock up the lobby he start laughing, and we started talking about the tenant, that came into the gate that Gladies want to jump on, I said O yes Gladies she was like a pit bull, when she saw that woman coming, and that woman she was afraid I saw that, Gladies said there is that bitch, that Gladies she was going to kick her ass, the police had to hold Gladies, he had a hard time holding Gladies.

Now on Jan. twenty two, David Montoya he still has not given me the dues money, that John had given to him to turn over to the new council, so what I did to keep my promise to the members, I took one of my check and wrote it, and open the account, from my account from Bank of America, check number six seventh four.

The bank we put the money into for the Louise Shell Tenant Association, dated three one 0 five, for three hundred dollars, in us bank.

Now on the twenty third of February, I had to send a letter about what Gladies had did to me, and about the safety of the tenants, after Gladies said that she was going to blow up the place, to the right peoples who could do about it.

The letter to Global property management group, Inc. attention: management.—We the tenants residing at the Louise shell apartments, located at 2101 no. Martin L. King Blvd. Las Vegas Nevada.

We would like to bring to your attention some health and safety concerns, the tenant by the name of Gladies Jones, who has been treated on several occasions for psychological problems.

The tenant Gladies Jones has displayed certain erratic behavior that was observed by many other tenants.

Ms. Gladies Jones, threaten to do physically harm, to several tenants in this complex. Gladies, throw a bag of human feces onto the Mr. David Patio.

The most recent episode, Ms. Gladies Jones, threaten to blow up this building. Ms. Gladies Jones behavior has been witness, verified and documented.

Per homeland security the statement of Ms. Jones made about blowing up the building, would be considered a terrorist threat.

We are bringing this matter to the management, because some tenants feel fearful due to this terrorist threat.

One would never know what Ms. Gladies Jones might do. Based on the Nevada State health and safety policies, as well as the Nevada State Housing Living standards, this is health and safety issue. It is essential that this concern be investigated immediately because some innocent person or persons could seriously get hurt. Thanking you in advance for your prompt attention to this matter.

Please respond to Mr. David Marshall, President of the Tenant Association. Sincerely yours, Tenants of Louise Shell Senior Housing Association.

Now after the tenants we did not have a manager in the complex, the tenants thought I was in management, because I was the president of the tenant council.

They would call me all time of the night, that there was something wrong about the things, that I could not do anything about, all I could do was explain to them, that I was not in management because I am the president, of the council.

That manager has a work order to fill out, when there was something wrong in our apartment all I can do is fill paper work out and the office will fill the order out. They give me letter about this complex is not safe, and this place is suppose, to be a secure property it is not, and everybody living here knows it is not.

And tenants in the building one, leaving rocks and cans in the door, so they can get into the building, and the gates to get into the complex, was broken most of time.

They said that the cops were called here on Sat. Feb. 26, 05 twice, and they left the gate open, and it is still open as she was writing the letter to me, there was a fight and it has happen before, peoples are coming and going from apartment 111, and 112, day and night writing by 109, there was five others tenants sign the letter.

Now I had to let the tenants know that, the duties of tenants council was, mediate—go between in order to reconcile, collect monthly dues the tenants to pay is one dollar a month, bring them together, coming together collected, that the tenant theory show own and all means of production, of the activity of the tenants.

At the month of March it was quite, all I did was enjoy Mary and sit and talk to the tenants, the ones who sit and wait on their mail, and say hello to those who come and go, and on march the sixteenth, the Corporate office sent Mr. Mazed to run the manager office, I talk to him about how the peoples are speeding around the complex.

On the eighteenth it was the tenants meeting, there was some new tenants came to the meeting, and some of the ones who came before, they was not there but that was ok, we had the meeting on the time and date we was suppose—to, have it and after the meeting we had some refreshment, for the tenants.

On March the Twenty I went over to see my cousin, Joyce, Robert and Michael Thomas, I got there about Three O clock, and on the Twenty first Joyce she had some things to do, she ask me could she bring Michael over to my house, I said sure bring him on, I would love to have my little cousin with me, we could hang out.

One day I was sitting in the lobby watching T.V. Mary my baby, she came down from the second floor where she live, I was sitting there, Mary said good morning and she sit by me, she and I was talking, then she said that she had to go someplace, when Mary she got up she rub her stomach, then she said that she had a hard knot, I said where! She said in her stomach then she ask me to feel it, I did then I ask what was it and did it hurt, Mary said no it don't hurt it is just hard, I said that she might see a doctor, she look at me with that sweet smile, I said ok, she said that she would call her doctor, then she left.

Now on March the twenty fifth, Mary she call me and said that she had appointment, for her doctor, I ask her did she want me to go with her, she said no that she could go by herself, I said ok that I would be here for her if she need me, she said ok that she would call me later, I said ok that I would be at home.

When Mary came from the doctor officer she call me, I was glad to hear from her I said hi baby, what did the doctor say, she said that she was coming to my apartment, I said ok.

David L. Marshall

When Mary she came to my apartment, I saw that she had something on her mind I ask honey what's wrong, she sit down and I sit there with her, she said that the doctor said that, she had Cancer.

Now after Mary had told me what the doctor said, I told her that the doctors was not God or Jesus, that they can make a Mistake also, don't take one decision find another doctor, before you can say that, then I said if another doctor or doctors say the same thing, then that she will not be along, that I will be here for her, whatever she need.

Then I explain to Mary that, she and I can be, it's whatever it is, and that all we have to do is pray and put it in God and Jesus hand, but we cannot give up please.

That day to me it was now special. Mary and I made love, something happen to me at that time, that after it put something on my mind, I could not explain it and now to this day, I can't figure out that feeling.

After Mary she left and went home, I close up my mind with anything that was on it, other than my God and Jesus, now I don't pray to my father or my big brother, I talk to them and explain to them, what I want and I am talking about, and if they feel that what I want or need, and if it happen that is what it is, and if it don't then that is the will of God, he knows the best.

Now God and Jesus I just meet Mary, and it has been a long time that I have had some one, in my life that need me, and that I believe that she love me, but we have our deference as many others do, and I love Mary also so please, please Father don't take her away from me now, I have found someone who I can put my trust in, now a doctor has said, that Mary had cancer please Father, don't take her away from me, I love her and I know that you love her also, please my Father hear me and that I need him and Jesus.

Now Mary she was still working, one day I was in the lobby I saw my friend Kopoe, she and I was talking she ask me, did I know that Mary had cancer, I said yes and it is a shame then I said to Kopoe, that I told Mary that she was not along, that I will be here for her that she and I together, can beat that cancer.

Kopoe said to me that, she was going to take Mary to see Kopoe doctor, that he was black and he was a good doctor, and if he said that Mary had cancer, she can believe that. I said to Kopoe thank, and now I know in my heart that Kopoe she, is a good person.

Mary she went and saw Kopoe doctor, when I saw Mary she said that, the other doctor that Kopoe took her to, he said the same thing as the other doctor said, that she had cancer. I said with she and I we can beat that, that was when Mary ask me a question, she ask me, that I know so much, was I God or Jesus.

That was when I got quiet for a moment then I said no. Mary she said that I act like it, then Mary said that she had appointment, on March the thirty at ten a.m. for treatment, and that I had to go with her, because the treatment was going to make her drowsy, and she can't drive back home, I said honey like I said to her, that I will be here for her.

Now after talking to Mary, I said to myself that I was a representative of my God and Jesus, I have part of God in me, and me in my God because I am his son, and Jesus has God in him and he is my big brother, who am I.

On the day of Mary treatment I was right there with her, she said to me before the treatment, that it would take three hours for the treatment, that I could go home and that she would call me, after it was over. I said no that like I said to her, that I would be here for her then the nurse, call for Mary, they took her into the treatment room.

After the treatment was over after three hours, the nurse came and got me that Mary she needed me, I went to the treatment room where Mary was, she was so weak, I sit down by her and took Mary into my arms, so that she could rest for a little while, before we leave the doctor officer, then Mary got dress and we left and came home.

One day I said that I was going to have passing through put on T. shirts, I contact Toney and had him to make the T. shirts, then I call Mary and told her what I had done, and when I get them back that I would give her one, Mary she said no don't give her one, that I had to pay for them and that, she wanted to pay for hers, because then she contribute to me in my future.

Now on April the fourth Toney he call me, to let me know that the shirts was ready, I said ok how much money I need, he told me, I said that I would be there in a hour, he said ok that he would be there, I went and pick the shirts up.

Before I got back home I stop and talk to Popeye, I showed Popeye the good Job Toney had did on my T. shirts, then I left and came back home, I showed Stewart the T. shirts he got one, and said that every one that live in here, should get one because that was all some was doing, was passing through.

Then I got a shirt and took it to Mary, she saw the T. shirt and read it and smile, she gave me the money and said, that now she can say that she help me, with my future.

Mary she was trying to cope with the cancer that she had, now before I ask Mary would she marry me, and she didn't give me an answer, so I didn't say anything else about it but I would do anything for her.

One day Mary came to my apartment and Mr. Brown, he had taken a picture of me Mary she saw the picture, and she said that she was taken that picture, I said that she can have it and that because, when she get ready to go to bed she can kiss me good night, she smile and said that she didn't feel so good, that she was going and go to sleep, I said ok talk to her later and if she need me, that I will be at home.

Later on I decided to put another poem I wrote, it was the first one I wrote called, unforgotten love. I was talking to Mary about what I was putting on the front, of the T. shirts. She told me to put, love dies, memory live forever. I said that was what I was going to do, that I was going to call Toney that day, and have Toney to make the other T. shirts up.

Now every time Mary had to go to the doctor for her treatment, I would be there for her unless I had some work to do, if I did I would ask Frank, Jean old man would he take Mary to her treatment, that I would take care of him, when I see Frank I would take care of him.

Now Mary and I we did not have any secret, she and I talk about anything and everything that, she and I wanted to know she told me something, and I said that she better watch some girlfriends, that was the same thing happen to my sister, Willie Mae. That was when I ask Mary again, did she call her family and let them know, that she need their help because she was sick, Mary said that she did, that was the first time she lie to me, I didn't believe her.

Now every Sunday morning I go and take my partner Popeye, to the grocery story. After I went and came back home, then I will call Mary to see how she was, her job gave her a medical leave from her place of work, one day I was sitting on the outside talking to Miss. Queenie, and Stewart he came out side then Mary she came out side, we all was talking then Queenie she left to go home, she had to fix herself some food to eat, Mary she was feeling bad I tried to make her feel ok, I started to play with her by tick her she didn't like that, she said David you better stop because she would hit me, then she said Stewart tell him that she will hit me, Stewart said with a little laugh and said she will.

After Stewart left to go back to work, Mary said to me that she had to go on a medical leave, I said that she can't work sick that I will be here for her, then I ask how long of leave that they was going to give her, she said two month, we sit and talk until Mary was not feeling good, she said that she was going and get some rest, I told her that I will be close just in case she need me.

Now after then Mary she got sicker and sicker, until one Sunday I had took my partner Popeye, to the grocery store and came home, I stop into the lobby to shoot the bull with Stewart, I found out that the paramedical had taken Mary to the hospital, I ask what hospital did they take her, no one knew where they took her, I said when I see Jean I will find out.

Every day Mary she was on my mind, I didn't know how to get to where she was, no one could tell me where she was, until look like something came to me, that Mary she don't want to see me, because she had lost so much weigh, and she don't want to see me.

One day Jean and I was in the lobby talking, we was talking about Mary she did not let her kids know, that she had cancer and that she need them, I said that Mary had told me twice, that she had told her kids that she was sick, Jean said that she didn't, that she, Jean had call them to see if they know, that their mother was so sick, so that the older daughter was coming.

That was when I said to Jean, that I don't know how Mary was doing, because she did not call me so that I could go and be with her, that Mary she don't want to see me, Jean she didn't want to tell me but she did, she said that Mary didn't want me to see her, like she was, I said that was ok that I still love her.

And one day Kopoe she was going to go and see Mary, she ask me did I want to go with her, there was Miss. Helen live in building two she was sitting there, I said to Kopoe know that I better not, she ask me why? I said that Mary, she don't want to see me, Kopoe said, how do you know! Miss. Helen said David he knows, I said that if that what Mary want, I have to respect her wish.

So now I had to get busy doing any and everything I could, to keep my mind clear that is and was hard to do, I start to cooking out with the others tenants, it cost me money but I was doing what I wanted to do, to have some others around me to have some fun with me, I would cook at four times a month, then in the monthly meeting we said that we was going to have a yard sale, for April the sixteenth on a Saturday it was pass, we ask for five dollars for a space and a table, to sell their things.

Now every day before the sale, we all was getting our things ready for the yard sale, I had my T. shirts to sell, and the others had whatever they wanted to sale, other than drugs.

Now Toni she said that she had a couch, that she wanted to put out on the yard sale, and that if I go and get it and bring it back, that she would give me fifty dollars after the sale, I said that I would, I Missed Mary so much.

That day before the sale it was on a Friday, before I went to go and get the couch for Toni, that was her day off my phone ring, I answer it was Mary." she said hi," some reason in my vision, I saw Mary putting things in her bags. I ask Mary why did she cut me out from her life, after she got sick I needed her and I thought she needed me, Mary said that she didn't cut me out, I ask then why didn't she want me to come, to the hospital to see her, Mary she said David you are a good man, too good. She said that she do love, then Mary she hung up the phone, that was the last time I talk to Mary on April fifteen 2005.

Now with my head looking down, I went and got Stewart and went and got the couch for Toni, after we came back and I was parking my truck, to get ready to take the couch off, I saw Mary daughter coming in Mary car, I look and Mary she was in there also, Stewart said there is Mary he spoke to Mary, I said hi honey how are you with my heart skipping, she just look at me without saying a word, her daughter said that she was getting ready to take Mary to the airport, I ask her daughter, that will she please keep in touch with me, so that I will know how Mary was doing, her daughter said that she would do that, I said to Mary that to take care herself, Mary with that pretty smile as she always do to me, without saying a word they left.

Now Stewart and I got the couch off my truck, and put it into the manager officer then I move my truck, and park it by my apartment, I look for Mary car park out there, they had left I guess her daughter just went right back out, after Mary saw me.

Now the day of the yard sale that morning, I had not got out side for the sale Stewart came to where I was, and call me but I was almost ready to put my things on my truck, Stewart said that they was waiting on me, I said that I was on my way.

After I got on the outside and put my shirts out, I saw Stewart I was going to put Toni couch out there, Stewart said that Toni did not want to put the couch outside, that she had someone else wanted to buy it, I said ok and went and took care of my own things, but Toni still owe me fifty dollars any way.

Then somebody ask me did I see Gladies, that she was out and back in here from the hospital, at that time I saw that BITCH Gladies, I shook my head why are she still in here.

After the sale was over I went home and put my T. shirts up, then I went back on the outside, I saw some of the others who sold some things on the sale, they said that they did ok with their sales, I said that I did ok also.

Now about April the twenty ninth," I believe that sometime when you are writing, back in time you can easily have a wrong date or time, but that you are still telling the truth," someone ask me when did Gladies move! I stated that I don't know and don't care then I said that my letter that I sent to the upper management has been answer.

Now I had another problem in my life, that Mary are going and went back to her home town," sick," and I might not see her anymore, and that I don't think that my daughter or my son love me, now my son, I have not talk to him until after July 2004 I called and left message he want call, or he might not get his message, now my daughter Jackie, I have not talk to her until after that July also, but I am ok with that, if they don't need me now, one day they are going to need me.

Now that Gladies has move now I will have some relief, and with the others, I will put that in God and Jesus hand, their hand are bigger then mind, then I go fourth and do what my Father, want me to do.

That Saturday May the seven, it was the Ky. derby I said that if Mary was here, I could run the names of the horse by her, she don't know anything about horse races, but I don't know either so I decided not to bet.

Now on Sunday may the eight, as I always do take my partner Popeye to the store, and come back home, this day I said that I was going to stop into the lobby, I park my truck and got out I saw Sheila, I spoke to Sheila, she said hi David, that she was so sorry about my lady Mary, I said hold it, hold it what are she talking about, Sheila said that someone told her that Mary pass. that was a hurt, Sheila said that she thought that I knew, I said no that I didn't know thinks, then I went home and wrote a note and got it to Jean or Frank, to call me that I need to talk to Mary daughter, and if she call her and have her to call me, I would be thankful.

Sure enough Mary daughter call, I was not home when she call, but she left her number for me to call her back, I did that was the first I meet Mary daughter, her name is Rhonda Knox, from Ruston, Louisiana.

She and I talk, she told me that she could not find my number, to call me that Mary she was not still in the ground, she did not tell me why, but she told me that Mary, her mother she love me, I said that I love her also, she said the day she was leaving she said, don't forget David picture, she said that she told Mary that she had it. Then Rhonda Knox Mary's daughter told me why that Mary didn't want me to see her, in the hospital. That Mary she didn't want to hurt me, the way she was sick and the way she was looking, I said she didn't want to hurt me, but she still did, Rhonda said that she know, then I told her that I had writing some poetry, that Mary loved, and if it be ok with her, that I want to send them to her to read at the funeral, Rhonda she said sure it was ok, I said that it would be there before the funeral, I got her address and said that I was sending it register, to her and that I would call her back, to see if she got it, she said ok.

That next morning I sent Unforgotten love, Passing Through and a copy of the valentine card, that her mother gave me, and my others words I wanted Mary to hear, that was May fifteen 05 I wrote this for Mary, after I found out she passed.

A letter for Mary when I first saw her I saw something in her that I could love, I just didn't know how to let her know.

Mary after I got your attention, I know then I was not wrong, I gave her my word, that I will be a friend of her for life.

Mary I had found the one for me, I gave me for her for our love to be as one, Mary I wrote unforgotten love, before your time, but my words was for her, as you had read and said it was for her.

Mary I wrote passing through, that we all will have to pass on some day, now that you had you have reach your destiny, and I have to cry.

So Mary I kept my promise to you, I love you then now I still have her in my heart, as you said, love dies, memories live forever, Mary her memories live forever.

So Mary I have your memories, and God and Jesus have you with them, they needy you more than I do.

Now after Sheila she gave me a card to send away, to get my book one publish. After I finish my book I sent it to TRAFFORD publishing, in Canada. That was on 04/ 18/ 05 first I went with Legacy plus package, the publish said that I should up grade my book, but money was a problem, but some where I got the money, it just came to me because I believe in God and Jesus, and if you have belief in God and Jesus, all thing are possible. I took my book from Legacy to Entrepreneur plus package, because I had and have belief in God and Jesus.

Every day I saw some of the tenants, I would always sit and talk to them, just to see or try and find out, what they want to do, that was the only way I would know, in the meeting they wanted to talk about, so I take out of my time and sit and talk to them.

Now, when someone want talk, when they should talk they want, but they will have plenty to talk about, when it was out of the meeting, but they did not know that, when every time I sit and talk to them, I was in a meeting.

Now I had to take the bull by the horn, and try to do something to make them happy, even thou it cost me money, I don't care or think about money, it's only something to make me or someone else happy, it change hands as life are passing through.

There is a cousin of mine in Lancaster, Ca. her name is Hattie Reaco, Hattie she and I call each other to see how,

David L. Marshall

time to time we are doing, and there is Hattie sister, Isabel when I call we talk before Hattie take the phone, I am a man who loves his family, I was telling Hattie about the T. shirts with passing through on it, Hattie said that she wanted one and send Isabel one also, I got their size and the color, Hattie said that she would send the money, so later on that day I sent the shirts to Hattie, later on she sent me the money for the shirts.

You see it get hot out here in Vegas, and at the sitting area in our complex, there is tables outside to sit and talk, but there was not anything to take the peoples out from the sun, I said to myself that if we had a canopy, that the tenant could be out from the sun, I said that I was going to run by my thinking by some of the tenant, to see what they think.

So at the monthly meeting, I can bring it to the members, and see what they think about putting a canopy up. Now at the time for the meeting, it was May the twenty at five o clock, 2005 when it was time to talk about putting up a canopy, in new business, I explain to the members about how it was important, to put up something to shade the sun while we was sitting outside, having some fun, the members gave me their ok, now I have to find out will the corporate office, with Miss Grand give me the approve to put the canopy up.

That was when I saw Stewart, and he and I was talking I said that the members, had gave me the ok and the approve to spend the money, to get the canopy then I said what do he think, Miss Grand she would give me the approval to put up the canopy, Mr. Stewart said why not Miss Grand she was a fair lady, she would let us put one up.

Then I said that I would send a letter to her about that, Stewart said that he think that it would be ok, then Stewart said that when I write the letter, that he would fax it over to Miss Grand, I said ok that I was going to do that now.

Now after Mary she had pass on and went to God and Jesus, I had made up in my mind that, I have had bad luck in a relationship with a woman, that I don't see myself with another woman, calling her my woman, that to make a commitment to her, because after Mary I can't see another woman, into my life and in bed with me making love, and having sex with her and she are looking for something else, like a commitment.

That was when I said, let a friend of a woman, just be a good friend. I use to go and do anything and everything, to get a woman into hers or my bed, if I could not get her in bed with me, I had to have her in my life some way, I would made her my sister or my daughter.

Now I will let a friend ship of a woman grow, to see where ever it go to be, I can't rush the sex to be or make a commitment, it want work.

You see if I had listen to my heart and my mind, what my father and big brother had gave me, I should have knew better, other than let my little head go where ever it wanted to go, well I can say this, it can't go anywhere unless I put it there, no matter how hard it was.

That was the same as the garden, Adam he did not listen, eve she had courage she was hard headed, a woman she do not believe in what some one tell her.

One day we was sitting on the outside, one of the tenant ask me why did Gladies, put that shit on my porch. I said because I would not go to bed with her, and that she was lucky, that if I was like I use to be, she would have been in the hospital, because I would have put her in there by my hand, and that now I am older now, I don't want to go into the system, that spell trouble and now I am too old for that.

When I wrote that letter and went and saw Mr. Stewart, I gave it to him to fax it to Miss Grand, he fax the latter for me.

Stewart and I we work with each other sometime, when he is off work on his off days, and if he wanted me to help him, the other day I was in my computer writing in my book, when I can't think about what I need to write, I go on the outside sometime, I walk around the complex, to get myself some exercise and think about, what I was going to do next, or just sit in the sitting area thinking, sometime my lady friends come out side, and sit and talk to me.

Now some things some peoples say, you shake your head now I know me, and I don't care about what peoples say about me.

Let me tell you something about me, that you don't know. I am the same as you are in a way, a user," yes a user" but you use peoples that, do not have anything, me, I use someone who have it all, he have it all from the things that man made, "or man did," now he only recognize but one that is his creation, now as one of his creation he use me, and he get jealous when I almost lean the other way, a man and his son are to be so close until, if another man give another man son anything that are difference, then he the son he have the termination to give, another man some attention that he should have, just like you see your woman with another man, yes he get jealous. And I would be jealous also, that is why I am jealous of my father.

Now he gave me all of him, now why can't I be him, I don't want to be the one who, want more from his father, all I want is his love, my father love, he is love.

Now I ask him what I need, when he give it to me I share my blessing with you, even thou if sometime it hurt myself.

At Holliday Memorial day, the corporate office Miss Grand, they give money to give a dinner for the Holidays Toni, some of the others tenant and me, cook the dinner for the tenant.

One day Stewart said that Albertson food store, had soda on sale for Pepsi, two dollars a twelve pack, he ask me did I want to go and get some, I said yes when? Stewart said when you get ready to go, so I went and got my truck and came back, Stewart and I went to the store, after we got in the store, Stewart saw a canopy it was put up in the store.

He look at me and said David, I said yes Stewart, he said look at that then he pointed to the canopy, we went and took a look at it," it was nice," I fell in love with it but only one thing, it was aluminum, but I knew then that we better get it now, soon because it might be going later, I said to Stewart that when I see Elizabeth, that I would get her and take her with the tenant, check book and get it.

David L. Marshall

While every day I was looking to see Elizabeth, the tenants was asking me about a Wednesday night move, I knew that I didn't have the time for no move, I have to work on my book. So I told the tenant that ask me about the move, that if that what they wanted to do, that I would support it with her.

And the craft class that the council would help them, with what they needed in the class, to have the money to get what they needed.

Then when I see a tenant they had others things to tell, about smoking in the hallway, about the rules Louise Shell senior have, now some of the rules they have, I don't agree with but, these are their rules I don't have to agree, with all of them but I have to live with it, or move.

How peoples telling their personal business to others, and later on the other person tell someone else, and it start like a match in a dry area of grass, light it and there it go. Then there is someone mad or disappointed.

Then the parking lot, parking in front of the office at the time of the mail man truck, I agree with that you and myself need our mail, but other than the handicap space, if you are not handicap don't park there. But the other parking space, there is no personal parking space, to your rule tenants can park as they please, manager should put up a sign to that affect, office parking only that will correct that problem.

Tenants or guess talking loud in the lobby, most of the tenants that live in here they can't, some can't hear so good, that make some peoples talk loud, big deal we all are over 55 years older. Some can hear and they still talk loud.

Then some want to have a neighborhood watch, I was going to go to metro police dept. and see how we could set it up. Toni asked me, what are, we going to do for mother day. We didn't do any-thing for father day, I had already talk to Toni about father day, I don't run behind no one," so I said to Toni, that yes we could have something for mother day, that I had talk to her before father day, so what we could have both days together, and call it his and hers celebration day.

Now we had in the bank then was $918.35 to work with, then one tenant said that the security guy, he put a parking ticket on his vehicle about, parking on a white line between the two lines, I said because the tenant park on a white line, he got a tow ticket come on. Then, we talked about having another yard sale in by Labor Day in Sept.

So with the concern of the tenants, after all I am not a manager of the complex, I am just the president of the council, I sent a letter to Global property management Group, Inc. ATT: all management, the letter too.

We, the tenants residing at the Louise Shell Senior Apartments, located at 2101 north Martin Luther King Blvd, Las Vegas, Nevada, would like to bring your attention to some safety concerns.

Many of the peoples that are leaving or coming into the apartment are speeding. We are seniors here, many of which cannot see, hear or walk well. The residents here are our main concern, but I, as president of the tenant association, am also concerned for your property. We I have asked the management a few times about installing speed bumps on the street to slow down the drivers.

We haven't had an onsite manager for months now, so who do we go to with this?

We are also concerned about the parking situation. We agree with you regarding parking in common driveways or on lawns, but we would like you further explain page 3, letter J in your book. Are you referring to parking between the white lines on the parking lot, or a driveway with grass to park on?

We are having an issue with tenants being ticketed and threatened with towing for parking their car just on the white line. Like I said before, we are all over 55 years of age and this puts an unnecessary burden on us. Though this is your rule and we are trying to follow it, we feel it was not right.

We are very concerned about the security here. When illegal activity is occurring, the security isn't to be found; however, he has plenty of time to ticket cars on white lines. We are acting as our own security at this point the lighting is a serious security concern also, as it is very poor.

We are looking forward to your assistance in making this a safe and happy place for all our residents. Thank you for your time.

Sincerely,
Tenants of the Louise Shell Senior Apartment Association
David Marshall
Acting President
CC. Frank Hawkins
Doris Grand
Richard B. Blue Jr.
Cory Knaus
All fax numbers:

Now that this maybe I can have some peace, while I am writing my book. The stages in my life was when God, put me on earth to stay.

Until he got ready for me to come home with him, now I was stumbling in life until, I was so bad I thought, until my father put a stop to what, I was doing, I got put out of School, that's where the fun was at, then I was all alone," I thought," I had to bring my parents back before I came back to School. The principal gave me five days to get it together.

Now after the fifth day, I went back to School by myself, I never told my parent, because this is my life, I had to take responsible of my own self, I had to do this for myself, that was my second chance.

My last chance is now. Because after I saw the light I ask for something then, that, on this day I found what I had asked for, to see my father. On this day he said that I wanted to see him. He said to me, look in the mirror and see what I see. That the reflecting images in the mirror, is what your father look like, I am you.

Now if I had went to School and gotten educated, other than being a fool, and did the first of my life as I have done the last, I would not have made so many Mistakes. Reading my books will show you that, all my grammar and Misspelled words might not be there, now it is me, all of my life story. I want you to realize that, all your life from a child, to the day God get ready for you, is a learning experience.

As I hear some peoples with all the illness that they have, in there body with the pain they have, to me sickness, in the body is how you treat yourself, from the wear and tear with the weather, that you have to take care of yourself, and watch what you eat. But the sole in the body that belong to God, you should take care of your body," God body," the sole is to be protected with God and Jesus, it is for you to take care of the body.

Now if you have read my other book one, of my pass life up to now, I guess you say that, this man is crazy, but think about what you have read, it was and is all about my life. My heart, mind, feeling, disappointment, happiness and my way that I love my God and Jesus, because they are me, and my God love all of us, not one but all, but you see God and Jesus they get disappointment to.

You know there is something in everyone I want to ask you one thing that I can't see? What do you see in me? I would like to know that, because I can't see myself what do you see, who or what I am! Please tell me.

While I am on the inside of my body, I can't see myself until I look into a mirror, all I see is a reflection of me, but after I get out from my apartment, and come out side what do you see about me? What kind of a person am I?

You see I am looking and I am trying to do something, I have to help someone else from a child or a grown up, that can't help them self, kids don't want to go to school and get their education, to go on with their life and their welfare.

All I see now is those who have drop out from school, and don't have anything to do or don't know what to do, those are trying to go through this world, with or without education they are wasting their life, some have it all some don't have, the drugs has brought them down. Drugs will bring down the best of you, if you let them. Do what I did to find God and Jesus.

Because every day, all days in my life I ask myself who am I, I talk to my father and Jesus, about my feeling inside of me, even if I can't see," blind," I still have to get to my destiny, like my heart and mind have eyes, I can see through darkness and go with my feeling, with that I can do anything with God and Jesus.

Now on June the first 2005, I received my renewal for my driver license that was on a Wednesday. On that Saturday the big horse race was running, the Triple Crown.

Now I am a man like this, I will do anything to help someone else if I can, and I don't like to ask others for anything, if I ask you for something, that mean that I really need what I ask for, my birthday is June the fifth.

Some know when my birthday is, that same Saturday of the race, someone said to me David Sunday is your birthday, and I said yes it is. They asked what was I going to do for my birthday, I said that I was not going to do anything, but just get another year older.

But now I had already said that I was going to, cook out for the tenants on the seven, for twelve o clock and that was all I was going to do.

Now I had got the meat that I was going to cook that day, because Elizabeth Johnson, Miss Russell, Miss Blackwell, Mr. Brown and some of the others was going to help, cook the side dish and bring it to the cook out.

That morning I got up and got my fire started in the grill, and went back to my apartment, and came back with the meat, and put it on the grill to started cooking.

While the meat was cooking and it got almost ready, those ladies at twelve o' clock they was ready to eat, I had to cut that meat, so that they could fix their plates, but you can't argue with a hungry woman. After we had eaten and had a good time, and we clean up everything, there is another lady live in here, name Miss Hattie she is a sweet lady, she said to me later that she put that meat, into her oven for a few minutes, and it was so tender. I said that I believe it but they didn't let me finish cooking, Miss Hattie said it was ok, I said thanks to her. Every day after that cook out, all we did was do whatever we need for our self, until before Father's day.

We was sitting on the outside in the sitting area, Toni she came out with Stewart, Toni ask me, what was we going to do for Father day, because we did not do anything for mother day.

That was when I explain to her," Toni," why I did not," but I did not say to her what I wanted to say," but all I said was that, I had talk to her about mother day before, but she did not follow up with me, to see what we was going to do, and after she did not say anything, she didn't want to do the dinner because, after all she is the coordinator.

Then Toni and I decided that, because we did not do anything for Mother's day, we would have a and her day, that was what it was his and her day.

You see I am a kind of guy, I study peoples that be in my present, I listen and hear, I check out their character, that is the only way that I will know who they are, and I am hoping that they are checking out me also.

While I am with them, I watch everything about what they are doing or do, I can be listen and watching other things around me, and they are talking to me they think that I am not hearing them, that I am brushing them off, but that is not the way it is, I have to see what is around me for my safety, and if I am with you, that make me look out for them also.

Now I can do two things at once, now I am not perfect and I am not trying to be, but I am no fool, you can't Misuse me one time, and come back to me, and do it again no way.

Now on the 24th of June 2005 I had already committee, to cook out for those who wanted me to, and I committee myself also for the 25th, I knew that it was close but if I make a commitment, I have to honor that.

After Stewart had fax the letter to Miss Grand, I was outside talking, Stewart he ask me did I hear from Miss Grand, I said no not yet, he said that he had already fax the letter to her, I said that she will call soon.

After I went home and check on my messages, one was from Miss Grand she ask me to call her back, I did call Miss Grand, she and I was talking I explain to her, that we was not looking for the corporate office, to pay for the canopy we already had it, all we need was the approve from her to put it up.

Miss Grand said to me, you already have it why didn't you wait until I talk to her, I said that was ok, I could take it back to the store, she said nowhere are it now, that she want to see it. I said that it was in my bed room," not to be funny," but it was in my bed room, I put it there after Elizabeth and I went and got it.

Then I said to Miss Grand that, it was too heavy for me myself to bring it over to her, but that I would get it over to her, she said ok.

Now I went and saw Stewart and Toni, I explain to Stewart what Miss Grand and I had talk about, that she need to see the canopy, Toni she said that she was going over to the office, and if I gave her a picture of it, she would take it to Miss Grand.

That was when I went to my apartment, and cut the picture of the canopy box, and took it to Toni so that she could take it to Miss Grand.

Later on that evening I saw Stewart, he said that Miss Grand had call him, and said that it was ok to put up the canopy, that he will have to be with me, because I don't have any contractor license, I said to Stewart when did he want to put it up, he said in the morning, I said ok that I will have it out there, about nine o clock, Stewart said that was a date.

That was when I saw Miss Elizabeth, she said that her son he was going to type the letter, that we was going to send to Louise Shell senior apartment board, that he was so busy now that he will get to it soon, I said ok that in the morning, Stewart and I was going put up the canopy, Elizabeth said they gave us the approval, I said o yes.

That morning I got up and got dress, and took the canopy to the sitting area in a little while Stewart came out, then we had some of the tenants came out to see, Stewart and I was working hard on putting up the canopy, then we had some speculators, making their theories and guesses the way it should be, I had to put them into their place, if they was not going to help, then keep their opinion belief and judgment to their self.

After Stewart and I finish putting up the canopy, Stewart he took his tools back into the tool room, I with the tenants that was sitting out, they said to me, that Stewart and I did a good job putting up this tent, I said thanks to them and said that I, myself hope you all enjoy the shade that the, council did for you with your dues money.

Now every day I would sit out to see and hear, what the tenants say about the canopy, I knew that some was glad that it was up, and some that sit and look out the window, with the fun we all having with our life, eating dancing to the music, laughing with each other now they don't like it, but who care, we are doing what we want to do, for out happing.

Now with the other canopy was up, I had to try and keep and make the tenants happy, after all like I had said before, we are all is over 55 years older, and some are sick with whatever they have, that they are sick with, that we don't have to long to live or longer, only God and Jesus know that.

But they and myself have retired, and we are living in a complex that don't have to pay, all that rent," thank to Frank Hawkins and Miss Grand," now all we have to do now is live and have some fun, if they want that.

Now I am the kind of guy who, after paying my rent, and I have paid all my bills, I have some left, so what I do is share it with someone else, that is what God and Jesus want.

So I sit down and started to think, so what I decide to do was, put up a sign on the canopy the days that I wanted to cook, or do something for them, I put it on the canopy because the lobby, was close after the office business day was over, but on the outside it is never close, the tenants could see and read what I was trying to do for them.

After we had one canopy up, some of the tenants ask me, why don't we get another canopy for the other side, I said yes we can but we would try, and find one that don't cost as much as this, the first one.

Then one day Miss Brown she was sitting talking to me, she said that, she saw a canopy in the big lot paper, that didn't cost that much, I said where is the ad, Miss Brown said that she had it at home, I stated to her that, bring it with her when she come back, or when I see her and she said that she would do that.

Sure enough Miss Brown showed me the ad, I look at it and said, that it was different from the first one, and that it was lighter, I said that soon we would find one, another canopy.

One day Stewart and I was at home depot, to get something we saw another canopy, Stewart said David look at this, there is a canopy almost like the other one we have, and it is cheaper than, the other one, so we look at it and we got it, after Elizabeth gave me the check book, Stewart went with me to get the other canopy.

The next day Stewart and I put that canopy up also, it was to me and Stewart said that the other one, was better than the first one, the tenants said the same thing.

Now we have two canopies up now to enjoy, I put up another sign up on the second canopy, the same as the first on.

Now, at least two or three times a month, I with the council we had something for the tenants, to have something to do, to have some kind of fun.

Now I was on the outside one day, and every day you can say, peoples in their vehicle that can't get into the complex enter gate, and they can't get in, and when someone else with their vehicle, coming out the gate and it is still open, they will drive through the exit gate to get in, that is not safe.

Even thou I have been out side with someone else, I see kids climbing over the exit gate, or crawl under the gates to get in, and when you say something to them, they look at you as you are crazy, and they go on to where they was going.

If the tenants guess could not call them on the gate box, and when someone come in they will drive through with their vehicle, now who do they look at," me," I said that we had already sent a letter to the board, to see what I or we can fix that.

Then I said that we have peoples living here, that they can hardly walk, see or hear to good, and that is not safe.

After I went home, I had a phone call on my answer machine it was Miss Grand, she wanted me to call her, that was what I did, not before I took a deep breath, and I let it out and said to myself, for to Elizabeth thank you Jesus, now I will have something to bring back to the tenants.

Now God and Jesus has heard my prayers, that was when I call Miss Grand and talk to her, she wanted me to explain the letter for her, I did about the content of the letter, she and I had a good communication," some had their own information about Miss Grand," but I don't listen to others what they say about no one, I have to find or know myself.

What I found out after talking to Miss Grand, she is not what some had said about her, I was telling her how all I wanted to do was, make the tenants happy and that I have told them many times, that I was not a manager, that I explain to them what the council duty was.

Miss Grand she was telling me how much it would cost, if they did all what we was asking for, I explain to her that I could put in the speed bumps, and put in the lighten with Mr. Stewart, with the spike to keep the vehicle, coming through the wrong gate.

Miss Grand ask me was I a contractor! I said, no, I was not! She said that to do what I was asking for, it would be costly, but she would take a good look at the oppose, then she ask me to contact her if there was a problems, that she and I can talk about it, that I didn't have to write the whole board, I said that I would do that, then she said one other thing to me," that made sense," she said Mr. Marshall you can't make everyone happy, I respected that wisdom from her.

Now I can see that my God and Jesus heard me. My sister Deloise, she call me from Chicago one day, as she and I we call each other, once a week, we think about each other that is love, you see my daughter Jackie, I love her dearly she is my heart as the same as my son John, after that 4th of July, she and I, we was not calling each other, unless if it was something important, that I, we had to talk about the family.

About two days before Deloise had call me, Jackie she call me, I was so glad to hear from her, after all I was not going to call her, after what she did to me. We talk and Jackie she gave me her apology, she said that if she had did anything wrong to me, that she was sorry. I said everything was ok, don't worry about it.

You know it was so hard for me a man, not to call his child or his child don't call him, I was trying hard after a whole year, now she is my child, I will take those words she gave to me, after all she was trying to reach out to me, now I will take that and build on that.

Deloise said, o Jackie call you, I said yes, Deloise said she call me to, that is good she said that I better talk to her," my sister," brother, then she Jackie must have told Deloise, what had happen. That Deloise had told Jackie, that she better call her daddy and talk to him, I said that she did call, and I told Deloise what I felt, that I am Jackie father or daddy if she want to call it that, but I am her father and Jackie, she is not my mother and she can't, be my father that is my job. And that I will not have her treat me as she is my father.

She is one of my children, and I love the others as the same as Jackie, that was when I told Deloise, that it was all most a year that I spoke to my daughter, that I love my kids, it is the way that Kee Kee, and Leveater they don't try to call, but they wanted it that away, I granted them their wish.

One day I was in the lobby, we all was sitting around waiting on the mail to come, Toni came into the lobby, she had another lady with her, a find lady to boy, that lady she made my heart took another breath, like my heart had eyes, I said ok, the way this lady look to me that, maybe my prayer for another manager has been answer, could it be a new manager.

That was when I said nor as by me being the president of the council, I know someone would induce me, then I said that the way things are here I can't say that, but if this find lady was another manager, well I think Toni is smart, she do have the sense to induce me.

Later I saw Glen and Killer; they ask me did I meet the new manager. I said no, I saw that find lady with Toni, that was walking with her, Toni she walk all around me and she, didn't say David this is your new manager, and induce me as the tenants president.

They said this, that they don't want me to know, I said that was stupid how can they hide it, they showed me how you can bring out something, that you see and hear I thought was true, about peoples around me.

One day just before we were getting ready to have a cook out, for Miss Blackwell, Miss Russell and Miss Dorothy.

Miss Elizabeth and I was putting up some things for the party, I had already ask Toni, to put the out-side function on the monthly calendar, as coming to gather. After Toni gave me my copy to put out, I saw that she had put on the calendar coming out, I said to myself coming out! I have been out so long, do she have a clue about what coming out is about.

Elizabeth and I was talking about that, now Toni dad he was out there with us, I said that I can't use this, I can't do anything with this, all she Toni had to do, was put on the calendar what I and she talk about, at that time Toni and the new manager, that I still do not know her name, pull up in Toni vehicle, and park and got out I call Toni, that could I see her for a minute, she came over to me and spoke, I spoke also, and I told her that she made a mistake, she ask how, I said that I we talk about coming to gather on the calendar.

Toni said that is what she put on the calendar, I said no, then I showed it to her, and I said that I had been out ever since, I was sixteen years old, on the creek banks in Alabama. That coming out I been there, I need them to come together, Toni said that she would change it, I said ok because I can't handle that.

That same day I said that, I have to meet the new manager on my own, I went into the lobby and I knock on the door of the office, she said hi come on in, I said that my name was David Marshall, and that I was the president of the tenants council, and that I had seen her before, but someone did not want to tell me, who you was.

She said that her name was Elsie Morgan, and she showed me her name, on her name plate on her desk, then she said Elsie like the cow, I said that might be, but I was going to call her Elsie or Miss Morgan, to myself I said she have a beautiful smile, and what I see she is beautiful all over, Elsie and I talk and I went back home.

On July the first was the cook out for the party, we all was having a good time, we had food to eat, something to drink and music to dance to we made it a party.

There was Miss Birdie, Miss Dorothy, Miss Blackwell, Miss Queenie, Miss Russell, Miss Mary Helen, Miss Hattie, my daughter Larissa came, Killer, Miss Elizabeth and others tenants was there, Elsie she came out also, she I knew that she was playing, she said ok you all have to take this some-place else, with that smile, I said get yourself a plate and eat some food, there was plenty. She said no that she had work to do, that she had already eating so have fun, I said to myself, you better know that was what I was going to do.

One day I was outside sitting, thinking about what I was going to write, when I get back home. And I was waiting for my first book to be in print, and get online, and thinking about how to bring peoples to gather, and I need money but I can't ask or take any money from someone else, I have to use what my father and big brother, gave and give to me, that it love and strength.

That was when I saw Elise coming out to where I was, she came out to smoke a cigarette, and I was sitting out, Elise she said hi to me then she said David right," I said right," she said that she will in time, know all the peoples that live in here, and that what she see, there are some good peoples living in here, I said you are right and some you have to watch.

That was when Elise she needed a light, I gave her a light then I lit myself a cigarette, we was talking and having our cigarette, I ask Elise could I fix a dinner for her, she said ok thanks, then I found out what she like to eat, or what she could not eat.

That day I told Elise that I had cook dinner for her, and that it was ready, but I need to know what time she wanted to eat.

She told me, I said that I will have it there for her at that time, so I went back home, and about a half hour before, the time Elise was going to be ready to eat, I got the food ready for her.

Chapter 3

Now I got the food ready to take it to Elise in the lobby, I took it there and put some of it on the table, I had to go and get the rest of the food.

On the way back to my apartment, I was thanking what I was going to say from my heart, how to receive or show her that I, we are glad that she are here, after all it took six months, for our complex to have a manager.

So I came back with the other food, I had fixed enough food for Toni, Stewart or anyone else, that was hunger if it was any left.

When I got back they was eating, I said you started eating before I got all the food here, and I had a speech to give for her, how I am glad that Elise are here with us, but now it is rune so eat up, I had my camera I had Miss Russell, to take a picture with Elise and I.

There was Elise, Toni, Miss Russell, Elizabeth, Sheila she came also you know and Mr. Wear, he was telling me how sick he was, and the things that he can't eat, I explain that you can eat what-ever you want, or drink anything that you want, but don't miss use it.

After we had finish eating, then I started putting the rest of the food up, to take back home, Elise she said David thanks for our dinner, now she had to go back to work, I ask Elise did she like it, she said yes she did," with her find self," I said to Elise that was thanks enough, then I said welcome to her, that she was God sent.

Now my daughter Jackie and I, I think that she had time to think about what she, had did to me, now we call each other like a daughter and a father, should be, because at that time I had step back, from my love I had for my daughter, but it was hurting me from my heart, now I can't divorce my daughter, because she are a part of me, because I am her father and I love my blood, that I pass on through my kids.

On the fourth of July I said that I was not going to cook, or do anything that day, but relax and rest, that was what I did.

Then on the fifth my daughter Larissa she called me that she needs me to come over to where she works, that she needed my help. I said ok that on the six I would be over, then I ask how was the kids, she said that they was ok, I said to tell them that I said hi, she said that she would.

Then I went to the sitting area just to relax, I saw my girl Kopoe on her porch, we talk then she said that she had some things to do, that she would talk to me later, I said ok, then I sit and saw some tenants or other peoples that know me, we speak then they go on to where they was going, then some of the other tenants would see me, then they come out and sit and talk, until they or myself was ready to leave.

On the morning of the six of July, I went to where Larissa work at the Salvation Army, she and I was talking she ask me, what was I doing on the eight, that was the Friday. I said that I had nothing to do what's up, she said that she wanted to have a barbecue, for the tenants like the way I did for Louise Shell, and that she wanted me to cook for her and them, if I was not busy, I said that I would be there about six, in the morning. She said ok because that I "David," like to start early.

Then Larissa she said that her reception name is Wendy, with another lady that lives in their name Mira, she was going to help and go with Larissa, to get the meat. then she ask me what else did she want, her to get from the store, I told her about the seasons spices for the meat, then I left and went back home.

That day when I got back, I pick up my mail and was sitting around talking, I mention that I was going to cook on Friday, one ask me where here, I said no where my daughter work.

That was when I told them, the way to get there if, they wanted to come by and that it cost three dollars, for the dinner. Miss Queenie said that I was trying to leave her, I said no Miss Queen not like that, my daughter she, need me, and a father I have to be there for my kids.

Miss Queenie said that she would Miss me talking and cooking, I said after I took her hand, that I will never leave her or the ones that appreciate, what I have been trying to do, that I know those peoples who disapprove, what I am, but that they have a problem I don't and all you have to do is call me, I said you have my phone number.

On the eight of July 05, it was the barbecue, that was when this guy he was a tenant over there, his name is Milton," no teeth," bare mouthed and he had just had a operation, he told me many things about his self.

He said that they, the doctors had cut open his chest, and operated on his heart, he is short fat and he was, and he is all fuck up.

That morning I was getting the meat ready, to be put on the grill he said some things to me, that made me took another look at him, what Larissa had saw him. He said that his meat had to be tender, otherwise he can't chew it. I said it will be tender I kept on doing what I had to do, then he said that, when he see other peoples cooking, that they has the tendency to take the dish rag, and wipe their sweat with it, he don't like that, now me I don't want that, I said hum if it was anybody other than my daughter, I would tell this half man something that he want like it.

Now, if I had to hit him because of what I want to say, because he would not like it, now that I didn't come over here to my daughter job, to hurt her all I came to do was help her, so I kept my cool and cook the meat.

After all the food was cook and we all was eating, sitting around talking shit, laughing I saw this white woman, big breast, blond and she was good looking. I kept on talking to Milton and Corin, but I could not take in a way my eyes off that woman, I said in my mind that she might be a resident, then I said no but, I don't know but I will find out later, I was looking at Wendy but, I found out that she was marry.

Now Larissa boss she came to the cook out, I meet her, her name is Regina. What a lady now I was like a dog in a hen house, I didn't know who was I looking at, Regina after the food had been serve, she jump right in and help clean up the kitchen, with Larissa.

Now Larissa she had a DJ spinning the music, she induce him to me as Maurice, I meet him and shook his hand, and said it was nice to meet him, I was getting ready to leave, I went up to Regina and said, that it was so glad to meet her, she said likewise, then I hug Larissa and said daughter, I would see her later, Larissa said ok daddy talk to you later, then I said good buys to some of the others tenants, Mira, Milton and Corin that I will see them later, then I left with Regina and that white woman on my mind.

Later on after I got home, you see we had a problems with those drugs dealers and user, out from where we live, we was doing a good job getting them out, there was one who live across the hall from me, name Ronnie, he was a big liar drug addict, he had his son with his woman, living in a one bed room apartment with him.

They were an addict also, I use to see him someone had kick his ass, and I said man what happen? He said well he and his woman had a fight I kind of smile and said, man that is what you can get when you get in a cat fight, they can fight also and you can't win.

When I see Rose that live across from me, my neighbor, I'll tell her that Ron, son that woman kick his butt, Rose said that his woman has seven sister, and all of them are rough, that was when I told Rose, after leaving her apartment lock her door, there was a reason.

Now I talk to Larissa when we need to talk, after all she and I are busy, if I needed to talk to her, all I had to do was call her, if she needed to talk to me, she know how to call me.

One day Larissa call me that, she had some problems at where she work, that they needed a maintenance man, and that if I take the job that, I would have an apartment free, that I have to live on the property, I said that, I could not break my lease agreement, and now that I am on social security, that I would have to get off, and I don't want to do that because if, anything happen that it would be hard to go back on.

Then she ask me, will I help her until she got one, I said ok, that I only can make so much money, before I had to stop by me on retirement, she said ok that she would not let me go over my income, I said if I did that the Government will penalize me and that I will be over to talk to her.

That day I was sitting on the outside, by the sitting area, I guess that some had heard that I had cook, for my daughter job dinner, some of the tenants came out to where I was, they was asking me, why was I going to move, I said that I was not going to move, that my lease was not going to be over until April the first 2006.

That my daughter she need me to help her, and as a father I have to be there for her, Miss Queenie she said that she was going to Miss me cooking, that was when I said to Queenie, if she need me for anything, all she had to do was call me, that now my daughter she need me to help her, and that I was going to put my second book on hold, just for now to help my daughter.

The day of July the eighteenth, I went over to Larissa job at North Las Vegas, Silvercrest apartment, for the Salvation Army, for a temporary position of building Superintendent, I fill out all the documentation to prove my eligibility, for the job and the letter Regina Dawson, sent from the Regional property manager, to me welcome.

On the nineteenth that Tuesday I started to work at seven o clock a.m. when I got there Larissa she was cleaning the windows, I got in there with her and clean the windows, there is a Church across the street for the Salvation Army, after we finish cleaning the windows, I started cleaning up the front of the building, and all around it so if peoples come in for business, it would be clean, then I started to see what I had to do.

First there was a wall that was pulling away from the building, I found some sand mix in the storage room, I took it and mix it with water and start fixing the break, then I had some speculator out looking, there was a guy that use to help, a white guy name Bill, he came and saw me working, he said that I was doing a good job on that wall, I said thank and kept on working until, I finish that break and found some others, it was hot as hell out there.

There was another lady who worked across the street, in the church, I saw her then Larissa she introduced me to her, as Brenda. I said after going back fixing those walls, man she is kind of find I wander is she with someone, I kept on working and said if it be, I would be close to her one day, but I would have to be cool.

While at work doing repair and fixing things that was needed to be fix that day, what I did was do so much that day, that I could do and think about the things that I was going to do, the next day after I get off work that day, I know what I was going to do tomorrow, I talk to my daughters, "boss," Larissa, what was facing me the next day, then I go home at 4: pm.

Before I get to my apartment, I stop at the lobby and get my mail, and talk to some of my neighbor from the complex that Miss me, and hear about those that don't like me, but because they don't like me, they can't do anything about it, but leave me along because I don't care, about what someone else think about me, only God and Jesus has my heart. And what people think that is on them.

You see I found out one thing in my life time that, when God and Jesus put you on a path to travel, a journey that God want you to do or go, it get hard sometime all you have to do is stop. Think, and ask your father and my big brother. Call him up and talk to him, he will show you the way and you will not go wrong.

With me I can't work without my supervisors God and Jesus, I have to live and be strong in order to be able, to pay my rent and my other bills when they come out, and to be able to help someone else, if they needed me as they are passing through this world. I don't like to ask others to help me, but if I had to do that, if they don't do it from their heart, I don't want your help I do mind from my heart.

Then I look at those who think that, I am a threat to them by their lies about me, I know what and who is in my heart, all the things that they think and say about me, I am still smiling with joy and that I am not the man that, Jesus is he is better than I, they lied on him and deceive him through rocks at him, he took that but he for gave you, but, not I.

That make you are not no better than I, would you take it? Now Jesus he gave his own life for you, but you don't even appreciate what he did for you, if you did you would not mistreat me, or your fellow man.

You know, I see and hear some think, that they have God and Jesus in heart, some they don't have a clue what's in their heart. I wish that they don't bring my father or brothers name out from their mouth, I call them, hypocrites.

After I get to my apartment and take a shower, sit and relax for a little while then I go outside, and sit and talk to the tenants that sit out, in the sitting area until they get ready to go back to their apartment, then I go back home if I wanted to go into my computer, I could or just sit and watch TV, relaxing, until I get ready to get into bed, to get up into the next morning.

That morning after I got up, and wash my face and start making some coffee, I took my shower and sit around drinking coffee, until time to go to work I had to be there at eight o clock.

At work I saw that white woman again, and when I saw Milton, I ask him what was the name of that white woman, with those big boobies with blond hair, was talking at the barbecue, Milton said that her name was Sally.

Now with that information about her name, I have to find out everything I can, to find out about her, and to do that I will use Milton, he will be the key he know her.

Now, what Milton he had already showed me about him, I did not approve him to be a friend of mind, but I only scratch the surface now I have to get under his skin, to get to the sole to see what he is about.

Now I could not ask my daughter Larissa, or one of the others ladies that live there, because after all they are a woman also, and they can't keep what I was trying to find out, because I had heard all ready, that how find I was, I don't see it but one thing that, there are so many hot ass woman, I ever seen.

So now I will work on Milton to see what I want to know, I got up into the mornings that when I get to work early, Milton, Donna ray and I would have coffee, before I start to work at Donna ray apartment, one morning I heard and saw something, that I had to watch.

Now, when I see something that don't look good, I have to watch to see if it was ok or not, now I have to open my eyes, ears and don't speech too soon until, I can put my hand on it.

Because it could be something that can harm, or hurt Larissa on her job, now if I keep close and treat Milton half way ok, he will trust me and I will find, what I am looking for soon or later, so I got through that day and went home.

Now I am still the president of the tenants council at Louise Shell apartment, and I am trying to watch my daughter back also, and the peoples that live in my complex, they are trying to say that I am stealing, they are all ways asking me about, the moneys that come from the Monday night moves, art and craft and bingo I tell them that I don't know. And I didn't know, I only wanted to know about was their monthly dues, one dollar a month.

And the problems that my daughter have, she need me more than someone who don't know me, now what do I do now, then I said resign from the council.

That morning I got to work, and took all the work orders that I had to do, and while I was doing that, I was thinking about what decision, to cut my time with my daughter, or resign from the tenants council, later on that day I was talking to Wendy, she ask me what was I going to do, I said I don't know.

Then before I got off work, I was in Larissa office we was talking, I explain my cessation to my daughter, about what the tenants was doing and that I was tiresome, Larissa said dad how can they say that, you are stealing their money and they don't have any, because most of the money after putting up those canopy, came from you and some of the others, what are they talking about, I said that I don't know, but I will find out then it was time for me to get off work.

Now I was trying to make up my mind, about what I was going to do asking God and Jesus, one day it came to me about what I was going to do, God and Jesus do things to help if you want it, all you have to do is ask.

One day I was sitting on the outside, talking to Miss Queenie and Miss Russell, and Miss Helen and her girlfriend came, they seem that they was coming from the grocery store, they had many bags that they had to take in their house, Helen girlfriend her daughter took them to the store, she is find, she was taking the bags from her vehicle.

That was when I heard someone call me, it sound as it was Miss Helen voice, I said to Miss Russell and Miss Queenie, that I guess that I will give them a hand, Miss Russell said hum, then Miss Queenie said David, you are a good man. I said that I try but they want let me, so I went and gave them my help.

When I got to where they was at, I took some of the bags then I ask, who bags was these that I had in my hand, that find daughter of Miss Helen friend said, that it was her mother bags, that was when I saw Miss Helen friend son coming, so I said to him that, I had his mother bags so take Miss Helen bags, and take them to her house, that is all it was, because the daughter she act as she was in a hurry.

Now that next day I got off work, and I came home then I stop to get my mail, and I was getting ready to go out of the lobby, Miss Helen she came out with me, they was doing something in the lobby, there was about ten peoples in there, I had already wave to the manager Elsie Morgan, when I walk to the lobby, I could see her from the window by her office.

Miss Helen she surprise me, she said that she didn't like what I did the other day, and that her girl-friend she didn't like it also, I had forgotten it I said what are she was talking about, Helen she said when I took her friend bags, without taken her first, that she didn't like that and that her girlfriend, she didn't like it also, that I was wrong.

Now I try to keep my cool but I want have no one, trying to make me like an ass, I said to Miss Helen, that I was trying to help them, now if I was wrong that she have my apology, but I didn't have to help them no kind of a way, and now after that I want help them anymore, then I start walking away I heard Helen hollowing, saying you are wrong man you are wrong, loud so that everyone in the lobby hear it, I kept on walking, shaking my head.

Now after I got to my apartment, I said that to myself I better resign, so what I did was call Miss Elizabeth and Miss Russell, then I explain to them that I was going to resign, from the tenants council, then I explain why I made that conclusion.

That I am tried, of the tenants asking me, where was the money from the move night, art and craft and bingo hell I don't know, I don't receive money from Toni to put into the treasure, she is the coordinate she has the money I guess, that she get from those nights.

And everything I try to do to help them, they don't appreciate it as they don't appreciate you and Russell also, now they are saying that I am trying to take over, hum, takes over what? They don't have no more then I, some might not have what I have that is love! Can they say the same for them self.

Elizabeth and Russell agree with me, they ask when was, I going to resign! I stated that I had already wrote my resignation, that I was going to take it to the office, and make copies and leave one in the office, for the manager, then I went to the office.

When I got to the office I saw Elsie, I spoke to her and ask how was she doing, she said that she was ok, I said find, then I ask her would she make five copies of this for me, and for her to keep one for her file.

Elsie she took the paper first she read it, and as she was making the copies, she asked me why did I want to resign? I explained to Elsie why I was tired of people trying to make me the bad guy and that I am stealing from them, I don't need that.

Then I explain that the other day I was in the lobby, monitor the games that the tenants was paying for to play," the money was to be put into the treasure, to have money to do some of the things, that they want to do with it later," Elsie she hand me my copies and she keep one, then she said that she just got here as manager, then she ask me, would I give her a chance.

That was when I said ok that I would hold the resignation, than I left and came back to my apartment, I started thinking about it very hard.

Later on I made up a Special meeting flyer, for July the 22nd 05 for the council at 5: pm, David Marshall—president—Russell—guide—Elizabeth Johnson—trustee—Grace Taplin—Trustee, Elect bodies.

That was when I took the Special meeting flyer, to the office to run off six copies to put on the exit doors, when the tenants come or leave the building, they would see it and read it, Elsie she said you made up your mind, I said yes I better resign now, because my daughter she need me to help her, but the peoples that appreciate what I was doing, I will be there for them but the ones, that don't appreciate me, I want be there for them.

Now I went home after I put up those flyers on the doors, I started thinking that there is some good peoples that live in here, some can be good if they reach inside their heart, and find what the heart is and for, some don't know, other than it pump blood through the body, in a cycle through, and through the vein, how could it do that without my father, God and Jesus.

Yes, I found God and Jesus. And I am glad and proud of that I have found them, because first I was lost, but now I have been found because I am a part of them and they are part of me. This is me that why I know who I am. Do you know yourself?

Now, I am going to let you know, some of me as I am about my kingdom I protect that. Now, if you can't and don't want to protect, yourself. If you are in trouble and need help, call me. This is me, that am all I can do for my fellow man.

When my mother she would whip me," beat me," and she would say that, she was beating the devil out of me. Now to this day, she did a good Job.

Now, don't think that, there is not a part of the devil in me, mother she didn't get it all out of me." have you ever say that was the devil, when you did something that you should know, that you was wrong, why did you say that?

Now when you have the devil in you, think about God and Jesus, they are you look in the mirror, see what you see. All you have to do, is tell the truth that is what will set you free, if not give some-one forgiven, you can fool me but God and Jesus, they already know.

Now, I have heard some Ladies, had said to some other that, why David, he don't get into bed with just any woman that invite him into her bed, some has said that he, "David," was a fag because he wouldn't go to bed with them, inferior remnant, that is not me as the dictionary reads, but I am myself and very careful.

In my pass life I would use a fine lady, I would work my way into her bed, there was not anything that I would not do for her, anything to just get into their bed. That was in my past. Some as myself, will say when they have her in bed, after she ask is it good honey, that is a mind bother, troublesome, if you say to her yes, honey, she got you.

Now I have had some it was so good, but a close mouth can't be feed, don't feed me I will know, if it was good, she don't have to ask me to tell her, because there is only two kind, a good big one, or a little one it is still the same, from a woman point, all I need from her is her friendship, or her love not sex.

Now in my lifetime up to now, I found out that there are things better then sex, God and Jesus. They make me feel good every second, minute, half an hour or hours of the day, sex is good only if, your mate respects you. God and Jesus will never leave you or for shake you. And they will give you all the respect that you need.

Now I have look inside of my heart, and back in my life time I ask myself, Father, and my Jesus, I don't want to resign from being president, of the council I am asking you, to give me my answer to what I am going to do, because I can't do anything by myself, all I can do is let you give me my answer, after all you are me.

That was when I got my answer, it came to me that I better resign because, these people are not going to change, they don't have anything and they don't want anything, all they are going to do is make my life, miserable, unhappy, wretched, mean and have all disappointment, so I can help the new manager, better if I resign because, I know what she has in front of her, after I ask God and Jesus to send her, I have to have her back.

Now with the new manager Elsie, I should give her a chance, but my daughter she need me, and that is love, but I will give Elsie her chance also, because I know why she is here in Vegas, I can help her in my own ways, if I get to close to her she is a lady, and I have all respect for a lady, she know how to push me back some. That is the way it is.

Now I had put down on paper, how and what I was going to do in the meeting, after Elizabeth, Miss Russell and I had already talk, I open the meeting the same as I had before, after the minutes and all reports was over, I let the members know how much money that, I was leaving behind and I explain to them that, they need tables and chairs to have, chairs to sit on while playing cards, bingo or whatever they was going to do.

And I also told them that I was going to, have the trustee Elizabeth carry on with my president, that I had left to go in the council, then that was when I told the members, that I was going to resign. I ask the trustee to read my resignation.

She I guess was as sadden as I was, I ask her to hand the letter to me, that I would read it to the members, the lobby was quiet.

So I took the letter and start reading, that to Louise Shell Senior council and coordinate, that on this date of 7/01/05.

That I the president of the council, will be sadden to inform you that, I have tried to show you that, all I wanted to do was do something for you to try, and make you safe and make you happy, in coming to gather.

But in my heart and mind you do not appreciate my goodness, and with no prejudice on the above date, I will resign of the head of the tenant council. Effective on this date, 7/ 22/05, time 5:07pm president of the council, I left

$478.30 in the treasure, and turn into the checkbook to Elizabeth, the trustee.

Now everyone there had something to say, Kopoe father he said before I got it approve, from the floor, he said that, what if they want let me resign? I stated that you all can't stop it, then Kopoe she is my girl, she tried to talk and stop me from resigning, but, my mind was made up about what I was going to do, that would not stop me also.

So I got a motion from the floor from Kopoe father, to expect the resignation, and I had a second, that is when I ask for the new manager, to speak to know her tenants, in the meeting Rose she got Elsie from her office, as she came to take the floor, I said that I was going to get up, and take my rightful place for me, I said that I will give them her manager Miss Elsie.

That is when I stood at the front door to hear Elsie, she have the beautiful smile, she said in so many words that, you run a good man away, Elsie started talking and said see David, he is standing in the front listen, that is my place now.

Now one day I was on the outside talking to Miss Queenie, Blackwell, Rose, and some of the others live in here, someone ask me how was Virginia? I had to think, then I said you are talking about Mr. Felton, wife, the guy that I had ask him one day, was he from Chicago, and he said that he was not from Chicago.

Then I told him where I see him on 74th and Halstead, what he was doing, drinking a tall can of beer, after he finish drinking the beer, he through the can away then he would leave.

All he did was smile, after that he would come out and sit, he and I would talk then he would, be ready to go home he and I say, see you tomorrow.

That was the last time I saw him, Queenie she said he was a ok man, but he drink beer that she had smell it on him, I said well I can't say anything about him about that, because I drink beer myself sometime, there is not anything wrong with it, Queenie said that she didn't mean it that away, I said that I know that, because the night before he pass on in to life, he had already told me that, the doctor took him off drinking beer, I said to him that day, if the doctor took you off then leave it a long, he said that he was, he told me also to watch some of the peoples, that live in here they don't like you, I said to him that I know, and the good thing about it, hum I know the peoples, he said you just watch them! Then I said that I would then I left, and went home that was the last time I seen him.

As this time now I have his home going celebration, in loving memory of Dec. Felton Childress, the Lord Gave it, April 25th, 1931 then the Lord took it away June the 9th, 2005, myself and Larissa went to his funeral, to show some kindness and sympathy to his wife Virginia.

Someone said to me how was my book doing, I said that I was waiting on my copy now, that I had paid the money to put it out, just waiting on my copy, they said good luck to me, I said thanks and that I had to go home to get ready, for work in the morning.

They would ask me, how my daughter Larissa was doing, I said that she is going to be ok, because I was going to be there for her, then I went home.

After I resign as the tenant council, some of my dreams has been shatter, for what I wanted to do for those old peoples, I had told some that after I had put up those canopy, that I wanted to plant some running roses, and put them between those trees where we sit out, enjoying ourselves and talking, with each other having fun.

And that I wanted to name them, from some that sit out and having fun like, Queenie, Blackwell, Mary Helen, Russell, Hattie, Kopoe, Miss Evelyn and Roseie and others are good peoples, I wanted to give them a rose garden, so that they can smell the roses. Now I can't do that.

That night before I went to bed the woman, that I saw where I am working with Larissa, she seem to be the same as I am, trying to help someone if that was what they wanted, and can't do it for themselves, Milton said her name was sally.

That morning I got up got ready to go to work, when I got there Wendy she was there, and also Larissa was there, I was there before them I just had not seen them, I said good morning to them, Larissa said good morning daddy, Wendee said good morning David how are you, I said that I was fine, and I got all of my stress out from me, Wendee she said what, I said that I had resign, Wendee said what you are quitting? I said no not here, remember when I told you that I was thinking, about resigning from the tenant council from where I live, Wendee said yes you did it, I said yes it would be too much for me, if I kept on as the president.

Wendee she said that she was afraid that, I was quitting from here we need you, I said that I will be here until you all find someone, who will and do the job that Larissa and you, are satisfy with them, because I will let them know that, I am not too far away if my daughter need me, that I will be there for her.

Then I saw Milton sitting in the lobby, I spoke to him and I had some work orders in my hand, I said Milton you want to help me, or you want to walk and talk while I am working, he said no that his son was coming over to see him, I said ok let me go to work on these work orders, talk to you latter that I had a hand full of orders to do. Then I saw Sally and said good morning, she spoke and kept on walking, I turn to watch her walk away.

That day I went almost through all of those orders, some was simple as changing a light bulb, unstopping a toilet, there blind need fixing, changing a garbage disposer, crack in the wall small things, I could not get in some apartment, they was not at home Larissa and Wendee, had already put out a notice that I was coming, if they was not there I put on the date and time, I was there on the orders, that I will try again another day.

Every day I saw Sally, I said that I was going to make her mind, that I see so much of me in her that I will get her, I said to myself that I was going to run it by Larissa, to see what she would say or think, if I made Sally my woman.

One day after I had gotten the building that, I could handle the apartment so that, I would not have to work myself to death, I was looking for things to do that is hard, then the grass it needed cutting I cut it, and some of the tenant over there was playing games, trying to get me into their apartment by myself.

One day I had a work order to do, Larissa and Wendee told me, not to go into that apartment by myself, because the lady name was Miss Black, she had told a lie on the other guy name Ruel, that use to work here as a maintain man, that he rape her and he had to go to court, there was a mess but he beat that, I said is she that black skinny ugly woman, with a brace on her hand, who with their right mind want her.

So I had to go into her apartment to fix, a toilet seat in her bathroom Wendee she went with me, All I had to do was tighten the bolt down on the seat we came out of her apartment.

Now when I found out that Miss Black, she was in the hospital that she had falling down, in the bathroom that something was broken, about the seat I fix that, all I had to do was tighten the screw back, where someone had loosen them, and by me fixing the seat on her toilet, I messed up her law suit. Wendee she went into the apartment with me, she and Larissa had already warn me about Miss Black.

Later after Miss Black came home from the hospital, I heard that I went into her apartment, with-out her permission, and that she was going to sew me, Larissa, and Wendee, I said she can sew me if she want to, that I had a job to do, and that she had put in a work order about her toilet seat, and my job was to fix it and that was what I did.

Now it is time for me to get off work, now after I get off work I go home stop, and get my mail and take my truck to where I live, go into my apartment for a while, then I go outside and hang out with Miss Queenie, Roseie, Miss Blackwell and some of the others tenants, that live in the complex where I live.

While we all was talking, I told them that I had saw this white woman that, is a care giver person that take care of two tenants, that work over where Larissa and I work now, and I told them that how much, of the goodness I see in her, are inside of me; and that I am going to try and get into her good grace; and that if I see a good person as I am passing through, this world I want to be a part of their life.

Miss Queenie she said, David there is someone out there for you, and that all woman are not all bad, and that David you are a good person also, then she was telling me about her son Greg, I said that I like Greg, that I only have meet him but once, and that what I saw in him was goodness, "I said to myself, Greg is a man as I am, trying to be good, I see God and Jesus in him," that was when Miss Queenie said to me, that Greg he is a minister and that he is a musician also, I smile and said to Miss Queenie, that I know God and Jesus didn't let me see, someone that was not good, I know a man because I am one.

Miss Queenie said David, one of these days you are going to find yourself a wife, out here one day. I said no Miss Queenie, I am not looking for no wife but a friend, just a good friend is all I am looking for, as I am passing through this world, that I have already been marry seven times, that is enough, now I will give the time for a wife, augment etc. bad moods I will give that time, to God and Jesus, I know they love me, and if you let me I could love you also.

Now I know, when I resign as president of the tenants council, because we was without a manager for about six months, so I sent a letter and I prayed on it, and I was not the only one prayed also, now Elise, Elise she came in as my, your manager where we live, now I thank you God and Jesus, for bringing Miss Morgan here.

Now I know what she is facing, now I can help her, but the only way I can do that is, resigning from where I am in order, to help her if she needed me, that is the only way I can have her back, that she don't forget that, is my word.

Now Elise she is a beautiful lady, find as I see her, that make me see life in another way, that I will be here for Elise if she need me, for what any help I can help her with, I am close by her or by the phone, if she don't see me; because she have a job to do as others has, because I am going to do mind, and a little of my time is for Elise, if she have a need.

Now my prayer has been answered, there are only three ladies here in Vegas that I can't put or lay my hands on, unless it is to help them, or want me to put my hand on them.

Now I am a man, and I carry myself as a man, but I see some men that will never change, for the better I had to change my life for the better, of myself.

David L. Marshall

Now I am not trying to talk about anybody, but there is a man I guess he is a man, everybody that put there trousers on, one leg at a time is not to say they are a man, my buddy Glen, as I see he is a good o Joe, what I see is that he himself, don't mess with anyone trying to hurt them, he only hurt himself, some of the things that he do, I would not escape that, I have did things that hurt me but, I know how to draw a line.

Now he is trying hard to get under Elise dress, but he is doing it the wrong way, every time he tell others his personal business, and what he was going to do keep it himself, peoples get jealous suspiciously and watchful of you, they will block what you are doing, they will let the one who you are trying to get to, and let them know what you are trying to do.

How he love his white woman and that, he don't mess with no black woman for a woman for himself, if she is not white he don't want her that is prejudice, Stewart he tell me everything that he know, about Glen business the money that he give to the white woman, and how he can't go over to her house on holiday, or he don't have any money to give her.

Now I can't believe anything that Stewart says, he is a big liar and everybody know that, but everyone know that Stewart and Toni are going together, but Stewart he want tell anyone about Toni and himself, I saw one day Toni she took Stewart wallet, after he said that he didn't have any money, and took out the money that she wanted, and she gave the wallet back to Stewart, Rose she was out there with me, I said to rose look, look did you see that, Toni she took money from Stewart wallet, and gave it back to him.

Rose she said you are late, I saw that before, now to myself Stewart he is no better than Glen, the white woman use Glen, and Toni she use Stewart, so how can the pot talk about the kettle, they talk about each other, I know they talk about me also but, I don't care one thing about it, I don't ask them for anything, I go to God and Jesus if I am in need.

Now in August on my calendar, things that I had to cancel because, now I am not over the tenants council, I can forget those things that I was going to do, for the peoples that live in here, now I have to live and look out for myself, I tried to look out for those out there, but they through that I was steeling, what a female body, some I would not touch nor go to bed with.

Now I have to help me because, I can't help you if I can't even help myself, I am number three in my world, God is one, Jesus is two and I make three, I had to cancel in August the 9th cooking breakfast, Rose birthday the 13th, then it was my God daughter Blessing birthday 17th, Miss Russell and I gave Blessing her first birthday party, and on the 18th it is Jackie birthday, my daughter in Alabama, I sent her a birthday card to say that I love her, and I always will love her.

That come back to Sally, that I always wanted to say something to her," Sally," but I could not find the words to say, until someone had said that Sally she, was leaving working over at the Salvation Army apartment, working with those patent, I said that I better say something now before it is too late.

Now I was standing in front of the maintain closet, I saw Sally coming by she stop and said hi, I said hello to her, then told Sally that I had a spot in my heart for her, she was shock she said o yes, then she said thank you then she walk away.

That was when I said that, I will write my phone number down, and when I see her again I would give it to her, when I was almost ready to get off work, I started talking to my daughter Larissa, before I leave about Sally, and that I was going to steel Sally, Larissa said daddy what you mean steel her, she don't have anyone she need help, that was when I told Larissa what I said to Sally, that I had a spot in my heart for her, Larissa said hum daddy, I said to Larissa would it be ok by her, she said yes daddy you need someone in your life, go for it.

Then it was my time to get off work, I was going over to my truck I saw Sally coming, her vehicle was park by my truck, she came out to her car, I said to her that I heard that she was leaving, she said well, she was thinking about it, I gave her my phone number and said to her, keep in touch then I got into my truck and left, with that woman with those big breast, with blond hair on my mind.

When I got home there was a light in my mind, and that light was Sally, she was on my mind and I was happy, and I showed it that is why I let that light shine, I open a door in my heart, so if Sally wanted to come in she can.

On the 20th that Saturday morning, I had to go over to the job for a couple of hours, Larissa she had gave me a beeper for emergency, and I had to go and make sure that the property, was clean from paper that blow from the wind," the wind is bad sometime in Vegas," then I had to dump the trash, then I was done about two hours.

Before I had made a promise to some of my friends," ladies," that I was going to take them to breakfast, that Saturday was the day, I told Larissa just in case she wanted to come, and bring the kids, I had told some like Miss Blackwell, Kopoe, Elizabeth, Miss Russell that I was going to treat them to breakfast, over to the wild fire casino, now I have a truck I could take two with me, Kopoe said that, she would bring some but she had something to do early, I said ok stop by after she finish.

So Miss Elizabeth said her vehicle had paper all over hers, so she took the papers and put them in the trunk, she drove and took Miss Russell with her, Miss Blackwell was with me, we got to the wildfire went in and got seated, then we order our breakfast I didn't see Kopoe, then she came with another lady name," Joanne," I said she was to come by herself, but she have someone else with her, I said ok that is alright Joanne might be hunger, I will do one thing, feed you if you are hunger, now I don't know Joanne but seen her, she live down the hall from me, when we are going or coming to or forth, from our apartment we speak yes we are neighbor, I said to myself, God and Jesus would not make a deference so nor can I.

So after breakfast I paid the tab, then we left and went home the ladies thanked me, I said that is ok did you have a good time? Miss Blackwell said yes we did, do it again. I smile and said we will see this is my pleasure.

Now Sally she was on my mind, I said to myself, she have my phone number now the ball is in her court, if she want to play we can.

Later on that day I went home, I had a call on my answer machine, it was from Sally, she was going to the union station casino, that she had a friend of her play in a band, and did I want to go with her, she left a phone number for me to call her back, so I did. After she told me what she wanted to do, I told Sally that I would love to go, then I told her what time that I would be there, and where I was parking at main street station casino lot, she said ok see you there, I said you can bet that I will be there, then I said ok with a smile to myself, and said now I got her attention.

Now at six o clock I got ready to meet Sally, her breast is like a softball clincher, and hair was long and blond, soon I will be there with her my luck is changing, I got to the main street station and park, when I got to the entrance of the hotel and casino, I didn't see Sally so I waited and I waited, then I said that, I told her that I would be here at 7 pm, by the parking lot at main street station, then I said to myself, maybe she have change her mind, but before I leave that I will go to the other end of the casino, to see so I start to walking to the other parking lot, to see if I saw her when I got there, but I look and I didn't see Sally, I went back to where I said that I would be at, and I waited and waited I didn't see Sally, I said let me make a call.

Then I went into the casino to call Sally, I did not have any change to call Sally, I saw these ladies sitting on a bench, by the phone I ask did anyone have change for a dollar, one lady she said yes that she think that she had it, then she started to look. She had the change, I said to her thank then I call Sally cell phone, after she answer the phone, I said that I have been here for an hour; I said that you had change your mind.

She said that she was on the other side of the parking lot, in the door for the casino on the other side, she said that she see me, I said ok don't move I am on my way, I thank the ladies again for the change, and went and found Sally.

That was when I kiss Sally on her jaw, and while she and I was walking to the Union Station casino, I was holding her hand, I said that I was going to leave that, I thought that I was stood up, Sally she said no we just got mix up, then we got to the casino and went in and got a seat, it was in front of the stage peoples was looking," black and white," the ladies I guess saw me holding hands, and hugging Sally they wish it could have been them, peoples that been together a long time, don't do that anymore.

That night I gave to Sally, her happiness and having some fun from then on, if that was what she wants or needed, Sally she acted as she was having some fun, I was happy also, she was enjoying herself drinking wine, white wine I was drinking a miller light.

The ladies and men was having their fun, the music was sounding good, they was dancing drinking Sally she said to me, that she had to go to the bathroom, that she will be right back, I order another round of drinks before she got back, after she got back she showed me a black lady, Sally she said that the lady was in the lady room, and she ask her that her," sally," seam as she and her boyfriend was so in love, I said o yes what did you say! She said that she told her that, he was not her boy-friend, that I was her husband.

Then Sally she pour on the love after that, she was laying back in my arms, every once in a while Sally she would kiss me, and smile. The ladies was looking and Sally was giving them, what they wanted to see, the guitar player he was looking at Sally, and there was a woman base player she was find, and look like she had on a wrap on dress, those legs was beautiful I had my eyes full, then Sally had to go again to the bathroom.

After Sally came back from the bathroom, I made sure that she was seated, but the peoples was having fun, but they was watching me, I said to Sally in her ear, peoples are just looking at us but they can eat their heart out, we and I are having a good time.

Our glass was empty I saw a cocktail waiter, I order another wine for Sally, I still had some beer we was there in the casino, for about four hours. Sally she look back at me and said, what are you trying to do, get me drunk, I said no but I am like this, when a woman is out with a man having a drink, she should never have to tell him that she need another drink, if he order another drink, it is up to her to say no thank, that she had enough.

That is when I said no that I was not, trying to make her drunk, because I don't want to be with a woman, and she is drunk, a real woman want get drunk.

So we got ready to go, we got to where Sally had park her vehicle, she gave the parking lot attendant, her parking ticket to bring her car, I said to her that if she can't drive, she can stay with me until in the morning, she start kissing me for real, the other side of me woke up, that kiss she laid on me, made me do strangely things that night. Everything started growing.

Now I had heard Sally say about on Russell road, that is where she live at and that was almost, where I use to work at Rhodes Ranch," Ranch by the road," was across warn spring almost by blue diamond road, Sally she was all over me tip toeing to kiss me, she was enjoying it.

Then her vehicle arrive I said to her again, if she could not drive back home, she can stay with me, Sally she said that she could make it, then she said that when she get home, she would call me, I said ok drive careful and I would be looking for her call. She left and I went and got my truck and went home.

On the way home my blood start coming down, after kissing Sally like she did to me, I wanted her, if I had gotten Sally coming home with me, I could have had some good fun with her, I know how to please a woman, I still had a hard felling in the middle, I got home Sally she call, that she made it home safe, I said ok I had a good time and that I would talk to her later on, she said ok good night.

That Sunday morning I got up and took my friend Popeye, to the store I was all in smile, I told him what I had found, and that was happiness, then he told me, what he had pass through his life, now, I fell him, because of what he told me, one or the other has walk in each other shoes, the same as I had pass in my life, he and I are on the same page.

David L. Marshall

As he and I was talking almost the same, if you put it all together, it spell the same hurt, with the felling about a woman how a woman has treated him and I.

Now I was on a cloud floating, with now I don't have no fear, after what Bernice and Mary she pass on, did to me Bernice she protein that she love me, but all I got was the same as they did to Jesus, but God is watching you.

Like Larissa said daddy you need some happiness, in your life. Then Larissa she ask me something, one thing I want do, is keeping my kids in the dark, and I could not deny her, she said dad you loved Mary, didn't you? I said yes that I did, and I Miss her, I keep her picture over my TV, now I am happy once again, Popeye after I got him home, and taken his grocers into his house, I had to go because I had another commitment, Popeye said man you got a good woman now, I said thank, that I would do anything almost to keep her, then I said about a sure thing was, you have to do the same thing to get her, or him, you have to do the same thing to keep her.

Then Popeye said that he would talk to me later on, then I got into my truck and went back home, later on that day I was watching the football game, Sally she call and want to know, if I wanted to go and have a drink, on her, I said that I had to go to work in the morning, that all I was doing was chilling out, she said that she had one more client to see, then she was off work, and that could she stop by, if that after last night you don't want to see me, and that you have change my mind, then she said that she need a drink.

That was when I said we will see, I gave the address to Sally how to get to where I was, in my complex, I had all the drinks I need to drink, I make wine the same as Jesus did.

Later on my phone ring it was Sally, she was at the gate she said let her in, she came to by my apartment and she saw my truck and park.

She got out I went and open the security door, from the hall to get to my apartment, Sally she came in I said welcome, make yourself at home and relax, I showed her around she got comfort, I fix Sally a drink, and I fix myself one then I said to Sally, if that she need another drink she had to fix it for herself.

Then while she and I was drinking our wine, Sally said David remember last night, you was trying to get her into my apartment, I said no, then I said yes, Sally said that she wanted to go home with me, but she didn't want me to know that, she was a bad woman. because she is not a bad woman, but she wanted me so bad that night, my third leg started to grow, I had already smoke a little cigarette, and I know myself after that, I wanted to go into her temple, body and worship her.

And if she give her prohibit for me to enter her body, I could make my way around her body, and I would see if she was worldly of my love, but before I go in, I want to check out the body of her temple, what I can see and feel then I will know, or think that I know about Sally, and what she feel about me.

After about five minute together along, she and I could not control our self, we was as our spirit was trying to connect, Oh boy how I love that, all I wanted to do was be like a blow torch, on a block of ice, when I saw that she was melting down, I made a toast in my mind and heart to Sally, that I was going to enjoy her and her body, what a night.

Sally she was all into what she and I was going to do, we were on the couch making out, Sally she said wait David dam, what are you doing to her that she was a good girl, then she got off the couch and took my hand, and she look at me and said, honey lets go into the bed room, I don't care where we was she had it coming.

Sally and I went into the bed room, I said to myself now I will go to work on this, and I will give her another pleasant and pleasing night, I saw that beautiful body of Sally, I had to make sure that I make it good to her, I went all the way out to make her feel good, man what a treat, and I was given her one.

That thing in my mouth that I talk with, is a red towel I have, I took it, and went all over Sally body, slowly, until I got back to where her head was laying, as I was going back up to Sally body, she was with a smile on her face, and she was relax and helplessly, now as I enter into her temple of her body, now I am in I could not stay long, my pistol went off, but after we did finish saying hello to our self, I was happy but, I told her that the next time I will stay harder, longer when we are making love, she said don't think about that, she loved it anyway then she kiss me, and that hard feeling came back again.

That was when I said to myself, that the same thing that put a smile on Sally face, I have to do the same thing to keep it there. No matter as we are in bed or not, I have to make her happy, now we are in bed I went back to work.

After Sally and I, had gotten to know each other, we was lying in bed, she was laying her head on my chest, she was rubbing on my body and we was talking, in my heart, I know that Sally was the one for me. Now each and every day at work I saw Sally, and when she was off work, we were together after she had done all her work.

When I had some time, I would go out and sit and talk to Queenie, Blackwell, Russell, Hattie if she was out there, Miss Evelyn if I saw her she is my sweetheart, there is Glen when I see him, he and I would ride to the State line to play our lottery, and I would see Mr. and Miss Lee, they would come out and sit and talk, then Elise when she was on break, we all talk I told them that I love Sally, and that I was going to put her name on my banking account, that she was going to help me with my other book.

Someone ask me, David how are your book doing, I said that the first one is at the publisher, and I was going to take it all the way to the Entrepreneur plus, package but it cost $ 1549.00 now it is in the LEGACY CLASSIC it cost $699.00 but when I get the money, I was going to upgrade to Entrepreneur Classic, but I am not worry about the money, I know God and Jesus will give it to me, I am working with my daughter until she find someone, to take the job because I can't work to long, so we was talking, I said that I was going to go and put something in my book, before Sally come to my apartment, then I will put it down and see what Sally, want to do then I left and went home.

Now sometime Sally she would just come by and call me, on the gate box where tenants code to get into the gate, I answer the phone and push 9 on my phone, to open the gate to let Sally into, to get to my apartment.

When she get to my apartment and park, I open the security door to my place, we come in side of my apartment and lock the door, then she and I get busy.

Now on pay day after work, I go to the bank and put my pay check in my account, and Larissa had me on Saturday and Sunday, on call just in case, that there was a problems over to where we work, only a emergence to call if it was.

Sally she was on call also, she got a call that someone had call off, and she had to go and see their client, and she ask me did I want to go with her, that it would only take a hour and she will be finish, I said ok I took my beeper, Sally said what are you doing with a beeper, I said that I had to keep this on the week end, that I was on call until Larissa, she can fill this position, Sally she said why don't you take that position, and you can have a free apartment, then we can live together.

Then I said yes, that is ok, but the worry from the tenants all time of the night, ringing my door bell waking me up for nothing, and I am on social security, and I only can make so much money, until I have to Quit the job, and that I was ok as I am, if I take that position and something happen, I said anything can happen, what if Larissa she might want to find herself another, better job and leave or the corporate office, they might want to give the job to someone else, and that I don't like paper work anything can happen.

After Sally and I went to where she had to do, we came back and go to my apartment, we had a glass of wine and Sally she had ants in her pants, she was all over me I got my little, big boy up, then Sally and I got busy again.

That was on the 30th of august 05, Sally and I was getting closer I like her, and I want to pass through, into my life with her be with her, doing things with her then I started calling Sally my wife, in the heart from God and Jesus. on that day I needed to go and get something from the store, but I was busy on my job fixing a door, I gave my money card and my pin number to Sally, she got nervous she was so nervous, until she put my card something place, and she could not find it, she said that she look and look for it, but she could not find it, I said that was ok that I would call and go into the bank, and change my card, and the pin number.

So after I got off work, I said to Sally that she follow me to the bank, so that I could put her on my account, she said why do you want to put her name on my account, I said if I had to go out of town, I need someone to look out for me and my bills, and help me with my book, she said that we better wait awhile, I said ok so I went and did it for myself, change my card and pin number from the bank.

Now in September 05 at work we got paid every two weeks, on the 2nd time go in, and on the 5th was Labor day, I was off work because of the holiday, and I am off on Saturday and Sunday, I was off three days, but I still had that beeper and I could not go or do anything but, work on my book, Sally she had to take care of her patent, no matter if it was a holiday or not she had to go, she ask me did I want to ride with her, now she has a cell phone if my beeper go off, I could use her phone to answer the call, I don't like cell phone.

So I said to Sally, ok I will ride with her and sit in the car, until she finish doing what she was doing, one of her patent didn't live to far from me, after she had finish all her client she needed to go to Wall Mart store, after we had gotten what we needed then we came back home, I would cook then we eat, food, then we have a glass of wine and lay around.

We watch TV. got tired of making love right then, we go to sleep after good sex you have to go to sleep, after we wake up I ask Sally was she hunger, she turn over to me and said hunger for what, you, that I make it so good to her that she want more, I said that is why I cook so good, just to please my woman any kind of the way I can.

And I have the time to do whatever, I had to do but that beeper had me held down, if I went far away and I got a call, I could not get there in time to respond the call, and that Larissa and Wendee with Miss Mira, had said that they wanted to have a barbecue for, the resident that live there where we work, it was to be after Labor day, because these old peoples are not throwbacks, because we, they are old they have family also as the same as I, they, we don't live with them but we still love them, I hope that mind love me, as so sometime they don't act like it but that is ok, as myself I am retire and wont to be by myself.

So they can spend Labor Day with their family, we will do something for them after Labor day, it is on the 10th without Grandkids all the time, we need sometime for our self also.

Now we have work and worry about our kids, and family for all those years through, the rain, sleet, snow all kind of weather, to make sure they could grow up health and happy etc. now that the one I have raise all those years, the mothers now why don't they do the same, for their kids spend time with them, love them and take care of their own.

Sally said the cook out is on September the 10th, I said hugging her yes then I said that now Larissa, are interview peoples to take my job after I leave, Sally she start to kissing on me the way I could not stand, I said ok now you are going to be in trouble, she said as long that I make her smile after, that was ok we made love again.

That Friday was pay day, I got it and sign it and I ask Sally, would she take it to the bank for me, she said that she would take it, but first she had to go and see another client, of hers and after that she would drop it off, at the bank for me, I said thanks then I gave Sally, my check and my deposit slip for the bank.

Just before Sally was going to leave to see, her others client she saw me I was looking for, something to do, I was caught up with my work, and ask me did I have time to smoke a cigarette, I said yes ok, Sally and I went outside by the smoking area, and I lit Sally cigarette and mind she and I was talking, as like every time one of those ladies, that live there specially the white resident.

They know where we was at here they come, I didn't care but when someone are talking, and some-one else jump into something that, don't mean anything, I know why it was because I am a black man, Sally she had already said to me that, I was the only black man, she had ever had been with," now did I believe that, no," and I myself take good care of myself, with the help with my God and Jesus.

And a white woman as Sally are, they was cock blocking but it was too late, Sally she also said that one of the client of her, she live there name is Pat, Sally I did believe that she live there with Pat, Pat had said that, David and Sally should take it slow, don't fall in love to soon, that was on my mind also, then Sally said that she had to go, one ask Sally where was she going, Sally said that she was going to work, I smile and kiss Sally, then she said again that, I had to cook on Saturday hum, I said yes, she said that she then she kiss me, and said call you when she got off, I said ok talk to her then.

After that I went into Larissa office to talk to my daughter, I didn't have anything else to do so I will, talk to her until it was time to get off. Larissa ask where was Sally, I said she was at work and that, I will see her after work.

Larissa she said daddy you love Sally don't you, I can't lie to my daughter, I said, she is ok yes I do love her, Larissa said she is ok but she need help, I said that I would do anything to help her, then I look at my watch it was 3:50pm I said, it was time almost for me to get off, Larissa she said ok daddy see you in the morning, that she was off to and that she was behind me, Wendee she said David she would see me in the morning, I said you can bet that, I was so happy and everybody know me, or Sally know that also.

Larissa call me back to let me know that, my grandson, her son Marcus would be with her in the morning, he want to see his grand daddy, I said o yes then I will have someone to help, and keep me company, I am going to have a good time, I said to Wendee and my daughter, that I would see them in the morning again, then I left and went home I was waiting on Sally.

Now every day I am with Sally, I am so happy until I was on a cloud, just happy until that Saturday of the barbecue, I started looking at Sally another way, but I still respect Sally because she is a woman, and that she is my woman I want her to, respect me for just me. I can't live here in this world by myself, I can't make it by myself that is why, I am putting her into my heart, for her but I can love another also, God and Jesus is love, I can spread that all over this world, that is the love of God and Jesus.

Now there was another lady that work at the church, that is still part of the Salvation Army, her name is Brenda, she seam that she is sweet, as I see, she wanted me to put on the grill some chicken wings, I did have them on the grill because Larissa, she got them for me, to put them on the grill.

So Sally she had to go to work, she came out to where I was cooking, to say that she was leaving going to work, that she would see me after work, I said ok did she want me to save her a plate, she said no that all I need to save is me, for her later, I said ok as Sally was walking away, Brenda she was coming to where I was, Brenda she said, David where are my chicken wing, that she was waiting on them now.

Then I kind of turn my head, I saw Sally she had stop, now I don't really know Sally and how she are, like or don't like, I said to Brenda you see my lady going there, Brenda she said o that she was sorry, I said that is ok what wrong, she said again that she was so sorry, I said don't stress about that, then Larissa came out to get the meat, I had to let the wings stay on the grill longer, because Larissa like her wing burnt, Brenda she wanted hers burnt also, so I said ok let me cook these wings, because all of these wings are going to be burnt.

After the chicken wings was ready and burnt, and was on the table, we all started to eating and talking, around the round table it was, Milton, Crayon she is in a wheelchair, she lost her legs, Judy she is in a wheelchair also, Joanne she is a good woman, she is in a wheelchair also everyone, but me and the staff talk about her, she is always pleasant when you see her, they say that she stink, she was not the only one you see.

Milton he said David, Sally she turn around after she was going to work, she was going to get on Brenda, then Milton said Sally is mean, I said she is ok I guess tell me more, when everyone had eating and was leaving, I said well I better go and stop and get my mail, and go home, Milton said yes you better because, you got a whipping coming, I start laughing and said not the way you think, but in bed yes that is a good whipping, then I said to Larissa that I was leaving, and that I would talk later.

Larissa she said o daddy, I said yes baby, she said that the guy that work next door, I said yes his name is Maurice Guice, she said yes that she gave the job of maintenance man, I said good that you know him and I met him, that is good when do he start.

Larissa said that he was moving in on Tuesday Sept. 13,05, I said ok good then, I can get back into my book, she said if that I could stay on until two weeks, to train Maurice. I said ok as long as you are satisfy, Larissa said yes that will give you some more money, to pay for your book, I said you are right then I kiss her on the jaw, and left and went home.

After I got home I stop into the office, to talk to Elsie about that Sally she was, going to be coming over sometime in and out, she will be helping me with my second book, and that I did not want the security person pulling her vehicle, that I need a parking permit, Elsie she said that Sally she need to have, her plate number, I said that Sally she had just got the vehicle, and that the plates has not came, I know that because I gave her the money for that, she was to pay it back, and when they get back that I would bring the number, back to Elsie she said ok then Elsie gave me a parking permit.

She made it out for apartment 152 building number 3 only, it was for 15 teen days a time, she had to do it that way because the agreement that I had sign, but I was thinking about that, she was not going to live with me, but she was coming to help me with my second book, then she go to work and do her job, and come back to help me in all ways, that I needed it.

Sometime it was too late for Sally to drive back home, so she is my lady anyway also, so why not cant she stay over with her man, and go to sleep and then go to work from here, after all I need help with my book.

After talking to Elsie and I had stop and talk to some, of the tenants they wanted to know how was Larissa, and when was I coming back to them, that they need me, I said one thing is this, that I never have left you, that I was here for them all the time, but a man have to be a man, and do what he has to do, that my daughter she needed me, and as a man I am, I went and help my daughter.

Now that I have never left you before, and I never will not do that now or ever, until you push me away if that happens, then don't blame me, it would be you, now after two weeks I will be here all the time, closer to you if and when you need me, just call me.

Now after I got home and went in to my book, Sally she call to see what was I doing, I said that I was putting something in to my book, what's up, she said o nothing that she just was thinking about me, that how much she love me, and that she is lucky to be with me, I said that I fell the same thing about her, then Sally said that she had to go someplace, after she get off did I want to take a ride with her, before I said yes, she said not that kind of a ride, I said take your mind out from the gully, yes I will take a ride both of them with you, she said thank you I love you David, I said you to see you when you get here.

But when some things are on my mind, I will do anything that I can, to ease my mind anything. Now what was on my mind was, after I had heard that Sally had a problem with pain, and I had heard that Milton had a heart operation, and that the doctor had to cut open his chest, and that Milton he sell his pain pills, to Sally.

Now I know that Donna ray she smoke a lots, but after when I saw Milton taking money, not four or five dollars, then I started thinking why Sally and Milton was so good friends, now I have to find out everything that, I can about Sally now I meant everything.

Now I did not know now but the pain and the pills, they go together, not that I can't put my finger on it, I can't say anything to anyone else, so I didn't say anything to Larissa, so I was showing Maurice what to do, and how the way, I did the job to make it easy for myself, and that he do things comfortable for himself, I wanted to say something to Maurice about, Sally and the pills and Milton, so I said to myself no it was not the time.

All I am doing now is giving Maurice the base of the job, he has to do it after the way I show him, his own way, I showed him how to fix those cracks in the wall, how in the morning after I got to work, clean up the property with paper that blow around, with the wind, clean and put the garbage out, so that the garbage truck can pick it up, then clean the windows, vacuum the floors, then check and see if the grass need cutting, clean the bathroom and laundry room, then I check the work orders and I do them, then if there was not anything else to do, I walk the halls checking to see if any others cracks, is coming through because the building is still selling, if I can't find anything to do, I will sit out in the lobby and talk to the resident, or sit in the office and talk to Wendee, or Larissa, until it is time to get off work.

On Tuesday September 13th Maurice he was taken his furniture, into his apartment it was time for me to get off work, I said to Maurice that I would see him in the morning, then I left and went home. Then later on Sally she came by, and after she was off that day she and I, just lay around and made love enjoying each other.

Now some say that Sally had a drugs," pain and aches," problem, now in Chicago, you can see a woman that have a drug problem, they are in the streets all the time, and they will do anything to get those drugs, but Sally she to me, was not like that she was with me all the time, we did things together, until one night I guess that Sally she would try me.

Now she had started to write notes, and lay them around for me to find, I would read them, on the mirror in the bathroom, she take lip stick and draw a heart, and write in it that she love me, now to me that is strange, I had said to myself why do she do that, she had already said that she didn't like her picture taken, I had ask why? She told me that she had been in a bad car Accident, and that she was all broken up, the doctors had to reconstruct her face, and that to her she was ugly, I would tell her that she was not ugly, that she was beautiful, and I was not just saying that, she is beautiful and find.

That night Sally and I had made love, now something happen I don't know what, or why she got up and got dress, she was mad for what, she started auguring.

And said that she was leaving, then she went to the door and left, I lock my door back and went back to bed, I don't like to argue and that I don't kiss no, woman or man I want kiss no ass, but a woman there are more than one way to kiss her, but not like this.

Then about 10 minute my phone ring, I answer it was Sally back at the gate, and want to come back in, I open the gate I thought she had left something, she came in and park I open the hallway door, she came I said what you left something, she keep on walking to my apartment, and went inside, Sally said yes I did leave something, that it was you that she change her mind, that she was walking out from the best thing in her life.

Now as I am, I gave her another chance, but she and I had a good talk, that I don't like no woman or man treat me, the way that they want to do to me, no way that is going on, now the very next time she want to make a move, she better think about what you want to do, because the very next time you walk away from me, don't stop, keep on going this was the first, now don't make that mistake again, she said ok then we made up by having sex.

Now at work I did not bring up what Sally had did, if I did Milton or Donna ray would not talk, if I needed to know something about Sally, so I let them know that I was, with Sally it was so good that I could not live without Sally, Donna ray, Milton and I was in the hall talking, they was going to their apartment, I was at work I said, that I was going to put Sally on my bank account, Donna ray she said, what. Sally she can't manage her own money, and you are talking about putting her on your account, good luck.

Now Milton he just smile with a shitty look on his face, "now I am watching Milton anyway," it was something about Milton and Sally, I am a man myself, and I have seen and did it myself get slick, but now I found out that, if you are thinking that you are slick, you can use another greasing, because if you think that you are getting over, on someone else you better think about it, because it could be you getting fuck.

Now after Sally she said no about my account, she start talking about her kids, she never had talk really about them, all but that she had two girls, now she are Missing them, then she told me about her dad, not her birth dad but her step-dad, and how much money he had, how he was over the mob, and he would send his boys and take care, of any one put their hands on her, and that she carry a 38 on her all the time, in her purse she said hold it, the purse was kind of heavy, but it could be anything in that purse, I don't think it was no gun.

Then Sally she said that her daughters, and Sally don't see eye to eye, I said whatever it is that she as the mother, should talk about it with them before it is too late, whatever it was that Sally herself, if that she had did something, then she should make the first move, and if it was something that the kids did, they should make a move also, but someone should start talking you are your family.

Then Sally she told me that her younger daughter, her name was Chrissy's, on September the 21st was her birthday, and that she was going to be 21 years older, then Sally said that Chrissy's she was a model and how small Chrissy's was, then she said that her older daughter, her name was Nicole, and that she live here in Vegas, with a big house on the hill in Henderson, and that Nicole and Sally they don't get along.

Then Sally told me that I was the first black man, that she had been with, then she said at one time she had everything, that she wanted in her life, and that Christy's wanted to come here in Vegas, for her birthday that she use to live here, until she left to stay with her dad in Ohio, I said ok we could take them out to dinner. When Chrissy get here then I asked Sally, where was Chrissy going to stay?

While she was here Sally she didn't know, that her older daughter and Chrissy's, they don't get along, I said well we can put Chrissy's up at the Texas hotel, or she can stay with us or whatever, Sally she didn't want Chrissy's to stay with her or me, because Sally she had to work and Chrissy's, she like to sleep in then Sally said no think.

Every day I go to work, until my last day on the 15th of September, I got off work and got my money order, for my rent I pay before time, so that I will know that it was paid, then no one can say that David L. Marshall, was put out from his apartment, not for paying my rent and I do all my bills the same way, pay as I get them, I was in the office paying my next month rent.

Elsie and I was talking I like Elsie, she is a good looking woman, and in my heart she is a good woman," how I know," I hear, listen, talk and watch peoples, all Elsie show me is goodness, then I said to Elsie that I was going to get marry, and that what I feel about Sally is, in the eye and my heart of God, we are already married, so I was going to put it on paper so, that everyone would know that Sally, was my wife.

Elsie she did not say anything while I was talking, she was doing her work then Elsie she said, that I, David L. Marshall want need a will, now at that time I did not hear what Elsie, had said after I got to my apartment, it hit me, I said oh it's a will, that all of my insurance-policies, book sell etc. I said no, no that want happen, now I had to find a way to fix that mess, that I have put myself into, thank you Elsie.

That Friday the 16th, time went in to get paid, for the next week, that day I got off work and went home, someone had stolen a VCR player from the lobby, after I went to get my mail, Elsie, Toni and others was in the lobby, doing craft Elsie she spoke to me, and said that there was a hundred dollars reward, for any information about the stolen VCR player, I said o yes, I need a hundred dollar, if I find who took it I want my hundred dollar, then I got my mail and went home, to get my mind together, I mess up and I had to fix it. Mary Helen her birthday was on the 17th, now that I was not over the council, I over look her birthday cook out.

Every day Sally and I was together, we go to work come home sit around, after I put something into my book, then on the 19th Sally and I was coming from, one of her client and she had a call on her cell phone, I found out that as it was her daughter Chrissy's, Chrissy's she must had ask Sally, could she afford to take her and her other daughter, out to dinner, I heard Sally said yes she can, that she had it.

Now I was in my mind wandering, what was that for then I knew, I was to get and have some smokes for Chrissy's, and that Sally she was to give it to Chrissy's, not for me to give it to her, so I went and got some smoke, for the 21st of September 05.

On Chrissy's birthday Sally and I took her with, Sally other daughter Nicole, we went to a Japanese restaurant, where the food was being cook in front of us, we all was talking about us, and how did I meet there mother," I explain when and how," then we took some picture, Nicole she ask one of the Japanese lady, if she would take the picture, she said yes then we all was on the pictures, then we had our dinner I gave my card, to pay for the dinner it was $80.00, after we all was in the parking lot, one of the Japanese lady came out, that she didn't put the tip on the bill, I gave her $20.00 for the tip, then I hug her daughters and we got ready to leave, they got into their vehicle and we did the same, on the way to the express way, we saw the girls in their vehicle, blowing their horn and waving to say good bye, we wave back to say be good now, then Sally and I went back home.

That next day Miss Normal Cottrell, she needed 10 T. shirts with passing through, I ask when did, she need them, she said before Friday because she was going to LA, and that her peoples love passing through. I told Miss Normal that she would have them.

That same day I had to upgrade my book, I had Wendee to fax everything to my publisher, that I needed to upgrade that was some money, I said well God and Jesus gave it to me, to do what I had to do for my business, and that I thank him, Larissa she said that she need an outfit, I ask Larissa when was she going, that to take Sally with her, that I was going to buy both of them an outfit, Larissa said what kind of money, I said whatever you see or want, you want hurt me.

Larissa said that they was going on Saturday, that was the day of payday and my last day of work, September the 23rd and on the 24th was the last drawing, of my super lotto plus numbers end, when I go to the state line to CA, I play for 20 drawing when I go, so when I see Glen he play also, sometime he and I go together, and stop and eat before we get back home.

After work I saw Glen and he and I was talking, I ask Glen when was he going to renew his lotto numbers, he said Sunday do I want to go, I said yes what time, he said about 10am, I said ok that I would be on the outside, by the sitting area.

That Saturday Mr. Brown and Miss Brown, was moving out from where we live, and moving out of town, and Mr. Brown already had ask me to help, with his son in law to load the truck, that he only can pay was a hundred dollars, I ask what time he wanted to load the truck, he said when his son in law and daughter get here, that they was to be here about noon, then Mr. Brown ask what time was it, I look at my watch and said 11:30am, then we saw a U-Haul coming to the gate, he said here they come, I said that I was going to go and get my, hand truck and that I was on my way to his apartment.

So I went and got my hand truck, and went to move the Browns things, we was putting the things on the truck, then Elsie and Stewart came to inspect, the apartment for the Browns could get there, deposit back. Then Sally she came looking for me, I didn't know that she knew where I was at, but she found me I induce Sally to the others, and I gave Sally my apartment keys, to get into the apartment.

Now I was busy she know how to get to the apartment, after we had finish loading the truck, Mr. Brown he paid me, he gave me a $125.00 he said that he did that because, I work hard, I said thanks, Mr. Brown he said your old lady is a find woman, and a white woman to man you got something, I said some time it look good is not, he said David you love that woman, I said in a way she is not what I though, he said that he want go into that, I said that I will find out what is wrong, I will put it in God and Jesus hand, and leave it along.

Mr. Brown said that some of these old women, in here they don't like that you are seeing, that white woman, I said not only a white woman any woman, that is not one of them, but they will get over it, that I was going to ask her to marry me, I said to myself that will fix my problems, when she say no.

What I am thinking about, what another friend of mind said to me, that make some sense you are pulling away, and don't know how to do it, without hurting her. I said he are right I can't hurt her without killing her, and I can't do that because I have never been in jail, only for shooting dice on the side walk, not for any other nonsense, and I want go now.

You see man have his system, and God and Jesus have their own system, I love and I have devoted all my time, for their system I know it work, tell God and Jesus what you want, put it in their hand and wait, you think that it is for right now, now wait and think about what God and Jesus, has for you what are you going to do with it.

That Monday Sally she was at work, I was not working any more, this, gives me the time to work on my book, number two of passing through. I took a break and went to get my mail, in the mail I had a copy of my book, and I got so happy man what a good feeling. Now my life in my pass is in a book, so that if someone else read this, they will I hope see the mistake that I made, as I was growing up to where I am now, and do some of my ways is good, and some was not so good but, I have to give in account of that, when I pass through.

No one else pass but mind, I was so happy I told Stewart, and some others that my publisher, sent me my first copy of my book, to check and see if it was ok, with the way they did my book, and if don't need any changes, or if I had to change some things do it now, before it go out to the public. I could not wait to call Sally, Stewart he ask me, did I have some more books, I said no not yet I have to read this one first, Stewart said that he want to buy the first book sold, then I said ok then I left and went back home to call Sally.

Now there is another friend a phone friend, that I never seen but she and I call and talk, her name is Bernadine Bronson, she is a friend of Val, who is a friend of my cousin Joyce Thomas, I do things for Val. that she can't do, as work on the house or move things for her, Val and I was talking about my poetry, that I wrote call Passing through, that one day I was going to write about, Val she said that she had a friend of hers, that is a principal of the school where she teach, that she write poetry.

Then Val she call Miss Bernadine Bronson and talk to her, to see if it was ok to give me her phone number, to call just to talk about poetry, I said ok now she, Val can give Miss Bronson my phone number also, that is how I meet Miss Bernadine Bronson.

Miss Bernadine had call and left a message on my machine, I call her back we talk as we know each, others all the time but if I see her in the streets, I would not know her, but if time pass and we don't hear from each other, we will call to see if one is ok. We always say that we were going to take time, one day to have dinner, but we still call to say hello.

Now with Sally and all the notes and cards, Sally leave laying around for me to find, all over the house and how she is always saying, that she love me so much, and Sally see some of my others friends, like Kopoe and the same as her daughters, that she love me and that I treat her like a Queen, when I got Sally on her phone, I told her that I got my first copy, of my book in the mail. Sally she seemed so happy for me.

Sally she said good that she would see me, when she get to where I am, I said ok then I hung up the phone, and I took a picture of my book, so when I see Larissa and Wendee, I could show them the picture of it, until I get the others books, that I have to have Wendee, to fax my bank card numbers to order, some more books to sell for myself.

Now after Sally came by my house, she had always said to my play sister Bobby Jean, whenever Bobby call me, or I call Bobby, I always let Sally talk to Bobby Jean, I also let Sally talk to all of my family or friends, when they call or I call them, I showed Sally my book she was all in smile, she ask me when have I talk to Bobby Jean, I said not after the last time she talk to her.

That was when Sally told Bobby Jean, that she and I could not keep ours hands off, of each other, she did not lie, I gave Sally my book to read, to find out my pass life and let her share the changes, of my life from the bad to the good way I am now, I saw the smile on her face that she was happy also.

Then the hands started to moving Sally and I, was all over each other we found our self in the bed room, now you know what happen then, yes it was good, after we finish making love she and I got clean up, she took my book and open it to read it.

That next morning I go up and went to where Larissa work, to send out a fax to my publisher, when I got there Sally she had the book with her, I didn't have it with me all I had was the picture, Larissa she was in the dinner room, Maurice he was in there also, Larissa saw me she said here is my daddy, hi daddy. I said good morning to Larissa and Marice, I said to Larissa that the publisher sent me, my first copy of my book.

Then I showed the picture to her and said, that Sally she have the book she taken it with her, Larissa she smile and said congratulation daddy, Maurice he said where is the book let him see, I showed the picture to him, he look at it and threw it on the counter, and said he want to see the book no picture, he was lucky, I started to put something on his mind. This is my daughter's job, and I won't disrespect her.

Now I started to say to Maurice, who are you? nobody but with a job, that I left for you that he can't handle it, because he don't know how to do it, he only got it because of my daughter, and I didn't need to work but helping my daughter, because she needed me.

Then I said to Larissa, that I had to order some more books to sell myself, that now I need to fax my order to the publisher, with my bank card number, to take the money out of my account, Larissa said Wendee will do it for me, I said ok when she get here, but when we got to the office, Wendee she was there with her good looking self, I explain to Wendee what I needed, she did it for me. I said thanks to Wendee.

At that time Sally she came to see Pat and Judy her clients, she Sally had the book with her, in her arms she stop in the office, and spoke and showed the book to Larissa, then Milton he came to the office to find some candy, Larissa and Wendee put out candy for the tenants, if they want some. Milton and I was talking he had his cell phone, that take pictures while Sally came through, Milton he was taking Sally ass as she walk by.

That day I order from the publisher 50 copies of my book, cost $548.96. I stayed talking with Larissa, Wendee and Milton, then Sally she came back to the lobby before I left, she ask me was I going back home after I leave, I said yes what's up, Sally she said that she would see me at home, I said well I better go home then, Sally said that she would be there after she finish here, I said ok and said to Larissa and Wendee, that I will see them later then I said to Milton that, I will talk to him later then I left, and went back home.

Now I know that Sally, she didn't have anything but herself, and I had said that if I make it into this world, of the hard times that if Sally are still with me, I would take her with me up the ladder, to a better place, and have a good times I want to give to her, but she have to help me also, because I am struggling and I know how to struggle, by going out and get what I need, not what I want you can't have everything you want.

Now Sally, every time I saw her she had my book in her arm, or at home she is in bed reading my book, she would come over to my apartment, and see some of my friends like Kopoe, Sally would say to them how much she love me, now after all I thought that I had the best.

Every day Sally she went to go to work, I made sure that she had gas for her vehicle, I would give her $20.00 every other day for gas, she was to give it back when she get her gas alliance, now I kept giving and money was not coming back, but I always would find a note in my shoes, in my draws everywhere she thought I would be using.

Then I still say to myself why do she do that, I don't want to read about how she loves me, tell me other than when we are in bed having sex. Other than I had to find it on paper to read, then Sally said that she wanted to write a book, that made me feel so good that someone, who want to do something for them self.

Now for what I did for myself, was my calling. I use to sing on stage with a 5 piece band, but I fall but I could not let life defect me, because I knew that God and Jesus had something for me to do, but I did not know what it was, so I tried everything that I think about, that would work for me, and the public could respect what I was doing, I ask my God and Jesus what do I do, but I keep on going.

Now Sally she want to write a kid book, I said why not that I would help her, any way I can, and I said to Sally that, why not help me with this book, two of passing through I am writing, and when it was time for me to write about, her and myself she can write how she feel, about what I write and that she can write what's on her mind, and heart into I put in my writing, Sally she said ok, I then said after I can't type to fast or so good, that after I hand writing on paper, that she could put it in the computer.

That it would be faster then she can fix the spelling, and cross all T's and dot all the I's, that was all she had to do and don't change anything, she said ok, now I am feeling good now that God and Jesus had sent someone, into my life that want to have something.

Now I have to do anything, almost to make her happy, that made good sex in bed make her look good that is what I have to do. Now that is all you have to do keep her happy, then you should have someone who, want to walk with you talk, laughing and having sex and will still be friends, no matter what, sleep together and stay together forever. You will have a friend for life.

Now you don't have to have sex with a woman, to have a friend for life just treat her, peoples the way you want to be treated.

Now the governor was given a rebate from DMV, motor vehicle, I went to the mail box on October the 8th; the check was in the box from DMV. I put it into the bank, Sally she was saying that her eyes was bothering her, that her contacts was scratching her eyes, now I don't want that, I said why don't she change them, she said that she would but, I said that I don't want her blind, Sally said me to.

Later on Sally she had to go and see Pat and Judy, her clients, she call me back and told me that, Donna ray had pass. I said that, I was very sorry about that what happen? Sally said that she was in her apartment, slump over on her couch, that Milton could not get in touch with her, he walk around to her sliding glass door, and saw her slump over on the couch, and call 911 they came and said that she was dead.

That next day I went over to where Larissa work, Larissa she ask Maurice and I, to watch Milton because Donna ray and Milton was close, I said that I would because Milton he was, looking sad yes because his friend has pass away, but I can't baby sit him, if I was over there I would talk to him, but I saw something about Milton, that I don't like.

On the 10th of October 05 on that Monday, my order was fill from my publisher my books came, Sally and I open the box of books, I took one and went and found Stewart, he was working in apartment, I sign the book for Stewart and I insured, Stewart that he was the first one, who purchase my book $30.00.

Then I went back to my apartment, and I only had 10 books to give away, I had to give one to my girl Elsie Morgan, and the computer guy that work on the computers, here at Louise Shell Senior Apartment, he was working on Elsie computer in her office, I gave him a book also, I know him from here and he show me that he, is a ok guy.

Now Sally, she didn't know anything about computer, same as I, before I meet another gorges woman that live in here, her name is Reba. Find now I can't have them all, I had a problem in my computer, I ask Reba if she could fix my problem, for me that I would pay her.

Chapter 4

Now I needed to have someone to do something into my computer, there is another lady that move here, her name is Reba, I was talking to Joanne, that live across the hall from me, about that I need to find someone, that know anything about computer, Joanne she said Reba she is good about computer, I said o yes then I will call her to see if she, can fix what I need in my computer, then I said to Joanne that if she see or talk to Reba, let her know that I want to see her, Joanne said ok that she will see her, and tell her to call me, I said thank.

On October the 11th before I had talk to Reba, about my computer, she came to fix my computer, Sally she was in the bed room reading my book, I ask Sally if she want to watch, about Reba and what she are doing, for my book in my computer, Sally she look at me funny and said no, I close the bed room door, and watch Reba while she was putting me, back on my right path.

The time was 2:p.m after Reba had finish with my computer, I asked Reba what did I owe her, Reba she said nothing, I ask her did she drink wine, she said yes sometime, I said ok that I had some homemade wine, then I gave Reba some then she left.

Sally she after I came back to the bed room, was smiling and said that she was so jealous, about that Mary in this book, I ask which one there was more than one Mary, she said all of them. I said after I kiss her, don't worry about my past that is what this book is all about, is my pass all I want and need is, keeping Sally safe and happy in our future.

Now a man he should want or need his woman, looking good if not you but me; Sally she wanted to order some cloths from Newport news, in I believe in Virginia, she wanted to use my bank card, that she was going to give me the money, after she got paid, I said ok but I said to myself, what about the gas moneys that I gave, she haven't gave that back, one night she got paid and gave me $20.00, she thought that she had did something.

So I let Sally use my bank card, she order from Newport news holdings was $170.00, that next day she needed to have her car payment, that the peoples was going to take it, if the payment was not in by tomorrow, that she was going to pay me back, like a fool I let Sally do that also was $350.00.

Now something happen I could not put my finger on, all the pass life of me and the women, that I had in my life, Sally she start to be a critical of my book, she even got mad about it, she started to say why did someone put, there company name on a book like this, that I should had read what I wrote," did I read what I wrote," I said yes I did read it because, it was my pass I wrote it.

Sally she said there was Misspell words, and that I talk in some places twice, I said all my misspelled words, and all of my grammar with everything, is me and no one else this is my pass life, that Sally or anyone else can write my pass, like I can without anyone else changing my pass, now I can explain only what is in my book.

That Monday I went to Albertson food store, I didn't see my friend Kim that work for Albertsons, I got my money order for my rent, and I saw this pretty lady that also work for Albertsons, she is black and work afternoon, with a pretty smile, I ask about Kim this pretty lady is a supervisor, she said ok David we don't play that, I start laughing and said ok, someone said what is Kim black or white, I said she is a person and a lady, no matter what color.

Now my daughter Jackie she had call me, that my younger grandson want a computer for Christmas, and Jackie told me how much the computer, was going to cost and if I could help pay for it, I said that I would send her a check for half.

That same day was October 17th 05, I wrote the check but I didn't have no stamps, I laid it on the table that I had to go and see Larissa, that morning and that I would get a stamp, and mail that check for my daughter, that morning I got up and left home, I forgot to mail that check.

Later Sally she came to see her client, she said to me that I had forgot to mail, that letter for my daughter, I said dam I forgot, Sally she said that was ok that, she mail it, I said thank because I had forgot to mail it. That check was for $250.00.

Now I call Jackie to let her know, that I had sent the check and to call me, when she get that check, Jackie she ok daddy, I said ok that I love her.

After about a week Jackie she did not call me, about that she had gotten the check, I stated to Sally that I had talk to my daughter, and that she still don't have that check, I said to Sally, did you put that check in the mail, she said with a attitude yes I sent it, it just haven't got there that it was coming.

Now seem like every day or week, Sally she needed money for something like she or myself, was rich, plenty of money, but she was only using mine, I made a big mistake when I put Sally, on my check account, I make the money Sally she spend it, now I after to put a stop to that, because I can't get anywhere like this, I don't want to kill Sally but I will about my money, but I am now too old to go to jail, I can't kill her but I can put it in God and Jesus hand.

Now my blood pressure it started to go up, and up Sally and I went to wall-mart, my head was killing me before Sally and I was going to leave, there was a blood pressure machine at wall-mart, Sally she took my blood pressure, she said that it was too high.

Now Maurice aunt name is Mary, she needed some work I had to do for her, finish putting up a shed, that her kids could not finish, that morning I went to fix the shed, it was hot as hell but I had made a promise, that I would fix it on that day.

While I was putting the top on the shed, the top panel was not falling in the right place, and I didn't have a hat on my head, and I didn't have any water I didn't have any because, I didn't think that it would take that long, to do what I had saw the day before.

It was so hot out there and I sweat so much, like someone poured water all over me," having sex also smile," one of her son he look out the window, he saw that I was in trouble in that heat, he came out and gave me some water," I thank him," I drink the water and sit down for a minute, and started back to work then the beeper went off, I said it can't be no body but Sally, what in the hell do she want.

She know that I don't have, want or need a cell phone I ask Mary, could I use her phone she said yes, and gave the phone to me I call Sally, she didn't want anything then she ask me, what did the lady I was working for look like, I said she look like a woman, is that was what she call me for, and don't call me about in my book, about those woman, women or ladies in my pass.

After I hung up the phone I went back to work, I was getting dizzy I was getting dehydrated, my water was low in my body, I kept on working getting dizzy and dizzy, until I got the top of the shed on, the door it was aluminum it would not keep anyone out, from the shed I call Mary sister or her daughter, I thought and I explain that I was going to, put up another door with plywood, that would keep others out.

She said ok what did they need for them to get, I said get a sheet of plywood 4x8 for the floor, and the door then I would come back, and put the floor and the door on the shed, then we went into her house I was so dizzy, she saw it and gave me some more water, and said how much do she owe me, I told her she gave it to me, and I said after they get the plywood call me, and I would come back and finish, with the shed with no more money charge.

After I sit there for a while we was talking, I said that I write poetry and that one name was, passing through, she said o yes she would love to read it, I said that I had one in my truck I would get one, for her I was still dizzy but God and Jesus, gave me the strength to go to my truck, got the poetry and gave it to Mary, and said to call me after they get the plywood, she said ok thank for the poetry, I said thank that I also wrote a book, about passing through.

Now I got into my truck and went back to where I live, I was so dizzy I was on my way to a sun stroke, and Sally beeping me and don't want anything but being jealous, about my pass life I still had that beeper, from Thursday night to Monday morning, then I take it and give it to Maurice, this was a Friday it is hot and I was getting sicker.

So I stop into the lobby to get my mail, I got out from my truck I saw Stewart, he look at me and said, David you don't look so good are you ok, I said no that I got so dizzy that I almost fell down, Stewart said get your mail and take that truck, and park it and don't move it, I said that I would and that what I did, I went inside of my apartment and call Sally.

When I call Sally and told her what had happen, she said, she on her way, I said that she don't have to come here, that I am ok. She said that she was on her way then she hung up the phone, about 10 minute Sally she was here, she said that she had to drive so fast, to get to me then she ask me how was I doing, I said that I was ok that I got dizzy because of the heat, Sally she said that I could have had a stroke, that we was going to go and see a doctor.

Because she could have cause an accident, I said that when I call her that I was going to be ok, that I had a good feeling about that, I will be ok don't worry, she said why don't you want to go, and see a doctor. I said why because doctors are not God, nor they are not Jesus they are just an instrument, and the instrument might find something, that I don't want to hear about, I made a commitment to God and Jesus, and they will take care of me, I promise that for you.

Sally she said ok that she had two others clients to see, and if I want to ride with her, I said what the hell ok, we left Sally she started to talking about my book, how she was so jealous of Mary, and those women in my past life, and that after she was reading my book, then Sally she said that it was a good book, but later on in my life it was going to jump up and bite me, I ask how? Sally said that she knew everything about me, and that I don't know anything about her, that I don't know her.

That was when I said to Sally, that I don't want to know about her, and her pass I don't care about things that don't concerned me, that I wrote my pass life because, after I started to grow I left my family, like a baby bird too big for the nest, but me not to go off to stay away, just for me to have room to grow, things to see, go and find out what I want to do in my life, but I always kept in touch with my family, to see if they was ok and that I was doing ok.

And I never had to go back for help from them, but I would help them if they need me to help them, if I could help them I would do that, this book explain to my family what, how, and who was I with, while I was not there with and for them, while they was growing up.

You see Sally, I don't care about your pass, but into the future I will know everything about her and some," I am doing that now," that is all I am thinking about is our future, Sally she said that she love that our future, I said that if I make it she will be with me, and my father God and my big brother Jesus, will tell me and show me the way, I will learn about you because you will teach me.

Now it was time for Sally to pay her car insurance, it cost $132.00 I let her pay it with my bank card, she was going to pay it back," like I said before I am watching her," on October 25th a cousin of Milton, she was here from the storm from Louisiana, Katrina.

Her name was Michelle, she needed someone with a truck, to go and get some furniture for her, from the Salvation Army store, Larissa she ask me so I did that for her, I took Michelle to get the furniture, and took it to her apartment that the Government had provided for the flood victims from Louisiana, here in Vegas.

After I finish with Michelle, putting her furniture into her apartment, then I went back home, now those headaches they kept coming, Sally she had stop and got a blood presser cup, to check my blood presser," now to myself, I know what's wrong," every time Coco talk to me, I would always say that Sally and I was coming, over to see her and her girls and the grandkids, also the same as my cousin Joyce, Sally she always had an excuse, that we didn't get there.

It was also when Coco daughter had her other baby, 10-30-05 I said to Sally that I had to go, and see my new niece, and my other niece and nephew Raffel and Miss Molly, she always said that she wanted to have a baby, and that she could spoil that baby, then she wanted to know the baby name, I said that right now I don't know, until I go to see her then I said that, will she stop and get a present for the baby, she said ok.

Now those head ache I know where it come from, the mistake that I made with Sally, and the new person as I am today, want let me hurt or mistreat anyone, or one of God creation when someone or something do me harm, I give it to God and Jesus to take care of my problems, his hands are bigger then mind, I just watch you harm yourself.

Now I had told Sally almost everything about me, from my book to now, how I am, she know about my life and my insurances that I have on me, if I get to be disable one insurance will pay me one Million dollars, and now my book sale and I am talking about marrying, a drug addict that is why my head ache all the times, blood shooting up it want stop until God and Jesus fix it for me, it is in his hand.

Sally she had made a doctor appointment for me, with some doctor that she know, name was Dr. Golbertson on the 27th of October, I didn't go because I didn't know where his office was, and that I know what she was trying to do, number one is Sally was trying to get my money, from my disability insurance, if her shifty doctors could have had me in their office.

Because if I was declare disable, the insurances that I have from the bank of America, will have to pay me one Million dollars, now Sally she, know that is why she wanted me to see her, shifty doctors just for my money.

On the 28th now I don't say anything about what Sally, was trying to do or raise hell about it, because in my prim time of my life, I would have kill Sally but now I let God and Jesus, take care of me and my problems, I live into my father system, I am trying to stray away from man system, Sally she had put on my calendar," he gave up," I wander what she meant about that, I don't know and realist I don't care, there is things that God and Jesus, want me to do.

One day, Sally, teeth was hurting, and that when she was going to make appointment, to see a dentist. Now any other time Sally she would ask me, to go with her everywhere she went, this time she did not say anything, about come and go with her.

She wanted to go along, I said something to her to that affect, she got defense and said that she was grown, and that I didn't have to go every place with her, now I said that I never had ask her, where she was going or could I go with her, I don't and didn't care, but if she was trying to make a fool, out of me I would find it out, and what ever happen is on her.

On the day Sally she had her appointment for the dentist, she said that she went and that she need, $200.00 for the dentist, I ask, why don't, you take checks! She said that she got it from the bank account. I said how she could do that without, my card or a check.

She said that her name was on the account, and all she had to do was give her name, and address and the bank will give the money to her, because her name was on my account, then she was at a drug store, that the dentistry had some pain pills described for her, that need to be fill that she needed another $200.00, for the Medicine then she ask was that too much, I said if she need it to stop the pain, go on and get it. Now after she got back to me, she had got a paper shear, the first thing she did after she taken out, the Medicine from the paper it was in, she went straight to the shear and sheared those papers, I said what, why did she do that, I could use that money that I spent for that Medicine, and put it on my taxes, she said I didn't know, I said you don't shred importation papers.

Now I am sure that I have to do something, because this bitch is trying to make me homeless, I did hear that she said that she would be with me, and live with me if I was in a paper box, I told her that is not me, so now look like she is trying that, but I will not let that happen.

Now every time I go to the lobby, to get my mail I say hello to Elsie, and whoever was in there with Elsie, this morning I stop to say hello to Elsie, the guy that work on the computer for Elsie, I think I called him See, he was in the office working on the computer, now I am looking like someone was dying, on my last leg. He saw something in me, that don't look to good he said, that when he saw me the first time, he said that he saw a strong, intelligent man that will try to help any and every one, who need him.

Then he said that he know that, he is a man give him my word, that I would go and see what is wrong, will I go and see a doctor. I hesitate for a moment and said that I would, he look at me eye to eye and said are you sure, I said yes I am, the next time you see me, you will see the change. He put it to me like a big brother or a little brother, he was concern.

Now I had put Sally on my business cards, as my business manager for my books, and my T. shirts. Thinking that she was the one for me, but now I found out that it was not true, I found Sally to be a white leech, and a white devil now one of us, have to go and I am not going anywhere, then I call on again to God and Jesus, please help me.

Now I am still thinking about all that money, that Sally took from me saying that she was going to, pay it back to me now she has going too far, it is time for me to take Sally name, from my bank account, that Saturday I went to the bank, to take Sally name off my account, they said that Sally would have to be with me, in order to take her name off my account, I told the bank person that this was my account, I had this account ever sense I came here to Vegas, in 1997 now because I put someone on my, account now I can't take them off, without them.

Ok I will go and get Sally and come back, I was thinking about the lies that Sally had told me, like last night I gave her $10.00 to get some gas, this morning she said that someone must have siphon it out, I know better than that, old peoples that I know don't know how, to siphon gas, she had the heart to tell me that lie.

When I got back home Sally she was in the bed, I said to her, get dress she have to go with me, she wanted to know where? I said to the bank that I want her name off my account, because I can't trust her with my money, at that time she played me, she started to tell me how she can change, and will I give her one more time to do right.

She said that she know how much money that she owe me, then she said you put my check in the bank, the other day that she was trying to pay it back to me, and please give her another chance please, I said ok this is the last time. The next day I went and move something for Maurice, and after we finish it was Maurice and a friend of his, Sally she had left me the word, not to leave before I saw her, I said what in the hell do she want, I went and found her.

She said that the peoples of Donna ray, they want to know how much to move, a couch and a table and chairs from Donna ray apartment, I said that I had to see what all they had, because I don't have any help to lift the things, I went to see, there was a young girl sitting on the floor, I ask what need to be move, then I look at that young girl, she look at me as to say no leave this along, they start to show me what all to be move, I gave them a price of $100.00, the boy he said no way he could get a cab, and move it for that, I said ok get yourself a cab, then I left.

The next day I was over there talking to Milton and Maurice, before I left I said in front of Maurice, we was standing in the front of the building of, Salvation Army, I told Milton that I know that Sally and he is, good friends so I am telling him that if Sally, don't straighten up and be the woman that I thought, she was going to be, I was going to put her out of my life, then Maurice he started to walk away, then I left and went back home.

That next Saturday Sally and I made love, she look like that she was trying, but I can't do anything about her pain, and I don't want no pain myself in the pocket, after the love making was over, I shower and got dress, Sally she had a client to see, I went on the outside to sit and talk, with who-ever was out there.

About a half hour I saw Sally at the gate, I said to myself, what is this why are Sally back so soon, so I went and open the gate to let her in, she wave to the others that was sitting out there, I got into the car with Sally, to ride back to where I live to building number 3.

Then I ask why did she come back this soon what happen? She said nothing we got to the apartment, we went inside the first thing Sally did was, getting her things that she had left here, I said what is this what are you doing, Sally said that she didn't want to stay anywhere, that she was not wanted.

She kept on getting her things, even that ugly doll she and Pat call Bonnie, Sally she had that ugly thing in the bed, while she was reading my book, I told her that I don't sleep with no doll, while it is made from rags, while Sally she was getting her things, I said to her when she pick up her things, keep them going I got up and gave her a hand, then I said give me back my truck key, and my apartment key, then I gave her car keys, then I ask for papers from the dental, and the pain pills I had to pay for.

Sally she said what, you don't believe me and that my problem, that I don't listen. I said you are right I don't because you never had anything, worth with merit to it, talking about but one to find a way to fuck me, out of my money then I help putting Sally things, on the outside by the door, then I close the back door and went and lock, my apartment door and went on the outside by my truck, one of my neighbor name is Cecil, he was outside by his car, I was at my truck if Sally try to do anything to it, I would try to kill her.

Then I saw Sally driving out, I said to Cecil that I had to put that white bitch out, away from me she is a theft, Cecil said you are right you don't need no theft, you send those away they are no good, I said now I have to get her name off my account.

After I finish talking to Cecil, I went and sit in the sitting area, I started to thinking about my bank account, how on Monday I have to call Sally, to meet me at the bank to take her name, off my account and give her the money, from her pay check that I put in the bank, I will give that for her because she need it, with the pain pills or whatever she use, all she are is a drug addict.

As long I get her name off my account, something was telling me that, the bank is still open go and see, if Sally had gotten the money already, I know that Jackie my daughter, she still has not gotten the check, that I sent to her. I said that I should but I can wait until Monday, that I will call Sally on Sunday, to meet me at the bank.

To meet me at the bank, then Mr. and Miss Lee and some of the others ladies, the had come outside to sit and talk, I explain to them that I was over with that white woman, you see some of the tenant see Sally at the gate, and Sally she had talk to some of them, now I don't want to see Sally anymore, Miss Lee she ask me for how long, I said never more. Miss Lee she said ok you are saying that now, it is over with her but, don't misunderstand now she is pretty, and find you might change your mind.

That was when I said you might be right and I promise this to you and all it is over. I also let Elsie know that it was all over with me and Sally I explain to Elsie why.

Then after I got back home I call my family members, that I had induce Sally to on the phone, how what Sally had did to me, and that it was all over that Sally she, was not what I thought she was going to be, but she showed me that she was no good, but a gold digger. Even to Bobby Jean my play sister in Chicago, I explain everything to Bobby, she said that the last time Sally and she, talk Sally gave her phone number to Bobby Jean, she said that she was going to call Sally, and Bobby she said that she was not going to, let Sally know that she know that we talk, to see what Sally had to say, that Bobby was going to call me back, I said ok.

Later on that night Sally she call me, I was watching a move Sally she was at the gate, she wanted to talk I open the gate, I went for that for one reason, her name was still on my account, and I don't want to have to kill her, or I might have to change my account number, so now, I have to be nice for now, so after Sally got to my apartment I let her in, she spoke I spoke back, I didn't have but one thing to say to her, that was meet me on Monday morning, to take her name off my account, I had some whiskey one of my neighbor, name Miss Fraizer who had gave to me, Sally ask me to fix her a drink, I said get her own if she want one, because things has change between us, it was all over.

Now Sally she thought that if she talk to me, it would make it alright, that I would still do anything for her, but she was wrong I use to treat her, like she was a Queen but now, she is nothing to me, I was still watching TV Sally she wanted to talk, I don't have no compassion for Sally, I don't have anything to say but you have fucked up, and it can't be fix.

Then Sally said that she would take her name off my account, after I saw a doctor, I said ok, but on Monday morning I want to see her at the bank, after Sally she saw that I was not interest in her anymore, she got up and said that I was not interest in her anymore, that she was leaving she got up and left, I lock my door back and went back to watching TV.

That Sunday I call my friend Coco, the one who use to work with me moving peoples, and I explain to Coco about Sally, and that I got to go and take Sally name off my account, now Coco son in law name Ray, he is a manager for a bank, I ask Coco was Ray at home, Coco she said yes hold on, she would let me talk to Ray, so I talk to Ray and explain to him, what I was going through Ray, he told me the same thing what my bank, had told me so I said that thank, that if I had to change my bank to another one, that

I was coming over to where he was at, he said ok if that was what to be.

Then Ray gave the phone back to Coco, she said partner Sally she didn't want to meet her, I said every time I ask Sally, to come on and go over and talk to Coco, or go and spend some time with my cousin Joyce, Sally she always had a reason not to want to go, Coco she said no she didn't want to meet her because, she would see through Sally and let me know, all about her.

Then Coco said you are a good man partner, and that Sally she was not finish with me, she was going to try to come back to me, I said not a chance it is over, then I said that I had to go and find Stewart, and that I will talk to her later and tell her, rest of her and mind," smile," family I said hello, Coco she said ok and be careful, I said that I would.

That Monday I went to the bank, and I wait in the parking lot for Sally, look like something came to me, to go back home and call this woman, I did that call Sally she was at Pat apartment, I told her that I was waiting on her at the bank, now I am mad as a wet hen what is this woman trying, to do get kill, I told her to get there to the bank, so I can get her name off my account.

She said that she had to go and see a client, I said what time could she be at the bank, and that time I would be there, she said about 1:00pm, I said no not a good time, that to be there in the morning, about 9: am, she said ok where on Martin L. King and Washington, I said yes, she said that she would be there. I said to myself, if she didn't, God will help her, because Jesus will be all over her and her soul, and that will be me doing that.

On Monday November 05 at 9:10am, Sally came and meet me at the bank, I spoke to her, we went into the bank and a bank manager, I see all the time I am at the bank, I gave her a T. shirt of Passing Through on it, she took care of me that day, when I got her Sally off my bank account, I took a load off my mind and back, I felt lighter because this problems is over with.

Later on I call my cousin Joyce, it was about 7:pm that night to tell her, that I got that thing, "Sally," off my bank account, Joyce said if she had the chance to meet Sally, Joyce she would have seen all through her, and she would never had a chance to hurt me, then Joyce said you know cousin, don't make that mistake anymore, I said no way we hung up, then I call everyone that knew about Sally and I, that she now is history and that I got, Sally off my bank account, they all said that I was a fool when I put her on my account.

Now I know, that I was trying to help or love someone, but now, I see that you can't help or love another, who don't want to help or love themselves, now each and every day after I got Sally, out of my life. I know some of the ladies that live in here, where I live they was watching me, to see how I was going to deal with the break up.

They always would say David Marshall, how are you doing, one of the others said, he, lost his lady, you know how he are doing. I just smile and told them that I was ok, and a woman is not my worry, I need love and money and that was the truth, and I was doing find look at me, what do you see a man is worry about a woman, that was no good no not me, and I am better then ok, I have a roof over my head.

All of my bills is paid and my truck is paid for, I am bless you just don't know, one day after Sally she had call me, to tell me that she was so sorry about, what happen about she and I, and that I just don't listen, I said don't worry about that, because time will take care of that, because she was right I didn't listen because if I had listen, I would not had the problems, I had with her because Sally, you are nothing, and I hope that she rot in hell for what she did to me.

And to that day, she still say that she was going to pay me back, now how can she pay me back, she don't have a pot to piss in, and no window to pour it out, and I have love for another, because I love me but I don't have any money.

Now the ladies that live in here, they see that I don't want that white woman, while I am walking around my complex, taken my exercise I see some ask me, when was I getting marry, that someone had told her that I was getting marry, I said at that time I was talking about it, that would make it number eight, she said what are you talking about number eight? I said if I get marry one more time it would be my eighth time I had been marry.

That person that I was talking to she said, after I said that no woman want to be bother with me, she said that I walk around like I own the world.

Then I said that I do own my world but I can't rule your, she said that I was the man for her, damn, that I was a hell of a man, then I went back to my walking.

David L. Marshall

Something must be with me I know, it is God and Jesus that is in me and some peoples, see that because I try to help them or love them, and if they don't like that I am sorry about that, because I know what they did to Jesus, I want take some of that talking that is ok, but don't put their hands on me, because I won't take that.

Now I said no not me didn't hit me, unless I am getting paid in a ring, and if I see something in a woman, that I like and make me want to be with her, and if, I make a commitment and marry her, don't try to change me because a signature on a piece of paper, she a woman want to change her man, "or woman," think about that.

For myself, I love a person for what I see for their own self, now if she change me, or someone else I don't know, but me I know they are not the same," an older lady she told me one day, to keep your woman, you have to do the same thing to get her, to keep her," now I don't know her anymore, she is adding on to things that I didn't know." not only a woman she is just a slit, deference from a man, think about that!

To me she would be like a stranger, I can't love someone who don't love me it won't work, after I call my publisher and upgrade my book, to be put on the internet book store, Miss Elizabeth, Miss Russell and I went to the bank, "USA bank," to take our names off the tenant council account, that was on November the 18th 2005, then we put the money in a bank draft, then we gave it to Louise Shell manager Miss Elsie, to hold until the council have another president.

On Thanksgiving day I did not do anything, but lay around and remember the pass, when my grandmother and my mother they was living, but God and Jesus gave me another thanksgiving day, when my daughter Jackie call me, to let me know that she was with my brother, Clifford Bennett I was so happy, that I talk to Clifford and his wife Annie P. Bennett, now I found them now I have to call my sister, Deloise hill in Chicago to let them know, that I found our other brother, so I did that so that they can call Clifford and Annie Pearl.

At the end of the month I receive a bank statement, I took a look at it and I was so disappoint, about myself I look over my statement, I took a paper and put down, what Sally had did to me. Number 1, license plates $242.00 dates 8-6-05 some have dates on it, some don't Burling coat fact. ATM $182.58, Fugi Restaurant ATM $88.10 Sally daughter birthday, Chili's restaurant $48.16, Transfer-funs from the bank $70.00 Sally she was over drawn on her account, Wall mart vision ATM $128.19 for contact in her eyes, Money for Pat and Larissa ATM $240.00 Sally let them have, date was 9-29-05, money tree, loan company check number 724 $349.50 helping her out for money she got, Royalty auto her oil change $17.00 for her vehicle, BHFC finance co. $325.03 her car payment, Farmers company. Visa $132.48 she never paid, cash with draw for her dr. $200.00 she went to the dental? Beside all of them, cash for med's for her $200.00 said it was from the dentist? The total is $2,222.04.

Now with the gas money, I gave her that was to give back to me, after she got her gas allegiance from the co. that she work for, $200.00 never got it back, that was $20.00 every two days for two months, on 10-14-05 Sally was trying to pay me back, she gave me her check to put in my account, $430.00 and I had $30.00 in a check paid for my book, put that in there also there was $789.50, put into my account that day.

Now after I got away from Sally, and trying to get her off my account, on the date of 10-31-05 that bitch she took out from my account, $789.00, and my daughter Jackie she never got her check, for my grandson computer.

On the date of 11-01-05 I got Sally off my account, but that was not all of my problems, there was some other things, that Sally had put on my account, for me to pay was Newport News Holding, still showing up on my statement, I went to the bank to find out why, was it still showing up on my statement, after I had gotten Sally off my account.

The bank manager stated that, the time that took the other off my account, the statement was already sent out, and it will show that but, the next month it should not be there, I said that I hope that it don't happen anymore. I left the bank and I went over to Larissa work, I gave Larissa a copy of what Sally had done to my money.

Now on December the six I had to go to see my insurance. I also have Farmers insurance, my appointment was at 10:pm I went, and gave my check card that I had change, my number then I went back home, and I call my friend Coco, that I got Sally off my account, but there was another problems that I had, I explain about the Newport News, Coco said what are you going to do, I said that I was going to wait until, the next monthly statement, and if it was still on my account, that I was going to change banks.

On the eight, Stewart he had something to do, and he ask me to take him and help him, that he would give me a hundred dollars, I said ok what time you want to do it, Stewart said in the morning about eight o clock, I said that I will be there by the lobby.

Then I went to say hello to Elsie, then I sit around waiting on the mail man to come, we all was having a good time, the mail man came his name is Lamont, he is a good mail man I got my mail, I had some bills, had come I went back home, I made out those bills and put them in the mail, for the next day to go out.

That Saturday I had to change my oil in my truck, I did that and did some of the things that I needed to do, like washing and cleaning up my apartment, I don't like to have my apartment to dusty, because you never know who are coming by, my grandmother always said, keep your house in order you don't know, who may be stopping by.

One the 13th I paid my rent, I have always like to pay my rent, and my other bills early, because you don't know what might happen to you, nothing is promise to you money or life. My social security goes into my account, also my truck company. Is paid from the bank, all of my company is paid by the bank. I have time to write about my life, I don't have no lady in my life, but I do have some friends, I guess?

On the 18th I needed something from the store, there is a store call Mario, I don't like this store but they had the things that I need, there is pan handling always standing around, begging when you go in and come out, I saw two of my ex sister in laws in the store, Betty Lou and Dorthy Mae they saw me, I didn't see them, I heard Betty she said, that man look like my brother in law, I turn around it was Betty and Dorthy, I said hi how are you all doing, they said that they was doing ok, Betty she said that she saw me, and said that you look like her brother in law, I told them that I had wrote my book, and it was on line then I gave them one of my card.

Now I never ask about Bernice or any others, in the family because they didn't nor do like me, but I gave them a chance Bernice, she fuck that up because I am doing just find, I got what I went to get, from Mario and went back home, and started cooking.

Now my cousin Joyce she had ask me, did I know a lady that live where I live, name is Lorraine Wilson, I said no I don't think so, I put my mind in operation I said no I don't, but I will find her if she is there, there is not to many ladies live here, that I don't know but, sooner or later I will meet them, what she look like. Joyce said that Lorraine is a good lady, she will hang with you, I had said that I didn't have anyone, to hang out with me other than playing those slots.

One day I started looking for Lorraine, now I didn't know what she looked like, all I knew was that she was from Chicago. Every time I thought someone was from Chicago, I would ask them was they name was Lorraine, they would say no but their name was, then they would tell me their name, then I would explain to them why, I ask for

Lorraine that my cousin Joyce, know her, her daughter and grandson.

Then one morning we all was in the lobby, talking drinking coffee and waiting on the mail to come, this lady came into the lobby and spoke, Toni she said hi Lorraine, I said ok this is Lorraine I ask her, did she know a lady name Joyce Thomas, she said I don't think then she started to think, she said know I don't think that she know that name.

Then I said that Joyce she was my cousin, and she said that she knew this lady name Lorraine, that live in here and that she had a daughter and a son, that her son Michael play with your grandson, she said I don't know, I said ok what I was going to do was, I have a picture of Joyce I was going to bring it out, and show her, Lorraine said ok do that.

On the 19th I was on my way out from the exit gate, Lorraine she was coming from Miss Blackwell porch, I stop and showed Joyce picture to Lorraine, she said o yes that she know Joyce yes she do, I had to go so I said that I would talk to her later, she said ok.

The next day Larissa was having a dinner for her resident, where she work Maurice and his friend, they cook I went over there to see my daughter, I saw that Milton he was sitting on the outside, from the kitchen I look at him and look away, I don't have anything to say to him, not even a hi. I saw Greg, Larissa husband with the kids, Melissa and Marcus, I hug them and ask how was my grandbabies doing, they said that they was find and went one the move, kids can't stand still, I went over to where Greg was standing, to talk to him.

Greg and I was talking, I said that I should go out there, there and put my pistol in Milton mouth, and make him give me my money, that bitch Sally stole from me. Greg he said what! I said o yes Larissa didn't tell you, he said no. I explain it to Greg, he said that is killing times, I said you are right, but Sally she was going to get hers, I know where she are at when I get ready to get her back; I have my time to do that.

On the 21st we all was waiting on the mail man to come, we all was talking and having a good time, Jenson he was out there also, Lucky he was in the lobby also, Jenson now he don't mean no harm, but there are some things that a black man, should not do, that is let a white man disrespect, a black woman, that is a no know.

Jenson he, had a money order in his hand to pay his rent, Elsie she is a sweet heart to me she are, a good lady friendly, sweet, looking good find she was sent here to work, as our manager of Louise Shell apartment, what we need and I want let no man or woman, misuse Elsie because I am with her, I have her back.

Jenson I thought that he was just playing, when he hand the money order to Elsie, to take it in the office for him, Elsie she said in a nice way, for Jenson to bring it into the office, he throw the money order on the floor, and said to Elsie pick it up, my blood shot up. But I could not say anything right then, because I want to see how Elsie handled this, but now I am so disappointed with that white man, but Elsie she handled it very good.

But she didn't pick up that money order from the floor, now I am fizzle splutter weakly, because if in my pass life, I would have been all over that white man, But Elsie she is the best, and I want that to rub off on me, because I need that help.

One day, I was outside, smoking, a cigarettes, when Elsie and Stewart came out there and sit, I said to Elsie, that she was making a good man out of me, Elsie she said why? I said there was a time when, Jenson did that to you, I would have been all over him, but Elsie you took care of it in a respected way, I love you for that, she said well.

Now I was going to cook dinner for Christmas, and invite Joyce, Robert and Michael my family, Larissa my daughter and her family, I saw Lorraine and invite her if she wanted to come, and I invited some others, now Elsie, she her kindness are getting to me, I feel something for her that I can't explain, but I love her," Elsie. I do.

Now on the 24th I started cooking my dinner for Christmas, because I don't want to cook all day on Christmas, I need time to enjoy my family, I work on my book two of passing through, while the food was cooking, sipping on my wine that I made.

On Christmas day I had to give my big brother," Jesus," a merry Christmas and how much I love him, and that this is his birthday, not mind but his so I am going to enjoy, my family with him on his birthday.

Now I call my daughter in Alabama Jackie, to say merry Christmas to her and her family, she said back to me marry

Christmas, and that she never got that check, that I sent for my grandson computer, I explain to Jackie what Sally had did, and that I do believe that she never sent it out, that I am so sorry for that, I was going to make it up for her and my grandson.

Then later on Larissa and Greg came, my daughter had a present for me, that don't happen to me no body from my family, give me no present but Joyce, now I have my other daughter she love her dad, I didn't open the present because I am to emotion, excited state of feeling I didn't want to cry, a real man don't cry, then Joyce, Robert and Michael came, Robert he had just came out of the hospital, Joyce she gave me a present also, I don't swap present, Larissa said dad open you present, I said that I would do it later because, I will cry and a man don't cry.

Greg laugh we all eat dinner and I said, take some food home with them, I don't want all this food for me to eat, I told Joyce that Lorraine she said that she was coming, but I don't think so she is not here, but I have my family then I let Joyce, show me how to use the spell check, on my computer she did then they got ready to leave, but this is a good memory for me.

That Monday night the football game came on, I was watching it then the sports spokesman said, that this was the last Monday night football game, I said o no what are we going to do, other than getting a sport from Cox TV.

Now I went and got my mail, I had a letter from the Salvation Army for a donation, I sent them a donation, what I could afford, but Sally not for me going to jail about killing her; I took her to the water to wash her away from me. It is out of my hand.

Now I love Vegas, Vegas is so beautiful and that there are some good peoples, live in Vegas but, it is hard for a poor person to live in Vegas, if they love to gamble, I know that life is nothing but a gamble, but not with something that you can't afford, if my luck is bad I stay away from the casino, and do something other to make my money, for me.

Then I start thinking about, if I had not lost that money now, I could have did other things with it, if I had not played that money, trying to win now in Vegas to me, I can make it because I know that I can't get rich, playing a machine or trying to lay a bet, to double it on the odds it is, the one who own the casino, is trying to do the same as I am, make some money I don't need or want all of it, just some of it and if I can't make some, I leave it a long because I have to live for myself, and my family.

Now after I got here to Vegas, I know now who I am, I set my heart and my eyes on God and Jesus, because I am one of his creations, that God made to see himself, man he made mirrors so that man can see him, what God and Jesus look like, look in a mirror what do you see.

You know talking to people they are not what you hear or what they are, I hear peoples say how religion they are, they don't have a clue about religion, so if you are so religious why, do you stick a knife in the back of peoples, throw stone at them then you go to church, and you think that everything is going to be alright, and thinking that God and Jesus love that, I want to ask you something truthful. Have you ever look into God and Jesus eyes, if you have never look into my father eyes, we don't have anything else on that subject, to talk about what you don't know, if you have never seen into those eyes, I can tell you something you want believe me, so let's talk about what both of us know, that we can relate to.

Some peoples say, that are man is like a dog, some say that, they don't want a dog, but myself, think every woman need some kind of a dog into their life, you see I am not a dog, but I am a black Stallion horse. Some say a man on a white horse, I don't use drugs it is to powerful, but it is not more powerful then God and Jesus.

You see I have never road a white horse, and I never will. But a black Stallion yes one with muscle so huge, standing tall black as midnight, strong ready to push, pull and run that is me, that black Stallion.

Now I am still racking my mind writing my past life, I think about the good peoples from Chicago, I use to work with, Robert. I call him my little brother. He still works at Wedgewood use to be, I call and talk to Robert, and I ask about my ex-boss Martha Laura, Denise Smith I was kind of sweet on her, then I talk to Betty Miller, I ask Betty if she know how to get in touch, with Jackie Child and to give Jackie, my phone number to call me.

Better she said David take her number and call her sometime, that when she talk to Jackie she would give my, number to Jackie, then Betty said that some of them was coming to Vegas, I ask when, she said soon, I said ok call me when they get here, I could show them around then I talk to Miss Trell Davis, I was telling her what she had told me, a long time back that I was too good to my woman, Trell said don't start anything, I start laughing and said let me talk back to Robert, I did and ask Robert to tell Denise to call me, Robert said that he would tell Denise.

Now on January the 4th 06 I was at home watching TV, the phone ring I answer it was Denise, she said what do you want, I said that I want to talk to her, don't she want to talk to me then I ask Denise, did she get marry that I had heard that she did, she didn't answer that, then I said that I was going to move to Louisville Kentucky, Denise she said, what are you trying to get close to Jackie Child, I said no that I was trying to get closer to her, she said that she was going to call me sometime, I said that I would love that.

Every day I get up drink some coffee, look at my computer to put some things in there, I said after I get my mail and sit around talk to some of the tenant, then at 12: noon I am in my apartment watching my soaps, and working on my book two of passing through, on Sunday January the 8th is Miss Russell birthday, that Saturday I went and got a card for Miss Russell, and put $10.00 with the card and gave it to Miss Russell.

Now I play the super lotto from California, I have to go to the state line from Nevada to California, to play the lotto it is about 48 miles away, it is a nice ride going and coming back, but when I play I play for 20 drawing, that is over two month so I don't have to go every week, to put in my numbers, then after I get back I go to the bank, and make a deposit if I need to.

Now on the 12th of January I paid my rent for February the first, I saw Lorraine we sit and talk in the lobby, then I had to go and get some work done, Lorraine she told me where her apartment was, then she gave me her phone number to call her, I gave mind to Lorraine that she can call me also, then I went back home.

You know I have always had said, that one day we was going to have a woman president, why? Because man has fucked up the country, it has to be a woman to straighten it out. Now I didn't say where the woman was going to be, when she is going to be a president, but on January the 16th on the news, there was a woman just won the president, in African.

One day Elsie, Stewart and I was sitting on the outside, Elsie she was on her break, she said that her son was coming in a couple of days, I said o yes when he get here that I was going to, cook a dinner for him, Elsie said thank, Stewart he try to keep up with me, whatever I say that I was going to do something, for some others he said that he was going to help me, he and I.

He said that he was going to take Elsie son, to a tit bar to get his hair cut, that the ladies cut hair with their tits out, Elsie she said o no you want, that her son was too young for that, I ask her how old was her son was, she said that he was turning 21 years old, I said that he already know, she said that she was going to keep her son, away from Stewart and I.

That was when I told Elsie what I was going to cook, she said ok that she will let that happen, but she was going to keep her eyes on Stewart and I, know titty bar, I said that when I was 11 years old, I lost my virginity, Elsie look at me, and not her son, Stewart said that when he get here, David and he was going to set it out for him.

That Saturday on January the 21st I went to the store, and got what I need for the dinner, Stewart after I said that what I had got to cook, he never said a word about how much money, that he need him to give back to me, I said Stewart he is a user like the others, all ways talking about how much money he have, I know as the same as the others that know Stewart, that he is a big no teeth liar, and I had gave Elsie my word.

That Sunday night I start cooking the food, when Elsie and her son get here, the food would be ready to eat, I work on my book while the food was cooking.

On that Monday the 23rd I brought the food, up to the lobby and Glen he was there also, he was trying to get into Elsie pants, she had no interest in him but he was trying, he us to be alright I thought, he eat like a pig he was hunger, he said hum David you should have fix, more of them black eyes peas they was good, I said this so that Stewart could hear this, that I fix what my money let me fix, Stewart was eating like a dog and a pig also, he didn't say David put this in your pocket, but Elsie and her son was my concurrence.

There was another guy that live here in our complex, he is a free loader a white guy I guess, he go through the lobby looking for food to steal, Elsie ask him did he want to fix him a plate, I didn't say anything my God daughter Blessing, Miss Russell had her for that week, I had her in my lap feeding her, that guy look at me and said no who cook it, Elsie said that it was her son birthday, he could have some he did.

After he left, I said to Elsie why he didn't put his hand, off into something that he was not ask, that I had got on him before about that, Elsie said o she see that she had ask him, I said right, Stewart and Glen is some ones who I had to watch.

On the 24th my girlfriend Kopoe, she is so sweet she said to me that God and Jesus, ask her to tell me to put passing through on caps, I said that to let me see if I could find, out who could put it on the caps, and how much it was going to cost.

Now I had some old pictures of my family and friends, that I was going put into my first book, I could not find I look and look for them, I said that I would never find those pictures again, so I went on with my book and put it out, I thought that I had left them when I left Bernice, but I knew that I was not crazy, I know that I put those pictures in while I was packing, so on the 26th we was in the lobby talking, I said that I had some old pictures that, I could not find and that it would be a blessing, if I could find then again, Miss Elizabeth she said what was the pictures in, I said it was in a tin container, Elizabeth she said that there was some pictures, in the draw by the TV, did I see them she went over to where they was, I saw the container I knew then that, they was mind now how did they get in the lobby, I never took then in the lobby.

Now the white guy name was John Hall, his kids and his wife took John, to California because he was sickly, John, he and I use to go round and around, we start talking about some things, John he knew that I was right, but he all the time try to make it to fit him, after they took John to California, he was there about two months or more, he past, on January the 30th.

Jenson he put a picture of John in the window in the lobby, so everyone who know John would know, that he pass on I said that I believe that if John, was still here in Vegas, he would have live a little longer, I saw that picture and I took it off the window, I thought it was mind I had took one just like it, and I didn't want it to fade, but later I found out that it was not mind, it was Jenson I took it back to Jenson, and said that I was sorry, that I thought it was mind, the next day it was on the news, that Mrs. Coretta King, Martin L. King's wife past on, John past on January 30th 2006.

In February 2006 I call Robert in Chicago at Wedgewood nursing home, use to be Wedgewood. I talk to Robert about Denise and how she was doing, I ask him to tell Denise to call me, he said that he would tell her to call me, on the first Denise she call me, she wanted to know what did I want, I said that I wanted to talk to her and was it a problems, she said no then we just talk about old times, I wanted to hear from her.

One day my daughter Jackie she call me, and said daddy guess who she had with her, I didn't have a clue, she said it was my brother Clifford and Annie Pearl Bennett, I was so happy to hear from my brother, we talk and talk he had forgotten about me, but he remember Dennice, Mack but he could not remember me, I said when I was younger he use to slap on my head, and make me go home, we was shooting dice behind the old gym, and I said that when I got big that I was going to kick your ass.

And after I left Brewton and I went to Chicago, and I went back to see Zeb, he had marry Agnes, Pluke's, ex-wife from Kelly alley, that I had saw Clifford then but I was not in no shape, Zeb. Had to knock down some one, because Agnes didn't want to dance with some man, he call, her, a bitch the fight was on; I had hurt my leg and Zeb. And daddy took me to the doctor, Zeb. Agnes and I was lying in bed talking, I saw Clifford and I said that I owe him an ass whipping, Zeb. Said sit my ass down because, I could not walk that was the last time, I had saw Clifford.

Then Cliff said that this was a good book, also my sister in law Pearl said that it was a good book, that they had to get one, I told them to get the address from my daughter Jackie, and go on line and get it, and that we have to keep in touch, we said that we will.

But later on Cliff call me at home for me, to send a book for him in Houston, TX. So that was what I did, on the 6th Cliff call me that he had gotten the book, then he and I talk about our health problems, and that he had talk to my and his sister Deloise Crosby Hill.

On the 11th my daughter Larissa call me, that her daughter Marlissa wanted me to go, to her School with her, that they was having a grandparent day, and Marlissa wanted me to take her, I said that I was happy to go and take her, it was for Feb. the 13th.

On the 13th I went and pick up my granddaughter, she and I went to her School, the School was serving orange juice and donuts, I was proud of myself sitting by Marlissa, smiling.

After the orange juice and donuts, my granddaughter she had to go to her classroom, I got into my truck and left, I was a proud grandfather then I went back home, and started to work.

Later I went and got my rent money order, and paid my rent I like to pay it early, then I saw some of my ladies friends, that I had promise to take them to breakfast on the 14th. They asked me, are we still going to have breakfast, in the morning. I said yes we were going about 9:00am. They said that they would be ready.

That morning at 9:am we went to have breakfast, and after the breakfast was over, we all went our own ways I went and got into my computer, to do some work in my book.

Now my home boy and friend Popeye, he was trying to get an apartment where I live, and he had gotten the apartment, he ask me to move some of his things on the 18th, into his new apartment, and later move some more, until the place he us to live and work, was taken over. I said ok that we could do that.

On the 18th after Popeye got off work, I went over to where he was moving from, he had another friend of his name is Anthony, to help load my truck, we put on the truck the things that he was taken now, then we took them and put them into Popeye new apartment, then I took Popeye and

Anthony, back to where they was at first, Popeye said David Lee, what do he owe me, I said man I can't put a price on a friend. He gave me some gas money then I left, and went back home.

One day my bank was going to send me, an insurance policy from Bank of America Company. On the 20th I receive the form from the Bank, I sign it a put on my daughter Jackie, Larissa and John Marshall as my benefactor, incase, I pass on. It cost $31.00 a month for $250.000 life policy that was not too much to pay; I throw more that away why not it has for my kids.

On the 22nd we all were outside talking, someone ask me, David Marshall. That they Missed me as the president of the tenant council, that the other David he don't know what to do, and that the others tenants want to know, will I take the council back as the president, I stated no, I can't go back. I gave them my all to try to make them happy, but what did they try to do to me, slander my good name, saying that I was stealing money, they didn't have anything for me to steal, all they wanted to do was discredit me, so that they can still steal from the tenants, that is all they was doing, but I was stopping them. I gave more than I could steal.

My friend Kopoe, her daddy he is in a wheelchair, he was out there also, he stated that he tried to tell them peoples, that David Marshall was not stealing any money, they only pay a dollar a month for dues, and if he was going to do something for others, he took money out from his own pocket, and do it for them to make them happy, and that if he was him, he would not take it back, I said, "dad," don't worry I won't take it back.

Then I said that there was only one way that I would take it back, someone said, what is that? I said only, if, Elsie, ask me. Then Miss Russell she said David, that her girlfriend had just drop her off, and she saw me and said that, one day she was going to sit out and flirt with me, I said that was ok she can do that, the others ladies do the same things.

One day I was at home working on my book, my cousin Joyce call me, that a friend of hers name is Rossland, her old man he make moves, and he have a low budget and he need some help, but he can't pay me. I stated that I also have a low budget, and that I will help him all he have to do is call me, and let me know where he was going and be, when he needed me.

Every time I talk to Joyce, she wanted to know did I call Rossland, I stated that I gave her my phone number, that she already had it, that if they needed me they will call me, because after I give my help or offer my help to someone, they will call after all I can't or want run them down, because I have things to do myself.

But on the 24th that Friday, I had talk to Rossland that I would be over to meet, her old man about 7:30am, so that was what I did, I ring her bell Rossland came to the door, everyone else was sleeping, that they was up late that night, and could I come back later on, that the girls was coming about 1: pm. I stated that later on that I had things to do, but for her old man to call me, that I would help him the next day, she said ok.

Now the next day I didn't hear from Rossland, or her old man but I was going to the lobby, I saw my neighbor Miss

Fraizer, she had things in her vehicle that she was taken out, to take to her apartment, I spoke and ask her did she need any help, Miss Fraizer said David no that she will be ok, and how was I doing, I said that I was doing just find, and that I had a book for her, she said David you got the book out, and how much did it cost, I said to her it would be on me," this lady is a real friend," how can I charge her.

Now I, when I was the president of the council, I wanted to do everything to help and make, peoples happy. I put up tents to take peoples out from the sun, in Jan. the wind was blowing hard, so hard until the wind blew down one of the tent, I saw it down but I could not put it back up by myself, peoples would call me and let me know, that it was down.

Then I would say to them, that they have to call or go and see the president, they said that is why they are calling me, that the president David Montoya he was not shit, I said then he have to call me to help him, that he work on other people property and homes, so he know what to do it was out of my hands, so about a half hour Montoya he call me, I went and help him to pull the tent back up, then he went and got some iron stakes, we knock them into the ground, and tie the tent down until he could fix it back.

That was when I told Montoya how to tie, the joints back together with L shaped brackets, across the top joints and put some on the bottom, that the wind cannot blow it down, now I saw that Montoya didn't know how to do it, or he didn't want to let a black man, show him what to do. So I said, if he go and take some of the money, from the council treasure and get what I need, to fix it because I was not going to take, no more of my money to do anything out here.

Now Kopoe sister came here from Michigan, I took her and Kopoe to a dairy cream, for ice cream it was starting to get hot, here in Vegas. One of my neighbors across the hall, she didn't know how to mind her own business. She got into mind business, I had did some work with Stewart, and what my neighbor did to me, was about in my apartment, about she though she smell weed in my apartment, that is my business and my apartment I pay rent at.

Now that was still on my mind, after Kopoe, her sister and I came back, I went and park my truck, with that still on my mind, I went to the lobby looking for Kopoe, I saw her and I ask Kopoe was she busy, she said no my brother what up, I said that I need her if she would, go with me that I have to talk to Joanne, she said come on then her sister she said, that she was going to, on the way I explain what Joanne had did, putting out that I smoke weed in my apartment, that is my business. Kopoe and her sister said you are right.

When we got to Joanne apartment, I knock on her door she came to the door, I ask her could I talk to her, she said yes come on in, Kopoe, her sister and I went inside, I said Joanne the night she came and knock on my door, about a cigarette, she said yes, I said that she said to me that, she smell weed in my apartment, and I said that it was the air freshen that I showed to her, she said I don't want to talk about that, with a high tone. I said well let me tell you this. What every in my apartment is my business, in a high tone. Then, she said.

Well when she came here, peoples said, that she was homeless. I said, and I was the first one to say, that you had a roof over your head so you are not homeless.

Joanne, she said that she was sorry that she didn't say anything, I said then how did others know what you said, then I said to her in front of the others, no matter what happens this it is warning for her, to knock on my door, don't, knock on my door for just anything. Then I left Kopoe sister, we walk out together, I open my door to my apartment, and I said, tell me what she smelled. She said nothing but dust, I said you are going to smell dust, we are in a desert and Stewart He has not change my air filter.

Now I didn't like what I had to say about Joanne, but you see, when God and Jesus give you something, use it. Why do you know how, where and how long to wait, but he will be there for you, give him a chance have faith in him, if you do that you will see, and know that he is so good, but I had to put Joanne in her place, my place is and was clean and it will be always, but a man have to do, what he have to do for himself, and this is for God and Jesus.

One day I was in the lobby, and Mr. Weakly he came and brought a card table, and gave it to Toni for the tenants to use, Weakly he shook every one that was in the lobby hand, and mind also I look into his eyes, and smile and said nice to meet him, now, he didn't tell me that his name was Weakly, someone had said that one of our council man, name was Weakly. Was coming that day and I was in the lobby.

About a couple of days after, someone said David, did you meet Mr. Weakly the other day? I said no. They said he was in the lobby the other day, I said he and I shook hands, but he and I did not meet, after I took a look into his eyes, I didn't need no introduction, I saw someone who, was just as I am, someone who want to help someone, show our love, as the same that God and Jesus, has shown us, you and I, Because I know him, because he is me and I am him. Now you can draw your own conclusion, about me I am just passing through.

When David Montoya taken down that tent, and didn't get the things that I needed to fix it, I was mad as hell, in my mind and out from my mind, I said some things bad about his ass, and I didn't and I still don't care, a Mexican cock sucker. After all that work to put that tent up, and the money that we spent, now everybody is looking at me, when are they going to put another tent up, it is hot and it is going to get hotter, I said don't look at me, you had the best but to you then, it was not good enough, you lie on me and didn't trust me, now what do you want me to do?

After, I had said, that everything in my life, that I try to do, to get ahead something happens, for me to reject or someone will steal it if they, see it or hear it. So I talk to my daughter about me writing, about my past and the future. Jackie, she said, daddy, that is your life in the past or into the future, I said it would not see me any other way, that you will be ashamed of, she said no. Now here I am. I know what, when and how I want to live it, "my life," not yours, but mine.

You see everybody I see and now, they have a Destiny! When I was a kid my mind was a wander, what was it out there in this world. When I got older, I went out to see for me, myself. Some was happiness, and some was funky but I made it to now, was looking at me every second of the day, I had to pray. For the good and the bad times that I had, God has done his job, that never stopped, has showed me most as I know, now go home and spread and show, what you know, all about love. He gave to me now I will give it back to you. That is my Destiny.

Now it was not easy for me, to get where I am today. I cried many days, real tears even as I lay fast asleep into my deep—a dream—I knew it was all so true. But as true as it seemed, I lay, at the foot of the cross, in my deepest dream I knew it was you in my thoughts. I felt a drop of moisten tears fall onto my face from the foot of the cross I laid. I took my hand and wiped the moist across my face to wash my sin for my life to take a better place, as I lay fast asleep with a smile on my face. I knew my life would take a turn around, and with new meaning that you would be pleased. Thank you, Jesus.

Now I had to thank my big brother every day, because my father sent him to me. That is why I still have to say every morning, when I wake you. Thank you, father and Jesus, for one more day. Now I don't have any money. Let me tell you what I think about money, Money is not everything, its good and its bad, how do you want to treat it? Man made money, God made man, as to be the same as he is; he made man to love another, not money. Man did that. Then God made a woman as the same as he did a man, to love, not money.

Ever since I came into this world, I came here crying about one or the other, money or a woman. When I came from a women, I was crying, it could not be for money, I didn't have any, but I had my mother, she was love, and I still share it that came from a woman. Thank you mother for your love, but I am still as this day, I am still crying.

To me, I believe you only have three times in life, you see, my first was when I open my eyes, to the world to see some things, but the rest someone had to teach me, the right and wrong, but it was up to me to build, on what someone had taught me. The second was when I got older, and went to Chicago, Ill. at that time everything that I touch turn to gold.

But it was not from God or Jesus, if it was I should have had everything in life that I needed; but those times was a test, how can I keep and protect what God and Jesus, have given to me, after I gave and not receiving anything in return, I started to fall trying to help or make someone else happy, that didn't want it, as I am passing through, trying to keep my head over the water, now I have another chance to better myself, because God and Jesus, still have hope for me.

You might say, David L. Marshall that man is crazy, but the only someone who say that is a devil, because I live God and Jesus every day, can't you see that!

On March the 5th Miss Russell said that, she was going to go and get my God daughter, Blessing and bring her over to see me, I love that little girl, I said ok with a smile, Miss Queenie said David you love that little girl, I said yes I do.

David L. Marshall

That Sunday was on the 5th, so I didn't see Blessing but that Monday morning, I saw her Glen he had seen Blessing before I did, he said Blessing there is your God father, then Glen said to me that, he had given Blessing a dollar, I said thanks, in my own mind I said you could have kept that, then Glen said that I had ruined Blessing, that she know already about money, I said o yes you have to teach them younger.

On the 6th my daughter Jackie she call me, to let me know, that my first wife Barbara Jean sister, Christen had pasted on, Jackie call me at 2:20pm by my time, I ask how was mat, Jackie said that he was doing ok she guess, I said what you guess, she said daddy she don't know, then I said do she know that, her brother John was coming to his aunt funeral, Jackie said that she didn't know, I said well I won't know, because he doesn't call me. Jackie, she said when she know, she would call me, I said ok honey that I love her then we hung up.

Some people needed some T. shirts that I make up, I had to pick them up from the guy, that made them for me, name is Toney, on the 9th I went and got them for the people that wanted them, after I took care of that business, I spent lots of time talking to Blessing, my Goddaughter, about what not to do, pulling up her dress, don't take to those that she don't know, and don't let no one put their hand on her, the wrong way. If they do, then tell someone about it, even to me.

On the 10th Miss Russell she was sick, and Blessing she was not feeling good, so I was in the lobby playing cards, by myself. Miss Russell said that she had called Blessing's mother to pick her up that, she was so weak that she was going up stairs, and that I keep Blessing until, her mother come to get her. Blessing, she didn't look good to me then she got sick started throwing up. I didn't know what to do I took Blessing, back to Miss Russell's apartment to her.

Chapter 5

THEN I WENT BACK TO the lobby to get Blessing things, I saw her mother coming, I spoke to her and I asked her, what is wrong with my baby, the mother said that she was at the doctor with her, the other day and that she was going to take Blessing, back to the doctor now, I said and let me know what wrong with my God child, the mother said that she would do that, so Kopoe and some others was into the lobby also, they said to me that they hope that Blessing, is going to be ok and keep a good eye on Blessing, I said all you can do with me is talk to God and Jesus, with me I don't have no power over Blessing, but God and Jesus has.

Now I am a man who will help anybody, if you want me to, now don't think that you are making a fool out of me, but you are not, you are only hurting yourself. Don't you never forget that don't play with me I am not a man to be played with.

Steward he, I thought was a good person, but to know the devil, you have to do some doing with him, in order to know him, I work with Stewart on Frank buildings, using my truck my time and my help, because some things

Stewart he needed help with, now this woman name CC, she help Stewart some times, she also work for herself, one day CC had a house from a real estate Co. she was going to paint, and there was some things had to be move out, to take to the dump I took my truck, with Stewart and I and did that for CC.

Another day CC had a job to paint a wall for Frank, a long outside wall Stewart and I was to, pull the dirt back so that CC could paint, and there was some trees also had to be cut, in order to finish painting, so she was to pay Stewart and I after Frank paid her, now that was ok I could wait, and Stewart and I was still running and working, on Frank building so I guess that God and Jesus was beating Stewart conscious.

He said that Frank had ask him, did he give me anything for my gas, and helping Stewart then he said, yes that he give me something," that was a liar, I have not gotten any money for three days," now I thinking in my mind that, Toni have taken all of Stewart money, and that she think that she can take mind to, she is not my woman and never will, she is not my cup of tea.

One day Stewart and I had some things on my truck, and I stop at the stop sign the traffic was bad, and a police on a motorcycle was coming, and a vehicle didn't stop hit the motorcycle, and the police I put the truck in park, and said Stewart did you see that, then I went with others peoples had stop, to see if they could help the police, the police he tried to get up, I said no don't get up that he don't know how bad he might, be hurt if he is hurt.

David L. Marshall

Then another police lady came, she ask did anyone see what happen, I gave her my card if she needed to call, then I got back to my truck and pull off, and took those things off my truck, and park and went to my apartment, after I got into my apartment and check my messages, one was from the police department, the female police she left a message that, they had gotten the accident straiten, and that she didn't need me and thank.

Now on the 17th of march Glen he ask me did I, want to go with him to the state line to play the California Lottery, I said ok why not I got my Lottery card, and Glen and I went to the state line, he Glen love his blues and he has some good tapes, as we was riding the music was sounding so good, then we got to the Lottery house and played our numbers, and we went back to Vegas and got back home, then I said thank Glen then I went to my apartment.

One day I was in the lobby playing cards, I heard some noise like two vehicle collided, I then saw Miss Queenie walking out, to the side walk I said where are Miss Queenie going, I went to where she was then I saw, where she was going, her son Greg was in an accident, now Miss Queenie she can't stand long on her feet, I told her to lean on me.

We was standing while Greg was waiting on the police, Miss Mary Helen and some others, came out to see what had happen, then Greg and I was talking about how, the devil was trying to stand in his way, and he was busy but he has God and Jesus in his life, and that the devil can't do him any harm, I said and you know that God and Jesus, will move those devils for you.

Then Miss Queen said Greg you go to the doctor, and get check out just in case he was hurt, Greg said that the steering wheel hit him in his chest, but he said that he was alright, I said but just let your mother know that, you will see a doctor then she want worry, he said that he would do that, then Miss Queenie said David, she got to go and sit down that her legs, was trying to hurt, I said ok that I will help her, so I help her to gate I see every and all things, I saw David Montoya wife and Miss Lee standing on the side walk.

And Elsie with some others was in the sitting area, I saw Montoya's wife as to say, look at this old woman with Marshall, she was trying to dance I looked into her eyes, she drop her head I walked around that devil, and took Miss Queenie to her apartment door, she went inside her apartment I went and stop and talk to Elsie, she ask me how was Miss Queenie, I said she was ok then Elsie she had to go back to her office, I went back to where Greg was at, and told him that if he need to take his tools, to his mom apartment, that I will put them on my truck and take them, to her apartment, he said ok, then I left.

Now I am still waiting to get paid from Stewart, for working with him at Frank apartment complex, and the work that I work for CC cleaning off that wall, so she could paint it now I am waiting fateful for my money.

One day it was a Friday Stewart and I was in the lobby, he said that CC got that check, I said o yes did she give you my money, Stewart said no she didn't, that Frank had a check for me that he was bring to me, I said what was that for, Stewart said he didn't know, I said some shit is about this but I will see it, and someone was going to, loose, a good friend.

Then the next day Stewart came to me, and said that Elsie had a check for me, and it was for $72.00, that Stewart still owed me $80.00, now I know that is not right because, the check that Frank left for me was, for gas that I had burn to take this bear mouth, ass Stewart, doing work for Frank, but I won't do anything or take Stewart anywhere anymore, that is a promise he better have some money, and no promise that he will pay me later, no more CC and Stewart owe me $80.00, for cleaning that wall for painting.

When I saw Elsie she gave me the check that Frank, had given her to give me, I said to Elsie that Stewart thinks that he got one over on me, then I explain to her what Stewart and CC had, thinking that they had gotten one over on me, but they better watch their self, I will put that in God and Jesus hand, and no good will come to them, that I promise.

When I use to be younger and crazy, they would get what they was looking for, a killing, now God and Jesus they help me, and proudly provide and make preparation for me, and I try to give back what God and Jesus, have given me and help and make someone else, the way I am now this I promise, the money Stewart and CC thank that they are taken from me, it will not do them any good, that I promise.

Now like I said before that one of Miss Russell friends, said that she was going to come and flirt with me so she did that, she and I call and talk to each other, on the 25th I had said

Passing Through Book II

I was going to cook, and let someone else enjoy what I am enjoying, so I let Judy, Miss Russell, Queenie and the others that sit and talk with me, that on the 25th I was going to cook.

Judy she is a friend of Miss Russell, she did everything she could do to help me, now I am trying to like it, now after the food was ready, and we started eating I was sitting, and Judy she was standing behind me, I saw eyes on Judy, she said in my ear these woman are just watching me, I said that was what I was trying to tell you, if you spent too much time around me, they was going to watch me to see what I was going to do, so they can have something to talk about, now if you sit down away from me, then they can't see anything to talk about.

Now after everything was over and I was getting ready, to take my things back to my apartment, Judy she had a soda cooler we was using, she hope me take the things to the house, I said that tomorrow I would bring her cooler back, to her house she said ok, and I could see that she was not ready to go, so she went to the bedroom with me, we was talking and I explain to her, to watch what she are asking for, because she might get it. She said that she ask for it didn't she, so what was I going to do about it, now don't bluff me I want stand down. I will make you show me that last card.

Now after I saw that card and showed mind, Judy she showed me that what in the hell, I have did she was trying to change me already, then she left and went home and call me back, and told me that to come and move with her, all the good things she can do for me, then she said when every

- 215 -

I make my mind up, to be with her all the time then I know where she was, then she hung the phone up in my ear, I said o no she didn't do that, that was the wrong thing to do, shut the door of her heart and mind also, I don't and want have anything else to say, to her anymore.

Now I didn't call Judy nor did I say anything to Miss Russell, about what happen when we are talking, I never say Judy name, but on the 28th Judy she call me to apologize, and that she was so sorry, and that she was not that kind of girl, then she wanted to know what she had did and said, like I said to Judy that, I don't have anything to say, she said please forgive her, I said that I forgive her, but I still don't have anything else to say, then I said see you and hung up.

Then I saw Mary Helen she said David, after the food was at my house she came by, to get her some but I had company and I was busy, I said busy how, Mary she start laughing and said you know, I shook my head.

On Friday March 31st Kopoe said to me that, she was having a set for her preacher a black tie, that she was trying to have it at Jerry Nugget, and that the ticket was going to be $25.00, but she don't know right now, I said ok let me know that I will get a ticket," she got one of my book," and my cousin Joyce she had call me before, that she was going to move they had gotten another house, I said ok let me know that I will help her, she is my cousin.

That Saturday Joyce said that on Sunday, she wanted to start moving, and I said that I would meet her at the old house about 9am. She said ok that some of Robert friends was going to help, I said that I would be there, then Joyce said that they was going to have a u haul truck, and with my truck it want take that long, I said ok see her in the morning.

That Sunday morning I got up and fix some breakfast, the phone ring it was Joyce, she ask me to before I got there to her, go and pick up some Mexican from the corner at M.L.K Blvd., I said ok how much a hour, she said about $10.00 a hour about three hours, I said ok I will pick up three of them, she said ok. So I got ready to go I went and got three Mexican, and went and got started moving Joyce furniture, that day we took two loads of furniture to the new house, and put it into the house it was almost three hours, Joyce said that we will get the rest next Sunday, she gave me the money to pay the Mexican guys, she ask me what did she owe me, I said just give me some gas money, after all she is my cousin.

That Monday I was sitting out with Miss Queenie, Mr. and Miss Lee, Mary Helen, Marie I call her my wife, Killer he came out, now he is drinking, he said that he us to be a boxer, I have a question about that, that I can tell you about, he might be a sparring partner.

He always talk about how he sell coats, shoes etc. from the trunk of his vehicle, I have never heard about a champ doing that, Killer he don't have any respect for the ladies, and he can't hardly walk or stand, if he fall down someone have to help him up, I had to pick him up many time, that day he got smart with Miss Queenie, and he tried to sit down he fell down, everyone out there started to laughing, I did to but I had to help him up, I said man you get smart and if you fall down, you can't get up someone can beat you to death.

And peoples they had a good talk about Toni, I know they was not lying because, I see and hear how Toni are, but I don't understand one thing about it, why do you know how Toni are, but they kiss and lick Toni ass, not me she are no more than I am.

On the 5th I was going to go over to see Larissa at her job, I saw Kopoe and I was telling her, she wanted to go also. so she and I went over to Larissa job, when we got there Larissa she and some others, was standing on the outside by her vehicle, she sell purses and shoes she saw my truck, she start smiling I said to Kopoe there are Larissa, she said where! I said there she said sure is my girl, I park we got out Larissa and Kopoe saw each other, they hug and cried I spoke to the others that was there, Larissa showed Kopoe the building, they was walking and talking I saw Wendee, she came out from where she was working, and hug me and said that she had to come and see me, that I still look good, I said thank Wendee then she had to go back to work.

Then Larissa and Kopoe came back, I was rested Larissa she saw that, because she know me I sit for a while, and I have to make a move, so Kopoe and I got ready to go I hug Larissa, and said that I will talk to her later, Kopoe said to Larissa girl that they will talk, then we left.

Now Elsie she like I said before, is the best lady I meet after Mary left me, "in death," God bless Mary and Elsie to, because I love her also, now I can't lose Elsie and I have two ladies, in my life that I love now I want say their name, but if and when they read this, they will know who they are, because I told them that I love them.

One I meet and I saw something in her, that I could love, in ways she want me to, and now I am falling to closer to her, I can't and I want even try, to go to bed with her because, I can't lose this love what I have in her, if I did that I would be the looser, not her. I have to keep that respect that I have for her.

The other lady is just like the other lady, but just one thing about this one, have you ever seen that commercial about, the miller beer, if you poke it you own it, so that was what I did, now I can't own it, but I will protect it when they need me or my help, and I will always love her and protect her, "why," because I know myself, she's still the same, as the one above I love them both, I want to keep them in my life forever.

Now I will give peoples the benefit of doubt, I will let you hang your own self, now after Stewart and C. C had tried to do me, I still gave him a hand I did that for a reason, this lady that live on "H" street, Montoya did that lady wrong, Stewart and Montoya are almost the same, they took that lady money to do some work for her, Montoya he and his helper messed up the work, and took the money the lady was looking for him.

Stewart after the lady kids came looking for Montoya, he showed the lady kids where Montoya live, he, Stewart said that the manager, Elsie wrote him up for that, I said that I would not like it, if someone showed someone else where I live, I would be piss off because if they don't know, then that is there problems. Stewart said that he didn't take that lady money, Montoya the check was in his name, and he didn't give him any money, in my mind I said, I bet.

So now I said that the lady has been through enough, I went on April the 6th and put two doors, on her house she was asking Stewart about Montoya, and how he did to her.

On the 9th was my daughter Larissa birthday, I was going to take her to lunch, but she was going to Arizona to work, at another Salvation Army place they have, so I gave her a card and put some money in it, to get her lunch.

On the 12th Toni she took the corporation money to fix food, for the resident of Louise Shell Seniors, after the dinner was over Joanne she was passing a card around, to thanking Toni about what she was doing, she gave it to me, I said no I want sign that, I did everything for her and the rest, and you never said thank one time, now Dora and Frank send money to feed your ass, why don't you have a card for them, it was their money not Toni, just as I did for you, and you didn't even say thanks to me, or Frank or Dora. Joanne said then I will get a card for you, in my mind you don't have to do anything for me.

Now I was talking to my daughter about, after 4-01-06 someone in Alabama want one of my book, she had to send the money order to me from them, and I had to send the book back to my daughter Jackie, for them like Len McConnice when he wanted a book, so I was going to set it up in Brewton, for account for Passing Through, and send 60th books to her to sell, and put the money in the account, one day it was going to be hers, mind is hers.

Then on April the 14th my son John, he finely call me, I told John that I thought that he was trying to devote me, he said no that was not what he was trying to do, I said well you don't have time to call me, now what up. He said that he was trying to get himself together, and then he said that his daughter Brittney, she was in Mississippi. I said how was she and call her and give her, my phone number, like you was to do the last time, I was in Maywood Ill, he said that he was going to call her, I said like all those years he, John was going to take some pictures, with my grandkids and send them to me, I never got them noting but lies about those pitches, so I said call Brittney so she can call me.

Just before I saw Maria, I call her my wife she was talking about Easter Sunday, she said as long as she can remember, she never had a Easter basket that she want, someone to buy her a Easter basket, I said watch what she ask for, Miss Russell she said he are right it might come true, I know what she was talking about, Judy her girlfriend.

On the 15th I was having a dinner for those who, purchase some T. shirts and a book of mind, it is a appreciate dinner and I went and got that Easter basket, and took it to Maria then we had my dinner, with my good friends.

The best day of mind was when I answer my phone, and my granddaughter Brittney, she was on the other end of my line, that was 4-16-06 she and I had a good talk, and we communicate together freely, I told Brittney to write me a letter, so that I could have her address, because I was going to send her a package, to see what I was doing in my life, and that she and I must keep in touch, Brittney she said granddaddy she would love that, then she said granddaddy she love me, that open my heart to my granddaughter.

On the 17th I call my publisher, to send out 50 books to my daughter in Alabama, now Jackie she have a post office box, and the publisher said it would cost too much, to send the books to a PO Box, so I gave my stepfather address to the publisher, to send the books to, that Jackie she would pick them up and I will follow them.

Now there was a new guy that move into the complex, I could see that he didn't have any furniture, because every day he was coming to the office, trying to get an apartment after he leave the complex, he was pulling a grip with him, I saw him about three days, then I found out that he got the apartment, I had to go to the store and get cigarettes. After I got back home, I start watching TV anything else to do.

After I got home, Stewart and the new tenant knock on my door, I open the door and said, hi can I help you, Stewart he said that the wrong door, I look at him and the other guy and nodded it my head to him, they left and knock on the next door, a man live there his name is Stewart also, I said to myself that Mr. Stewart, he must be selling that couch that I took to his apartment, that Joanne gave him to that guy.

Then I smiled and said that God and Jesus has a plan for me, what about Toni and Stewart are trying to do to me, trying to take my kindness for weakness no way, like that day of the yard sale, Toni had me to take a couch from her house, and bring it to the complex and put it in the yard sale, she was to give me $50.00, I never got the money.

And Glen he was in bad shape needed money, he sold his big screen TV to Stewart, Stewart he call me that morning, that if I would take the TV about three blocks, I said ok I did went and loaded the t. v on my truck, I was going to tie the TV down on the truck, Stewart he said that he was going to ride on the back, so that he can hold the t. v so it want fall.

Now as I was driving, I said to Stewart knock on the cab of the truck, when I was to turn to take TV, he said ok, I kept driving then it came to me, I said that I will bet my life Stewart, was taking this TV to Toni house, then I saw what I was thinking, we took the TV to Toni house, I said ok Stewart and Toni know that I, would not do anything for Toni what she did, so Stewart he use me the last time.

We took the TV off my truck and put it in the garage, then we left I didn't have too much to say, because I know now what to do. on the next day I had cook and we all was eating, my God daughter Blessing she was here with Miss Russell, I had Blessing in my lap feeding her, that the next day we was taken Blessing back to her mother, so that was what Miss Russell and I did, and we came back home at four o clock.

Then I saw Stewart he said David, Toni want to know how much did I charge, to take the TV to her house, I said $25.00, he said ok that he would tell her, that next day I saw Stewart he gave me that $25.00, I said thank, in my mind it want happen no more.

On the 20th after what Stewart tried to do, what he did to me I know, that God and Jesus are putting something on his mind, and Toni also because all I have for them are, good morning because it don't cost me anything.

My lady friend Elsie and I was on the sitting area, having a cigarette and talking, Elsie said David, after you came through the gate early, she thought that I had Stewart in my truck, I said no, that it was little Joe I took him to sell his cans.

After smoking Elsie and I went back to the lobby, she went back to work, I stop and talk to Kopoe dad, Glen, Miss Blackwell, Toni and Miss Helen was doing some craft, I got ready to go home, I stop by the office and let Elise know that, I would be at home if she needed me, she smile, she to me have a beautiful smile she said ok David, I went home.

After I got back home I call Elsie back, to see if she want some snacks, she said yes, I told her what I had, she told me the ones she wanted, so I took it to her in the lobby Toni, she was trying to see what was in my hand, Glen and Kopoe they was still in the lobby.

Then I went into the office, to give some sweets to my sweet heart Stewart he was in the office, I gave Elsie her cookies and went back home, I had already saw Stewart, I got back home and said fuck Stewart, he is not a friend of mind, what he tried to do to me I gave it to God and Jesus.

Now there is a lady name Reba, she gave me some help before with my computer, she is a lady that if a man with any sense, he could be happy with her, one day I was out in the sitting area, Reba she came through the gate, and call me over to her vehicle.

After I got to her vehicle, she had a lady with her, I took a look at her and my heart stop beating, for a moment she is and was so beautiful, Reba induce me as her sister, I said nice to meet you then I said to Reba, that she and I had to take her to dinner, before she leave then I ask how long was she going to be here, she said until Friday, I said ok that I would see her later, Reba said when did I want to go to dinner, I said that their time is mind.

Sure enough Reba and I took her sister to dinner, after dinner we went to the casino at Union Plaza, my luck was so bad I could not do anything, Reba she went to another machine, her sister and I was on the table playing black jack, I was losing and her sister she was winning, she gave me some chips to play, I got a little luck and Reba sister she start losing, I gave her some chips that I had, so she could get back what she lost.

We played and played then Reba she came back, she had lost but she got hers back and quit, so it was late we went and got Reba vehicle, and on the way back home Reba sister, had to be at the air-port her plane was to leave at 11: am, and Reba she had to be at work that morning, she was going to take her sister to the airport early, I said that was to early that I would take, her sister to the air-port all she had to do was call me, when she got ready to go, so we got that together, then we got to the complex, I said to Reba and her sister after I got out of her vehicle, to call me now when she got ready to go.

That morning I got up and found little Joe, I ask him did he want to ride with me, to take Reba sister to the airport, Joe he said yes he would ride with me, so I went back home to receive Reba sister phone call, she had already call me and left the message on my machine, I tried to call her back but I could not get through.

So I went over to Reba apartment and knock on her door, her sister came to the door, I said that I got her message, and tried to call back then I said are she ready to go, she said in about a half hour, then she said that Reba wanted to leave her keys, across the hall with Jean, I showed her Jean apartment, she knock on Jean door, she came to the door and Reba sister said that, Reba want her to leave her keys with her, Jean she said ok.

Then Reba sister said to me, that she would be out in a little while, I said that I will be in the center waiting on her, when I got there Joe he was out there, we wait then I saw her coming, I went to her and took her bags and put them on the truck, we left and she wanted to go and get something from the store, I found what she wanted to get, then we went to the airport.

After we got to the airport, and found the plane that she was on and took her bags, off the truck she hug me, and said something that stuck in my mind, she said that I was a good man, and she think that she have found a friend for life, I had that same feeling I said a friend for life, that was my words I would say, I said that no matter where she was or at, if she need a friend call me anytime, that she want to call and if she could not find me, call Reba she know how to get me, she said ok and have a safe drive back, I said thank and she have a good flight going back, then Joe and I left and went back home.

Some of us was sitting out talking about our bills, I told them that I pay my bills as they come in, some say that they wait until the last day before, they pay their. I said to myself peoples don't pay their bills on time, is giving away money, by paying on time you can save late fees, reconnection fees you can save all of that.

Then we start talking about our pass life, one said David you always talking about, the bad things that I did in my life, now that I was a good man, what and how made me change my life, I said it was God and Jesus made me the way, I am today. I told them that I saw something everyone should see, it was the light I saw.

One of the ladies said why don't you have a woman in my life, after Mary pass, I said that there was no one I was interesting in, because I tried it with that white woman, and you can see what happen to me, then I said that, a woman she want a man to give her a commitment, I can't do that, I have already given my commitment to God and Jesus, my commitment is, that I will try to help someone who needed my help, because God and Jesus help me, while I am trying to get closer to the light, while I am passing through, going to the light.

That is why I haven got a woman into my life, I have been through seven wives that is enough, and if I get another one you will have too much, to talk about because it was not one of you, and I can't and I want take another lady through, all of that whispering about me that would be going around, that would be a liar.

On the 25th we all was sitting on the sitting area, in the morning time we was waiting, on the mail man come and there is a very lovable lady," she is white," but I don't see color her name is Betty, she came out to sit, and she was waiting on her daughter in law, to pick up her baby her name is Jazzy, a sweet little girl, Betty she saw how Jazzy was looking at me, she said look at Jazzy how she is looking at David, she like David, that was another star over my head, and love to my heart.

Now this other friend lady I talk to, when she was not mad at me her name is Miss Helen, she love to tell others what to do, and she is a nice lady but, she should stay out of others peoples business, she is to bossy, on that same day of the 25th, I had to put Mary Helen in her place, "again," she has a busy nose, I had forgotten my watch on my arm, we was outside talking, I look at my watch to see what time it was, I had forgotten it I said that I knew that, I felt naked that I forgot my watch, I better go and get it.

Now I had a cup in my hand I had something in it, I pick it up and started to get up, Mary Helen, she put her nose into my business, she said David don't put anything else in that cup, I said when you are out here in this sun, I will have any and whatever I want, because you are 50 per cent of water and 50 per cent dirt, so you need liquid, fluid.

Then I left and went and got my watch, and fix another drink, I started thinking about what Mary Helen had said, I open my refrigerator and got out 4 sodas, and I took them back to those that was there, when I got back Miss Queenie she had come outside, that made 5 others now I only had 4 sodas.

Before I gave them the sodas, I said to Mary Helen in front of, Mr. and Miss Lee, their grandson, and Kopoe daddy, was there first I told Mary Helen that, I was not her husband and she was not my wife, and not my grandmother nor my mother, so don't never tell me what to do.

Then I gave the sodas out and told Miss Queenie, that I was going to go and get her one, Mary Helen she said to Miss Queenie, here take her, I said ok then that I was going to go, and get Mary another soda, Mary said that was ok she don't want one, now I am not going to kiss her ass, because she was in my business.

After I had told Mary Helen off, Reba and I was talking, I told her that I had to tell Mary Helen off, she said what! I said yes she got into my business, then I explain to Reba what happen, she said I know you did, I said yep it had to be done.

That night I went home and made some call, I call my play sister Bobby Jean in Chicago, and talk to her then after that I, got into my computer and did some work, in my book two, then I went to bed, sometime I get lonely and wish that I had a good lady, into my life but she have to be right, if not soon or later, I will find her out, that call for a break up, then I watch TV and try to sleep but I can't sleep, sometimes I put on my cloths and walk around the complex, for about six times then I get tired and go back home, and go to sleep.

On the 26th after I got up and put my clothing on, I went to go to the cigarette store and got a carton of cigarette, I smoke first one, then I came back home I had fix some chicken salad, my neighbor Rose I gave half of the salad to her, there are another man live next door to me, name Stewart also, he is a strange man he can see me coming out from my apartment, the same time he are he speak then he ask, has the mail man run, how do I know he was leaving his apartment, the same time as I am, I just say no Mr. Stewart I don't know, he said oh, ok have a good day.

When it is cold outside in Vegas, he have on a short sleeve, and if it is so hot outside you can hardly stand it, he have on a sweat shirt with a hood on it, and he have it over his head.

Rose and I was still talking in front of her apartment, Stewart he came back with his mail, I said to him on the mail man has ran hum, Stewart said yes, sure he came and going, I said to Rose that I better go and get my mail, that I was looking for a letter from my granddaughter.

Then I went and got my mail the letter, was here I was looking for from my granddaughter, I pack up some T. shirts, a book of mind and some others papers, I wanted to send to her that was what I did, then I call Brittney, short to me for Brittney, I told her that I had sent some things to her, and I told her what it was, to look out for it, Brittney said ok granddaddy how was I doing, I said that I was doing find, then we talk for a while I had to go, Brittney said granddaddy take care of your-self, that she love me, I said to her that I love her also.

Now I had gotten a coon from Rose old man, and someone else had given me a rabbit, I had a roast in my refrigerator in the freeze, I took it with the coon and the rabbit, and I cook them and I gave some to others, that wanted some of it, they loved it Joe said that it didn't taste like no coon, I said that I soak it in red vinegar overnight.

 you know we have all kind of peoples in this world, there is some are beautiful peoples of all color, we all look like flowers, that mix with the others color of peoples, we sew the seed with others, I call it God and Jesus garden of his creation.

Man he think that he sew the seed, he are just an instrument for God, so man you are wrong, God and Jesus use you like he use me, he use all his creation the way he see it, the way he want you to be, he can do anything that he want to do, and there is not anything you can do about it, you can't stop God nor Jesus but sometime man try.

The doctor, are a doctor nothing but a man, an instrument for God. Every one of God creations he has something for them, just believe in him. God use Jesus and God use you, now I am going to use you.

That night Theron he ask me to take a ride with him, he saw trying to find some picture frame I went with him we was talking about peoples, and how they are, some are good and some I don't know about, those who don't know what is around them, they keep to their own self they don't care, what is around them until, something happen to them then here they come, I myself, want to see what is around me, then I will know how to deal with it, I am looking for my future, if God and Jesus see it for me.

On the 28th I had fix myself some food, and I always try to look out for Elsie, I took her a plate after I got to the office, Stewart he was in the office, Elsie she smile and said, peoples are going to say that we are going together, they are going to start a roomer, I said, what is my name! Now who are they? My name is David L. Marshall then I left out.

That was when I saw Miss Queenie, and I ask her was she hunger, she said that she had just eating, then I saw Miss Russell and took her to my apartment, and fix her a plate then Mr. Jenson, Joe and I saw Kopoe and fix them a plate, and for Kopoe to take her dad a plate, I call him dad also, then my friend Lorraine she came and fix her a plate, for her daughter Karen and her son Pierre also, then I saw Reba the food was leaving so fast, I had enough for Reba if I didn't, then I was going to take her to dinner, same as Miss Elizabeth. Now I can see that Stewart, God and Jesus was beating him, because he was trying to make a fool out of me, he could not hardly look into my eyes, he better beware of peoples and names in high places.

Now on the 29th at 2:10am, God and Jesus woke me up to think about, how Stewart talk about Glen, now when Stewart is with Glen he talk about me, Glen tell me, and when I was with Stewart, he talk about Glen, but I would not tell Glen about what Stewart said, because Stewart is a big liar, and he will say something that I never said, so I just say o yes Stewart is a trouble starter, bear mouth ass, only kiss Toni ass.

You know and I know that if you don't have anyone, else in my life it is ok sometime, you get lonely, On the 29th I always ask God and Jesus, that I am so tire of these no good women folks, and I ask God to send me a lady from you God and Jesus.

That all of my life I was looking for a good woman, lady and that I have been marry 7th times, now all the ladies or women I have put my hands on, and I talk to, they want to change me, if anything about me to make a women or lady, see in me that make her want to be with me, don't change that you saw, if she or he do that you will have a problem, arguments, often reasons to dispute, then there comes the Divorce, and the hate that if you never change a person, you could have had love because, they was the same as they was when you or me meet them.

And I need someone to talk to, and made love to and they make love back to me, now when you ask for anything from God, and you don't specify what you want, he will give you what you was asking for, now after I ask for a good woman or lady in my life, I didn't say to go to bed with, and make love to her also, I meet one of those lady that God and Jesus, answer my prayer, now this lady she is so sweet, nice, friendly, beautiful with smile like a rose opening in the morning, and how closer I am growing to her, this don't mean that she is my lady or my woman.

Because God and Jesus sent a good person to me, in my life time that she is ok with me, that doesn't mean she has to be my wife, lady or woman, just a friend a good friend, God he don't send you or give you something, that is no good. Everything God sends you is good, and this lady is the one I asked God and Jesus for. Her name is Elsie Morgan.

Now, like I had said before, I do not know anything about computer but write, in my book anything else I get a friend, if they know I ask them, on May the 1st I had ask Reba would she come, if she had time and fix the spelling for 20 pages, that the spell check mess up for me, that I had put them on paper so that, she would see what I was talking about, she said yes, then after a little while Reba came and fix my problem.

On the 2nd of May we all was sitting on the outside, I saw David Montoya taking out from his apartment, a big TV taking it to put on a truck, I said to Stewart, Montoya he must be moving he is putting a TV on a truck, Stewart said o yes he got to go, I ask Stewart now is the time to beat Montoya's ass like he said that he was going to do, when he move, with that stick you got for Montoya.

Stewart said that when he saw David Montoya, out from this complex, I gave a little smile and said to myself, Stewart is someone that is like a tea pot, putting steam off he think that I am a fool, like the others that live here, I know that Stewart is a big liar, and a coward. On the 3rd, Montoya got his others things and moved out, a little while after, I found out, that after I had resigned, Miss Elizabeth and I closed the account for the tenant council money.

She and I put the check in a draft, so the other president of the council, could put the check into account for the people, the other president name was David Montoya, and the vice president is Miss Blackwell, I found out that Miss Blackwell she had the check, now, she knew that Montoya he was going to move, Miss Blackwell she gave the check to Montoya, why did she do that, I found out that Montoya wife, thought that Blackwell and David Montoya, was going together and not only his wife, others said the same thing.

Now at the next monthly meeting for tenants, Blackwell said that Montoya was going to bring, the money back for that meeting, I saw Montoya truck that he drive came to the enter, to the gate Blackwell she came out to meet him, I saw that no one told me, then Montoya left and Blackwell she came back, I said ok he came to bring back that check.

In my heart I love Elsie, I have to be respectable to her she is a lady, I am not the man who are trying to, get into her pants, "let me explain," again that all my life I ask God and Jesus, to bring and put a good woman, lady into my life not to have sex with her, he didn't put Elsie here for that, she was put here to do her job, that the corporate office with Frank and Dora, put her to do after I sent that letter to them.

Now my job is to protect her from those snakes, all I have to do is love and respect her, and see that no one else disrespect her, as I had promised. And look out for her not to be looking for sex, is not all to love to be a sex slave, but love her for herself. It could be amazing that if, I could find another lady or woman like Elsie, but I don't think so, that I could have sex with and love her, as I love her back. Now get your mind back to what I had said.

That I am not trying to have sex with Elsie, because if, I had sex with Elsie, that would make me a looser, I would lose too much, more than money that is the respect, that we have.

Now I needed to find some more pictures of my family, I call my sister Deloise Hills in Chicago, we talk about what I was looking for in the pictures, she had them and sent the pictures to me, with some others things that I was glad, to get it, then I went and copied the pictures and sent Deloise her pictures back to her.

One evening I was in my apartment putting some things, in to the computer someone knock on my door, I open it, it was Joanne. She said, "Hi David" she was smiling, she had a mango in her hand, she said that Reba, gave it to her to give it to me, that she kisses it and rubbed it and it was sweet, I smiled and said ok I will see Reba later.

On that day the tenants was having a yard sale, I was going out the gate Blackwell said to me, David did I want to put something out there, I said no that I was too busy to sit out there, peoples in here not all don't have no money to pay, for my life because they don't like me, because I have something that they don't have, I love everybody the same as though they don't like me, but that is not my problem, that is their problem, they should work on it.

And if someone want a book of mind, they know where I live and they can call me, then I will go to them but good luck to them, I went and came back home and did, what I do each and every day, if that was what I wanted to do, that same day it was the horse race in Ky. I watch the race to see what horse was going to win.

Because in two more weeks there was going to be another race, be four the tripper crown horse race, then I will make a bet on the winner, of the Kentucky Derby.

That Sunday I went and took my buddy Popeye, to the store as I do all the time if that, when he need to go he would call me, now Elsie she really don't work on Sunday and Monday, but this Sunday of May the 7th Elsie she was at work, I went and spoke to her and I let her know, that if she needed me I would be at home, Elsie said thank David, then I left.

That Monday morning I got up thinking about, the books that I order from the publisher, to be there in Brewton, Alabama, when I get there, I am going after my daughter Jackie call me, and said that her sister Noonie said, after the aid in the paper, that I should come to Brewton, so I got in touch with my cousin Joyce, and she had AAA air and auto travel to get my ticket.

So after Thinking about the books I call my daddy, in Brewton to see if the books was there, I sent them to daddy address, daddy and I was talking after the book has not came, that I was coming for the 1st of June, and that I was going to stay with him, when I get there because Jackie, she live so far from town, and staying with him I would be in walking distinct, to do what I am going to do in Brewton.

After I finish talking to my dad, I went out on the outside I saw Kopoe, I said to her that I will be right back, that I was going to write a check for her affair, she said ok, I went and wrote the check for the church, and came back and I gave the check to Kopoe.

The rest of the day was and is like the same, of the others I work on my book for a while, and stop watching TV, I get tried, of watching TV, while I am thinking about what else, I was going to write about an how, then I go outside sometime Elsie, she was out there we have a cigarettes, and talk and when her break was over, I walk her back to her office open the door, to let Elsie into the lobby, then I leave and go and do whatever.

That next day my daughter Jackie call me, and said that the books was there, that they had just came in the mail, I told Jackie that she have to keep records, about whatever she was going to do, if it was from or for passing through book," for taxes," and that her records should be the same as mind, and that whatever she was going to do, she must let me know what she was doing, and how just in case of the Government.

Now, I try very hard to be a good person, it is a hard thing to do to try to be, firm, resisting pressure, solid. Some peoples they are, difficult to understand, harsh, unfeeling difficult to bear, now what all those peoples think that they, has gotten over on me! I can't blame them I have in my pass life, did the same thing. So I forgive those but, I can't forget what they did and how they did it that is my learning.

You know what burns me up, when someone says when Jesus comes back. He never left. You have to recognize him, when you see him, know him, and treat him with value and respect. Try to take me off the path that God and Jesus have put me on, to follow theirs that is not mine to follow. So take me as I am or leave me alone.

Karen and her mother Lorraine, we was talking about cooking some barbecue meat, I said to them let me know when they wanted to do it, Karen said what about when mother is off, she is off on Wednesday and Thursday, so we decide on that Wednesday, I said ok bring the meat to me, so that I can soak it in vinegar to make it tender.

Now the kind of man I am, if I was cooking and someone else want some, I can't turn down a person that was hunger, so I went to the store and got a bag of chicken wings, and on that day I put those on the grill, for others who ask me for some, the other meat on the grill it was not mind to give, Kopoe she brought herself some chicken wings, out there for me to put on the grill, I didn't mind I call them my friends, even though they are not mind.

Some others came out we start talking about death, and where and how they want to be burial, and what not to do after they are dead, I said for myself, I want the doctors to take whatever, that they can to help someone else keep living, and take the other that is not needed for someone else, and burn the rest, and to my daughters and sons take some clay, spread it out and spread my ashes, into the clay and work it into the clay, and make hands out from the clay and my ashes for them.

On May the 11th I was working on my book, and watching the news on TV they said that Floyd Pattson had pass, and that he was 71th years old an ex-boxer, I went back working on my book, until I get tried then I will take a walk, outside.

We all was sitting outside Elsie, Miss Queenie myself and some others, I saw this vehicle coming through the enter gate, one ask me who they was, I stated that I didn't know but, they look like the man that was cooking on the grill, the other day, Elsie smile and said David walk with her, we went to building #1 then I knew was going on, I said to Elsie, not that black guy live at the end apartment, someone else said he was funny and the other day, he ask me for a cigarette I said man, take two one for later, and that white guy is with him o no.

Now Lorraine she have a grandson his name is Peirre, the son of Karen when I first saw him, I saw in him myself when I was a child boy, now I am glad that, I am close to the grandmother as she and I am close, he is a good kid he play baseball with a team, and every time they have a game, I want to go and see him play ball, to let him know that he have a friend out there, watching him and cheering him on.

The day of mother day, every time it come I am sad, I am sad because my mother has pass, and when she pass I lost my best friend, and I Miss her every day of my life, but, on mother day I wish that she was here, but I see others that have a mother, caress her.

On the 16th Joyce birthday I am so busy, that I forgot my little cousin Michael and Joyce birthday, so I said that, I was going to make it up for them, about their birthday then I said that, I was going to give Joyce a check, to take them out to dinner, she said ok.

About an hour, Joyce call me back about the check, that she could not cash it in a restaurant, I said ok pick me up and I will go to the A,T,M, machine, and get the money, Joyce said ok that she would be over in a little while, I said that I would be outside, it was Elsie, little Joe and I sitting out talking after 7pm, Elsie she was waiting on someone to pick her up, and I was waiting on Joyce to come, then I saw

Joyce vehicle coming, I said to Elsie that my ride was here, that I will see them later, she said ok David see me in the morning.

Then I went with Joyce to the bank, and I got out $60.00 and I gave Joyce and Michael $20.00 each, for their birthday then Joyce said thank to me, then she drop me back off a home, and I went to my apartment because no one else, was sitting outside to talk to.

Then after I got back to my apartment, I started thinking about what little Joe had said, before that someone sent a bug into the mail, to Mr. Jenson address, I said what that is black magic, Jenson must have did something to someone, now they are sending him a message, and it don't look good later on he will feel, what they have did to that bug, to get it to him.

Now I take little Joe to the can yard to sell his cans, I don't charge him but my truck don't start, for nothing it cost me to move my truck, so I tell him to give me some gas money, he give me $5.00 for gas, now that I found out that Joe he hustler can, to put money on the books for a woman, that is in jail, no more, I don't move my truck for someone else I don't know, and in jail to what do that look like, to me I was a fool.

You know I am bless, I am so bless that I have my good health, and my truck is paid for, a roof over my head, food to eat and I don't have so much money, that I can throw it away but God and Jesus, they give me what I need and if I had some over, I try to share that with someone else, but, now that they don't appreciate it, I know God and Jesus will show me what to do.

Now after I got away from Sally, and I had ask God and Jesus to send me, someone into my life he did right in my eye site, and I didn't recognize it until, I heard the word Elsie the cow and Hittler, started to spreader around, I didn't like that she was so sweet.

Now I feel she don't need that, she needed to be more respectable, then calling Elsie names that she are not, now I call her sweet names, that is what I see into her. now all I have to do is show her that she is loved, and everyone should respect her for that, and don't let no one else do things to her, that I want do, and all I want to do is love her, the way she want to be love.

To me, I believe that Elsie was and is the one God and Jesus, sent to me into my future, now I know my destiny, and let no one stand in my way, women always said that a dog is a man, you have to train a dog, I was train by the best you can't train a man, when he is already train let him be what he are, that is a man.

In my pass I would love and Miss use a lady, but now, I had found out the treasure of love, the riches, stored wealth or valuables the love of a lady, I have meet some good ladies now again, like as you know some like Miss Marilyn Wicket, she is a sweet heart I take her to the grocery store, sometime when she have to go she will call me, and I take her.

Like this lady that I never lay my eyes on, that I talk to on the phone name is Bernadine Bronson, the voice I hear from her she is a sweet heart, peoples that I don't know but I do know them, by the way they talk and carry themselves.

Some has said that, what that white woman had did to me, and I had to go out from my race, and got a white woman that I got, what I deserve but I disagree, what is white they are talking about, a woman one of God creation a person, let me show you what I see about white is nothing but a back ground for to see black see black, let me explain, can you take white with white and get a color, no it will still be white, same as black you have to have a mixture into you, or whatever you are trying to do, to get color. That is why God made us this way. "Black and white."

But as a black man I had and I steel having a hard time, I have to work harder in order to get, to my destiny where I want to go or be, I had to fight, and know how and when to back down, I had to eat something I didn't want to eat, now that I found my father and my big brother, to show me the way, and now I am bless why? I found God and Jesus.

One day we all was sitting on the outside, some was having a break, it was Elsie, a Mexican guy that live here in #3, he and Elsie was sitting on one table talking, and the other table was full, I was standing talking to and from both tables, Elsie she said David, I walk over to her and said yes honey," now Elsie she can speak Mexican," now I don't know what they was talking about, Elsie she ask me don't lots of men love her.

That was when I told the truth about me. I said yes it is, me I will let her know, that I love her in many ways that I omit that I love her because it is true. Like an old man said before, seeing believes I show mind.

Now that I found love from someone, other than that white woman who was trying, to use me that Elsie she was not like that, that is why I love her. Now Mary she can rest now, that I found love without sex.

When I was with Sally, Mary she was not satisfy she came to me, in my head she was the head aches, that I was having she was letting me know, that I was in trouble and that I was killing myself, so fix the problems that I put myself in, the head aches stop after Sally left, now Mary she can rest she have not been back, like that.

Sunday, Elsie she came to work that day, she call me to see if I was busy, I said no what is up, the wind was blowing hard and the canopy curtain, they was blowing also, Elsie she ask me, would I come and help her take them off, so that the wind could blow through the canopy, other than blowing down the canopy, that was when I went and hope Elsie, a woman, lady that I will do almost, anything for her.

Now Lorraine grandson Peirre his team have a game, on the 22nd Lorraine and I was at her apartment talking, we was talking about ladies, and how they want to have a commitment with a man, and that commitment come with not to talk, or have anything to do with another woman, that this is hers.

Lorraine said, that I had been with, a lots of women in my life, that I had a harem. I said no I don't what are you talking about a harem! Lorraine said that I had so many women that want me, I said well, I can't help that, then I said that I was going to the game for Peirre, Lorraine said that she had to work, I said that I was be there with him and Karen, cheering him on.

Before the time the game was starting I saw little Joe, I said that, I was going to the game at Dolittle, and did he want to go, he said yes, so he and I went to the game, when we got there watching the game, a guy walk by Joe and I sitting on the tail gate of my truck, found out that Joe he knew him, they start talking about the old times they had.

When Peirre was at the bat he strike out, and he through a bat he was mad, I saw that, after the game was over his team lost, Joe and I left and I went home, later on that night God spoke to me, from my heart to give Peirre a little wisdom. I call him and ask Karen was he at home, she said yes he was, I ask could I speak to him.

Karen she gave Peirre the phone, I told him that God had me to call him, to give him something in the way of wisdom, to not get mad because he didn't hit the ball, but after look at what you did, and think about it and build on that, and find a better way to hit it next time, by getting mad don't make it better, but it will give you low esteem, and then you will never know why you Missed that ball ok, Peirre said ok thank for that, I said that every game they play that I will be there, he said that they had another game on Saturday, I said that I will be there.

Now I had receive my ticket to go to Alabama, and I had already ask Theron, to take me to the airport, and pick me up after I came back, now I was going on Delta air line, leaving 30th of May 06 on a Tuesday at 11:30pm, and arrive in Atlanta at 6:12am now in the pass, I didn't like the airport in Atlanta, I had to walk to far to get to my next plane, to Pensacola Fla.

One day Miss Queenie ask me to do some things for her, on the 26th if I was not busy, I said that what time she wanted to go, she said about 9:am then she told me, what she wanted me to do for her, I said that I would be there at 9:am that morning, Miss Queenie said ok that she would be ready, and that Greg he work so much, and he didn't have time to take me, I said don't you or Greg worry, I will be here for you when Greg don't have that time, and he know that because he and I talk, Queenie smile and said she know it.

On May the 25th I talk with my granddaughter Brittney, and she told me some things that I didn't know, my son John is like me in a way, and another way he is not, I took care of my kids even though, I was not with them all the time, I had many women in my pass life, that to this day I am sorry that, I played on another heart, but one thing I can say is this, my kids asked me for something, if I didn't have it right then you could bet, that a little later they had what they ask for, and if I had more I gave them more.

Brittney she told me that I had another grandson, I said what are you talking about another, grandson where, all that I know is about little Johnnie JR. and where is the other one. Brittney she told me about one of his nieces "John my son," I stop Brittney and said hold on back this up, what are you saying that John, he went with, one of his nieces.

Brittney said granddaddy I don't know that her mother know, she gave her mother the phone she and I talk, then she explain to me how that was, I said John know better than that, even though it was Milton niece or not, his mother was marry to Milton one time, it was still wrong for him to go, with his stepfather niece and have a baby with her, he was bold as I was.

That Sunday the 28th Joyce was having a birthday dinner, at her new house and for me to come, and bring someone else if I wanted to, I said ok that I would see her there, I had ask Lorain did she want to go with me, she said that she had to work and thanks for asking, then I saw little Joe and ask him, did he want to ride with me that, my cousin was having a party about 4:pm, Joe said that he would go with me.

Later on I was at home relaxing watching TV, the phone ring, it was Lorain she ask was the invitation still good, I said that Joe he was going after you said, that she had to work, she said that she had call off, I said you know I have a truck, three was to be kind of crowded in the cab, Lorain she said that Karen has her car, then she said go on and have a good time, maybe next time she can go with me, I said you can bet on that.

At 3:30pm I went and got in the truck and got Joe, than he and I went over to my cousin Joyce house, for the party.

After we got there I had to go on the grill, I know that if she needed me to help her, then Roseland she came I spoke to Roseland, she ask me did I bring some of that wine I make, I said that I forgot to bring it, Roseland said you better go back and get it, I said ok after the chicken on the grill is ready, to be taken off then I ask Joe did he want to ride, when I got ready to go and get that wine, that I forgot, Joe said yes he would ride, I said ok and went to check the grill.

After I taken the chicken off the grill, Joe and I went back to my house, to get the wine when we got through the gate, some of the tenants was sitting out, I wave to them and went to my place and got the wine, and went back to Joyce house and gave it to Roseland, she pour me some in a glass, and Joyce she had a singer playing a piano he was good, we all was having a good time mixing, talking no arguments even Joe, he saw someone he knew they had a good time talking, then I saw this find lady coming, with a bowl in her hand I spoke to her, as I knew her.

Now Michael my little cousin he was on the outside, I ask Michael, who was that lady, he said that he didn't know, I said hum she is a good looking lady, I went back inside the house and I sit down, and listen to the music this same lady, she had a plate in her hand and she sit in a chair, right where I was sitting she start talking to me, have you ever talk to someone, that you don't know and want to know them.

They are talking to you as they know you, now not to be a fool I will ask question, and the best person to talk to is my cousin, I went to the kitchen and went into Joyce ear, I said that she and I had to talk, a little while after Joyce said to me, what did she need to talk about, I said that lady that sitting there talking to me, are she marry.

Joyce said o yes she are, and that I know who she are she was the cleaning lady, I said man I didn't see that now I will hang my head, I went back outside and talk to Michael, I said man now I know who that lady are, Michael said who are she, I said that she was Joyce cleaning lady, Michael said now he see it now, I said when you put your face on and, in other clothing peoples don't look the same, she is looking dam good.

Now I meet Roseland old man he make moves, and another lady she start singing with the piano player, she had a very good voice, we was having a good time Roseland and I talk, about my book, then I said to Roseland that in the second book, I had to be very careful about what I put in there, then we all went on the outside the guys, and one of the ladies was out there smoking a cigarette, we all was talking it started getting late, I went back inside and ask Joyce, was Deniece coming she said that she was, Deniece is a friend of Joyce.

So I stayed for a little while longer, then I said to Joyce that I had to go, then I told Joe that we have to get back, then I said my good buys and Joe and I left, and went back to where we live at, then I went into my apartment.

Now, I had packed my things that I was taken to Brewton, Alabama. that Tuesday May the 30th I call my brother Clifford, and talk to him my sister in law Pearl, Clifford said that she was in New York, I said that tell her hi when she got home, that I was going to Brewton on the 1st of June, Cliff said o yes that he didn't know when they, was coming back to Brewton, right now he didn't know then he told me that, somebody went into the house they had in

Brewton, and stole the air conditional out from the house, I said o man peoples are curl, then Cliff said that he would talk to me, after I came back have fun, I said that I was going to work.

On the day before I left, Elsie and I was sitting in the area having a cigarette, she ask me when was I leaving, I told her that she know that I love her, she said that she know that, I said that anything that I could do for her, anything that I was the last person, she could rely on and the others turn their back, get in touch with me she would have a friend. She said ok David she would see me after I come back, and have a good trip.

About 8:30pm Theron took me to the airport, and said that he would see me after I came back, that he would be here to pick me up after I came back, and have a good time. I said ok thank that I will take work, and put some pleasure into it should be a fun time, then I went into the port and got check in, and went to where the plane was leaving from.

Now that I know where the plane was leaving from, I went back to where the slots machine was, to try my luck. I had on my T. shirt Passing Through, peoples in the airport was looking and reading, and saying that is right we are just passing through, I said thanks then we talk, and I told them about my book, and gave them one of my card to get the book, and my phone number if they wanted, to get a T. shirt or the book.

Now I lost $20.00 in the slots machine, I said that was enough my luck was bad, then I went back to where the plane was leaving from, then I waited and peoples was reading, and saying passing through, I said with a smile thanks then I pass them a card.

Then it was time to board the plane, after they call the area for the seating mind was 29D, I got there and put my bag in the baggage department, and took my seat and buckle up, waiting for the plane to take off. I was happy that I was going home, to see my daughter, grandson, daddy, Zeb and Carole my sister in law and my brother, then I started thinking about butch," Charles David Russell my brother, if he came home and I could see him, it would make my trip worth the while, all I want to know is he are alright, I would know that if I could see him. Where are you?

Then it was time for the plane to depart from the port, I got relax and start thinking about what, was I going to find when I got home, I was thinking about every time when I come home, after my mother pass, I got surprise that I, after I leave Brewton in my mind and heart, I don't want to go back but, I have a daughter, grandson, a dad and a brother that don't care about me, if it was not for them I would not be home, for a long time.

After the hours in the air we got to Atlanta airport, and got off and found out where I had to go, to get to Pensacola, Fla. I had to wait for that flight, after it came I got on and got to my seat14C, put my bag in the baggage department and sit down, and buckle up waiting on the plane to departure, from Atlanta to Pensacola, Fla.

After I got to Pensacola and gotten off the plane and, got to where I was had to be pick up, I waited and waited there was a parking lot tender, he and I started talking I tried to call my step dad, and I could not get through, I call my daughter Jackie she was not at home.

Then I said to the parking lot tender guy, that I don't like cell phone one is that, I don't know how to use them, now that I got here from Vegas, he said you are from Vegas, I said yes that I came here to go to Brewton, Alabama, about my book that I had written, he ask me what was the name of my book, I told him Passing Through. He said Passing Through that he heard about that book, that some want to make a move about it, I said that my cousin in Vegas, she want me to hold off on a move right now. He said that he read about it.

Then now I was still waiting on my brother Zeb, and Smitty a friend that I went to school with, it was about a hour now, and they are not still gotten here, I said to myself, "and I was thinking," where are my brother when I need him, maybe they are not coming.

The lot tender he ask me, did they know what time my plane was arriving, I said yes they know because my daughter, ask them would they pick me up she, call me and said that they would be here, I gave her the name of airline and time the plane arriving, he said that maybe they will be here soon, I said me to then he went to check on his lot.

Now I started looking at the cab stand, I said if I take a cab and they are still coming, then the lot tender came back and said that they still not came, I said no that I was thinking about taking a cab, but if they are coming they will Miss me in the cab, he said then why don't you give them a few more minute, then he showed me where they pick up at, so I walk over to there and I waited, I tried to use my cell phone it was being an ass.

Then I went over to the cab stand to see, how much it was going to cost in fair, to go to Brewton, Alabama, the cab driver he look it up, I could see that I was going to get fuck, so the driver look it up and told me, it would cost me one hundred and fifty dollars, I said thanks and no thanks, I walk back standing and waiting and praying, and asking myself where is my brother hum.

Then about another half hour, they came with that they was waiting, on me over on the other side, I said what other side there was where the plane land, that every time I come here Jackie she, pick me up here by the parking lot, Zeb he could not talk straight when he was asking, Smitty d-d-d didn't we wait hours on the other side, waiting, that they came here a half hour before the plane came, then we got to Smitty vehicle I put my bag inside, and we got inside and left the parking lot.

Now there is a gate going out to pay for the parking lot, I ask Smitty how much was the ticket, he gave it to me I paid it, then we was off going to Brewton. Now you can feel when someone is telling a lie, because they can't let it go that is a conscious. So I started talking about the things that I use to do, and did in that area when I was a kid. Then I was looking as we were riding, remembering the things and places that, I been and the things that I had did.

So just before we go to Brewton, I ask Zeb and Smitty did they want a beer, Smitty he said that he don't drink, Zeb he said that he didn't want one, so Smitty he stop so I could get me some beer, and I had to get some change, so I can pay Smitty for picking me up from the airport.

We stop at a store that sell almost everything even some beer, Zeb and Smitty they got some coffee, I ask was that all that they wanted, they said that was all they wanted, I gave the lady behind the counter a $100.00 bill, then I ask Smitty what kind of cigarettes did he smoke, he told me, I told the lady behind the counter to give him two packs, and when she was going to give me my change, I said to her not to give me a $50.00 bill, she look at me and said how did I know, I said that I know lots of things peoples don't know, that I know.

Then we left and started moving on to Brewton, Alabama. I gave Smitty $45.00 for picking me up, and I had a carton of cigarettes for Zeb, now we got to Brewton we got to Burntcorn creek, I smile and said to myself, there was when I lost my vanity, now it is a memory.

Now coming through town in Brewton, I was looking and thinking how Brewton was not the same as it used to be, when I was a child. Then I said to Smitty that I had to get myself some Hennessey, stop so I could get me some, Zeb and Smitty said that the liquor store has been move, they took me to where the liquor store was, I went and got my Hennessey, we went and pick up Zeb truck, that was park at the store they, get beer, cigarette and coffee from call mom and par, we go the truck and went to dad house.

We got to dad house and got out of the truck, he was in the living room he came out to greet me, we hug each other than dad said come one in, I said that I was going to stay with him, because Jackie she live so far for me, to do what I came here for, dad said that I was at home yes I could stay, I gave dad a $100.00 for him not because I was going to stay there.

Then when I got seller down, Zeb and I went to see my girlfriend Deborah Ann Smith, that was marry to Rag Smith that not to long pass on, this time I found Deborah Ann sober, why because after Rag pass she went to the hospital, doing not to good now she are not to be drinking, but I know Deborah she want stop drinking.

When I saw Deborah Ann, she asked David Lee, when, did you, get here. I said that it was about an hour, the first thing Deborah said was give her a drink, I said that I will if someone take me, to the beer store that I would get a case of beer, Sutt, he said that he would take me, so we went and got the beer and came back.

And some other that I don't know, or was younger then I, and I what saw into them that, they was cool with me like Robert Earl, I meet him at a party they took me to, then I saw Barbara Jean my ex-wife sister daughters, Christean, she just pass about three months, God keep you Christean, I talk to them for a little while, and I had forgotten my cigarettes, he was going back over to where we was, and he said that he would bring them back.

You see I just meet Robert Earl but I am a man like this, I don't meet know stranger if they respect me, I have to respect him. And the others that I meet and talk to, but I was having fun and working also, then I meet Smooth, and there was another woman I meet, the other time I was at home her name is Argue, I spoke to her now I don't know who, what or how peoples are I sit or stand, listen and don't ask question unless you know, the one you are asking the question to.

We was drinking smoking having fun, time fly when you are having fun, now my brother is an old man, he said about 10:pm that he was ready to leave, and if he leave I am leaving also, because I didn't have no way to get around, if I did where was it I could go so we went home, I said that I was going and sit on dad porch, Zeb said don't you want to stay here, I said no that daddy might be looking for me, that I would be at dad on the porch. later on I didn't see anyone driving some was walking, they stop and talk then begging, for a cigarette or a beer, I woke dad up and went to bed, I said if I was at home it would be plenty, of places to go.

The next day after daddy got up and gotten himself together, I get up and get myself together I fix breakfast, for dad and myself then we sit on the porch, and talk until Zeb come by, then we go to the spot where Deborah Ann live, after Deborah Ann get up and come out, when I was there, I could see every one that I know, and don't know, and know each and everything, that I wanted to know, and some that I didn't want to see or hear.

Everybody know Deborah Ann that party in Brewton, and they love her even myself I love her, she to me yes she like to drink, but show me one that don't like to drink, unless you have did it so much you Misuse it, and it hurt you if you drink, but by drinking is not the only thing that can hurt you, you can drink too much water it can hurt you, eating too much can hurt you, too much sex it can hurt you also, talking to much can hurt you.

Don't peoples say that is sin, "what is sin?" now to me sin is when you Misuse yourself and others, that is my opinion everyone have that, now every time I go home Deborah Ann she, let me know what was going on in Brewton, and when no one else wanted to have anything, with me and I was sitting on dad porch by myself, Deborah Ann she would find somebody driving, and come and get me so that I want be along, while I am away from home.

Now the yard was full of peoples drinking, and I was still buying beer for them and Hennessey for me, those peoples there can't afford or can't drink the best, until someone else buy it and they mooch on them, I know because Baba, Nick my brother Dennice brother, every time I see him he want to sing, he think that he can sing I saw him, they had to take both legs off, he is in a wheelchair and still drinking.

That day I put my bottler down and Zeb my brother, pick it up I said Zeb you don't drink Hennessey, he pour almost a half cup of my Hennessey in Nick cup, I was mad as hell, I told Zeb that these peoples don't drink what I drink, and I don't drink what they drink, other than beer all they drink is vodka, I stop drinking vodka years back.

Now my brother he has went back to a baby, he have to go home and get his nap at 12: noon, he said to me that it was his nap time, we left and got home I said that, I was going to walk down to dad house, he said drive his truck and put it in dad yard, now it was only a half block from Zeb house, I said that it was only a half block that I can walk, now, I didn't want to drive that truck, it is a piece of junk wires hang down, a homemade switch to start it, I said ok then he had to show me how to start it.

So I drove the truck and park it in dad yard and got out, and went in the house dad he was watching a baseball game, he love his ball game and always has, my step daddy now is 95 years older, and he get around good and peoples respect him, I had some beer in dad refrigerator, I got on and was drinking my beer, and talking to daddy I got sleeper.

Before I told dad that I was only going to sleep about two hours, that by then Zeb would be ready to go back out, later Zeb he came and woke me up, still in my sleep, I saw Zeb standing over me griming, I didn't like what I saw at that time, I said to Zeb to go on that I was steel kind of sleeper, and when he go and come back, that I would be ready, he said ok and he left and I went back to sleep, I was tired.

After I did get back up I sit and talk to my step dad, then Zeb he came back, and we went back to where we was at the spot, before we got to Deborah Ann, I ask Zeb where is Len McConnice, that I have not seen him while I was here, he said that Len was over in a lot over there early, in my mind I said what is over there, I said well maybe I will see him before I leave, we park in Deborah yard and got out, Deborah said you got enough sleep, I said yes then Argue she gave me a beer, from her cooler Deborah said ok, I said what is that for, Deborah said before I put my thing, into one of these women that I better talk to her.

Then Deborah she said that Argue want you bad, I said not me then Zeb he was talking to another guy, about pouring some concrete for someone, and I was watching Sutt, he is a short ass fat guy that, every time you see Argue he was there with her, or he was coming he work at ma and pa store, I was trying to place them to see what is that, he and she going together but she is trying to flurt, with me in front of him.

Now I found out one thing in life is this, don't jump or leap into anything, that you don't know anything about it, Now the guy that Zeb was talking to, about doing concrete, I saw him going over to Argue and kiss her, I slightly smile and said find out your pry before you leap. Then I ask Deborah what was he to her, Deborah said her old man, I said ok thank.

Then I ask Deborah what was his name, she told me Anthony and that he is nothing, she can do anything she want and he, know that she is nothing but a whore and he know that, Deborah told me something about them two, that all he was as I see it, he was a pussy and I am not talking a cat, even a cat will scratch if you doing it wrong, but a pussy, it will get fuck and make only two happy, the one who is pushing and the one getting push on, the third one is Anthony who watch, what was going to his woman.

That was when I said that, I was going to put into my next book, that I was going to say that Deborah Ann, she are the queen of Brewton, Alabama, some look at me and said what! Deborah Ann. I said yes, that everybody knows her and will do anything for her that is the way you treat a queen. Because I feel the same as you do.

Now Zeb and I went to the store, I was thinking about putting some things on the grill, I go the meat and I wanted to do it the next day, that was on that Friday of the 2nd of June, Zeb he stated why not do it on Monday, now on the 5th was my birthday, that was ok.

That Friday everybody saw me, asking when was we going to start cooking, I said talk to my brother Zeb, that I was just passing through, trying to show some love that was when, I saw nick, he still had that cup in his hand, that Zeb had pour my Hennessey in, I said dam Nick you still have that same Hennessey, that Zeb fuck up from me, Nick said man that Hennessey is bad, I said then why didn't you say no, and walk away to talk to Smooth and Robert Earl.

They was the only one who treated me with respect, they when I ask them anything, they would say yes sir or no sir, now I found out that Zeb was jealous of that, he ask Smooth or Robert one, that they don't say yes sir or no sir to him, I said man it is all over the world, that is jealous why do others, have to be jealous of another why? When God gave us the same things or thing, in the God I can't see why.

After later on Zeb he had to go home, Deborah and I was with him in the truck, now there is another man name Bay Ruth, he take care of the dead, I saw him he said David Lee, that he see that I am still with Zeb, then he said that Zeb was no good, now, they talk shit all the time, to me it was a joke, I smile and said o yes he is no good, Bay Ruth said, that's right he is no good, then Bay Ruth said ok Zeb and David Lee, see you all in the morning then he pull off.

Now after the way Zeb treat me I better listen to Bay Ruth, now Zeb he got his self a coffee, and we took Deborah Ann home, and she got into her house we left, and on the way to Zeb house I saw lights on in the C C camp, there was a ball game if Zeb was here in Vegas, with me I would had ask him would he like to go but, everyone is not like me.

Then Zeb and I went home, I knock on dad door he open it and said, o yes David you made it back, I said o yes he was watching the ball game, we started talking I went and got myself a beer, and I had some more Hennessey that I didn't, take out there I kept it in the house with dad, then I said to dad that, I was going to be on the porch, he said ok come in whenever I wanted to, I said ok that I need to think.

After I was on the porch for a little while, I saw this vehicle coming I look, then it park I said it got to be my daughter, the lady she got out it was my daughter, I was in smile she had just gotten off from work, we hug and went into the house, and sit and talk to daddy until, I said to Jackie my daughter, that don't she have to go to work in the morning, she said yes she do at 6:am, I said that after I look at my watch, that it was after 10:pm I said where is my grandson, she said that she have to call him, to see where he is at.

Jackie call my grandson and found out where he was, and that she was going to pick him up, then she said to daddy, granddaddy see you later, then I walk Jackie to her vehicle.

That was when I said, when did she want to take care of the business at the bank, she said that she was going to be off on Monday, and we was going to go on Monday morning, I said about 9: am, she said that was ok then I hug her, and she left to get my grandson, I went back and sit on the porch, drinking my Hennessey.

Later on I saw another vehicle coming and stop, someone said David Lee from the vehicle, it was Deborah Ann she got someone to pick me up, to hang with her, I went with her to the spot, where everyone be drinking, this time of night there was a few peoples, on the street other than the polices, we was sitting in the yard I counted 6 polices, in a group I said dam it is bad, in this little town as someone had said it was, I can see this in the city, I said it is just a hand full of peoples live here, what is this I wander.

What I was seeing is that Brewton as a problems, and the problems was not from the good peoples, that live here in Brewton it was from the drugs dealers, that the white man had put into the neighborhood, to bring down the black peoples and their neighborhood, because all the money that they can make by selling drugs, the black peoples don't have that kind of money, to bring drugs into their hood. Where do drugs come from to be there?

To me, when you are dealing drugs there is only two things, that can happen to you, one is the jail house, and the other is the grave yard, and the only thing the user can get is, use all your money that you can live on, and when you don't have any more money, you have to turn tricks, steel from others, in order to get the drugs, while the dealers ride around with gold vehicle wheels, big gold around their neck, that is drug money Misuse it, can get you in the grave yard, and when the police catch you, you can go to jail or get kill.

Now it is not the police, it is the ones who bring on the problems, on them self, the police is only doing their job, I love peoples no matter what their job are, do their own job, I was sitting in the yard with Deborah Ann, her daughter and other ladies, was standing by the side walk said that they want, be remove and that they are a tax payer, and was not doing anything wrong why me, that can't live their own life and working, why me get the one who giving the police the problems, not them they want to be left along.

They have to be off the streets after 9: pm, no matter how old you are, I saw the polices walking 6 deep, I spoke to them they spoke back friendly, I didn't see what the polices was doing, but carrying out their order doing their job, but how can the police do their job, while they have to dodge bullets, because the peoples was shooting at them, and the vehicles tires was to be off the side walk.

You know while I was a child in Brewton, we didn't have this problems but time change, and this change is not for me, you all should revamp your life, and make it better for yourself and your kid's, do the right thing where you live, and the others live.

Now it was getting late, I had to walk back to where dad live about a mile, I said to Deborah Ann that I was going to crash on her couch, until later on this morning, Deborah said that was ok, that I could sleep with her, in her bed and curler behind her, I said then Rag would get me for that, I would be ok on the couch, we went inside to go to sleep.

Deborah Ann had the air condition turn up so high, it was so cold I started to wake Deborah, to turn down the air but I took the pillow, from the couch and use them as a blanket, and pull them up over me, later on I woke up and saw the sun light, I got up and use the bathroom and left, after I close the door, then I went back to dad house.

That Sunday morning after I got to dad house, he had just gotten up, he said David you just gotten home, I said yes that, after Deborah Ann pick me up last night, I was out there with them at Deborah house, in the yard to see what I was going to write about.

It was so late I didn't want to wake you, so I stayed with Deborah until it was day light, then I said that after I clean up, that I was going to fix us some breakfast, so I went to the bathroom and clean up, and fix some breakfast dad and I eat, and sit and talk.

Later on I said that, I was going to go for a walk, now there is a church across from where dad live, it been there for as long as I remember, I told dad that I was going to go for a walk, so I start walking, I got across the church the parking lot, going to the next street I look back and saw Zeb truck, going to get me.

Then I turn around and went back, to where Zeb park he had gotten out from the truck, going to dad porch I call him, he look around and saw me, he said where was you going, I said just walking and looking, then we got into the truck and left, there is a guy that I know, he could hit a ball when he was younger, he was sitting on his porch, his name is Pie Moore.

We stop and talk to Pie Moore for a while, then I thought about the t. shirt, that I had on Deborah Ann said that she wanted, that I was going to leave that shirt Passing Through, on it for her before I leave Brewton, I said that she could have it, but she have to wash it, she said that was ok she will wash it, I had forgotten the shirt, so I said to Zeb that

I would be right back, that I had forgotten the shirt that Deborah Wanted.

Zeb said take the truck, I said that I wanted to walk I could see dad house, why drive I said that I needed to walk, so I did and came back with the t. shirt, we sit there for a little while and left, while we was going over to Deborah Ann, Zeb ran out of gas now it was hot, too hot to push a truck with all those tools on it.

But he had a little gas in a can, a very little so he tried to put it in the tank, he was wasting it I took it and put the gas in the tank, he prim the gas up by pushing on the gas pedal, the truck started in my heart I said, thank you God and Jesus.

Now we had to get to a gas station, my heart was in my hand in my mind, I said God and Jesus please, let us get to this station before the gas run out, sure enough we got to the station at ma and pa station, Zeb got some gas and I got some soda, for him and myself you can't buy beer on Sunday, but you can get it from the boot leggier.

After we got to Deborah house I gave her the t. shirt, and I said this is for the queen Deborah Ann, they start laughing and said ok Deborah Ann, she said that is right I am your queen, then she smile, then Deborah said David Lee, did you sleep good last night, Zeb said what do you mean did he sleep good, he stayed all night with you, Deborah Ann said so what you have to, so what is the big deal.

Later Anthony and Argue pull in to the yard, and got out with some beer in their cooler, and Argue she hand me a beer, I said do you thank that your old man want that, Argue said what do you mean, I said after the other day I got into his ass, that I heard that you are not to talk to me, she said forget him, then I took the beer.

We all was sitting around talking joking around, but in every once in a while Anthony, he be just looking at me, then Suet he came and park and walk over to me, and put his hand out to shake mind, then he brought up, something that I was going to forget. About how I had to talk about Anthony about talking about, his woman in the public, Argue.

It does something to me when a woman and a man, in the public and he low rate his woman, so that everybody to hear and know about her, take her home and do whatever.

Now I heard Argue said that Anthony he knew, when he first meet her, that she was a no good whore when he meet her, then Argue she start crying and grab a bottler, and through it had beer in it, then she was looking for something else to fuck him up, I guess he got afraid of her now, that she have going off on him.

Now he wants to talk to me, it was not my business but now, he opens the gate when he wanted to know, what I thought about it. I told Anthony that he was an ass hold, and that he was not a man, anytime you are in the public with your woman, or any woman and you put her business, into the streets, he said that he didn't put her business in the street, I said o yes you did when you told me, and everybody else out here heard you.

Now she was truthful to you, then he said that he already know about her, I said do you hear me, I said that this woman was truthful to you, she told you the truth when she first meet you, that she was a no good whore when you meet her, now, you had two choices, one to walk away and the other is to deal with it, now you chosen to go with her now, now deal and play with the cards that, life gave to you.

Then I said what you should do was go over and hold, kiss this woman and tell her that you are sorry, and treat her like a woman and a lady, because, if I take her to Vegas he want see her anymore, if he did she want talk to you, now get yourself together and keep this woman, or leave her along.

Then suet said David Lee you are right, now I know that but I don't want to talk about it, until I write about it when I get back to Vegas.

Now Zeb he had to get his nap in midday, he ask me to take him home and take the truck, and come back after he woke up, I said no you take it and come back, after you wake up, he didn't like it but don't tie me down.

Then Smooth he came, we was talking then a friend of his came by, I said to Smooth did he want to go to the store with me, then we can get some beer, that Zeb wanted me to get bread, muster, plates for the party etc.

Then Smooth ask his friend did he have anything to do, he said nothing but go by, and check on his house, then Smooth ask him to come on and, let get some beer and

David L. Marshall

some things Zeb wanted, to get for the birthday party for David, Zeb brother.

After that we left and went to the store, over cross burn corn creek, where I found out about making love, what a memory then I smile, we got to the store and got the things, that we came to get and took it to dad house, then we left and went to check on the house, of Smooth friend he said that it was ok, we just riding drinking some beer looking, I was looking at the woods that was there, when I was a kid.

Now there is fabric homes over in there, the grass is so green and pretty, the houses sit in almost the middle of the property, it was beautiful over there it took my breath away, we rode around for about an hour and a half, then we went back by Deborah Ann, when we got back there was not to many, peoples sitting out there, then I heard again about Anthony and I that Friday, words fly around, they ask me that after I had gotten on Anthony, later on that night that I had to get, into Anthony behind again.

That was when I said that Anthony, he didn't want to leave that along, I told him that he was a jack ass and a punk and that I didn't have to talk to him, he still did not like it but he better let it go, because I have.

Then suet he came and said, David Lee that he was going to another house, and drink some beer and did I want to go, I said ok then another guy he went with us.

When we got there the host I had saw her, and talk to her in the yard with Deborah Ann yard, and there was Walter he was there, the other day Walter he got two dollars, from

- 268 -

me until he went home, that he was going to give it back, I gave it to him he was drinking, then I saw Kate, they call her war-war, she is so beautiful with, that smooth black skin I can't forget that, then I saw Moot Hubert, I haven't saw Moot Hubert since school he and I was talking.

Now, I am not nobody fool, I keep my eyes on Walter because he lied to me, he haven't gave me my money back, but two is not anything for me but a liar, I can't stand and if you lie to me, something happen to you can't understand.

Now Walter, he was feeling good he order a half pint of gin, the host she gave it to him, then after Walter open the gin, he gave the host her money, I saw other money in his wallet, I said what is this by that time Walter, he sit the half pint down it turn over, and lost almost all of the gin in the bottler, everybody else started laughing I said, that if he had never lied to me, that would never happen, he owe me two he got from me the other day.

And now he are showing me money, and he show money and don't give me mind back, now the wind started blowing Walter, he had lost his wallet in the chair, and someone saw it and pick it up, and said Walter let him see his wallet, Walter he look for his wallet and he could not find it, the guy he gave Walter his wallet, then Walter started talking shit to the guy, he was trying to tell Walter, that the wallet was in the chair.

Chapter 6

WALTER, HE TOOK HIS WALLET and look inside, the wind took the ten dollars from his wallet, and Walter he did not know it, I saw the ten dollars but someone else saw it, at the same time I did, they pick it up and went and sit down talking, Walter he found out that ten dollars was going, he got mad swearing that, if whoever got his money better give it back, because he was not going to lose no money, and that with that hatred on his face.

That was when I said again, if Walter haven lied to me and trying to fuck me, he would still have his ten dollars, that's was why he lost it. Then Walter said that he was going to go and get his son, if he did not get his money. Someone said Walter is trying to get his son kill, we all still was talking about that.

Then a white guy came up, the yard was full he claim, that he was looking for his dog, he started to describe his dog, a pit-bull with two white paws on his front foot, there was another dog that was tied in the yard, look almost as the dog the white guy describe, but it was not the dog, he was given a hundred dollars, for anyone see his dog and bring him back to him.

Then after he already saw the black peoples, was having fun laughing and drinking talking, the white guy said can he have a beer, I sure enough start looking at him after he said that. Someone gave him one he open it, and start drinking it and kept on talking.

Then after he starts asking personal question, about thing you don't talk about, when the other is a strange. That was when I ask the white guy, you are trying to find out some things from us, now, who are you? He said why? I said we don't know you, and you don't know us, now, what are you looking for. Then he walks away from me, later he left.

Now it started getting late, now after reading back, you can see what I did after Zeb brought me home, do I have to explain. Sit on the porch looking, and go to bed.

Now it was time for Zeb. He got ready to leave and go home, Deborah Ann and I got into the truck with Zeb, he wanted some coffee, he stop at Mom and Pa station to get some coffee, after he got his coffee we drop Deborah Ann home, then we went home, I woke dad up to let him know, that I would be out on the porch, dad he got up and unlock the door for me, when I got ready to go in and go to bed.

While I was sitting on the porch, I saw a vehicle with the lights on, when it go to me I saw that it was my daughter Jackie, she park and got out, I said hi honey how are you! Jackie said that she was ok only that, she had just gotten off work, and she was tried and she has to go back to work, in the morning at six.

That was when I said, that she didn't have too much time to sleep, it was then about 10pm and that she had to drive, a long way to get to her house, then I ask Jackie where was my grandson, she said that she have to call him to see where was he at, then Jackie said where are granddaddy sleep, I said no he was watching the ball game.

Now dad he didn't have any cloths on, I open the door and told daddy that it was Jackie, did he have any cloths on, dad he got up and put on some cloths, Jackie and I was sitting talking, then dad he came back into the front room, we all was talking, then I ask Jackie about Brenda my daughter mother, that I didn't see her at the party.

Then Jackie said that her mother don't party on work days, and the party was on that Thursday night, then Jackie call my grandson Sharn that she was on her way to pick him up, then Jackie got ready to leave to pick up Sharn, she told her granddaddy that she would see him later on, dad said ok Jackie come back again, Jackie said ok then she and I was walking to her vehicle.

That was when I ask her what time in the morning was she and I was going to the bank and take care of the business. She said it open at 9: am that we would be there by that time, I said ok that I would see her then I hug Jackie, before she got into her vehicle there was a female walking, Jackie she said daddy watch her all she want is to turn a trick, and she is not clean, I said thanks but I don't mess with anything. Then Jackie left to pick up my grandson, and her son.

Later on I was still sitting on the porch, another guy came by and spoke he call me by my name, now I could not call his name because I didn't know it, but I spoke as I knew him he and I was sitting and talking, the next time he ask for was a beer or a drink, I gave him one now, dad he need some work on his house I was talking to the guy.

About doing some work to my dad house, he told me that he will do anything for Mr. Charles, "my dad", and that he would do it for me, I said ok that I would send the money to my brother Zeb, and get the things that he need to make where I grow up, in the house I use to live in.

Now when I was a child and was growing up, my home town to me was so big and it was together, now in around town what I see now it sadden me, run down building drugs all over on the streets, and Jealous in peoples that live there of another, look like God and Jesus came out of me, tears started to flow from my eyes of what I saw, and heard I woke daddy up, and told him how much I love him, the tears would not stop rolling from my eyes, dad all he would say was, I know son, I know that you love me, the tears would not stop until I went to sleep.

That morning dad and I got up and clean up, I fix breakfast after that dad and I sit on the porch talking, Zeb he came by and stop spoke, and said to dad and I that he had to go down town, to take care of some business, that he would see us later then Jackie came, Zeb park to say hi to Jackie, she and I was going to go and take care of our own business, from the bank that was one thing I came here to do.

June the fifth my birthday. I keep on every once in a while say that, the day was my birthday that was just like throwing it into the wend, no one care not even my daughter but that was ok, Jackie and I got to the bank and took care of the business, the lady that took care of it she was so nice, her name is April B. Crawford she is the branch specialist, of Colonial Bank of Brewton, Ala. I made her smile.

After Jackie and I left the bank my cell phone ring I answer it, there was Lorraine and her daughter Karen, they was calling me to say happy birthday, then Jackie took me back home to dad house, she had some things to do I sit on the porch and talk to dad, then a man and a child came and stop got out of their vehicle, and the man he said uncle Charles, the child a boy he was smiling dad said now who is that, then the man said uncle Charles this is Ambus, then now I know him it been a long time my cousin, we embrace he Ambus induce the boy as his grandson, we was sitting on the porch talking about old time, Ambus told me that now he was a preacher, and that he was also into music and it was on line, Legions of soul music.com Go, then I gave him one of my card for me book.

Then Ambus he had to leave and get back to Pensacola, Fl. And that for me to keep it up whatever I was doing, that I am looking good then Ambus and his grandson left.

After Ambus had left, I said to dad that this is good for me, to see my peoples that I have not seen for a long time, about that time my brother Zeb he came back, we was sitting on dad porch I told him that Ambus he just left, Zeb said o yes that he wish that he was here when he came, that he had to talk to him about some things, now Zeb he have a beer shack right down the street from dad house, between Zeb and Carole house, Zeb he said to me that we had to go to the store, and get the things for your party, I said ok we went to the store.

After we got to the store and we got the food, I was out of $80.00, but that was ok with me, as long as we have a good time this is my birthday, we left the store and came back to dad house, and put the meat into dad freeze, then Zeb and I went to his shack where the beer was at, and he was looking for another guy to clean up the place, for my birthday party.

Now it was not my cup of tea but, what can you say I was a long ways from home, but at home and not you know what I am saying. Deal with what you have and that is not anything. Then the guy that Zeb was looking for came, then we clean up the place it was a dump, but like what I said before what can I say, I am a long ways from where I live, deal with it.

Then after the cleanup guy finish, I took dad rack back to dad house and let him know, that I put the rack back into the shed, dad said ok then I went back to where Zeb was at, I saw Polly and spoke to her she was in a hurry, then Zeb and I went over to Deborah Ann house.

Now after we had gotten to Deborah Ann house, I could see something that I didn't want to see, but all you have to do is listen to your surroundings. And you can find out what you want to know, it started to get late everybody was asking me, what was we going to do, I said talk to my brother I live in Las Vegas, not in Brewton.

Now I can see that Zeb don't know where to have my party, I overheard Deborah Ann and Zeb talking. He and Deborah had talk about having the party in her yard, she had to do things with her yard, then Zeb he talk to suet about having the party in his yard, suet he must have said that we can have it in his yard, then Robert Earl heard me say that it was my birthday, I said yes that today I was 64 years older thank you God and Jesus, that I made it to this number that is a blessing.

Then Robert Earl said happy birthday man, that he doesn't have anything to give me, I said that was enough more than my daughter, grandkids, my brother or my other family did but that was ok.

Later on it started getting later, Zeb was getting ready to go to suet house to start cooking, we all was getting ready to leave Deborah house, Smooth he said to me David sir, you can ride with him, I said ok then I went to go over to Smooth vehicle, someone else said to me that Moot Hubert, he had fired up the grill to cook a birthday party for me, now I was in the dark and in the middle of this, I said that I don't know this was my first hearing this, that if I had knowing it on Sunday that I would know this, but now I have to go with my brother.

Then after Smooth and I went to dad house and pick up the meat, and took it over to suet house to be cook, I told Smooth to come on and lets go, and get some beer and come back, he said ok then we went to the store, and got some beer and I was looking on the shelf for some Hennessy, but there was any there.

Then Smooth said to me that the cook she like Malbo rum, I said ok then I will get that and it will be for the cook, the man over the house and myself, that I had spent too much money sense I been here with them, that now let me see what the rest are going to do.

Now Smooth and I got back to suet house, I took the Malbo rum into the house to give it to the cook. I saw the cook was Argue, Anthony old lady well that was ok I explain to her, about the rum then I pour myself some in a cup, then I went out on the outside and sit down, there was peoples everywhere standing sitting on their vehicle, I was sitting on a picnic table talking to Smooth, then I saw suet coming out his house I call him, he came then he and I walk over a little piece, from the table I explain to him about the rum in the kitchen, I through he was ok with that after all I paid for it, no one other help me.

Later on Anthony, Argue o man he came out from the kitchen, and came out to where I was sitting. At the picnic table and he ask me where was the rum, I said it was in the kitchen and that was it going to stay, that was when my brother Zeb, he came up to me and ask was it some rum in the kitchen, I said yes it was and that it belong to me, and that I will give it to anyone that I want and feel, like to giving it to because, I paid for it with my own money, and if I wanted to pour it out it was mind, that was when Sutt said to me, David Lee if you don't want to act right, that I could leave off his property, that should me something that I was been sit up, that was when my brother. Zebbede Bry, told me that he did not care, if he never seen or saw me anymore or again.

Now that was when I ask him, did he mean that what he said, Zeb he said yes that was what he said, I said once more did you meant what you had said. Zeb he said it once more yes, that is what he said, then I said done deal then I got my bottle, and pick up my beer and took a walk out from Sutt property, not before I let everybody that was there, that I was mad as hell then I through the beer bottler, into suet yard and said fuck this I don't need this, I started walking going back to dad house.

As I was walking I saw a vehicle coming behind me, I heard Robert Earl said David come on get in, that he was going to take me to my dad house, I got in Robert said man that he didn't like what happen, I said yes Robert but that was ok, that I only have two more days to be into this hell, then we got to dad house, and I got out of Robert vehicle and thank him for ride, he said man don't worry everything was going to be ok, I said that I know once again thanks, Robert said no problem then he pull off and left.

Now I was sitting on the porch, I said to myself that I didn't have too much time to stay here, in Brewton now my own brother he don't want me for his brother anymore, I took a drink of my rum and close the bottle back, I saw a vehicle head lights coming and park. When the peoples got out I saw, Smooth, Deano, Robert Earl and Zeb, they wanted me to come on and come back to the party, I said what party how can I party after what had happen to me, then Deano said man Zeb he didn't mean that, then Robert Earl said that is right David sir, Zeb he didn't mean that he didn't love you, I said you don't know anything. That I know that Zeb don't have any love for me he never has.

That was when I said, that I saw his hand close as he wanted to hit me, when he was mad at me when I was there before I left the party. Then we woke dad up he came to the porch to see, was everything ok out there, we said ok it was ok then I said that I would go back with you, because you didn't dump your brother but my brother dump me, so that I was going back because you want me, then I said that I don't know how much fun, I will have but I will go with you, then we left and went back to the party.

When we got back to the party, I told Argue to fix a plate before I went back home, so that I could take it to my dad. She said ok and that she had some fish ready, and that the stakes is not ready, that she was bringing me some of the fish that was ready. I said ok so she did bring the fish to me, I was sitting talking to Diana they was playing cards, "tunk" I didn't have no mood now to party it was not in me, I took out a picture of Elsie and I from my wallet, and stare at it and said to myself, Elsie I love you and if you don't have the same feeling. For me as I have for her, that I don't have anyone else to love, but God and Jesus.

Then I look into the kitchen I saw Zeb, and some of the others playing cards me, I shook my head and said what a time I had, every other ladies came up to me and tried to cheer me up, but I tried to have a good time but it was not in me, then Sutt he came up to me and said that he was sorry that happen, I said that was ok don't sweat it.

Then it was getting late, I ask Argue did she have the plate fix for my dad, she said yes that it was in Zeb truck, I ask her would she do me a favor, and get it from Zeb truck and give it to me, that I don't want to go into his truck, then

Zeb he came up to me and ask me, was I ready to go. I said to him no way that I was going to go anywhere, with him that I will walk back to dad house, he didn't like that he hollow woo, then he got into his truck and left, Deano, smooth said that they will take me back. Going to Deano vehicle Anthony came to me, to shake his hand that was not for me, I walk away from him and I told Deano, to keep this guy away from me, I don't have anything to say to this man, I will go to jail.

That was when Deano walk over to Anthony, and told him to leave that man along in a way, that he could understand don't fuck with him, if Anthony he didn't leave me along that he will have a problem with him, then Deano ask me would I shake Anthony hand for him, Smooth said then if Anthony mess with David again, that he will have the flood, or the ground to kick Anthony ass, I shook Anthony hand to leave me along then we left, they took me to dad house, I woke dad up and I explain to him what Zeb had did, dad said David, you telling me that Zeb did that, I said yes he did dad, dad he said what is wrong with Zeb, I said that I don't know but he got his wish.

Now on that Tuesday morning I got up, and fix something to eat, I saw that I didn't have any cigarettes, I said to dad where could I walk and get me some cigarettes, he said right up the street there was a store, I said that I was going to the store and get me some cigarettes, dad he said ok, then I left going to the store, now I start walking looking for the store, I walk all the way up to where Mr. Knock had a store, long time ago but it was like the others stores that have falling down, not anything was there to get me some cigarettes.

Now I look and didn't see anything so I keep on walking. Going to the shopping area up to where Deborah Ann live, I got there and got my cigarettes, and as I was still walking open my cigarettes, I stop at ma and pa store and I got myself a beer, and after I left the store I saw Bay Ruth he was sitting in his truck, I spoke to him, he said hi David where is Zeb, I said that I don't know, then Bay Ruth ask me did I want a ride, I said ok why not then I go into his truck, he ask where was I going.

That was when I said that I was going to see if Deborah Ann, was sitting on the outside, then Bay Ruth said didn't she go into the hospital last night, when she was at the party, I said what party. Bay Ruth said that he heard about that, and then he said didn't he tell me that my brother Zeb, was no good, I said now I know.

That was when we saw Zeb standing in someone else yard talking. Bay Ruth said there is Zeb now and did I want to stop, I said no go on that I will sit in Deborah yard, just in case Smooth or someone else come by there, so Bay Ruth stop and park and got out, and sit and talk to me, he said that he can't go to a hospital, I said why, he said when they see him in the hospital, peoples say that they are not ready yet.

That was when I kind of laugh and said why that was, he said that he was a mortician, and when the sick see him coming, they think that they are ready to die. I said that I don't blame them, because you drive a meat wagon and the sick don't want to see that, or the man who takes the remains away, then Bay Ruth said that he was going to go and get himself a sandwich, and did I want one. I said no that I had something to eat this morning, then we saw Zeb coming Bay Ruth and Zeb did there same thing, when they saw each other talk about each other.

We sit and talk for a while then Zeb ask me, did I want to ride by the house, now I don't hate my brother but he don't like me, but that is on him not me, because he and I had the same mother, and we can't change that now if he don't want to see me anymore, my daughter and my grandkids still live here in Brewton, and if and when I want to come and see them, that I am coming now if my brother don't want to see me, then let him leave town.

Now he and I went to his beer shack and he told me to get myself a beer, I did and I had my note book with me, I asked him the names of the peoples, that I saw and talk to while I was in Brewton, he told me after I wrote their name down, and what I want to write about them, then I said that I still have not seen Len McConnice, that I have to see him before I leave Brewton, Alabama.

Now Zeb and I was at his beer shack for a little while, that was when I saw one of my cousin name Elave McGown, she has a sister name Cat, now it have been a long time that I had seen Elave, I hug her and told her that I had talk to cat, and I wanted to know how was she doing. She said that she was doing good and that one of her daughter, live at a house right by Zeb shack, I said o yes then I ask her was Alice Fay still living, she said yes that she live in the house on Zion hill, where the Redmond use to live, I ask how was she doing, V she said David that I didn't want to know, I said that bad! She said they are shut in the house all day and come out in the night.

That was when she had some things to do, and that she would see me and how long was I, going to be here. I said that I was leaving on Wednesday that my plane leave at 6:45 pm, then she said that she was going to try, and see me before I leave, I said ok then Zeb he was ready to go, he and I saw Polly and talk to her for a little while, then we went to Deborah Ann house, and saw Deborah daughter and ask her how was her mother, she said that she was ok and that she was coming home to day.

Then I saw a guy he asked me that, did I see Len McConnice and if not, he showed me Len nephew. I told Len nephew that I wanted to see him before I leave Brewton, and ask him to stop and see over to Deborah Ann house, Len nephew said that he would tell Len that David Marshall, want to see him. I said thanks. Then I saw Kate "war-war," she was getting out from her truck, with that find ass she came into the yard, and there was no seat for her to sit down, I got up and gave her my seat. And I stood back looking at the peoples having a good time, now the most of the time I was looking at Kate "war-war," with her find ass," Zeb he was sitting right by where I was standing. Then Kate ask Zeb, was that talking about me, was this brother, Zeb he said with a frown in anger yes, Kate said want you induce her, Zeb he said hell no. She said that was ok, that she will induce herself that was what she did. She walked over to me and said that her name was Kate. I took her hand and start to kiss her hand, I said nice to meet her.

That was when I ask Kate, could I put her name into my next book that I was writing, she said yes with that pretty smile, that she would love that, then Kate went and sit back down, then Dennice my brother that pass on, his x old lady

Minnie Pearl she came, and she said David lee how long has I been here in Brewton, I said that I got here last Thursday morning, then Minnie Pearl ask me how long was I going to be here, that was when I said, that I was leaving on Wednesday, it was the next day.

Then I ask Pearl how was my nieces and my nephews doing, that I never see them when I come home, she explain to me that, the kids that she and Dennice had, that she already had them when they meet, but Dennice he raise them as his own, and that he had did a good Job. And that they was doing find, I said that it don't matter, they are still my nieces and nephews, Pearl said to me thanks, then she and I started talking about fishing, she said that she go all the time, Minnie Pearl and I talk until she had to go.

That was when Hardy Little came out and took a seat by me, then he and I sit and talk for a while, that was when I saw Len McConnice coming I smile, and said to Len that he still look the same, that I have been looking for him ever since I been here, Len told me where he and Hattie live. I said man while I am walking and don't have a ride, to get around others don't tell me anything.

Now Len and I sit and talk about the old pass times, then Len ask me how long did it took me to write my book, I told him about two years, after I lost some of my work and had to go back and back track, and rewrite it because I am not too good on computer, then I said to Len that I would love to have, one of our old football picture from the team of the Trojan.

That was when Len said to me, that he would go and get one for me, I said would he do that for me, then I tried to give him some money to pay for the copies, Len said that was ok and that he had talk to Wade Hooks, and gave him the way that he could get one on line, that Wade Hooks he wanted one of my book. I said thanks to Len then he left to go, and get the Trojan football team when we kick ass, with the other teams we played.

Now after Len left we all was still sitting on the outside, some was drinking and some was not, but just talking. Then Deanom, his mother she came and look at me, then she look at Zeb and said Zebedee, are this your brother, Zeb said yes, then she look back at me again and said what happen to you Zeb, that was when the war started I saw the anger flair up, Zeb said that was all right, that my brother want be here after he leave, and that he will still be here in Brewton, because my brother was just Passing Through.

That was when Deano mother said to me, that she was Deano mother and she extend her hand to me, I said that it was please for me to meet her. She said likewise with a smile, everyone else out there start to laughing. Zeb he was so mad that he was smoking. Now it was getting kind of late then my daughter Jackie, with my grandson came, to see what time I would be ready, for her to take me to the airport. I told her that we could leave about 4: pm tomorrow, then Robert Earl said to me, David man this is your daughter, I said yes it is and that Sharn is my grandson I hug him.

Then Len he came back with the picture, some of the others started to leave, Len and I started looking at the pictures in front of Jackie vehicle, it was kind of dark I said to Len that I can't recognize, anyone but me because from my number was 80, and that the others I can't recognize them, it been a long time, Jackie said that she don't know, then Zeb he look he could not recognize any, then he got ready to leave.

Len and I kept on looking and we did the best we could. I said well I will see when I get back to Vegas, what I was going to do about them when I get back, that I just might put them into the book like it is, then Len left Misty Deborah Ann daughter, and Smooth had got some beer and offer me one, I took it and said thanks, then Bay Ruth came back and said David Lee, he hand me a vhs-120 tape and said, that Len said to give it to me, I said ok thank it was from Booker T Washington reunion. From 1959 and 1969 reunion we had.

Then Jackie was ready to leave, I said to Smooth and Misty thanks for the beer, that I hope to see them in the morning before I leave, then Jackie went by where her mother stay, and rode by we saw Nunnie's son riding his bike, I said that when I come back that I was going to, have a party for them just the kids, he said ok then we left I told Jackie that, Betty Ann she had fix dinner for me, then Pee Wee he came," Pee Wee is Betty Ann brother," that I have not seen him after school, and that he is still my cousin Pee Wee, just gotten older.

Then we got to dad house I saw that Zeb truck was in his yard, I said to Jackie drop me off at Zeb, that I want to see Carole my sister in law, and talk to her for a little while before I go into the house, Jackie said ok she stop I got out, and said that I would see her and my grandson at 4: pm tomorrow.

Then Carole and Zeb both was sitting on the porch, I went and sit and talk to them and showed Carole, the pictures from our old football team, and the tape that Len had gave to me, and that now that my job was over here in Brewton, Alabama. That I have everything now that I need for my next book, now I will be leaving tomorrow, that Jackie was to pick me up at 4:pm to take me to Pensacola, that my flight was leaving at 6:45, now all I came here to do is done, now I have to go back home. Carole said did you have a good time, I said it was ok that all I was doing here was to see, what was going on in my home tome, now I know what I see and that I am sadden about it, but I can't do anything about it but write about what I saw, heard and seen. Then I saw that Carole she was going to sleep, and Zeb he went in side of the house, so I said that I might not see her before I leave, that I love her and that I hope to see her, when I came back. She said ok David Lee, have a good flight, I said ok then I left and went to dad house.

I got to dad. I woke him up to let him know, that I was here on the outside, dad he open the door for me, he ask me how was my day to day, I said that it was better than yesterday, that was when I told him what Zeb had did to me. Dad said to me, you tell me that Zeb did that to you, I said yes he did but that was ok, but he ask for that and that is what he want, and all I have to do is let him have his wish, but it would be hard for me to do, after all he and I had the same mother, and I nor him can change that, but I can let him have what he ask for, that was his wish but tomorrow, I will be out of here going back home.

Dad said how could Zeb, treat you like that you are his brother, I said dad it is like this, I still have some family here in Brewton, my daughter her kids, now I will be coming back to see them and you, now. if Zeb don't want to see me anymore, then when I get back to see my kids and you, then Zeb he have to leave town, because I want never stay away from my family that I love, because of Zeb don't want to see me anymore, I was born here but I want die here I hope.

After talking to dad he went back to bed, that was when I got my things, and put them back into my bag to be ready, to leave Brewton Alabama on tomorrow, then I went to bed.

That morning dad and I got up and got clean up, I fix breakfast then Zeb he came to pick me up; I don't hate or dislike my brother. But I am a person that respect's another desire. Now, that was my brother desire not to see me anymore, I respect that.

Zeb and I went to Deborah Ann house, I saw my cousin Pee Wee and the others, that sit under the tree then my cousin Betty Ann, she came out from her house, she don't live to far in the same block, I thank her for cooking dinner for me, and that I would see her whenever I came back, if the lord spares me and her to live that long, then Pee Wee he had went and got some wine, we was drinking the wine and talking then Pee Wee, he went some place, I said to someone where did Pee Wee go, they said man Pee Wee don't sit or stay long anywhere, he have to move around, I said just like me, I have to move around.

Now it was getting late Zeb he said David Lee, it was almost his time for his nap, I said ok then I told the rest that was still out there, that I hate to leave them but I have to leave now, and that I would see them when I came back, that I hope when I came back again, I hope to have a move crew with me. Someone ask me what did they want them to do, I said that I don't want actors all I wanted was, them to be them self then Zeb and I left; I went back and sit and talk to dad.

About 4:pm my daughter Jackie and her son Sharn came, it was time for me to leave and go to Pensacola for my flight, I got my bag and hug dad and said to him, that it was nice to see him and staying with him, that I would call him when I got back to Vegas, then I put my things in Jackie vehicle, and got in then I said to Jackie, come on and go I said that because my dad, he don't want me to leave him he never do, when I come home and it was time for me to leave, he will cry and it make me cry, a man don't cry unless he is hurting.

On the way going to the airport, Jackie and I was talking about her vehicle, and how it was doing while she was driving, I said to her why don't your uncle Zeb help her, and find someone to fix it, she said that peoples don't want to help you do anything, I said that if I was here that I could help her, keep it running.

Then my grandson and I, was talking about how, green and beautiful it was going to Pensacola, Fla. I said that if and when my book Passing Through, do well that I was thinking about moving down here, in Pensacola that I would be closer to my grandkids, and my daughter. Then I look over at Jackie gas hand, and said that she need some gas, but I didn't have enough money in my pocket now to get her any gas, but when she got back get some money, from the account and get her some gas, that she could write a check.

Then Jackie said daddy this was a saving account, I said that my mind was going that I had so much on my mind, that I forgot that it was a saving account, and that when I come back again that I could open a check account. Then my grandson saw a house that he like, I said if it was a grace of God and Jesus, and when Passing Through do well that I would buy myself one, and that he could come and stay with me, and enjoy it with me, he said ok.

Then we was almost at the airport, Jackie she said daddy what plane was I leaving on, I said it was on Delta, then we saw Delta Jackie she pull over to the sign say Delta, and park I got out and got my bags then Jackie and my grandson, they got out and I hug Jackie and I said, that I would call her after I got back to Vegas, then I hug my grandson and told him, that I don't want him running with those bad peoples, and gang members, he said ok. I said promise to me that he won't then he promised to me that he won't then I went into the airport to get check out.

When I got to the check in gate, I had to take off my shoes, I said that was why that I wore sandal, so that I would not have to take off my shoes, because others peoples they have to take off theirs shoes also, and that they might have fungus, and that I don't want theirs fungus.

After I got all check in and was going to the gate, where my plane was going to leave from, I had a pain in my back I grab my back, and said oooohh this arthritis is acting up, and why now because I have a long ways to sit, now and on the plane why now, then there was a young lady saw me, she ask me was I ok, I said yes other than this old arthritis is acting up, she said that she know about him, that she has it also, I said to her thanks for caring. She said that was ok.

Now I have plenty time to think about, what I saw and heard in Brewton, Alabama. What my dad told me about he had a daughter, that I didn't know other what, my brother" butch" Charles David Russell had told me, way back. This young lady came to take daddy down town, and I was induce her as Elane, she said to me that she had heard lots about me, then dad drop his head, and said David this is his daughter and that, he had just told her about that he was her father.

Then Elane said yes that it throw her a loop also, that she could not find the words to say, she was stun speech less that her whole world, was turn up side down, it was a hard pill to put down, she didn't know what to do, then dad he had to go down town they left, man dad he cheated on my mother, but what can I say, I did it to other ladies also they was a mother.

Then I was thinking about those young men's that live there, they are a fool shooting at the polices and running. And the next day they were laughing at it, as it was funny. Now don't they know that the polices, especially the white polices the got a kick out from it, boy I had that black boy running through those woods, those nigger can run but he can't hide, that he can get him whenever he want to get him, that he know who he is, he will get him later.

And those guys don't have no job, and riding around on their vehicle with gold wheels, how did they get them from drugs, and the white man know that, because the white man gave the drugs to them to sell for him, and he know exactly where he put his drugs, into the black neighborhood, to destroy his own and leave the white man along.

And those young ladies that are there, I feel sorry for them they love a no good man, that don't care anything about them, if the men's that is with them why don't they get a job and take care of his woman, a woman that let a no good man layup with her, and give her a house full of baby's, and she have to go to work and take care of the man, and the baby's to. She is a fool get her a good man, and treat him right.

Now that arthritis it was doing it thing, and I could not do anything about it right then, but let it hurt me until I get home, then I will take myself some Aleve to stop the pain, but now I have to bear the pain and think, now I am so glad that I got out of Brewton, Alabama when I did, otherwise I would have been stuck there, thank to my real daddy "Mack G. Crosby". Now today, what I see it bring tears from my eyes, and the tears is blood that comes from Jesus, tears and blood from sorry of the one that are still there.

As I think about how those peoples in my home town, they don't have any places to go, to see but trouble. I saw the light. I know my Destiny and with God and Jesus, I will get there as I am Passing Through this world, that don't belong to us it belong to my, father God and Jesus. Now they don't know about money, it was made from man to make you do evil, harmful things to others if you don't watch it, you have to know the good things to use money for, at one time I didn't know how to treat money, for the good of mankind I Misuse it for no good, but today, this day I know how precious with great value of money, to live and help other live that is less fortune. Love of money.

Now it was time for me to Board the plane for my flight, with Mr. Arthritis and all, I got my Boarding pass to board the plane, from gate 02 zone 7 I got on and found my seat 21D, put my bag in the compartment and sit down, the Arthritis pain was so great I wanted to cry, but I know that I had a long time to sit, after the plane take off, there was another lady and a child sitting by me, I wanted to strike up a conversation, but I said to myself no keep my mouth and words to myself.

So after the plane was ready to take off the older lady, I guess that she was the younger one her mother, she said hi to me, I spoke back hello, she ask me where was I going. I said that, I was going to Vegas, she ask me have I ever been to Vegas, I said yes that I live there, she said that one day she wanted to go to Vegas, I said that it was beautiful in Vegas, she said that she had heard it was beautiful, I said one day that she should visit Vegas, then I told her that I had just put out a book, she said o yes.

Then I gave her one of my card, she said ok Passing Through. Then she said that it was the truth, that's all we was doing was Passing Through. Then she shook my hand and said Mr. David L. Marshall. I said just David Marshall, then she told her daughter that this man he wrote a book, her daughter look at me and said hi, I said hello to her, the she said is this the way, on the card to get the book, I said yes it was, she said that she was going on line and get it, I said thank.

After we was in the air going to Atlanta, and I was twisting and turning my back was killing me, but all I could do was twist and turn until we got to Atlanta, after the plane landed we was getting ready to get off, this lady she said to me that, if she did get to Vegas could she call me, that she would know someone there, I said that I would love that. She asks was there a Miss Marshall there. I said no call me whenever she got to Vegas, she said that she would then we got off the plane, she said talk to me when ever, I said likewise then I went to find where my next flight, was leaving from.

Now in the pass I didn't like the airport in Atlanta, it was like a horse shoe to me, the area for the flight you need to get to, look like you could see it across to the other side, but if you did not take one of the ride, you had to walk a long ways to get to where you need to be, but now I didn't have to go too far, to get to where my flight was to leave from, to go to Vegas.

It was 8:28P when I got to Atlanta, my Elapsed Time was 1:13 my seat was—21D, I sit down and watch all those find lady, that was coming and going through the airport, and seeing those find lady and you can't get one, all you can do is look and shake your head, and wander and say I wish, but you can't have any and every thing that you want.

Then it came into my mind again about my brother Zeb. And how he treated me and what he said to me, I said to myself that, I can't worry about that, that was what he wanted and I have to respect that, and I have to live my own life and go on for myself, because I don't need that stress. Because stress will kill you and I are not ready, because God and Jesus are not through with me.

That was when a lady came and sit by me, she spoke to me and I said hi to her, she ask me where was I was going. I said that I was going to Vegas back home, she said that she was on her way to Vegas, to meet her boyfriend and that she have not been there, I said that Vegas was beautiful and there was plenty things, that she can do and see, and some that she might not want to see or do.

That was time to board the plane at 9:33P Nonstop, to Vegas Miles was—1747 Confirmed, and I would be in Vegas at 10:50P, after I get there to Vegas my buddy THERON, he took me to the airport for me to go to Pensacola, and he would be there at McCarran Airport, to pick me up at 1050P in Vegas, I got on the plane put my bag in the compartment, and took my seat my back was killing me still.

But I had to make the best of the secretion, there was two others lady sitting beside of me, my back was hurting me so bad I didn't want to talk, after the plane took off in the air I lay my head back, and I was hurting so bad that I could not sleep, hum I didn't want to sleep anyway, because I snore bad when I am tied, and it can be bad all I did was toss and turn, when we almost got to Vegas, the lady that was right by me she said that, she was so glad to be here so she could get off this plane, I said was it her first time in Vegas, she said no that, she have been in and out of planes in the last few weeks, until she are tied.

Then she told me what she was doing, that her daughter she play softball and that she have to be with her, and that in and out of planes and hotels, and that it was getting the best of her, I told her that, I had just put out a book call Passing

Through, and that I was coming from Brewton, Alabama. And that I felt the pain traveling can get the best out from you.

Then the plane was ready to land, after we got ready to get off the plane, after it had stop I got my bag and was standing, waiting to get off the lady she said good bye to me, and have a good life, and that she was going to get Passing Through book, that I wrote. I said thank to her, I had already given her my card, and then we got off the plane I went to the parking lot, to find THERON.

Now at the airport in Vegas I get lost every time, this time I did it again, I walk around to see where was THERON, I ask Question where to go peoples pick up, after getting off the plane, one lady said to go to the low lever, I went to the low lever that was wrong, I went back inside the airport and ask a porter, he sent me the wrong way I said man what is this, then I heard THERON voice, I look up it was THERON I said thank you Jesus, I got to him he and I went and got his vehicle, and was going home.

THERON he said David man how was your trip, I said THERON man, it was hell. He said what, what happen; I told him how the peoples and how my brother had did to me. THERON said dam man and how he was sorry, that how the peoples treated me, then he said your own brother treated you that away, I said yes man they almost, all of them was so jealous of me and why, I don't know. Then a tear came into my eye, I was getting emotion, I get that away when someone takes kindness for a weakness.

About that time THERON he asks me, did I had to stop and pick up anything before, we got home. I said no man unless you need anything, he said no that he can't think anything, then we got home I saw the complex sign, from LOUISE SHELL SENIOR APARTMENT, I said thank you God and Jesus, I am home thank you Jesus. Then THERON park his vehicle, I got my bag out and said to THERON thanks, that I was going inside of the apartment and call my daughter, to let her know that I got home ok, and then I was going to go to bed. THERON said ok David man, that he would see me tomorrow. I said ok if it was the will of God.

When I got into my apartment, I put down my bag and call my daughter Jackie, she was a sleep at that time of the night, she answer the phone, I just wanted to let her know that, I had got back home ok, she said ok. Then I told her to go back to sleep, that I would call her back later and that I love her, she said to me ok, then I hung up the phone and fix myself a sandwich. After I had eating my sandwich I went to bed, in my own bed and said once again, thank you my God and Jesus.

That morning I got up and put on some coffee, and I take push up every morning, so I took my push up and wash up my body, then I fix myself a coffee and drink it, now Karen she had save in my computer, you see I don't know too much about computer, but write in it. Karen she had saved about 80th pages for me that I had already put into my computer, before I went to Alabama. To go back to work in my book number 2, of Passing Through, I turn the computer on and went back to work.

That was on the Eight of June o six, after I had put the things that I wanted, to put in my book at that time, I turn it off and went out on the outside, to get my mail when the mail man run. And see a friendly face to say hi David Marshall, Welcome back. I sit at the sitting area where we all sit when we want to sit, vehicle going out the gate the driver would wave, and I will wave back. The only friendly face I saw was Elsie at that time, she had someone with her showing them something, and she saw me and smile and said to me, Welcome back. I smile at her and said thank, then I went into the lobby for my mail.

The next day I had told Jackie, while I was in Brewton that I was going to send, some T. shirts back to her to sell, so I got every kind from Passing Through—unforgotten love and Just a Messenger, and box them up and send them back to my daughter Jackie, and the rest of the day was just a regular day, doing what I wanted to do if any. Elsie at her break she would call me, and ask me was I busy, I would say no. she said that she was going to have a cigarette, I said ok where was she going.

Now it get hot here in Vegas, and the canopy that nigger Mexican guy Montoya, after he took it out from what I put up, in the sitting area to take the sun off peoples head, there was no shade out there, so we had to find some shade to stand, to smoke a cigarette. So Elsie she would tell me where to meet her, or she would say to meet her in the lobby, because sometime she would have someone in her office, when she was on her break, I would turn off my computer and go and meet her, for a cigarette and after the smoke was over, Elsie she would go back to her office, and I would say to her that I would see her later, then I would go back and do whatever I wanted to do, I am retried.

That Saturday night I went to bed and after I went to sleep, I had a dream that kind of worry me. Now I have not seen or talk to Barbara for a long time. She was in my dream that night June the tenth. Seam that she was trying to tell me something. And that the dream was so clear and so plain, I could touch her but she didn't say anything, but she was trying to say something and I could not hear what she was trying to say. Then I woke up, now Barbara she was my ex-wife my sons mother.

Now that dream was still on my mind, I was on the outside at the sitting area, there was another lady sitting out there, she and I was talking then I ask her, about the dream that I had, to see if her are another could tell me what it mean. She didn't know, now every morning when I get my mail, I get Miss Queen mail also, she and I was talking before I got her mail box key, I was standing by her porch waiting. The mailman, to finish putting the mail into the boxes.

Then I was telling her about my dream. And I ask her what was it, Miss Queen said David, there is something that you are doing, or there is something that you should know, and you don't know and Barbara was trying to let you know that. I said whatever it is still on my mind, then I went and got our mail, and came back and gave Miss Queen her mail, and we talk a little while longer I said, that I better go and get back into this computer, and put some more into my book. Miss Queen she said ok David talk to you later, I said ok then I left and went back home.

That was on the 12ᵗʰ of June Karen son Pee L, he play baseball little league, they had a game to play that evening, I promised him that, I would come and see him play ball that is what I did. After the game was over I went back to the complex, when I went through the gate there was some tenant, sitting on the outside. It was KOPOE, Miss Blackwell, Louise, Mr. And Miss Lee, I went and park my truck and came back.

Now I came back because, I didn't want to go into the house that early, so I sit and talk with them, then Karen with Pee L came back to the complex and stop, Pee L he got out and thank me for coming to his game, I said that was ok that I in joy it, and that I would be to all his games that he play, seam that he was proud of that, he said thank to me then they left

After they had left Miss Lee said to me, David what, you went to see the kids play ball? I said yes that give me something to do, other than staying into that computer going back, into my pass write about the bad and to good, thing that was in my life. Because I had a bad pass life and some was good now, it was not all bad.

But the bad I had to change that, and the good things I had to keep that, and build on that and ask God and Jesus. To forgive me for the bad things that I had done, I ask for their forgiveness.

Now on June the 11ᵗʰ it was my daughter, daughter's birthday her name is Melissa, so that Tuesday I got a birthday card, and put some money into it, and I took it to my daughter Larissa job, so that she could give it to her daughter from me, after I got there, Marcia and Melissa they was in the vehicle, Marcia he is my daughter son.

They was ready to go someplace, I said that this was the right time, in another minute that I would have Miss you all, I hug my daughter and gave Melissa her birthday card, and said happy birthday to my granddaughter. Now Marcia he was mad about something, I said to him what was wrong? Larissa she said that he was mad because, his sister she was going to go to L.A. and he can't go that he have to stay at home, I said that was ok man, that I would come and pick him up tomorrow, and he and I could kick it together ok. That kind of made him happy he said ok, then I ask Larissa to bring him to work with her tomorrow, and call me, and that I would pick him up.

Just before Larissa was going to leave, I ask her where was Maurice? Maurice he was the maintenance man. That took over after I left from working for the Salvation Army. She said that he was on the back watering the grass.

So I went and found him and kick it with him, for a little while. Maurice said to me that, if Milton had any sense, and not did what he did." Milton he started going with that white woman that I was going with Sally. And start given my daughter a problem, after she was so good to him." We all could have been kicking together, I said yes, but Milton he was just like others that want whatever I had. But he was not the man that I was, and am. Because I found out that Sally she, was nothing but trash.

Milton he was nothing but an ass. I stayed and talk to Maurice for a little while, then I said man, that I was retried and that I had a lots time on my hand, and that I don't want to stop you from his work. That I was going home, and put something into my computer, and that I would talk to him later, he said ok David see you later on. I said ok then I left.

I going to my truck, I saw some of the tenant that live there, that I know. I stop and talk to them for a little while, they wanted to know, when was I going to come and cook for them again, I said when my daughter call me, and want me to come to cook again, they said ok and stay as I am, I said ok then I went to my truck and left, and went back to where I live, and did some work into my computer.

After I got tried, I turn off my computer and went on the outside, and sit out on the sitting area, then my friend I guess Elsie, she came out and sit and talk and smoke a cigarette, then she went back to her office. I was still sitting out there thinking, about what I was going to put into my book later, then another lady and little Joe came out and sit, and we all was talking then I said, that I was going and get some work done, because that book can't write it by itself, then I said that, I would see them later then I left.

Now after I got back home, my phone ring. It was my friend Reba. I said hi baby how is my Reba, she said that she was find, and that she wanted me to make her, some of that good barbecue sauce that I make, I said ok when. She said tomorrow, and how much would it cost. I said only for the ingredient that I had to get. She said ok. I said that she could pick it up after she got here," Reba she use to live in building 2" she said ok then she said.

That, she had to come and see Joanne tomorrow," Joanne she lives almost across the hall from me" and that she can get it then. I said that it would ready for her that was when I ask Reba how was her sister? She said that, she had just talk to her sister, and that she was ok.

That was when I said, that the next time that she talks to her sister, say hello to her for me, she said that she would do that. Then I said that, I would see her on tomorrow. Reba said ok then she and I hung up.

That next morning I got up, and went to the store and got what, I need to fix the barbecue sauce, then I came back home and fix the sauce, for my friend Reba with her find self. Then I let it cool off and put it into a container, for Reba to pick the sauce up.

Later on I got a call from Lorraine, that Karen and she wanted to take me out to eat, because I had did so much for them, and one hand wash the other. So I said ok, Lorraine said that they was on the way to pick me up, that was from building 2 where she live, and I live at building 3 they came and pick me up, we went and pick up Lorraine check, where she work then we went and ate. After we got back home, Lorain and Karen, they went someplace they had to go, I went to my apartment.

After I got back home, I turn on my t. v and my computer, and put something into my book, then it was time for my Soaps to come on, I watch all my Children, one life to live and General Hospital, those are my favor Soaps that I watch. Then I watch Divorce court, sometime Oprah or Judge Joe

Brown. After that I need some air, so I go out and sit in the sitting area, to get some air and talk to someone.

While I am on the outside I smoke myself a cigarette, sometime while Elsie is on her break, she come out and sit and talk then others, they come out sometime for a little while. Then after they leave and go on by them self, I think about things that I should put into my book, I go back home and work on my book number 2, of Passing Through.

The next morning I get up, sometime I walk around the complex, to get myself some excise. The excise made me feel so good, that I was ready for anything. I mean any or everything that come my way. Until later that day Elsie, after she got to work I was putting something in my book.

Later on that day Elsie she calls me that, she was going on her break, and did I want to have a cigarette? I said ok where she will be at; she said that it was not to hot today that we could sit in the center I said ok that I would see her out there.

So I turn off my computer, and went to meet Elsie out in the center, where we sit talk and smoke cigarette, she was telling me about," now she and I talk to each other about, life in general," all of the medication. That she had to take, I told her about that light stroke that I had before, and that now I don't take that medication, that I don't need it that, now I take care of myself.

Now I remember, that someone else had said to me, about all of the medication that Elsie was taken, but I don't listen or put into the truth, about what man or a woman tell me. They can lie.

Now after Elsie had explain to me, about all of the medication that she had to take, and what it was for, I was sadden about her, it hurt my heart, tears form into my eyes, I love Elsie so much until I felt the pain, that she might had. Especially, when she said, that one day that her body mite shut down any day.

After she and I had finish out cigarette, and Elsie went back to her office, I saw Lorraine she was in her apartment, she ask me to come in. I did that Karen she was there also, I was looking so sad Lorraine said David, what wrong have a seat. I did and when, I started telling them what Elsie had told me, with the emotion in me tears form again into my eyes.

Lorraine told Karen to give me a tissue, Karen she did. Then I said why, why do my God take the good peoples, and let the no good peoples live with no problems. Then I said that God know the best, what we know not anything.

Lorraine said that Elsie had told her, the same thing to her before. And that God he know what he are doing. I said that I know but to me, it was not right, when she told me that it was on June the 16th 06. I found out in my heart, that I was in love with Elsie so much.

After I, left Lorraine apartment I went back home, Elsie she was in my mind, about what she had told me, I prayed to my lord father and Jesus, to put their arms around her, and keep her healthy, safe and loving as I see her, now after that I didn't have any mind to put, anymore into the book.

The next day Coco and her daughter, was having a birthday party for Raff, Coco grandson, and he is my little buddy, I promised that, I was coming and I also had promised, to be at Karen son Pee L baseball game, now I had to be there for both of them, Raff birthday was at 1:pm. And Pee L. game was at 5: pm.

So I, took one of my T. shirt Just a Messenger. To take it for Raff a birthday present, so at 12:30pm. I went over to Coco house for the party. And gave Raff the T. shirt he was so happy, I think then I gave Molly and Gianna, they are Raff sisters some money, to get them self-something.

After I spent sometimes with Raff, Molly and Gianna, and the rest of the family, I told them that, I didn't want to go but that I, had to go and make good on another promise, for another kid, he had a baseball game I promise to be there, and that I had a good time, and that I would see or talk to them later. Then I hug them all and Coco she, walk me out to my truck before I got to my truck, she and I was standing on the porch talking, then I said that I better go, then I hug Coco and said to say hello, to her friend Green, she said that she would then I left.

So I, stop to my apartment to get something and pick up, little Joe and I took him to the game with me, after all Pee L. team lost after the empire cheated. The empire had a cousin on the other team, but it was a good game, I in joy the game but I don't know about Joe, he saw some peoples that he had not seen, for a long time seem to me he in joy himself.

After the game was over, and Joe and I got back home, that was all he would talk about, that was when I saw that, he had a good time, he told everyone in the complex that David and himself, was at the game that Lorraine and Karen son play with.

Now, I only see or talk to Elsie, when she was at work that Sunday, she had come to work I didn't have anyway, to know that until she call me. She had something that she had to do, that had to be done, she are the manager of the complex, she had call me and ask me was I busy, I said no not that can't wait what up. She said for me to meet her for a cigarette! I said ok where she would be, she said in the center. I said that, I would meet her there.

So I turn off my computer, and went to meet her, Elsie and I was out in the center of the complex, at the sitting area smoking a cigarette and just talking. Then after we finish with our cigarette, she said to me, that she had to go back and finish with, what she was here to do, and that she would talk to me later. I said ok then she went back to her officer, I walk her back then I went back home.

Now, after I got back to my apartment, I didn't go back into my computer, I just sit back and lay back on the couch, doing anything but thinking, about what I was going to put into my book later. And about Elsie also about how much I love her.

A friend of mind call me, that he wanted one of my book and that, he was coming over to my apartment to get one, I said ok that I would be at home, he said ok then he and I hung up the phone.

After he got to my place, and gave me his money for the book, he wanted to take me out for lunch. I said thank, but I could not go now that, I had someone else coming for a book, he said ok then he said to me sign his book, I did to love from David l Marshall to my friend, Kelcie Banks forever.

Then my friend Kelcie, he said that he was going to eat, and after that he had to make another run, I said ok man, and that I would talk to him later. Now Kelcie Banks pictures are in the back, of book number one of Passing Through.

After the others peoples came for their book and left, the rest of that Sunday all I did was, lay around and watch television and rest, because early my granddaughter Brittani she had call me, to say happy father day to me. That Sunday was father day. Then later on my son John he calls me, to say happy father day. I was surprise, I told him that Brittani she had call me early, he said o yes. The rest of that day, I was at home along all along.

That Monday morning I got up, and got myself together, and went and put that money into my account, at the bank of America. The rest of that day it was a normal day for me, if I didn't want to put anything into my computer, for my book I didn't, all I did was sit in the house, got rested I went out on the sitting area, if there was anyone out there to talk to, I would if not that was ok to.

Now, when I had things to do for anyone else, I will put it on my calendar so I could not forget it, because I am the one who, will help others that cannot help themselves, so I help them and myself also, because I have a truck and it need gas to run it, and maintenance sometime need it to be done for it, I don't charge a lots money to help others, but I can't run my truck for nothing. So I help them to save money and have a little for myself.

On the 20th I had to take Miss Annett, she need me to take her to a laundry, to have her laundry done and clean, and that the next day I had to take her back, to the laundry and pick it up again, in order for her not to take a cat bus, and wait and wait on her to do what she had to do, I save her time she might have to go to others places also, of what she had to do, I was there for her and others if, they needed me.

That day I took Annett at 9: am to take care of what, she had to do and brought her back home, the rest of the day was all for me, to do what or ever I wanted to do, until later on that day I call my granddaughter Brittani, down in Batesville Mississippi and talk to her, I ask Brittani had she heard from her dad, she said that her dad was mad with her. I ask for what? She said that because, she had call me first for happy father day, before she call him.

He was second to be call. I said well, what was wrong with that! Brittani said granddaddy she doesn't care, he will get over it. I said that he will one day, then she started telling me how the way, her daddy treat her, he want send her no money, to do the things that she needed for School, and that she is 14 teen years now, and in high School and that her daddy, he always lie to her when he said that he was going, to send her something to help her.

Then I said that he was wrong. That now that she is a young lady, he should be more concern after all she was a girl, now she is a young lady, and that she need money for lady things, now if she was a boy child they are not expense, as a girl, young lady or a lady they need things, now I am not saying that a boy child, don't need things they do, but not like a girl child.

And that he should look out for her more then he should. Because I didn't turn my back on him and David Jr. nor did I turn my back on Jackie either. Because I was not with them all the time, that don't and didn't make me not take care of them, I did my best, I tried to do anything and everything for them, when they needed me, I did everything in my power if I could, to take care of them.

Because their mother, and I was not together, they was doing their job away from me, because we could not get along together, I will take my hat off to them, I think that they did a good job with them, it was not up to them because, after they grown up and went their own way, in their own mind of the way they wanted to go or do, now they are a grown-up mature adult person, with their own mind, whatever they do is on them.

That was when I talk to Brittani mother, she also told me about how John was, that John he never has did for Brittani then, and that he was not doing anything for her now. That was when I said to Brittani mother, remember when Brittani was born, that I told you that if you needed help with the baby, that all you had to do was call me, that I would help you the best I could, she said yes you did.

That was when I told her, that I know my son," peoples always said that, the apple don't fall to far from the tree," now I don't know what kind of tree they was talking about, that is a lie. Me myself I, have never been into the system, not like my son he is a two times looser. Read my book number two of passing through, you see I told Brittani that, I will try and do my best to help her sometime, of things that she needed because my son he suck, to me he have should been suckling other than pocking.

After talking to my granddaughter I said to her that, in a couple of days look into the mail that I was going to send her some kind of money anyway. She said ok thank you granddaddy, and then I told her to not run with no gang nor, use any drugs off the streets. She said that she would not do that, I said thank that if she did, that her mother would call me and tell me, then I had something to do, I said to Brittani that I love her and tell her mother that, I would talk her later. Brittani she said that she would tell her, then she said to me that, she love you granddaddy, I said you to honey then we hung up.

Later on that day, a friend of mind she came to see about me, she ask me how was my day doing. I said that it was doing ok so far! That I had just finished talking to my granddaughter, my friend she said what, your granddaughter, that I don't have any grandkids. I said that was not all, that I have great grandkids also.

She said what! You don't look as you have grandkids, and that I don't act like that in bed. I said because the snow on the mountain, that don't mean that I am cool, I said that she in joy and like it, because I don't play fair, she said that it make it so beautiful, then she push me back onto the bed and said, you bad boy then she kiss me, after that it was going on, until later on that morning.

That morning after my friend left, later at 10: am I had to go and pick up Miss Annett, and take her back to the laundry, to pick up her laundry and bring her back home. So I did that after I finish with Annett, Miss Mary Helen she call me, that her vehicle would not start, it is a new vehicle. So I went to see what was wrong. I open the hood and check the battery, it was low in water so, I put some more water into it, and there was another lady out there with Mary Helen.

Her vehicle was park beside of Mary Helen vehicle, she had some jumper cable, she hand it to me and said to use her vehicle, to jump the vehicle. I did that, but it would not jump. I said that it was her battery that it needed to be charge, so I took the cable off the other battery; I ask the other lady how was her battery! I ask her to turn off her vehicle, she did I open it and saw that, the water was low also.

So little Joe he is the brother of Mary Helen. He had some water on his porch I took the water and add some, to the other lady battery. Mary Helen she said, that she was going to call a tow truck, to take the vehicle back to where she got it, because it was time for her car checkup. Then she would let them put a new battery, in her vehicle. I said ok, she said thank to me. Then I left and went back home.

Later on that day I saw Mary Helen. She said that she got a new battery. That was wrong because her vehicle didn't start, I said every once in a while, that I would check her battery, otherwise was she ok. She said yes, I said long as she was ok. That I would see or talk to her later, then I left and saw Elsie, she said David want to smoke a cigarette? I look at my watch and said why not.

Elsie and I was sitting talking and smoking our cigarette, some of the other tenant came out, we all was laughing and talking until, Elsie said love to sit longer but, she had a job to do, then I said that I was retried and in a way I was not, so I had thing to do also. So I walk Elsie back to her office door, and said that I would be at home, if she needed me then I left.

After I got back home, with Elsie in my heart and mind like also. With the other things that I have to do, that I have to put in place before I can do it. The rest of that day it was a normal day, if I could help someone I would, and if not the other time was mind.

In the morning, at10am, I had to take Miss Queen to her doctor appointment, and take her to the bank to get her, rent money order to pay her rent. So I did that and came back home, the rest of that day was for me, if there was no one else needed me. Sometime it got lonely and restless but. As lone I had something to hold on," that was my fancy." That I have and but I can't have it, for myself.

But you see I am bless, that I am never along or lonely, not as long I have someone better then I, and you also. What I have is God and Jesus. I don't have to smile every time you see me, my life are like yours, sometime happy, pleasance, delight and with satisfaction. We all have a bad day sometime you and I, but we can get over it, as long we keep God and

Jesus in our heart. We all have some problems. But you can try and put a smile, on my face.

The next day I had a buyer for a T. shirt, I didn't have that size that she wanted, so I told her that I was going to order some more, and that I would have it in two days. She said ok and she wanted to know, could she pay for it now and pick it up later, I said yes, she gave me her money I said that I would call her. So I call Tony to order 30 more T. shirts deference sizes, he had a problem this time with my order, he was going through what every marry couple go through.

He Tony could not find my words that I had given to him, that go on the T. shirts of just Passing Through, and put D.L.M. on the back after the poetry. I had to take it to him twice, and he still didn't do it like it was to be, but I can live with that, the next day I went and pick the shirts up, just to say that I was not satisfy, the way the change of my way, that is my way that I pay for, I started not to take it that away, but I could live with that ok.

If it was not what I gave him to do for me, it was not the same thing. I call him on that. He said that he made a Mistake, and he wanted me to change the name on the check, to his name I thought Tony was his name, but I did that for him, later on I found out that he was not what he was. Next time I should not take things, like it is with their face value.

When I was the president of the tenant council, no one who wanted to work or help me, other than Miss Elizabeth Johnson and Miss Russell, they were the trustee of the council. They were the only ones tried to help me, with the council. All the rest of them that live there, hum, I don't have to call no names they know, who they are.

Now that they ran, not ran me no one run me anywhere, they made me so disappoint that I resign. To see what they was going to do, Elizabeth, Miss Russell and I went to the bank, and took our name off the account, and put the money left into a bank draft check, and gave it to the manager of the complex, to give the next head of the council, after they got one.

Now you made your decision about me, you live with that. Now you want me to come back, as your councilman I am so sorry about that, now that I am going on with my own thing. I can't go back if I did that, I will lose ground that I have made. I tried to make you all happy, while you are old but you didn't want that, so now I have to look out for myself. After all I am just Passing Through.

That Sunday I took my buddy Popeye to the store, as I do every Sunday morning. The little money he give me to take him, it help keep gas in my truck, so that when I had to do some work with, someone else as moving job or just pick something up for them, that they can't get into their car, I would go and pick it up on my truck.

After I go to the store and come back and, take his things into his apartment, sometime I will have another person that needed me to do something for them. Like Miss Marlene she is a lady friend of mind, when she have to go to store, she would call me the night before, after I finish with Popeye I go home and call Marlene, to let her know that I was ready for her.

After I wait on her in front of the lobby, and she come and get into my truck, we go on to the store, I wait on her while she shop I will play the slots, until she are finish Kim my friend, that work the cash register at Albertson food store on Crag, she always say that I am a good person. Sometime she give me a hug Kim she is a good lady, she have a man I never seen him, if she did not have one with me, she would.

Anything that I could help Kim, if she needed and I was able, and I could provide it to her, all Kim have to do is call me, yes Kim she have my phone number. While Marline and I are leaving the store, I said, good bye to Kim that I will see her later. Then I take Marlene back to the complex, where we live and take her things into her apartment then I leave and go back to my apartment.

After I get home, sometime I will do something and sometime I want. Only if there was a game on t. v I would watch it, or just lounge around. Sometime my phone will ring and on the other line, no one will say a word just hold the line, to me that is stupid when someone do that.

That Monday Pee L. they had a ball game I went Lorraine, she and Karen was there but Karen, she was at all her son game anyway. After the game was over Lorraine, she wanted to ride back with me I let her, she ask me did I want to go and play, the poker machine. I said that my money was funny but why not, so she and I went to Texas we didn't have any luck, so we came back home, I saw Lorraine into the building where she stay safety, then I went home o yes Pee L. team won the game.

Now they had another game to play, the day after the other game so I was there, they won that one also. I was proud as a friend could be, kids doing other things other than doing drugs, and gang banging. The other day I saw my other lady friend Elsie, she ask me how was the game last night. I told her how it was that they won. I was going back home, to put something in the computer.

Then Elsie asks me to hold on. That she was going on her break, and did me want to have a cigarette with her. Now Elsie she, know that I will drop anything for her. I said ok that I will be waiting in the lobby, it was hot that day as the others days, I said to myself that, I had fix it so that peoples could have, something over their head to shade the sun, but we did had two canopy that I, we put out there now, the other president after me, he did not care about the tenant, if he did the canopy would still be out there.

When it was time for Elsie break I ask her, where we were going to find some shade, sometime she and I would go to the back of building two, there was some shade sometime, she and I would sit and talk to the Jenson, and ask them about Lucky. Lucky he was sick he had cancer, and it was bad he and I use to sit out, and he would nod off, I would call out to him to see if he was ok. He would say that he was ok. But I saw something in him that, I could not help him with. Only God and Jesus could help him.

After Elsie and I finish our cigarette, I would walk her back to her office, and see that she was ok or going to be all right.

Then I would go back home and be lonely, or try to make a better life for myself.

The next day I was feeling kind of down, then the phone ring it was Elsie. With her voice that just picks me up, you see in my heart. I was falling in love with Elsie. I was standing to close to the edge of a cliff, if I made one more step, I would fall off into the gate of hell.

Elsie she was going on her break, and wanted to know that, if I was not busy did I want to smoke a cigarette. I go out and sit and talk to her, I love talking to her she make lots of sense, Elsie and I, can talk without any augment. I can talk about anything to her that I don't want anyone else to know. It will never go any farther.

Each and every time I, am with Elsie the feeling that I have for her, just keep growing and growing more, and the more I said to myself. David Marshall you have to back up stop this, thinking about something that is not going to happen. Hum this feeling is real from my heart. Can't I have myself a fancy the power of my imagination, why not?

Now there was another lady friend of mind. Name Kopoe Brown. She was out of town and that she was to be out, for a month. On June the 29th Kopoe she calls me to let me know, that she had got down in Alabama safe. And let the other know that she was ok, that live in the complex. I said that I would do that, then Kopoe she said that, she was telling me about how good, and how she was in joy the watermelon down in Alabama. Then she hung up the phone.

Now when Kopoe was here at home in Vegas, she love herself some watermelon, that was all I could hear from her, after I had heard from Kopoe, I saw someone else to let them know, that I had heard from Kopoe. That was old news. Because Kopoe she had call and told each and every one, that live in the complex the same thing.

Some said that it was a joke, but I didn't get it I didn't know that. So I went and got the keys for Miss Queen mail, I get the mail and do anything for Miss Queen, that was a promise from me, to Miss Queen and her son Creig, that I would do the same, as I did to Elsie and her son that is my promise, to look out for them and that is what I do.

Now it was after 10am. Miss Elsie she came to work, I was coming through the door into the lobby, and I saw Elsie, Miss Norman and others was in the lobby also. Elsie she saw me and extend her arm to me, I didn't know nor I didn't see what Elsie, was doing so I kiss her hand. Norman she saw that and said, don't be kissing or let David kiss Elsie hand. That David was her man.

Now they all was just funning so I just smile, and said that I love you all and I got Queen Mail and left. Later on I saw Elsie she explains to me, why she had put her hand out for me to see. I thought that she wanted her prop. You see before I had brought Elsie a bracelet. I saw it and said that it would look good on her, so I got it for her. She was letting me know that I saw it.

Then Norman she said that, she was going to take my picture off her refrigerator, I said that it was like, taken your heart out from her body, but don't do that. Because the other half of her heart belong to me, and that she needed both half, I am her other half of her heart.

On July the first that was on a Saturday. I use on Saturday to wash my cloths, that day I don't do anything but, lay around and think about, what I was going to do the next week. Now if no one needs me to help them, I take that time on Saturday and Sunday, to hand write what I was going to write, into my book and into the computer.

This Saturday I took my cloths and went to the wash area, and put them into the washing machine, to start washing. When they was almost finish washing. I saw little Joe he needed me to take him, to the fiesta hotel casino to cash his check, I told him that I could take him, after my cloths finish washing. And put them into the dryer. Joe he said that was ok he could on me.

After the washing machine had stop washing. And I put them into the dryer, I went and got my truck and got Joe, and took him to the fiesta to cash his check. After we got there and got inside of the casino, Joe he was looking around as he was kind of lost, then he start walking to where they cash checks, then he stop to use the wash room.

Now I don't carry too much money into my pocket. I had only $7.00 in my pocket, now I don't get broke for no one, so I took $2.00 and put into the machine for poker. Just to play until Joe cash his check, and came back. I was only playing 50 cent at a time. Now I would only catch 3 of a kind every time, this time I started to play the max $1.25, but I didn't do that, the next time I deal the machine gave me 3 aces. I felt then that I was going to hit the 4th ace.

But now it was too late to change that, I throw away the other cards that I didn't want to keep, and deal again the machine gave me the forth ace. I said now why didn't I follow my first mind, and play the max but I did win $200.00 because the kicker, was a duce. Now I could not complain just thank God and Jesus for the $200.00, after all I only played 50 cent.

Then I took that out and cash my ticket, about that time Joe he came back we left, and when we got back to the complex, my cloths was still drying I saw my friend Elsie. She was in her office she stop me, to come into her office I was telling her, that I had just won $200.00 and did she need any money, she said no. I said ok that if she don't need any money, that I was going to put it into the bank.

Now I all ways know that Elsie, she was independent self-reliant woman. That is why I just love her to death, I tell her that all the time. If there was another woman I told her that, she would have wanted it all. But Elsie all I can say is, in her mind that I love her, and if anything that she needed from me, she could get it and she knows that.

Now my cloths was finish drying I went and got them, and I said to Elsie that if she needed me, that I was going to the bank and the post officer, to send off some t. shirts for my buddy Anthony DeVries. Anthony I call him my white brother, and when I come back that I would be at home.

Now later on that day, Pee L. team had a game to play I went to see the game, after all they lost. I left the park and went back home, and did nothing but watch t. v and relax the rest of that Saturday. Sunday and Monday, before the

4th of July. Everyone in the complex knows that I love to cook. Only if they in joy them self-eating when I cook, just have some fun they wanted to know, what was I going to do on the 4th of July. I said that I was not doing anything. They wanted to know what Louise Shell was, and the manger was going to do anything. Or the tenant council was doing anything. I stated that I don't know that they have to ask them to find out.

Now if peoples can't use you. They don't have anything else to talk to you about. They only are think about them self-need. Now on the 4th I fix myself some food, and sit around all day doing anything but rest, watch t. v and eating.

The next day I saw Elsie, she ask me how was my 4th. I said that it was just another day, she ask did anyone else did anything. I said no not as I know, now she was busy I went home and fix myself some food, and put something into my book. Later on that evening I was walking around. As I do every evening or night if I can't sleep, any way I saw Elsie. She ask me to walk with her, it was kind of dark.

While she was putting some papers, in the others building on the doors for the tenant, so I went and did that with her, until her finish. Then I went back to her officer with her, it was at that time 6:p.m. she only had one hour left before she get off, at one time I would sit and talk to her until, she get off and see her to her vehicle safe. But those old jealous hot pants lady, they don't want to see a younger woman then they is, see her with me.

After Elsie was in her office I went home, I knew that no one was going to mess with her, and let me know they are not crazy. After I got home Pee L. he came to see me, just to hang out and spent some time with me, while I was working on my computer in my book. I love kids in the pass and now only, if they were not bad kids.

Now they could be bad, if they have enough sense to listen to someone. I can't deal with a hard head kid that, think that they know everything. But they don't know anything because I was a kid once, I was a bad ass also but I knew that, if I disrespect my elder. I knew what was going to happen.

After Pee L. was ready to leave my apartment, I let him out and lock my door, and went back to working on my book, on the 7th my daughter Larissa she, call me to see if I was going to be at home? I said yes that I would be home. She said that she was coming over, that she had something to talk to me about, I said ok. Then I kept on working.

Later on Larissa she came by, she and I was sitting and talking. She wanted to see if I would help her, fix a dinner on the 14th for the tenant that live there, where she work. I said that she knows that I would help her, and then I ask her what time on that day, that she wanted me there, she told me whatever time that I, wanted to come by. I said that I would be there about 7am to get started.

She said ok, that day she was having ribs and chicken for the grill, I said ok then what she had to do the night before, was to soak the meat in red vinegar, and when I get there that I would take it from there.

David L. Marshall

Then Larissa she was getting ready to leave, I said that I was going out also, so she and I went on the outside, she and I went to the lobby. After we got inside I induce Larissa to Elsie. Elsie was on her computer, she said hold on for a minute after Elsie, had finish of what she was doing. Elsie said that it was good to meet you, they started hug each other and start talking.

Now I was not going to sit and listen, while two female are talking. So I went into the lobby and start watching tv. after they had finish talking I heard Larissa, said to Elsie girl we will talk. Then I walk Larissa to her vehicle, and said that I would see her later, then she go into her vehicle and left.

Then I went back home. And later just before Elsie got off, I went back and sit with her until she got off, then I go back home. And do whatever that I want to do.

Later on the 8th the peoples that live here, was having a yard sale. It was hot that day. And while there were no more tents out there anymore, they had to move the product that they were selling. They had to put them into the lobby, out from the sun. I was sitting outside in the sitting area smoking a cigarette, Miss Blackwell daughter Linda, she walk up and sit down where I was, and started talking to me that she had made something that, she was going to put in the sale.

That she was out all night having herself some fun, and that her mom she wanted her to, sit and sell her things but she was tried, and she don't want to sell her own things. I said that she works all the time and that she need time for herself sometime. She said that is the truth then she went to the lobby.

Now Linda she is a find woman, I was looking at her while she was walking to the lobby. All I can do is watch it. Because my counter name he had already, told me that Linda was a mean woman, and that she play softball and she keep that bat, and that she will use it, you see while I will stay from that.

On the 10th Miss Queen she has a doctor appointment at 10: am. So I will get up that morning and get ready, and pick her up and take her to the doctor. So that was what I did. I took Miss Queen to the doctor officer for her appointment. After the doctor saw her and they was finish, I took Queen to get some Popeye chicken, after she had her chicken we came back home.

Later I went to the lobby just to get away, from the computer. Elsie she have not call me to have a cigarette, but I went to have one anyway, I saw Elsie, Mary and Challa coming back from smoking a cigarette, Mary she saw me and look at Elsie, and start laughing. I said ok you all don't need me anymore hum; that you have thrown me away like an old shoe, but that is ok. Mary she said David, David we just finish out cigarette, you can go out and have your by yourself.

Now after the way these women want to act, I can back away and let them see that, I don't want to go to bed with them. They don't have what I am looking for, that is a mind. All they have to give to me is a piece of ass, I can get that anywhere on the outside, if I did that in here of the complex I would be in trouble. Do I want that no I don't, I want a mind to help our self to go farther, into life if she was my lady.

I can get a piece of ass, anywhere as female have always said that a man was a dog. But I use to be one of them now no way. But now to this day I want a mind. If I can't get that I don't lay around with anything. Female now these days are only looking for, what some man can do for them, and that is around money. If he had money they will think that, he had a woman in love with him, but don't get broke, when the money is going the love fade away.

Now but Elsie what I see in her, she is an independent lady. Not looking for a man for his money, she is finding and she is smart, she is smarter than I am in a way, I have the base of book smart. But I have street wise with mother wit; I am no fool I act like that for you, to show your hand.

Now I have that book out there into the public, passing through about my pass life. And I need some help to marked it. If Elsie was a friend of mind she could help me, with the marking and she also will be helping herself. Now the others that I know, what can they help me with, other than give me a piece of ass, I can't put that into the bank. But they will try to get into my pocket.

Now when I see what I want and need, some others are trying to block that from me, a friend ship with a Female that is the devil. Now when others are trying to be friends, that is a block I see that but, I want say that for Elsie she has her own mind, so I will let that be what I see about that, and move on I have heard some said that, if they can't have David Marshall, Elsie she can't either.

Some white hair old woman, she said to me one day that, she see that Elsie and I was growing to close, that they was going to block that, I said to her that she or anyone else, could not stop anything that I am grown, and that there was not anyone else in my life, that I can't talk for Elsie. But this is from me. She and no one else can stop anything from me.

Now if Elsie let some other stop, what she want that is on her. There is others find smart lady out there, if there are one for me I will find her, all I have to do is wait and treat the other, as I want to be treated and move on. Now I love this lady Elsie so that, I was going to Misst calling her sweetheart.

And doing thing for her, like when I see or saw something that, I thought that she would like, I would get it and surprise her with it, like a man that love a wife that was not his own. But now my fancy is cracking like a find line, in a mirror I have to walk away slow.

How can peoples get into others peoples business, and let theirs go liken I don't get that. And peoples laugh into others face, and talk about them when back are turn, what kind of peoples they are?

They don't know anything about them. Some tell me David you don't want Elsie, she is too intelligent for me, then they say now don't say that you are not intelligent, but not like Elsie she have high stander," high maintenance" I said how do you know.

David L. Marshall

That is when I tell them that, Elsie yes she are smart and I am also. Smarted then you are why! Because you showed me, that you are not so smart, if you was then you would not have talk, like you did. And that I am smarter then you because, you would go to bed with me, but I want go to bed with you. That I why my street since are better than your, you don't have what it take.

I saw the change in Elsie. And the friend ship I thought it was, it hurt but what the hell you have to be hurt first, in order to be heal. I have been hurt before and it want be the last. That is life.

Then next day I saw my home girl Evelyn Pullman, she had some old school pictures, showing them to me and she and I was trying to see, who was who now that it was a long time. She was showing me the ones who she recognize, I said that it was a long time, and that we all are older now and has change, that I can't recognize them now. Evelyn she said that she has forgot also, later she took the pictures back to her apartment, I sit there for a little while longer, and then I went home with Elsie on my mind.

Now on every second Wednesday of the month, my social security check get into the bank, and every time I get a bill in the mail, I write a check for it and send it out, I hate bills but they have to be paid. Now in these days I don't Missuse my money anymore, I will pay my bills when I get them in the mail, and make sure that I get my rent money order, into Elsie hand make sure that it is paid early.

And if I had any money left, and wanted to use it I could, everything else was paid. On the 13th I saw on the news that, some fool was shooting at polices and they can't win.

It was not too far from where I live, I said it don't matter where you are. There is going to be a fool out there the streets now, these days are not safe. It is the same as it was when I was in Alabama, in June.

Now I came back home in Vegas, I see on the news the same as it was in Alabama, when do the hate stop? Where do you or me draw the line, that was the same night, Betty, Robby, Armond and I was sitting on the outside, there was 3 or 4 polices cars, going to the street over from us, I said that on the news that someone, had road up on a bicycle and shot at the police, they was ready to leave after that.

Then next night I was walking around excise my legs, my old bone I saw many polices cars, they was blocking two streets no one could go into there, the lights was just like Christmas time on the polices cars, while I was walking I saw someone, with a long case in his hand. He was checking vehicles, I didn't know him but I knew who the vehicle belong to, I ask him what he was doing. He said that he was seeing if his vehicle was lock.

That was when I said to him that he didn't live in here, and who did he know in here! He said art was his cousin, I ask him where did art live! He said over there. He was pointing at building 3 that is where I live, I told him to get out of here, and if I saw him in here anymore that, I would hold him for the police.

Then I said that I should take that case away from him. Because he might have stolen that case, then he left out, I kept on walking looking at the polices lights, when I got over to where Jenson live, he was on his porch smoking a cigarette, I said hi Jenson did he see that guy, just walking

David L. Marshall

with that case by the street. He said yes what was with him! I said that I had to run him out from here, he was checking vehicle to see if they was unlock.

That when he was checking Miss Evelyn, and Miss Blackwell daughter vehicle, I knew that he was looking for, something to steal. I made him leave out from here, Jenson said that he might want to get shot, and if he mess around in here he will get shot, someone have taken things off his vehicle, and someone had broken my truck windows before, and it cost my money from my pocket, to fix it. Then I went back to walking until I went into the house, to go back to bed.

On July the 14th it was Larissa dinner, for the resident that live where she works, at the Salvation Army Apartment. I got up and went over to Larissa work, about 6: am to start the fire into the barbecue grill, to start cooking. Larissa she had not got to work but I could get into the building. I went into the kitchen to see, if she had the ribs soaking in the red vinegar.

When I got into the kitchen I didn't see the meat, in a little while I was there, Larissa she came to work about 7: am she said hi daddy. I said good morning where was the rib that was to be soaking into the vinegar. She had forgotten to soak the meat.

Chapter 7

NOW THAT WAS NOT GOING to be an easy day for me, she said sorry daddy that she had so much on her mind that she forgot. Now I can understand that I said that was ok, so what I did was, put the meat into some warm water, to finish thawing it then I went and started the fire, in the grill. I went back in the kitchen to clean the ribs.

Then I ask Larissa did she have any meat tenderizer, she said that she did she gave it to me. As I clean the ribs I put some meat tenderizer on it, and then after I finish that, I put some of the ribs and chicken, on the grill to start cooking. Then I sit down and lit a cigarette, then Miss Mira and some others of the resident, they came out to say hello to me. I know some of them when I use to work there, and some of them are new resident, that I don't know.

Now the dinner was going to be pot luck some of the resident that just move there I didn't know. One of them came out with their dish to, take it into the kitchen after she came back out her, and open my grill to see the meat that was cooking. I stop her and told her don't do that. She said op that she was sorry, I said that was ok. She went back into the dining room, Larissa she started laughing.

Then she said to the lady and said, that is my daddy and he doesn't like anyone, looking into what he was cooking. And that he don't mean no harm he is just like that, now it was a hard and hot long day, after the food and everything was ready to, sit down and eat I let them get their plates, then I got myself one.

Now Maurice the Maintenance he was spending records, the music was sounding good and everyone else, they was having a good time eating. After they had eating they start dancing even the pastor, from the catholic Church he was there, with his family they was dancing to the music, having a good time Larissa she induce them to me, we all was having fun.

Now Larissa she had ask me to invite, some from my complex to come to the dinner, I did that at the time we was eating no one came, but later on Lorain and Karen they came, it was almost over with Larissa, Mira and the others was cleaning up, the dining room but there was still some food left. Lorain and Karen I induce them to my daughter, Larissa.

They Lorain and Karen got some food and eat, after they had eating we all were sitting back talking. Then the music I guess it sound good to Karen, she got up and start dancing with her own self. I would have dance with her but I was beat, I walk over to the D. J stand and told Maurice, that I was beat and that I was going home, and kick up my feet and relax. He said to me did I want a beer to help me, after

I got home to relax. I said why not that I could drink one, so he and I went to his apartment, and drink a beer.

After the one beer we came back to the dining room, and I told Lorain, Karen and Larissa that I was going home, and kick up my feet and relax, Larissa she said ok daddy and thank for everything. And that she would talk to me later on, I said ok then I ask Lorain and Karen, what they was going to do. They said that they are going home also, so we left going through the lobby to my truck, there was some of the resident sitting there still, they said David thank for everything and they, will see me later.

After I got to my truck Lorain and Karen was in their vehicle, I left going home. After I got home, I went into the lobby and got my mail. I saw the woman that I love her name is Miss Elsie. I spoke to her and I went home, because it was a long and hot day.

The next day I got up and got clean up. I had to take Annett to pick up her cloths from the cleaner, at 9:30am. I did that and came back home. Then I needed to do some washing for myself, but I was still beat from the cooking yesterday, by been on my feet all that day the fore, all that day I dad was just relax.

That night in my heart and mind, that was 7-15-06 God and Jesus came to me, to not let me forget that I am in love with Elsie. But in my heart and my mind I love her so much. I think about her all the time day and knight, she are there in the pass and the future, no matter how she treat me and the others, how they try to keep us away from she and I.

Now I know that there is age of 19 teen years between she and I, what is age have to do about love, I love her from my heart age is the years that I have live, and I am still here on this earth that God put me on. Now am I wrong to love someone, or not to love someone because of age. No I don't think so that is just a number, I call it wisdom, and all I want to do is make Elsie happy.

Some lady slide around to see if, Elsie and I was sleeping around with each other, but there was anything to see, heap see but no one knows, if it was they would never know. If there was a woman that I was sleeping with, everyone would know it, because if she saw me talking to another woman, she would tell them stay out from my man face that would be a big problem, so I keep my thing in my pants.

Even Stewart he said to me one day that, Elsie and I must have broken up, he age more than he was to see what I was doing. I should have told him don't worry about, what Elsie and I are doing worry about the money that he and C. C. owe me, from cleaning that wall that day, so that C. C. could paint it for Frank, that I never got paid for, it was $80.00 that she and he owe me. I use to take him around doing work for Frank, and when I stop at the gas station he wanted to know, what I was doing. I said that my truck don't run on water, even if that water cost also, he never came out from his pocket to pay for gas.

Now Stewart he wants to know about business, he better get a life for himself and stay out from mind. I know what I am doing I am grown, full grown 64 years old.

Now as every Sunday, I take Popeye to the store when he want to go, to get his grocer after he finish getting and paying for them, he and I will stop by the slot machine, and play slot poker. Then after we win or lose our money, I take him and his grocer home. Sometime there is another lady friend of mind, her name is Marilen, sometime if she needed to go and get something. She will call me, and I will take her to the store, to get her grocer.

On July the 16th I took Marilen to the store again for her grocer, and took her back to her apartment. And I went home along if there was a ball game on tv. I would watch the game or work on my book. Then on the 17th I got my rent money order to pay for the next month. That same evening I was working in my computer, it started raining now we don't get to much rain in Vegas.

That Monday evening it started raining so hard, the power in the building went out. That shut down my computer. I said man now that I was going to lose everything that, I have put into my computer. After the power came back and I attempt to get it back, into the computer for my book. I could not get it back no way or long I try, I could not find it.

To me it was all going everything that I work on in my book was going. I shook my head and said to myself, now if it was not on the hard drive. That it was going to be so hard to write it back. I had already rack my brain to do it first, now if I had to do it again it was going to be hard, if I had to start all over again. Man that is not what I want to do.

But what else can I do if it was not on the hard drive, but start over again. Now I don't know too much about computer, but write about my pass life. What I have to do now is, to find someone who knows how to go into, the hard drive to see if my work was still there, until now I will let it along.

Now the other days I don't have anything to do, I try to find someone who can help me, with the computer to find my lost book. On the 20th Miss Queen she had another doctor appointment at 10: am. Now the day before she had said that, after the doctor appointment she had to stop by the bank. I told her that I would pick her up at 9: am. Because before we get to the doctor, we had to get to the bank first, that the doctor office was not too far away.

And that the bank open at 9: am we will stop at the bank first, and then go to the doctor office. Miss Queen she said ok that she would be ready, then I left and sit outside and smoke a cigarette, I didn't see Elsie she was in her office working. So I smoke my cigarette and went home.

So on the 20th Queen and I went to the bank after that, we went to the doctor office. After the doctor finish with Queen we left the office, I ask her did she want to stop and get some chicken. She said no that she had something at home, so she and I went home. Now I can't do anything in the computer, because I can't get my book back on the screen, the rest of that time and the days after, no one else needed me to do anything for them, I just sit and watch tv and sleep.

On the 24th Miss Queen she found two more checks, that she had Missplace and she call me, to let me know that she had found them, and she wanted to take them to the bank. Then she said that what she was going to do, with those checks was cash them. I said ok see her in the morning. The rest of that day I was trying to find someone, who knows about computer.

The next morning I got up and took Miss Queen back to the bank, so she could take care of her business. And she had called the Pharmacy for her medicine, at CVS/ Pharmacy that was going to be ready, when she got there. So we stop and got her medicine and went back home.

On the 27th another friend of mind, that I never lay my eyes on her. She had called me and left a message, I call her back her name is Miss Bernadine Bronson. She and I we call each other, sometime to say hello and how we are doing. She and I keep in touch with each other, even that she and I never seen each other. Sometime I would say to her that, one day when she is out my way, that she and I should have dinner? She said that would be ok, we could do that.

On the 29th there is another lady that I knew her name is Pat. She work on computers, I said Pat that was a blessing that I saw her, that something was wrong with my computer, she and I went to my apartment so Pat, she could see what was wrong with my computer, she got back my book on the computer, I was so happy until, she said that I needed a new computer.

Pat she said to me that she was trying to move closer to here, and if she could find apartment closer, she could help me with my computer. Then she said that she needs me to help her move something. And she said that if I help her, she would not charge me for working on my computer. I said ok that was good for me because I don't know anything about computer. Then I ask Pat when she was ready to move her thing! She said on Sunday if it was ok with me, I said it was after I go and take my friend to the store, she said ok Sunday was ok.

Then I said that she have to come and get me, so that I could follow her to where she was moving from, she said ok that she wanted to put some of her things in storage, and on the next Saturday she had to have everything out from the apartment. I said no problem see her on Sunday about 10: am. She said ok then she left, I went back into my apartment happy but, thinking about a new computer that I cannot afford.

That Sunday morning I got up got ready, and took Popeye to the store and came back, and waited on Pat to call me. Later on she calls me she was at the gate that, she was here and ready to go. I said ok that I was on my way, I went and got in my truck and Pat and I left.

We had to go all the way to bowling highway to where Pat was moving from; after we got there she said that there was another guy coming that was going to help us. I am the kind of guy that doesn't waits on anyone, so what I dad was ask Pat what was going. She show me I start putting them on my truck, after I had almost loaded my truck, the other guy came Pat, she induce him to me as Larry. I said to Larry that it was nice to meet him.

After we had got what Pat was going to put in the storage, I tie mind down on my truck we went and put them in the storage, then we left I went back home. Later I saw Pat she was taken something to Theron apartment, I gave her a hand she said that she was house sitting for Theron, until he came back home. He was out of town. Then after that I went back home it on the 30th of July 06.

That Monday the bug man he came to spray my apartment. He sprays every apartment once a month, Stewart he was with the bug man. After he had finish with my apartment, he saw my dolly. I have a good dolly that I use, when I am moving someone, he said David that is a good dolly that you got; I said thank that it cost me a pretty penny. He said but it will pay for itself, it is not one of those play dolly.

That was when Stewart said David. There is a lady he know she need to move something. And Stewart he asks me was it ok, if he gives her my phone number. I said sure give it to her and have her to call me, that I would move it for her. He said ok then bug man said see that is money, I said yes it was that I need it then they left, going to another apartment, to spray for bugs.

After I had move Pat things the first time, she said to me, David do you have $299.00. I said yes and no why? She said that she had a Sweepstakes Clearing house, credit voucher with a Discount that I could get a new computer, for $299.00 and that I do need one.

So I said ok why not. So I took my check book and wrote a $299.00 check and sent it off, for a new computer. Now I could not afford it but. I had to have it for my business of writing my book. On August the 5th Elsie son Mark he came to visit his mother, now it was just like the first time that I meet him, I cook a dinner for him. This time I did the same as I did the first time, Elsie she had told me that when he got back to Tex. He told all his friends about those black eyes peas that I had cook for him.

So after Mark had loved those black eyes, and that made me feel so good. I cook some more for him, with some pork, corn bread, and I took some Apples and took the core out, and stuff them with sweet potato and bake them, that was the first time that I had tried to fix that. I call it Apple potato desert it came out ok, that what the others told me.

After we had eating and sitting around talking. My God daughter Blessing she was in my lap, still eating Elsie she said something that, she was going to tell Stewart that I was talking nasty to her, I said to her that I don't and want talk to her like that. Because when I talk nasty to her, it will be for her and my own ears only, Elsie she said to me that, I was right that I don't talk to her that away.

After we all had finish eating and I had clean up the lobby, Elsie she call me into her office I went in. Mark he was in there also, he had a present for me he said that, it was not much but that was all he could afford. I said that it don't matter how large or small it was, it was the thought of the given. I look inside he had a T. shirt for me, from the Tex Longhorn football team. I thank him and embrace him that put some good, into my heart he had did more for me, then my own family had ever did.

They never gave me anything in my life, other than about what they want and needed from me. Elsie son Mark had made me feel so good. He and I were standing on the outside, in front of the lobby talking. One of the ladies, live here, she saw Mark and said that he was Elsie son. Mark said yes mam. She said that he was a good looking man, then she look at me and said just like David. She said now David he could teach you something.

Because David he know how to run. David he is running from these women's. I smile and look at Mark and said o yes that I am, running away from them. The lady she walks away laughing. Then Elsie she came out from her office, it was her day off anyway she was ready to leave. Going to her vehicle Elsie she said David, thank you for everything and that she would hug me but, I said that I know there was some are peeping already, to see if they can have something to talk about. Then I said that see her in the morning and Mark, talk to him soon I hope then they left.

On the 6th my granddaughter Brittani she calls me, from BATESVILLS MISSISSIPPI. She said that she had giving her brother John Marshall 2nd. My address to write me, I said that was ok and that I haven got it yet. And that it might be here soon in the mail, she said that he need a lawyer and polices, had a trump up charges against him, and that his grandmother Barbara Jean. His and her dad and aunt were not going to help, and that his mother she was trying all she could, to get a lawyer for him.

He said that what they had on him was a lie, and that he was railroad. I said that they all say that when they get catch, why was he running with a bad crower, he already had a mark on him for the first time. And if he was trying to do something to better himself, I could see that he should have been busy, trying to work or looking for work, he would not be in what he are now, other than giving his peoples a problems, and a head ache peoples don't have money to give away.

Then I said that maybe I should have did my son, what my mother did to me to straighten me out. Put something on my ass she said that she was, beating the devil out from me. I was a bad ass when I was a child. Look at my now I am clean from the system.

Then I said to Brittani. Think about this little John now he is a two time loser, just like his dad that is my son, and like myself I never have been like that, going to jail into those peoples system.

Then I said that I don't have any money to help him, I can hardly help myself. And when my own son John, he did not do what I told him not to do, when someone had rape his aunt. And he did it anyway; I didn't do that for him he was my son. He should have listened to me let the law take care of it. Like the older peoples had always said before, if you make your own bed hard you have to lay in it not me.

Now on August the 7th I got a letter from my grandson John. The Illinois Department of Corrections in Pinckneyville IL. It was the first one that I had receive from him, I read it and I said that it was my son all over again. Like he wrote it the way he talks. What up pop, now is that away to start a letter no. it is not the way to say hi, I don't have the best of training mentally and morally provide by Schooling. But I know better than that, young people's stay in School if you have Quite, then go back and get all you can.

The second letter I got from my grandson John Jr. he needed some money that I don't have, that was $3500.00 he said that was for a lawyer to take his case, but the lawyer he would start the case, if we could come up with $1500.00.

To take the case and to pay the rest as the case was going on into the court. I don't have that kind of money. I guess that because I have a book out, that I have money think again.

Then he sent me some pictures of his kids, they are some find kids two girls and a boy. Robin A. Marshall age 8 years old, JA'NYAA J. Marshall 3 years old, and John w. Marshall 3rd. 1 years old I never meet them. But I only seen John the second only once, if I saw him on the streets I would not know him.

Now I can't help him this is on him, he wanted me to send him a T. shirt of Passing Through and a book of mind Passing Through. I sent them to him that was the best I could do, also in the letter he said that, he had 3 great kids and he really needed to get back to them. That he can't see another guy raising his kids, now he should have thought about that before, whatever he has done.

Then he said in the letter that, in my younger days that I had lots of woman in my life, yes I did but I knew how to stay out of trouble. Other than when they wanted to kill me some tried, but I am still here out of the system of the law. Now I have my things to do for myself, I went to the gas station and got $20.00 in gas, and did what I had to do.

Now I try and help anyone who needed me, so I had to take Annett to the cleaner for her cloth, and came back because I had to take Miss Queen, to her doctor appointment at 10: am. I did that everything that I had to do and came back home, now I was thinking about Elsie how beautiful she are, so I went to a flower shop and order some flower for her, to be deliver to her on the 11th about 10:am., when she got to work. On that day I waited and I waited on those flowers, to be deliver to Elsie so that I could see her smile, when she see them.

No flowers came it was about 12: noon the flowers still was not there, so I call the flower shop to see why the flowers, was not here now I had paid $60.00 for those flowers. The lady she said the flowers were on the truck and that they were on the way to 2101 north Martin Luther King Blvd. Now I waited until 1: pm I call back.

It was the same o thing the flowers, was on the truck and they was on the way. Then I said ok. Keep them on the truck that, I was coming and get my money back. Because now at this time it is no good for me, because I had order the flowers for 10: am now it is in the pm. I said that now I was on my way to get my money back. You should have said that you could not deliver; I will be there for my money back. That was what I did. I got my $60.00 back that I paid for those flowers.

Now one of the tenant, that live in here he had cancer his name was Lucky. He and I would sit out in the sitting area talking. I would keep my eyes on him while he was out there, because I could see something into him. That I could not do anything about it, because it was the will of God and Jesus, and no man can enter fear with that not even the doctors, they can make it comfortable for you until, God and Jesus get ready to bring you home.

The cancer it had got so bad in Lucky, one day he and I were on the outside talking. I saw him starting to drift off I saw something in him. I said to Lucky are you alright he open his eyes, and look at me and said that he was ok, then as I was watching him he said to me, that the cancer was going too far now. I said that he was going to be all right.

Then he drift off again I ask him was the sun too hot for him, he said no that it feel good. I said to him why I am asking him those Question was, that I saw and see something in him. Lucky he looks at me and said you see it to don't you! I said yes I do but he was going to be ok. Later on the cancer put Lucky all the way into the bed, to stay there that the doctor had said, that they could not do anymore for him.

Now Elsie and I with Mrs. And Miss Jenson and some others, tried to make it comfortable as we could for Lucky, but the other was in the hand of God and Jesus, Lucky he had stop eating as his house keeper had said, but he like insure. One day Elsie and I were over to Lucky house to see him. I gave his house keeper some money, and told her to go and get Lucky some insure.

Now I ask Lucky when I buy this insure, would he drink it for Elsie and I, he said yes he was so weak. The lady, she went to get the, insure and came back, Elsie she took a straw for Lucky to drink the, insure. After he drink it I told his housekeeper, every time it run out get in touch with me, that Elsie she know how to get in touch with me anytime, that I had the money for his insure.

She said ok. August the 12th that was on a Saturday night. That Sunday morning Mrs. Jenson he call me, and he said David Lucky pass last night, I said what time was it. That Lucky he knew that he was ready, that is why he always said that, he was going to be ok. Jenson he said that it was about

10: pm or 11: pm. When he went to Lucky apartment to check on him, that he didn't hear Lucky and he call out to him, and he didn't respond he knew that he was going.

That was when I said that now all his pain is going. Then I ask Jenson had anyone had call Elsie. He said no, I said that I would call her and let her know. So I call Elsie and told her that Lucky had passed, last night that Mrs. Jenson had called me this morning. She said ok then I hung up, I had Miss Marlean at the 99cent store, she was shopping.

Chapter 8

O N THE 13TH OF AUGUST it was another friend of mind birthday, her name is Coco I call her to say happy birthday to her, she and I talk for a little while then we hung up, and after I was in Alabama about my book, a school buddy of mind that I went to school with, he call me. I have seen or talk to him after school days, his name is Otis Redmond.

Otis he said that he got my phone number from Len Mcconnice, another school buddy we went to school with. Otis and I was talking about my book Passing Through, I was telling him how to get one, he said that he was going to Brewton," he live in Mississippi" and that he would get it from my daughter. Then he said that he was going to keep in touch with me, we hung up.

Now as I always do after the 2nd Wednesday, I get my rent money order to pay my rent for the next month. On the 14th I did that. Now I have been marry 7th time in my life, now I am not bragging about that, to me now it don't make no sense, and all the woman I had sleep with, and broken their heart. Now I had got my heart broken also, now to this day what did I prove, not anything.

David L. Marshall

Now I want to do the right thing and find, a woman with a big heart like mind, that I can love and she can love me back. I can't find one to trust me, or she have been Mistreated by someone else, and she don't trust anymore. Now I am the same way she is, but if she love me as I love her, I could try it again.

Now that I have saw and found Elsie, all I have is a fancy. Now I love her but I can't have her. She is just a friend. She and I see each other while she are at work, because I live there where she work. Now what that white woman Sally did to me, on the 15th of August 06. Elsie and I were on the back of the building two, smoking a cigarette I said to her. If and when it comes time for me to meet God and Jesus, to leave this world and I know, where she is at, would she marry me?

Elsie she said to me that I was not going to die. And that she will never get marry again. I said that one day I was going to die, she said why? I said that then I want need to make a will, then she was ready to go back to work, I walk her back to her office then I went back to my apartment.

Now there is lots of lady that would love to be in Elsie shoes now. There is another lady that just move in to where we live, I see her and sit and talk to her, one day I said to myself and some of the others, that the old lady that sit in the lobby, that talk kind of fast. For some reason I had saw her before, but I can't think where I meet her.

On the 15th I was going to the lobby, before I got in there was a find lady coming out, leaving out from the building. I look at her and said man she is so find, she should be mind.

I spoke to her she said hi, I was looking back at her, she stop and look back and said. Doesn't she know me? I stop and look at her and I said that she does look formulary, and then she asks me did I know a lady name Bernice Jordan. Then it came back to me.

That was when I said Shellar, she said David Marshall she and I hug then she said, that her mother live here. I said your mother! She said yes. I said where, she said come on then she and I went back into building.

She took me to her mother apartment, and knock on the door, I start to slap my own face. Her mother she came to the door, Shellar said to mother do you know this man, she look at me and yes she sit and talk to him in the lobby. Shellar said no mother don't you know who this is, this is Bernice ex man David.

Then I got some more hugs she said David, she had keep on looking at me that she know this man. Then she said David how are you, I said mom that I was doing find, and that I keep on looking at her before, and said that I know this lady, then I said that now that I know now, that I can rest my mind. Her name is mom Ruth.

The next day this lady name Roshall, she asks me to take her and pick up some x rays, from the Veteran hospital at 11: am. I said ok. So at that time I was taken her to the hospital, she and I was talking about how these old lady, was trying to get me into their bed. She asks me what I was looking for in a woman. I said one who love me and respect me, for what I am.

David L. Marshall

She said to me that I wanted honesty, and that I will never get that. Then she said that she know what I need. I said to her, that she doesn't know what I need. She said all I need was, for her to take me to her bed, and give me all the loving that she could give to me, I said that I can get all the love and sex outside, of this complex and all I wanted in there, was the love from their heart and respect, from them.

Man what a trip, now my truck was not running to good, when I go about four blocks, it would cut off but it would start back. After I got finish with that crazy woman, and took her back she wanted to stop at the lobby, to get her mail I stop to let her out, after she got out she was mad because, I would not jump in bed with her, she slam my truck door I said ok now, you break that window you pay for it, then I said to myself, that was the last time she get in my truck.

Now my daughter Larissa she had said, that one day she was going to have me, to move her that they had house now. I said when! She said that she would let me know, then I told her how that crazy woman Roshall did, Larissa said well daddy all those woman want you, I said that they had a problem not me. Then I said to Larissa call me, when they were ready to move, so that I want have anything else to do, she said ok.

Now on the 17th I saw and was talking to Mr. Jenson, I found out that Lucky had been cremated already. That's his wife and the kids. They didn't want to have anything to do with Lucky. That was when I said, that Lucky he never talk about a wife or kids, Jenson said that Lucky never talk about them. Then he said that Lucky he was a mean man,

I ask Jenson what about Lucky things in his apartment, he said that he and Miss Elsie, was over seen them. Until to see if the wife and the kids was coming, I said you are right because peoples like that, if someone take them they will raise hell about them, no matter how they don't want to have anything about him, peoples are funny.

When I saw Elsie, I was telling her about what Jenson and I, was talking about. Elsie said that the wife had all the say so about, what go out from Lucky apartment, and that no one go in until, she see what the wife and the kids, was going to do. I said to Elsie that was a lonely way to die.

That Saturday my cousin Joyce she came by, to see me she had some time to kill, that she had a client to see and she was early, Joyce and I was at my apartment talking I said, that the mailman had run and I need to go and get my mail, then I said to Joyce come on and walk with me, she and I went out and we saw Stewart and Elsie, I induce Joyce to them, Joyce she look at Stewart, and said that she heard about him.

Stewart he was fixing a window, and Elsie she was cleaning up the glass, Stewart he didn't want me to hear what, Joyce had said he had a shitty look on his face, I start laughing and said what is it tell me, Joyce she didn't say what it was, that she heard about Stewart.

The window got broken out because, this guy was trying to get into here every day, looking for apartment until he got in, he had told some that God and Jesus, had brought him here from L.A to preach. I said what if I could have got away from killing him, he would have been in the Misst of God and Jesus, that guy is not shit.

That I had taken him to get something for his apartment, and his woman said that she had given it away, I said that he had to pay for my gas, for bring him there anyway. That he had said that he didn't know anyone here in Vegas. And it took so long to pay me, I got mad and said he could have the money, and he had all kind of woman crack heads, coming over here and he treated some lady in here, now he had a problem.

The way the window got broken was those crack head woman, he had coming to his apartment kick his ass, woman like them have no moral. They will do anything to get that crack, I mean anything and God and Jesus, brought him here to preach, I don't think so that was the devil, and his crack.

On the 21st of August a friend of mind, she came by to my apartment to get a copy of my book. After she got the book she wanted something more, but I could not do that for her. Because it would not be right, because I had someone else around my heart that, I love and I think that I would be cheating on her, until I see that I can't have her or I can have her, I will never make love to another. And she was all in my mind.

On the 24th I had to take Miss Queen to the bank, to get her money order for her rent. After I got back, I saw Elsie she and I was talking and having a cigarette, she said well David, peoples are saying that you and I are going together, then she smile. I did to because I could not be that lucky.

Then I said to Elsie. If she and I are going together, that was ok with me if it was true. "Now I wish it was true, because I do love her" on the 26th of August is my older sister Margieree Smith birthday, I had said that, I was going to Chicago for her birthday. But I could not afford the trip right now, because I was doing my second book and I need the money.

On Friday September the 1st. Annett she had to go to the bank, and get some money so that she could pay her rent. So I took her to do that, and came back and went into my computer, and start working on my book, and while I was working, I was also looking at my soaps at the same time.

Now on Saturday and Sunday I try not to work on my book. That is time that I can think about what, I was going to do next. On Saturday like I said before, I do my washing sit around, on the outside sometime Mr. Lee he was out there, he and I sit and talk about things about our pass, and if anyone else is out there, he and I would talk to them, until Mr. Lee wife come she sit for a while, then they leave and I would go back home, unless I see my baby Elsie" yes she are my baby to me" she and I would smoke a cigarette, until she go back to work.

That Tuesday September the 5th. I call my publisher to upgrade my book, to the best seller. Now, I know that I want and don't have a future, with Elsie but if I can have her friendship. That is enough for me, every time I see and talk to another woman, I don't feel the same about them, like I do for Elsie.

There is something about her that I can't let it go, like the older peoples always had said that, you want everything that you can't have, because you want it so bad and some, you can afford and some you can't afford it. So I will stay into my book working, hopefully one day, one day God and Jesus will make preparation for me, to have everything that I need in my life.

Until then I will do the normal things that I can do, that is helping someone if they need me, if not staying in my own place in my own life.

On the 14th of September it was Lorraine birthday, and it was also my brother Clifford in Huston, Texas, birthday. Betty she wanted to have a party for Lorraine that was to be on that Wednesday. Betty she was going to WAL* MART, to get a cake and other things for the party. I could see that she could not go, and do it all by her so I went with her, to help her if she needed me.

On October the 16th, it was going to be Elsie birthday, and I need to see what I was going get for her, that she might like while I was looking at, what I thought that Elsie would like. Betty she told me what Lorraine wanted was some jewelry. I overheard what Betty was talking about, no one tell me how to spend my money.

We went and got what Betty was going to get, and I got a birthday card for Lorraine, and sign it and gave it to Betty, so that others could sign it also for Lorraine. Then I wrote a check for $20.00 for Lorraine, and gave it to Betty to give to Lorraine.

Because I had something else to do that day, for Peat and Doris they are the niece and nephew, of my other part of my heart, Miss Norman Cottrell. "Smile" now on the day of the party, later on I finish with what I had to do, and came home Lorraine and all was in the lobby having fun.

As I was coming to the lobby door, Elsie she hold the door as I was coming in, she said no man aloud then she open the door and said, that I knew that she was playing. I said to Elsie yes I know that. Then I walk over to Lorraine and said happy birthday, now I had made some money, I said did she want the cash money or keep the check? She said that the check was ok that she could put it into the bank.

Then I said to Lorraine, if I gave her the cash money, then I could tear up the check, and it would save me some paper work later, she said ok. Then I tore up the check and gave her the cash money of $20.00. Lorraine party was almost over, so Elsie she fixes a plate for me, so that I could take it home with me.

Later on I saw Theron and said that, on October before the 16th I need him to go with me, to find and get something for Elsie birthday, because I could trust him. Theron he said ok just let him know, now like always I do after the second Wednesday, when my social security check get into the bank, a couple of days after I go and get my rent money order, to pay my rent for the next month. To get it over with and if I need to spend money, that it would not affect my rent money it is paid, this was on September the 18th Elsie she is off on Sunday and Monday, we have a drop box. So I drop my money order into the box, Elsie she will give a receipt later.

Now my rent is paid for the next month, on the 21st my granddaughter Brinnti it was her birthday, I had already sent her a check for her birthday early. So I call her to say happy birthday to Brinnti, and talk to her for a little while, and I told her that her grandfather love her, she said that she love me also, then we hung up.

Now Coco daughter and Coco son-in-law they was getting marry, on the 23rd of September 06. I could not get there I was out of town, taken care of something for my book number one, of Passing Through. I said that I would call them when I could, because business come first, they would understand that.

On that same day my daughter Larissa, she and her old man they was moving, into another apartment, I could not even help them.

That Sunday I call my sister Deloise Hill in Chicago, Ill. I had not call her, she and I talk at less once a week, to see if she and I was ok and find out, how the rest of the family are doing after all, they don't call me. Then I call my play sister Bobby in Chicago, she is just like my own sister, she and I call each other all the time.

Now something was wrong with my computer, I was still working with it until my new one came, I could not get the book back on the scream. I saw Pat coming from Theron and Pat and Sheelar they were standing, on the side walk talking. I explain to Pat what the computer was doing, she said David what have you done! She came with me to my apartment, to fix my computer.

While she was working on my computer, Coco she call me, I said that I was just going to call her. But right now someone was working on my computer, and after she leaves that I was going to call her, that I had just got back.

The way she was talking she didn't believe me," why" because she said that I was slick," now" I could not talk right now because, Pat she was there working on my computer, and if I don't take care of my own business, who else will. A man he should do what he have to do, in order to keep on going.

Now my truck it was running kind of bad, I ask Elsie would it be ok, if I put a gas filter on my truck in the parking lot," in the rent agreement we are not to work on vehicle" she said it would be ok if, as long it was no mess. So I put on the gas filter and after driving my truck, it was still doing the same thing.

The next day, I was feeling down, why I did not know. I call my cousin Joyce, just to have someone to talk to sometime life are like that, she and I talk for a moment she was busy, she said that she would call me back. But she never did. I went later on the outside and sit, and smoke a cigarette there was no one else out there, but me.

Elsie she was at work she was busy, she have a job to do also. I just needed someone to talk to, I saw one of my neighbor she and I was talking, I was telling her about my problems, she didn't want to hear about it. She said that she had her own problems that she was sick and she went on and on, I said ok sorry that I burden her. Then I left and came into my apartment.

And I shook my head and said to myself, that I listen to everyone else problem, let them just let it out. Now I need someone to hear mind, and nobody want to hear about mind. But I do have someone who are not, too busy to hear me they want turn me away. I turn to God and Jesus. After talking to them I felt good about myself. The next day, Miss Queen she had her appointment at the doctor, at 10: am. I took her there and came back home, I had move Miss Goseton daughter, and she didn't have any money right then.

So I saw Miss Goseton she gave me a check for the money, she had all but $5.00. that she would have it later on that day, now I use to read my horoscope every morning, when I was in Chicago, one told me that one day I was going to move, to a faraway land, now I am in Las Vegas I didn't think that I would be here.

Now I don't take a newspaper anymore, but sometime when I do get one, I look for the horoscope in it to read, there are sometime good in the stars. About mind that is Gemini. So now if it was good I keep it, later on for my book two of Passing Through.

Now, everyone has a dream or had one, time or another if you have never had one, I did and I still have one now." Dreams of voyages to far distant places may seem unattainable, they're not, though. It's just a matter of planning and determination, one step at a time. This was what my horoscope had told me on Friday, April the 22nd 06.

On Thursday, May the 5th 06. My horoscope read/ the coast is clear again. Gather with friends to celebrate. Whatever you've accomplished is something you didn't have before, so it's worth a party. Now that mean all of my worry, about what ever in my life or on my mind, is free and the things that I have learn now, about in my life I have accomplished that, I know more now then yesterday, I am ready to party.

Now everyone has only two lovers, one of mind is my woman; the second is the love of money. If you don't have the money, you cannot have the woman because, the two go together.

On Sunday, June the 28th 06 my horoscope read/ it look like a great deal of money is coming your way, but there are restrictions. It's as if you're being tested to see how responsible you are. Take care.

Then on Thursday, June the 30th my horoscope read/ speaking of money, there's quite a bit of it hiding in your own closets. Instead of buying all the time, try selling. It could be fun. Now I have that book and T. shirts on hand, so go out and sell them.

Now I try to keep my body in shape, and keep up my appearance the best I can, now if someone need me to help them, no matter what I have on it want matter, at this time someone need me. And I am proud of myself. On September the 27th 06 my horoscope read/ use affirmations. Stand in front of the mirror and say 10 times:" I will have fun"; "everyone loves me"; and" I look great." Amazingly enough, a few minutes of this will probably change your day.

Now Elsie her birthday is October the 16th. She is a Libra. I read her horoscope it read/ run rings around the competition. You might be the wind beneath someone's wings or the light that brightens someone's darkest hour. That was in September 27th 06 horoscope, Elsie she are the wind beneath me, and the wings that keep me flying high, and she do brighten my darkest day, every time I see her.

She is my strength, my power and my control. Because I do believe that she know, there is many ways to evil, everyone have their own thinking, and be leaf. Someone one day ask me, what do I think about evil? Now God and Jesus gave me, what I should know about evil.

That I should go back to his creation that, he put here in his garden was that serpent. And it was one of his older creation, was the devil. Take off the" d" what do you have, evil. Bad, harmful, what is bad or harmful is sin. So my best advice is, treat everyone the way you want them to treat you, because the one you Misstreat might be a Son of God.

Money, talking about money and the love of money and a woman,—Love of Money—and the love of a woman\ Money is not everything, it's good and it's bad, how do you want to treat it? Man made money, God made man, as to be the same as he is, he made man to love another, not money, and man did that. Then God made a woman as the same as he did a man, to love, not money. Ever since I came into this world, I came here crying about one or the other, money or a woman. When I came from a woman I was crying, it could not be for money, I didn't have any. But I had my mother, she was love, and still share it that came from a woman. Thank you mother for your love, but I am still as this day, I am still crying.

There was a man that, live right next door to me, his name was Stewart, when I first meet him, he was standing on his porch rocking I spoke to him, he and I talk for a little while, I had to go back inside of my apartment, I said that it was good talking to him, and that I would see him around, he said ok. Then I said to myself, that man he may be the one who I could talk to, to find our him or what he are, right now I like what he are talking about, someone to learn more that I know, while I am passing through.

Now every time I will be on my porch, I would see him on his porch meditation. I saw, him on the outside. We all sit sometime in the middle, of the sitting area reading his Bible. Now all the time peoples who you see with a Bible, or always talking about, how much they go to Church, and how they are working in the Church, and how much they are working for God and Jesus.

Now don't get me wrong that is good. But the Church it was built by man, and the Bible was writing by man also", "good book" the door of the Church is lock some time, with a key. God he build this building of mind, and this heart of mind is never lock, the door of my heart is always open.

Now don't get me wrong about what I am saying, reading the Bible will keep you inform about, what who wrote about that they want you to know, they can't tell you no more than they know, they was not there in the beginning, but believe in God and Jesus they will show you, what you have to do in here they live.

What does man know he was taught first? Other than that he would not have anything else, to talk about, man he will deceive you but God and Jesus want, I don't put no trust in man, Stewart he was a nasty not clean man, in his apartment around him was smelling, now if he can't keep the outside presentable, I don't want anything from the inside.

Now he got put out from his apartment, and had to move. He asked me could he store some of his things, into my apartment until he could come and get it, now I am not the cleans man, but I am not the nasty man also, so I told Mr. Stewart that I was sorry, that I could not do that." I have been in that man apartment before, putting up air filter for the maintenance man Stewart, to help him. That apartment smell like a dead fish" that odor stayed in my nose about two weeks.

Now after Stewart that live next to me, he had move and left everything in the apartment, and said to the manger of Louise Shell, the way I see it do what every they wanted to do with it, he can't take it with him, he didn't have a place to go himself.

Now the day that the maintenance man Stewart, and Elsie had started cleaning up that nasty apartment, I saw Elsie moving those things, I told her that I was going, and get my hand truck and give her a hand." Others are on their own" now after Elsie had did what she had or was going to do, her help from me stop she knew it, she said to me thinks David. I said anytime, then I took my hand truck back into my apartment, now if I had not gave Elsie some help, to get that place ready to be rented, it would take the maintenance man Stewart two weeks or more, to do it and that will give Elsie stress, and she don't need that.

That Tuesday October the 3rd I saw Shan, the lady that work for Frank Hawken, pretty lady find white woman yes she are. I look at Shan and smile to her, that if I had known that she was going to be here, that I could have cook dinner for her, Shan she said that want stop anything, that she will be in here for all the week.

Then I said ok, what about Thursday the 5th. Shan she said that would find," in my mind I said not as find as she are". Then I said that I would see her on Thursday. Now every time, I say what I was going to do for someone else, you can bet someone" mostly women" are going to stick their hand or two cents in there, why. I didn't say that I was going to have, someone else fix a dinner for Shan. I said that me, David L. Marshall. Was going to fix her dinner, I don't need nor want their help, unless I ask for it.

The people I am talking about she know, she started telling me how lone she knew Shan, I didn't ask her for that, then she wanted to know, what all I was going to fix, I told her. Then she said that she was going to fix the Mack and cheese, now I should have told her that did I ask for help.

Now if I had did that, they would have had something to talk about, because I know how these peoples think in here, because Elsie she sometime have to tell me, be nice. But the money is coming from my pocket, how are she helping me, she want to help herself.

That Thursday I had cook the dinner, it was raining kind of hard, Elsie she ask me where was we going to eat, I said that I was going to take it to the lobby, she said ok then I took everything from my apartment, and took it to the lobby. Lorraine she did the potato salad and the Mack and cheese.

But anyway Shan and Elsie they in joy their self, that was all counted for me, to see a smile from Shan and Elsie, that made me happy now I don't know, why others try to come in between of my happiness. On that same day I heard that, someone had said that, David he cook for all three of his woman today, the one who brought the bone, said that one was black and the other was white, I said some see and no one know.

That was the time some had told me, that they see that Elsie and I, was growing to close together, and that they was going to break it up. I told them break up what, what is to break up a friend ship. Only two can break that up her and me.

Now I know that these woman are not going to, let this friend ship be in peace, and I have promise to her son, that I would take care of his mother, when I made that promise to him, and he believe in me. From my heart that promises I marry Elsie. She are my wife from my heart, I cannot walk away from that, now if Elsie come up to me and say David, she want a divorce, and if that is what she want, she got it because I am just passing through, there will be another out there want and need that. Until then I will be close to Elsie, one way or another.

Like I had told Elsie before, that I don't want to lose her, and how much that I love her. I didn't only tell her how much I love her, I told others also and anyone else, who ask me about it also, I told her no matter who I am with, or where ever I am if she need me, I am coming or going to her.

On, October the 6th, I started to tell Elsie that she don't need me, to be there for her all the time, that she had all the looking out from others, and if or anytime she need me, all she have to do is call me, I will be there for her. Because now she are in good hands, that I was going on and finish this book.

Then I thought about Mark her son, and the promise to him I made, I want walk away from that, now this is for real also, I am falling in love with Elsie, I am close to the edge of a cliff of love, if I go any farther, I will fall over and I want know where I land.

So I just have to stay back some, so that she will know that I still have her back, and always will until she divorce me. One night I had a dream and Elsie she was in it, I thought that she was drunk, and was with some guys that I know, I told her that she better watch herself, that those guys was for no good, then I woke up.

On the 11th I got with Theron and went to the jewel store, to get a birthday present for Elsie. And with Theron and the clerk of the store, and myself we made a determination, that Elsie she would love the ring that we was looking at, it is a birthstone ring for Elsie, that was what I got for her.

Theron after we was leaving he said man, that ring was not cheap and that Miss Elsie, she will love it. I said you think so, he said yes she wills if she doesn't she are crazy. I said anything for my baby, and then I said early she got mad when I call her baby, now I want say that anymore to her. Then I told Theron that I was going to give the ring to Elsie, on the 14th because Elsie she is off on Sunday and Monday, and Monday is her birthday.

Theron said that he will bet that Elsie love that ring, I said that I hope she love it. Now the ring was on my mind, and I could see that my friend, and that she was not my friend anymore, the way she try to avoid me. On the 12th I said that why do I have to hold, this present until the 14th. That I will give it to her on that day, I went and got it and took it to the office, to give it to Elsie.

Now I also had a birthday card with the ring, so Stewart he was in the office with Elsie talking, I knock on the door she start laughing, and she said come on in. I gave her the present and said happy birthday to her, she smile and said thank you David. Stewart he said is it Elsie birthday, I said yes on the 16th.

Elsie she start looking at the card, she put it back into the envelop and said that she will, read this at home with a smile she said again, thank David. I said ok and went back home, the next day I went and got my money order for rent, and gave it to the office Elsie she said that, she was not going to open her gift until her birthday, I said I hope she like it. Then I left and went back home.

Back in my mind and the feeling from my heart, I have lost a friend. Because for some reason Elsie she are acting funny with me, as so she don't want to talk to me, or have another cigarette with me, she would go for a cigarette and I was out there, she would see me and go another way, avoiding me.

That was when I said to myself; ok that is what she wants she got it. But she owes me some kind of a reason why, she don't need my friendship anymore, I due that much. That Saturday on the 14th I was working on my truck again, I could hardly work on my truck, without Elsie on my mind and why, she are walking away from a friend.

It was so heavy on my mind until it hurting my heart, the pain I could not hardly bare it. I had to find out why. I saw Elsie standing on the side walk talking, to a guy from building 6 I said that I will wait on her.

Now Elsie and Stewart was cleaning up another apartment, she had the hand truck in her hand, I waited until she finish talking, she said so dry hi David, I said hello then I ask her Elsie, could I ask her a Question. She said sure, I ask her what went wrong with the friend ship, that I thought she and I had, I saw something in her face, eyes and from her mouth, that I didn't like it. She went off on me and said that she was busy, and that I see that she are busy, and that she don't have time to talk.

Now I didn't want to hear that, all I wanted to know was our friend ship over, she said that we still have a friend ship, from the highs but she have work to do; now I know that. So the last thing I said was, that I hope that she love her birthday present, then I walk away but I still have my memory, she cannot take that away.

Then I said man, where did that come from I never take her, away from her work or stand in her way, from anything from her. She said that she didn't have time to talk to me, that is ok all I ask was a simply Question, are we still friends or not! Then she said that we are friends from the highs, so I will seller with that and go on with myself.

Now I was afraid to say what I wanted to say, so I had already given her present to her, and she don't have 5 minute for me so be it, but I still hope that she love her birthday present that is all I want.

Still working on my truck thinking and shaken my head why, why and feeling hurt. No not hurting but disappointed. But I still have God and Jesus, I put all of my trust in them, man or a woman will walk away, and leave you hurting.

It look like the devil was in Elsie but I never seen it before, for her to turn her back on me, but I can't turn away from what God and Jesus, put in front of me I ask for this, so I have to deal with it, until she tell me David get out from her life, until then I will always be around somewhere for her.

When you have a pain in your heart you can't, put your hand on it to smooth it. The pain will always be there. Write or put into words, I said what every happen I don't know, but whatever it is or was, it was not as bad as it seem. Because I respect the feeling of another but, I also have to recognize myself and my feeling to, in order to respect you or another, talking to myself.

Because one day she will see that I was a man to know, she only see what someone else said to her," a good man is hard to find". And to this day now I know that, so after I finish working on my truck, and went in the house I could not stop thinking. I keep on talking to my father and my Brother, God and Jesus will see me through.

You see if you keep God and Jesus with you, you will always have someone to talk to. I had to talk to them, the ones who could ease my pain from my heart. Because I had lost a friend and it was a prevalent to have or had a good friend. They are hard to find and I am not getting any younger, but in another way I am as younger as I feel.

Because I have the tool to work with, I think about those who have pass on before me, one day I had to do the same thing as they had to do, after all we are passing through this world, thinking about Mr. Felton Childress pass on June the 9th 05, and to leave a loving wife Virginia behind, and Miss Roise Parker who made a deference, in Alabama when she made up in her mind, to sit other than stand on the bus, she pass on October the 24th 05, and another friend of mind from my hometown, Hurdo Jones Jr. every time I went home he wanted me to sing for him, he pass on March the 4th 03, memory.

Now like the old saying the road has to end somewhere, now Elsie she makes me happy when I, know that I could laugh and talk to her, but now it is just a memory. No one can take that away from me But God and Jesus, why can't I have that my happiness. Now I have earned that when I change my life.

Now I want be hurt anymore by a woman, they have their own life let them live it for them self, now if that is what my friend want, she got it. One day Stewart and Elsie they was working in the door, of building two I had to go through there, to get to my apartment I spoke to them and kept on walking, I didn't have anything else to say, I heard Stewart say hum I smile and went on, going to my apartment remembering what I did have, now it was all over.

Now the way I am now, I almost fall what I had ask before from God, and he granted it to me not to fall in love anymore, that I can't walk away from. God he do strange things sometime. Now I can walk and hold my head up, I still have my pride.

Some of the tenant they had ask me, what was we going to do for Elsie birthday, I said that I don't know what, they was going to do but I know, what I was going to do. I had already spent all the money that I was going to spend, that was enough. "I didn't think anything about it until" Kopoe she ask me to ride with her to go and get, some donuts for the resident that live in here with their coffee.

There were two friends of mind I thought, was on the front talking, one was on her porch and the other one, she was standing on the ground talking. Kopoe and I was at her vehicle I spoke to my friends, they act as they had mush in their mouth, after Kopoe and I was in her vehicle, she said David what was that? I said that, I don't know.

After Kopoe and I went and got the donuts and came back, my two friends they was still on my mind, what was that I saw about my friends, that I would do anything for them in reason. But that was ok I want let that worry me, because the way I see it, one of my best friend has walk away from me, I don't have anything else to lose.

And they thought that they were showing me, what they were thinking about me. For Stewart retirement dinner it was no invite to me, they had a party for Elsie birthday no invite to me, even some of them they stop talking and was speechless to me. Like I care, they only showed their hand to me.

Now I know what to do, mind my own business and keep on going. Every day I still do the same thing that I do, get Miss Queen mail and get mind, if someone I see and want to speech to me, I speech and talk to them or, I sit in the sitting area and smoke a cigarette, and get ready go home and work on my book.

The day after Elsie birthday she was at work, they were spraying the apartment for bugs, "bug man he was there". When they got to my apartment Elsie she was at the door, while bug man was spraying the apartment, Elsie she said David thanks for her present. I said that was ok glad to do it, did she like it. She said in a proud way, yes. Then they left what she said and how she said it that, lift me up I felt good.

Now I don't know what someone had said, I could see then that she know that, I don't want anything from her, but her friendship only, why did I always tell her that, I will never disrespect her if I did that, I would lose her for good. If anything else she would be the same as, those other women.

That is my man why do you have to be in his face all the time, that thing belong to her. I could not talk to another woman unless, after I get home, I would hear about it later. I would be in jail, "why" because I would have put my own self in the system, then I would have to deal with it.

Now the way I was going to the edge of beyond love, God and Jesus pull me back from the edge, the edge of falling in love with Elsie, now all I do is speech and do the same, as I always do get Miss Queen and my mail, she are my life saver I can talk to her, when the others want.

Miss Queen she always has the time to talk to me, and I do the same with her. Be there for each other to me she are, just as my mother and my grandmother they pass, but in Miss Queen I see and I hear, my mother and my grandmother and I have, all the respect for Miss Queen my parent still live on, both of them peoples like Queen, they keep me going on my right path.

On October the 17th about 8:30 pm I was sleeping, I started to dream there was a lady in my dream, I didn't know who she was, but she was here with me in my house, she went to the bathroom after she came back, she look into my bedroom. I was lying on the couch, then she came and lay down beside of me, and she starts kissing on me, I was in the mood then after she kisses me.

Then I put my arms around her, and start kissing her back, I was kissing her on her neck she was in smile, I knew that she like it. I was going kissing on her all over, so that I would know every spot that she love, she had not too long hair, she had on a flair dress, then I woke up now I didn't want to wake up, I said to myself who was she, God who was she I tried to go back to sleep, but I could not.

Later on my new computer came, after Shellar had to go on line and check on it for me. They on that day they sent part of the computer to me, that the other part was coming and that, I was to have $75.00 to give on the other deliver, I call Pat to let her know that part of the computer had come, she said that she was at work now. I said that all I call was to let her know that, part of it was here.

The others days I was looking for the rest of my computer, that Monday the 23rd the rest of the computer came, I gave a check for $75.00 on deliver. Then I call Pat back and told her that the rest of the computer had come, she said that on her off day she would come over, that she also had to check on Joanne computer, I said that I would see her then.

Now that Tuesday the 24th Miss Queen she had a doctor appointment, I was taken her there I said to Miss Queen, that my computer had come, she said sure enough she was glad that it came. After her appointment was over and we got back home, I saw Robin. And told her that my new computer had come, and when Pat get my book off and put it into the new one, she could get the old one, she was happy.

On the 27th there was a neighbor of mind, wanted me to take him to the airport, and that he would buy my gas, I said ok and I saw little Joe and ask him, did he want to ride with me, to take my neighbor to the airport, and after then he and I would stop and have some breakfast, Joe said ok what time, I told him about 6: am in the morning.

That morning I got up and Joe he came to the apartment, we took my neighbor to the airport, and stop and had breakfast, after I had paid for the breakfast I took the change, and put it into a poker machine, and hit 4 deuces.

Then I said that I had won my money back, then I cash out and Joe and I came home.

That Saturday the 28th time change on the clocks, and that Monday I had to take Miss Queen to the bank, I did that and came home waiting for Pat to come, and work on my new computer so I could give, the old one to Robin so I could go back to working on my book number two, of passing through.

That Tuesday Mr. Lee, Joe and I was sitting out in the sitting area, like we always do talking, Mr. Lee wife Miss Lee she was coming to where we was, there was this crazy man that, was a cousin of art he was sitting there also, I don't like to talk to peoples when they don't, have respect for another.

He have a woman and they live in the same building, that I live in he saw Miss Lee coming, he said here come his woman, I said man that is this man wife give him respect. He kept on Miss Lee she said hi her name is Miss Lee, then Miss Lee said to Mr. Lee was he ready to go home, that fool he said if Mr. Lee don't want to go, that he was ready. I said man you know that you are wrong, and that he doesn't have any respect and, if he did that to Mr. Lee he would do the same thing to me.

Then Mr. And Miss Lee left and that fool he, was trying to talk to me I told him to, never talk to me anymore never. Then I left and went home then Pat she came, to fix my computer after she work and work on it, she got it ready and got the other one ready, so I could give it to Robin, then Pat she went to Joanne apartment, to work on Joanne computer Pat she would come and, see into mind to do something for Joanne computer, Joanne she came to see my computer and said, David this is a good computer that I have, I said thank then Joanne she left.

That same evening my neighbor that just moves into, the apartment that Stewart moves out from, her name is Jennet. She and I were sitting and talking on the outside, that guy he, I saw that he had a problems a big one.

Now I am not stupid, I know when someone is talking about me, I heard him talking crazy I didn't say anything. So when I got tired of hearing him, I got up to leave something said to me, don't go now so I sit back down, because that man he was drunk and crazy, later on I left and went home to work on my book.

Later I got tried and turn my computer off, and took my walk as I do almost every day, I saw a police car going out, I said hum I wander who was the police here for, I kept on walking. Just by building too and three there is a dumpster, I saw Miss Elizabeth going home she stop, she and I was standing by the dumpster talking, about what she and I was thinking about, what she and I wanted to do, to help the tenant.

This fool of a man I guess he had a death wish on him, he walk up on me with his hand behind his back, and push me in my chest with his chest, right then I push him back and said man get back, you don't know what you are doing, then I ask Elizabeth to come and go into the office with me that, I was going to report that fool.

Because if he do this again may God and Jesus bless him forever, Elizabeth and I got to the office, that fool woman she was in the office, with Elsie and James the new maintenance man. The fool he was in the lobby also, saying that he was going to say that I hit him, I said if I had hit him everyone would know it, I wait for a while then I went to the office window, and knock on it.

Now I had to get one or the other attention, to come out here now otherwise, we was going to have a big problem out here, James he came out, I told him what had happen. James he said they was taken care of it, don't go back in there. I could not let it go with that, I just told James what had happen to me; I want to know what is happen.

Then James he came back and said that, the woman in the office is that man woman, I know that, James said that she had call the police on him. And that there was others complain about that fool, he was going to get evict just wait. That is ok but tell me something, I went back home.

After had talk with James about that fool, that they was going to take care of the problem, now I had a leg to stand on as long that, fool leave me along. Now I am ok but he doesn't cross me, never. Otherwise I am not responsible to what was going to happen, now everything and about the others days, was ok also. I am a busy man and I don't have time for a fool.

On November the 7th I took Annett to the store and came back home, I had just taken my shoes off, and fix myself a cocktail to relax, and do what every I wanted to do, and some that I don't want to do. Just watch my soaps on tv then my phone ring, I said o no who are this calling now, I answer the call it was my other part of my heart, Cottrell in building two she needed me to take her to the store, I could not turn her down.

But I was relaxing and she is my heart, I said that I was on my way, and that I will be in the lobby in a minute, to pick her up. I put back on my shoes and went to the door, after I was out the door and going to lock it, that fool he was coming to the apartment where he live, he started that same old shit, now, this is time to put a stop to this ass hole, for good. Now when I go to my truck, I go to the back door it is closer.

He was still messing with untidy confusion, in the same old shit. I had to go over to him, and let him know, that he and I better go to the office and, iron this out now because, one of us are going to get hurt. He was making a pistol play I am not afraid, I kept on walking and talking to him because, if I get within 5 feet of him that gun, want do him any good.

He was saying that, I was going to die to day keep on coming, I said don't you worry I am coming, and that he was going someplace also, if he are not careful, then that drunk and crazy man he said, that he don't care and that he was not going anywhere, now I am mad as hell I could smell the blood, that was rushing to my head.

Then he said that if I was looking for, the lady from the office they was sitting outside, that I don't have to go too far. And that he doesn't care any body was going to do anything to him that made me much madder, and then he slam the door to his apartment. I went and saw Elsie and Mrs. Jenson sitting out talking, and smoking a cigarette.

As mad as I was, I said to Elsie that, the same man he was still messing with me. If she, don't stop him, that I will. Elsie she said holds it hold it lets go into, her office. Mrs. Jenson she left and Elsie and I went to her office I was smoking, and it was not from a cigarette.

After Elsie and I was in her office, she call Toni and ask her to come and sit in, Toni she came I explain to them, that I was tired of this man messing with me, and that I was not messing with him, leave me along. Because I don't have to live like this now, I don't know what his problem is and that I don't care, but he is trying to give me one, and that I want take it, not from him or anyone else.

Elsie said why I treated him; I said what, threaten him that was a lie. But after I had knock on Elsie office window, I said that someone better come out here, because it was going to be a problem, now what I did say was that I promise that. Because no man put another man in the place where, he get into trouble for a no good man, that he is not worth it tell someone.

Now he had already bump up on me, now who has been threaten then she was telling me, about what was in the lease agreement, otherwise she was saying that you can't protect yourself, I knew what was in the lease, it don't say that you can't defend yourself. After Toni left Elsie said to me, she know that I will listen to her, she said David stop threaten peoples. I said ok but a promise is not a threat.

While I was still in the office, Elsie she call the police for me, she and I both talk to the police, they was going to send someone over, they also told Elsie to not let me leave. "Why" because the police could hear how mad I was, Elsie she said that he want leave. While I was waiting on the police I was quite, I had things on my mind, I had to have and take the time to think. About on long mountain the lady, she want me to move with her to make her happy, now if in time she see that she was tired of me, and the good treatment I could give to her, and she find someone else better, then I, where would I go or do.

Elsie she was busy doing her own job, then she look at me and said to me, what was I thinking about? I said O nothing but passing through. Then I saw Miss Cottrell she, was ready to go to the store, I said that now after this had happen I, could not go to the store right now, that she and I would go after the police get here, she said don't worry what she wanted to go and get, it could wait take care of my business, I said ok.

Then I went back in the office where Elsie was at, Elsie she said did I explain to Miss Cottrell, I said that I did she will wait. I sit there for a little while, then I said that the polices was not coming, Elsie she said that they said they was busy, I said they are not going to do anything about it, so I was going to find myself, another apartment because, I am not messing with anyone here or outside.

And that I was not going to let anyone walk on me, I cannot let that happen, Elsie she said before I find another apartment, the guy he would be out of here, then I said to Elsie that, I would be at home if or when the police get here, she said ok. Then I said that I had some phone call to make, I left and went back home.

After I got back in my apartment I call my cousin Joyce, I left a message then I call my daughter Larissa, and left a message. Then I call my friend on long mountain, and talk to her and explain what had happen, she said no, that she know that I want let anyone, walk on me to get my things, and bring them to her house.

Then Larissa she call me back and said, that I could move with them if I wanted to, but I love my private later after Elsie, get it together and send that guy out, I could come back now that I want let no on walk on me, then my cell phone ring I answer it was Joyce, I said that Larissa was on the other phone, that I would call her back.

After I call Joyce back, she wanted to know what had happen! I explain to her what had happen, I told her that I was going to move because, and I want let no one walk on me. Joyce said that she don't blame me, Joyce said that she had already call Doris, and told her, that someone was messing with her cousin over there.

Then Joyce she said that she was close by with a client, and after that she would come by, now she are busy and I had already call the police, that I was going to be ok.

About a half hour Elsie she came and knock on my door, that the police was here and they was out back, talking to the guy, she ask me to come on but for me to go through, the other door and walk around there. I said ok, and then Elsie she went back outside. I came out and walk to where the police was.

The, polices was with that fool man talking to him, one of the police walk over to me, I shook his hand he ask me what had happen, I explain to him what had happen. The police said that I don't have to live like that, and that they was going to talk to the man, like he was a pussy then the police he turn to that fool, the police he was trying to discredit that fool, but they had a hand full talking to him.

Now, after listen while the police was talking to him, I know what his problem is now, like I said before he was crazy. Like the way he talk to the police he don't care, the police threaten to take him to the crazy hospital, he didn't care now Miss Russell, she had already told me and Elsie what that fool had did, to my God daughter Blessing.

He tried to give her candy and he had a play grenade, and he tried to give it to Blessing that was a no, no Miss Russell said that she went off with him, that was when I said he was crazy, and he needed some help. He was drinking alcohol and taken medication with it, because after the police and Elsie found that out, they went into his apartment to see what he was taken.

They found the medication and the alcohol bottler, was still in the apartment everything was in there but, the big belly man that drink with him, after the police had talk to that fool, they ask him was there someone to call, to let them know where he was going because, they was going to take him to the hospital.

That was when I said that Art, Elsie she said Art that live in building 6, I said yes and did they want me to go and see, if Art was at home. Elsie said will you, I said sure then I went to see if Art was at home. After I got to building 6 I saw Art he was standing out on his porch, I spoke to him and ask would he go with me, to talk to his cousin I explain to Art what had happen.

Art he said David, that he was so tired of his cousin, and he had already told him that, he better not keep on starting trouble with others peoples, they was not messing with him, then Art he said David that he had to live here, and that he was not going to let his cousin, mess that up for him that he was sorry, that he didn't want anything to do with it, because he had not seen his cousin for years, while they was kids.

That was when I ask Art would he do me a favor, and come with me and talk to Elsie and polices, and let them know something and me also, Art said ok David that he was doing this for me, because I was a dam good man. then Art he came back with me, to talk to Elsie and the polices, after Art he had talk to the police, and gave them what they needed to hear, now they had made their decision, what they was going to do.

What I had heard I felt sorry for that man, now I am bless and I know that, there are some I see and know they are bless also, but they don't know it. They are bless in the way God want them, as long they get up in the next morning they are bless, stop complainant God know what you need, he are our father we are not his father.

We are all his children I am part of my father, the police said that they was going to take that man," Art cousin" to the hospital so they could validate him, they ask me what did I want to do, I said that all I wanted was to be let along.

The police said ok that they only could hold him for 24 hours, then the hospital will let him go, I said that I could live with that, as long he just leave me along. The police said that guy he don't have all his facility, and if he mess with me again call them, they would come back out then he would go to jail, I said thank and if they don't need me anymore, I was going back to my apartment.

The police said they had all they needed, then I said to Elsie that if she need me I would be at home, she said ok then I went back home. After I got there about 5 minute Elsie she call me, to call Miss Russell to see if she want to file charges, on that sick man for what he try to do, to Blessing. I said ok that I would call her.

So I did call Miss Russell but no answer, so what I did was went to Miss Russell apartment, she was at home I told her what Elsie had said, now I didn't go back to my apartment right then, I saw Elsie and told her that Miss Russell, she was coming on the outside. So I went to the sitting area and sit down.

The police they had sent that sick man out, they was still here to see what Miss Russell, was going to do they was in front of the lobby, Miss Russell and Blessing came outside, and talk to the police, after I had saw that Miss Russell she wanted to let it go, because that man he was a sick man, I was ok with that then the police they, started playing with Blessing and giving her police things, and let her play with the stroll lights, on the police vehicle and the siren, then I heard one of them said that Blessing, she was a pretty little girl and take good care of her, then they left.

David L. Marshall

Later on I saw Elsie she and I was talking she said to me, David. You didn't press any charges to that guy and, that I and Miss Russell had the chance to do it why, I said that after listen to everything that I had heard, I said to myself that this man is sick, and he need some help I could not send him to jail.

Elsie she said that she know because, I was not that kind of person. While Elsie and I was still outside talking, Art he came back to say think to me, not putting his cousin in jail. Then Art he explain that his cousin was sick, and how much he love Elsie, Art he said that his cousin could not see, anyone but Elsie, I said he and many others.

The next morning I got up and put on some coffee, then I took my shower I saw another friend of mind, she are so sweet in her own way, she and I was in my apartment talking, and having coffee she ask me why didn't I and Miss Russell, bring charges on that man and get him out from here, that he should not be in here.

Then I said that she was right, and to me it would be wrong because, that man he is sick and that the manger insured me, that they was going to take care of it, and that I do believe in that they will. Now after this he might get some help, and let the entire pass be by going and keep on going.

My friend lady and I was still at my table talking, I ask her to tell me something why, or what is the deference of a threat and a promise, she said when you promise someone something, you can break that. And you carry out your threat. That was the same thing that I know, now I know that I didn't threat that man, I hope him get some help.

Then I ask my friend why it is every time, God and Jesus want you to do the work, they want you to do. Someone or something try to get into the way, why don't peoples let me do my job, what my father and my big brother want me to do. Then she hug me and the tears start flowing from my eyes, then she said that she feel my pain, and don't give up keep on going and keep on doing what, I always have been doing that everything, was going to be ok because I was a good man.

That was what I needed to hear and I felt it, soothe my heart I said thank I needed that. After I had to cry on her shoulder, and she had left I had to do something for Annett, so I went and pick her up and took her, to taken care of her and came back home.

Now I had went into my computer and found out, that I could not tell how many pages I had, that the numbers of the pages was not there. That was when I call Pat to one day, she was over here to take care of it for me, later on Pat she call me back that she was at work, and that she could not talk right now, that she would call me back.

Later Elsie and I was on the outside talking, and she and I had smoke a cigarette, and she was ready to go back to her office, she ask me was I still going to move. I said that I don't want to," in my mind I don't want to lose her from my life" then I said as long that guy leave me along, Elsie she said that they was going to take care of that, and that she want me to stay.

Now if I move away that I want be close to her, if she need me." I know and she know that I will, do anything for her"

I said that I want leave she smile, then she went back to her office, and I came back home. Later on Pat she call me back and I heard, what she had to say and I didn't like it.

She and I had agreement if I hope her move her things, she would keep my computer going, if I need it until my book was finish, Pat she the first time when my new computer came, she sit it up and when I was to take her home, she ask me for a Pepsi cola, and that I should do that much for her, I stop at the service station and, got two cans of Pepsi and gave it to her, then she wanted more Pepsi.

So one day Theron and I went to the food 4 less, I got a 12 pack of Pepsi to Theron to give to Pat, and I got a 12 pack for Theron and we went home. Now Pat she are calling me talking crazy and slick, that I got a 12 pack of Pepsi for her and, she don't even buy no 12 pack, that she only buy 24 packs and do I know, how much it cost to work on a computer. That piss I off I said to Pat.

Did she know how much it cost to move someone, then she said to me don't talk to her, like those women in the street. That was when I told Pat that she want do me, the same as she do those men out there also, then she come down and talk to me with sense, that was when I told her that was ok, that I will get someone else to do what I need, that mean her and mind friendship was over.

What I had to do for Pat to get her together, on July the 30th on that Sunday, I went and move Pat things and put them into storage. It took 4 hours it should had made $280.00, she only gave me $25.00 for gas, then the next week I move the others things, into storage it took 4 hours I should have the same money, as the first time but I was living out my promise, that was my word.

Now Pat she was trying to get apartment in here at Louise Shell. She kept the apartment for Theron after he was out of town, after Theron came back there was apartment available, Elsie ask me to tell Pat, for her to stop by her office and let her know, if Pat still wanted the apartment, I said when I see her after I did see her, I gave her the message from Elsie.

Later Elsie said that she had talk to Pat about the apartment, and that she didn't want it she was waiting on, the apartment over on Owen.

When Pat found out that she had the apartment on Owen, I went back to the storage and move all her things, to her new apartment. And now she want to get slick and renege on our agreement, that she and I had made, she is no more than those no good women like, she are that is why I don't want her as a friend of mind.

On the 9th there is another lady that lives in here, her name is Jackie. She is a find woman and a good looking one also, she use to sit out with us with Joanne talking, she needed me to take her and get a love seat, and bring it to her apartment. I told her that when she got ready, to call me. Jackie she said ok.

Now when she did got ready she call me, she and I went and got the love seat, I took it to her apartment and told her how much, money that I wanted to bring the love seat, to her apartment, she said ok as soon she got some change, she would give it to me. I said ok and left and went back home.

That Friday the 10th I was at home, making notes to put into the computer for my book, my play sister Bobby Jean call me, one of the lady that I went with her name is Candy, she was on the line talking also on 3 way, from Chicago. Candy and I we start talking about the good times, she and I had in the pass when I was cheating.

Then I ask Candy to take off all of her cloths, and take a picture of her and send it to me. Candy she said what, Bobby she ask me what was I going to do with it, I said then when I get lonely for Candy, I can look at it, Bobby she said and do what, Candy said that don't matter what he do with it, that when she get here in Vegas that she would have, the real thing and that is her, "Candy."

Bobby, Candy and I was on the phone for about an hour, then there was a knock on my door, of my apartment it was Elsie and the carpet man, with the lady that just move here, next door to me in the hallway, Elsie she ask me did I have some maxide, roach, ant and spider killer, that there was a roach crawling up the wall, she need to use it I gave it to Elsie, she use it and gave it back to me, and said thank David, I said anytime.

Now as I was talking to Elsie, Bobby and Candy was still on the line, they heard everything that I was talking about, after then I said to Bobby and Candy that, I had to go someplace, and that it was so good to me had talk to Candy, and that I was going to watch the mail for my picture, that to give it to Bobby to send it to me, because Candy she had a husband now, and she can't send it to me.

Then I got ready to hang up the phone, I felt something from Candy she are not happy, that is why she are still in love with me, and I know that Candy she only marry her old man because, what I had told her. Candy she one day said to me, David, Jackie is your lady right, I said yes, then Candy ask me what about her, I said that she was my lady two. After that Candy she just fade away from me, and got marry.

Now Candy I still love her but, I still want to know to know this, when I was in Chicago after I had move to Vegas, I was visiting Chicago and Candy she, did not find a way for just a minute, to see me give me a hug a kiss or whatever, that would have brought me back to my pass, now I can when I talk to Candy that she, still want me.

Now I take all of my dreams, from the heart and my mind serious because, I do believe that dreams do come true, after all we live for a dream. On November 13th was on a Monday night, I had a dream that I was in jail now, I don't know how I got there, and everything that I did to get out, I could not find a way out that is a bad feeling. Now I was in a rage, I was in a dream that if I wake up, I would have something to think about, and whatever took me to that dream, God and Jesus take it away.

Peoples of the mind think about, what you are doing. Something without thinking, can put you in places that you don't want to be in, why, not thinking. Stay free of trouble if not, you cannot get what God and Jesus have for you, you are in jail and can't go when you get ready, you don't know when God and Jesus, will need you, so stay out of jail and treat others the way you want to be treated.

The next day I saw Elsie, I was outside smoking a cigarette thanking, about what one of the lady I know, she said to me about another friend of mind, that she was using me she don't want me, I said that it don't matter to me, about what someone care about me, it only matter for me about, what I feel about someone else. That is love for me.

Now I know she was telling the truth, she was telling me something that I already know, but like I said before it is a dream, who know that it want come true, I can dream the same as Martin L. King Jr. I am trying to get to the top of the mountain also, when and ever I get there, I want the one I love beside of me.

Now I was saying in my mind that, I wish it could be Elsie but nor. After I was leaving Elsie she call me back David, where are you going that she had a break, and she saw me leaving and that, she was coming out with me for a cigarette, and that I was leaving man what about that.

Now I said to myself, this find, sweet woman with that sweet smile and sweet voice, how can I walk away from her, I turn around to in joy all of that in her. Then after she and I had finish our cigarette, I walk her back to her office and I went back home, still dreaming about if she was mind, what I could do with her and how, much I love someone so much, but I feel good about my dream, it is a test of life.

Now I am all the time thinking about others that, are less fortunate then I, now I was thinking about cooking something out on the grill, just to try and bring someone together, out on the outside to in joy I said nor, peoples don't respect you are appreciate you for, what you are trying to do to help others.

Now if I ask Elsie what she want on the grill, that I was going to put something on it, she would say that she don't want anything thank, if she did she would never tell me," why I don't know" but I do think that if she did she would appreciate it. She is the one that I am trying to make happy, and myself also.

On the 16th I had taken some food, to my other part of my heart, and the tenant they was playing bingo in the lobby, after I had deliver the food I saw Elsie, while I was leaving going back to my apartment, Elsie she was coming out from the bathroom, she was drying her hand with a paper tower, now at the thanksgiving dinner I had promise, to get Elsie an apple pie" she should me that she love apple pie" she saw me and shook her head up in the air," I know what that mean" she didn't say anything she went to her office, I went home and call back.

After she answer the phone, I said hi honey do she want her apple pie now, or could she wait until tomorrow, Elsie said well that she could wait until tomorrow, and don't go now. I said ok. Look like something said to me, David put your shoes on and get into your truck, and go and get that pie I did that and came back, I was at the gate to open it to get in myself, I saw Elsie and two others lady sitting out.

Going through the gate I said to Elsie, by pointing at her and said you, Elsie she look around and look back at my truck, and said who is you talking to, I said you come here for a minute, she came to my truck and said, ok you that I know her name, then I gave her pie to her she was happy, and now I was also.

So I went back home with a smile on my face, for Thanksgiving Annett she was out of town, and she had come back home, she call me to let me know that she was back home, I said that was ok and how was her trip, she said it was great, I said that I would talk to her later, she said that she need to go and get her cat, I said ok when? She said tomorrow. I said that would be a good time, see her in the morning, she said ok then hung up.

On Saturday November the 18th that was a big thing going, the smoking band was all over the news, trying to have peoples to stop smoking. Now the way I see that is, the tobacco company is still growing tobacco, and the stores are still selling the cigarettes legal, appointed and permitted by based on the law. And everyone on this God earth, have a right. Now why separate the right or the wrong, we all have the right to smoke if, that was there chosen.

And also was on the news was that, Ruth Brown the blues singer pass on, November the 21st Miss Queen she had to go to the bank, and she also had a doctor appointment, I took her to take care of what she needed to do, and came back home doing what I needed to do, for myself working on my book until Pat, she call me back piss me off, I need her to honor our agreement, get my computer in order.

Now when it was time for me to go and take Annett, to get her cat from the cat setter, she said that her daughter had taken care of that, for her mother. Now, on thanksgiving day Miss Elizabeth she had gave me, a Christmas sock every time I look at it hanging by, my t. shirt case it made me feel so good, to know that someone care. Elizabeth she had given me joy and love. On the 24th my cousin Joyce she call me, she and I was talking about my 65th birthday, and other things that needed address, then I said to Joyce that, I was going to close my second book, in January and later that I was going to start the third one, then Joyce said to me, why don't I wait until I get to be 65.

Then I could have a big celebration on my 65th birthday. I said that she had something there, yes, I could have a big birthday cook out, yes I was going to think about that, Joyce and I talk about two hours, she said that way I could write about my 65th birthday, then close the book then, I said that I would think about that, then Joyce and I hung up.

The 25th I call Joyce back to say that she had a good ideal, and that I had thought about what she had said, and that was what I was going to do.

Later I was talking to someone, they don't like white woman with their black man, I had to tell her something about my opinion, about that the white woman she, was no more than the black man in slavery, now today it is better but back then, the white woman she was no better than the black man, in away. The only thing that, separate the white woman, and the black man is the skin.

The so call white skin, there was a time the white woman she, didn't have no rights in the business world, the white man he would not allow it, for her to have any thinking and talking, about his business other then she having a baby, he was not satisfy for his own woman, he had to have my black woman also, yes to day and back then the black man, he also had the white woman, the same as the white man did the black woman.

Whenever there was a meeting in the mind, the white woman she was shut out, the same as the black man no matter, how smart they were. Now the white man he would listen to the black man, about what he had to say because, the white man he knew that the black man, he was no fool.

The white man he use the black man in many ways, even though his black woman. The black man he invented almost everything, look around yourself the black man he had no, power or money like the white man, to do anything about what he had invented, but now the white woman she have a black man, with something on the ball she, will be right with him if she had anything on the ball.

Now some of the white woman have access, to the white man money that is one way, the white man he don't want to see the black man, with that white woman, so the white woman should love Martin L. King Jr. as the same as the blacks, because she have come also along ways in life.

On the 27th a lady friend got me a gold chain rope, after when I got back home I said to myself, that I was bless thank you God and Jesus. The next day Miss Queen she didn't know, as she was going to put up some Christmas lights or not, on the 28th I did put up the lights for her, now when I get Queen and I mail, sometime she would tell me not to get her mail that day, because all her bill are paid, and only was in the box was junk mail, so I could skip that day, I said ok if she needed some water put up, I did it for her.

Sometime I see Elsie in her office busy, I get the mail and wave to her and leave, she are busy doing her job I just let her know that, I saw her to just say hello to her. And if she was not too busy I would go to her office door, and say hello to her, she would sometime say sit down you have a minute, have a seat. Then she finish with what she was doing then, she and I would talk for a little while, and then I said that I would be at home.

Sometime when I don't see or talk to her, for a day she would say David, that she did not see me yesterday man, I said that she was on the phone busy, so I can't stop her from work, so I wave to her. Then she would ask me did I have a minute, I said sure anything for her. She and I go out and smoke a cigarette, and talk then after we finish, I would walk her to her office, then I go back home and work on my book.

The next day my other part of my heart, she needed me. I took care of what she wanted done, then we was talking about the smoking band start, all I could say was what was told to me, from Elsie it start when you sign on your new lease, after that you could not smoke in your own apartment.

On inspection day James the maintenance man that, he took Stewart job after he retired, he was with Elsie, when they was to inspection my apartment, I was writing something that I was going to, put into my book. After they came

David L. Marshall

into my apartment, James he said hay David, I said hay James, Elsie she said O you are working, I said yes then I said James, did Elsie tell you what she did to me the other day, Elsie she start laughing, James said no what she done now, I told him about that apple pie.

Elsie she was still laughing she said that right, that she wanted some apple pie, and that was what she wanted an apple pie, and that was what she got. David he went and got it for me, I said O yes I went and got it, keep a woman satisfied and happy, you will be ok trust me on that, try it.

December the 1st the smoking band was heating up, now peoples when they want to smoke, they can't smoke in their own home, to me this is trying to take someone rights away from them, and that is not right everyone have rights, if you can't stand the cigarette smoke, and I want to smoke that is my right, don't try to take that away from me, now I will respect you because you can't stand it, I will move away back from you, I have right also the same as the ones, that can't stand the smoke.

You know what about everything that is in the air, just flying around that you cannot see, and the other that you can see, you are taken in all of that you don't have any complaint. What about that Elsie and I were talking about that, now after the others tents we had up and the wind took it away.

We didn't have one now I was going to try to, raise the money to at least get one of them, Elsie she was also thinking and trying to get one, also out there she sit out there on her break, and in joy herself a cigarette out from the sun, she was also concern.

12-02-06 I had wash my cloth and took them home, and came back because Elsie she needed me, I went back to the lobby to see what she wanted, she said to me don't go anywhere that, the guy that was having the marathon, and needed us to help with the water volunteer, they was bringing another canopy over here, the marathon was to come through by, Martin L. King Blvd. Coming from downtown on the 10th, I said ok.

The guy he would call Elsie trying to get to the complex, Elsie she would give him the direction, she said that she guess she told him right, I smile.

Soon the guy he came with the canopy, he and I was ready to take the canopy off his truck, he said that it was heavy, I said come on and lets go with it because, I have pick up more than that heavy other than this, then he and I took it off the truck, and lay it on the ground I open the box.

After the guys had left I saw that the same canopy that, they had brought was just like the other ones we had up. So Elsie and I was trying to see, how could I anchor it down, after all the guy said that it was going to be temporarily, so I told Elsie that I had to put it up on Monday, or Tuesday, she ask me why. I said that I need a drill to, drill some more holes that the ones that, was already put in want line up with the others, I showed it to her, she said that she was going to call Toni, she might have a drill.

So Elsie and I went to the lobby she call Toni, after talking to Toni we still don't have a drill, so Elsie she call the guy back and explain that, we don't have a drill that David and Elsie, we was going to put it up, the guy said just anchor it down because, it was only temporarily. I said ok that I know what to do, I told him about iron stakes that, I was going to go and get them and stake it down, he said ok.

Now Elsie she said that, at 2:pm she could go with me, to the home depot and get what I needed to put the canopy up, then Elsie she said for me to drive my truck up there, that I could ride with her but, what the peoples would have to say, David and Elsie are riding together, I said that she was right, that I would meet her there, she said at 2: now on her break, I said ok that I would let her know, that I was going.

Now I went back home and did not anything before 2: pm. I took my truck and went to Elsie office, and let Elsie know that I was going, she said ok that she would meet me there, I left going to the home depot, got there and park waiting on Elsie to come, later on she came and got the iron stakes, we got 6 of them, then Elsie she said that she had to go, over on to another property for Doris to do something.

Then I said well that was ok, that I could do it myself see her later, she said after she finish she was coming right back, then she left. I went back to the complex and, start putting up the canopy after I started, some would see me working they would ask, did I need some help, I said yes that I do you are going to help me, one said yes that he was coming right back, he live in the same building that I live, I said to myself right.

Now Theron he saw me and said that did I, want to go with him to get some donuts, I said that I was busy and could not go, I keep on working later on Miss Annett, she sit out there with me talking, then Theron he came back with some donuts, and said this was for me because he was no able to help, I start laughing and kept on working, later on Elsie she came back I had the tent up, and was cleaning up the area.

Elsie she said it look good and that she was trying to get back, and who hope me anybody, I said you know it was no one that wanted to help, I said Theron he brought me some donuts want some, and that there was another guy from building 3, he was coming back you know how that was, she said yes thank David Elsie she left, and said for me to come by the office before I go, I said ok.

After I finish and went to the office, Elsie she call the guy to let him know that, it was up and talk to David he knows, Elsie she hand me the phone, I talk to him and let him know how and what, I had did he said ok thank that we all, should be very happy to have Elsie with us, I said that he and I know that, then I gave the phone back to Elsie, she said to me come back before she get off work, I said ok that I would be back.

Now on Saturday Elsie she gets off at 5: pm. I went back about 4: because she had to lock the door, after that she had so much work she had to do, otherwise she could not do her own work, after going to another complex to work, she was behind in her own work, I stayed with her she didn't get off then, until 7:30pm then she said to me, see me on Tuesday. I said ok and have a good weekend, she left and I went back home.

Now on that Monday I was waiting on the mailman to come, later he came and left I got mind and Miss Queen mail, took Queen mail to her and put up some water, for her and was going back home, I said to myself no that, I was going to see if Theron was at home, to see if he want to move that tv now, he had ask me before he wanted to move it.

Chapter 9

S O I WENT TO THE elevator and got on and went to the 2nd floor, that is where Theron stay, I got there and knock on the door, Theron he open the door, I said hay man how are you doing, you want to move that tv now I have time, he said yes man come on in, I went inside and went to his bedroom, to see what and how I was going to move the tv. then I unplug the tv and took it into the living room.

Now after I got the tv all plug in, I found out that he need another cable on it, I said that I think that I have one at home, I told Theron that I would be right back, I went home to get the cable to hook up Theron tv. on the way back I was going to the elevator, I saw Miss Jenson she ask me did I have a minute, I said yes what is it, she said that Mr. Jenson and her want to thank me, I said what for? She said because I put that canopy up out there, I said ok thank then I went back to Theron apartment.

The door Theron had left it open for me, I went and put that cable on I saw that, I need a splitter I had one at home, I told Theron that I would be right back. I went and got it and came back, and got Theron tv right, then I said to

Theron that the tv was ok now, he said David man thank you, I said hay man glad to help, and then I went home to my soaps.

The next day Annett she wanted me to take her, to get some ice tea every time she and I go to Wal*mart, they was out of the tea she like, so I was telling her about the food 4 less store, that I had seen it there. So now she wants to go to the food 4 less.

So I did that for her and came back home, later on that day my next door neighbor Jennet, and I was sitting out like she and I do some time, almost every day after 3: pm because she like to watch the same soaps, the same as I do she and I watch the same ones, she and I be out talking about those soaps, what was happen and what she and I, trying to see what the writer was going to, let us see now.

Jennet and I was sitting talking, she said where are Elsie, I said that I don't know, they think that I should know, Sheller she was I guess getting off work, she was getting out of a vehicle like, she do every time I see her at that time. The day before her, Sheller had taken up a collation, that James father had pass in L.A. he had already told me that before, James and I talk.

And Elsie and I was talking in her office, I brought up that James father had pass, Elsie she said see that I didn't get that from her, I said o no James he told me himself, Elsie said and they always saying that she, tell me everything what was in this office, I said who ever said that tell them that I said, that was a lie.

Now Sheller she was at the gate to come in, she was saying something to me, I could not hear her and that it was so rude, to talk loud out to someone. Jennet she look at me, I look back to Sheller and said to her that I, could not hear her she was acting ghetto. She got closer to where I was at; she didn't even speak to Jennet that was so rude.

Sheller she start talking about Miss Queen, that she was taking up collation for James, and Miss Queen she didn't want to give one, I said hold on now Queen she didn't have to give, only if she wanted to that was her money. Sheller she sure enough got ghetto, I saw Elsie coming in with her vehicle and park, Sheller she got loud. I said to her Sheller leave that along, she kept on talking and talking.

Now Elsie she was out of her vehicle, and coming over to where I was, Sheller she kept on talking loud, I said to Sheller why don't you leave that along, Elsie she walk around me where an ash tray, was sitting to put cigarette buts in, she put her hand on my shoulder, and put out her cigarette Sheller she was leaving, walking away and still talking about, Miss Queen I just look at her, Elsie she said to me are you ok. I said yes that I was ok then Elsie she, went back to her office, Jennet and I was still out there talking, I start thinking about how Sheller was, peoples always talk about God and Jesus, how good they are, what about you God and Jesus are in you, and if they was in some I can't see them, God and Jesus only show themselves, through you.

Now the smoking band is all the news and the woman that I know are in my news, talking about what they don't know, they don't know me. They just have to have something to talk about, speculation. They might talk about me where as it was good or bad, if they do I would know about it the who, want and what it was and should be, I will hear about it some way or the other, it will get back to me, I might not say anything else about it, but I would know.

Miss Elizabeth, Elsie and I was sitting out talking, I said well there was another rumor, going around. Elsie said what was that, I said that she and I was marry because, I will do anything for you like a husband, would do for his wife. Elsie said well I am your wife and I, I said yes you are in my heart, but not on paper.

Elsie said to me and Elizabeth yes and others, on the weekend she was and the others days, for someone else. now I am always thinking about my pass, and how I treated some women that I am not proud about, now that Elsie have come here I saw something in her, that I could love and make believe that, she are with me and I can make up the wrong, that I had did in my pass, and leave the other along." If it was not broken don't fix it" she and I think get along good together.

Now this other lady that I use to be with, she was on my mind her name is Jackie Child, she and I had a kind of good pass, she was on my mind I found out, that she was back in Kentucky staying there, before I had talk to my brother Robert from Chicago, that use to work with me, to see if someone know how to get in touch with Jackie.

Robert said that Pam, Jackie Child niece she work in the basement, that he would let Pam know that, I was trying to find Jackie, I said ok then I ask about Denise, Miss Trurell and Betty Miller, Robert said that Miss Trurell and Betty

Miller they are standing there, I said O yes let me talk to them, Robert he did that I talk to Trurell and Betty Miller, she said that she talk to Jackie sometime, I said will she call her and have Jackie to call me, that she was on my mind, Betty said ok then Betty gave me her phone number, to call her sometime, I said that I would do that.

Now I never heard anything from Jackie Child, until I call Betty Miller on December the 9th. Betty and I talk for about a half hour, she gave me Jackie Child phone number, I said that I was going to call her, and I thank Betty Miller for the phone number, then I ask how was my ex-boss lady Laura, and the others that I had doing with, Betty said that they was ok, I said ok Betty that I was going to call Jackie now, she said when you talk to Jackie, tell her that she Betty are doing find, and that she are always thinking her, I said that I would do that talk to her Betty later.

Now the peoples that gave us the complex that 3rd canopy, that is with the marathon that was going on, the 10th they was asking for some voluntary, to help give out water to the running, I told Elsie that to sign me up, she said that she had already did that, then she gave me a paper to sign I did, and that was that.

On the morning of the 10th Elsie she had got those that she could rely on, she know that I was going to be there, and there was Mary Helen, Blackwell, Louse, Miss Jenson, Lorraine, Toni, Elsie and some others was there with us out there, I can't think about their names right now, but I know the faces. We were out there on Martin L. King Blvd. And Washington, in front by the bank of America at 5:30am that Sunday morning, we had to pour up water in cups, when the running came by and wanted water, we hand it to them and they keep on going passing through.

That morning day, I fill up many cups of water for those runner, when the come through running and need water, we hand it to them while they are passing through. I had fun myself I saw Elsie she had a brome, in her hand I smile and said, what she have a brome in her hand, she don't know what to do with it, then she came to the end of the table, where I was at and ask me was I ok, I said yes, Elsie said this is fun don't I think so, I said yes it was as long she was ok, Elsie she start saying water here, get your water here water in the hole, I start smiling as I was pouring the water.

Now I wanted to say something else to her about that, now you don't know what I am talking about. Channel 8 was covering the marathon, now I had heard Miss Blackwell said that, Elsie she and Toni was ready to leave, and that she and Mary Helen and Louse, was staying I said to myself, I better leave now also otherwise, I can't get back home I don't have my truck.

So I look over to the bank I saw Toni and Elsie, they was ready to leave I went over there, and ask Toni could I hitch a ride with her, she said sure, I got in and went to where we live, Toni she could not get to close to our complex, because the streets was still block, so Lorraine and I with the others came with Toni, we had to walk the rest of the way, to the complex others peoples was out cheering, for the runner.

Now after I got back going to the lobby, James he was on the phone then I heard him say, did you want to talk to him then he gave me the phone, I said hello, it was Elsie on the phone, she ask me to try and get in touch with Louse, and let her know that she just didn't leave her, that she had got a call from her boss, that she had to go and get ready and come to work, I said that I would try to get in touch with her.

Elsie she said ok call her back and let her know, before she get to work, I said ok that I will call her back. I went and found Kopoe she was at her dad apartment, I spoke to her dad and ask her, did she have a way to get in touch with Miss Louse, Kopoe said yes and that she had saw me and Lorraine on tv. I smile and said O yes, then I explain to Kopoe why I was trying to get in touch, with Miss Louse.

Kopoe she said that Monique "Miss Louse" she will find a way back but she will try, to get in touch with her and let her know, I said ok thanks then I went back home, and call Elsie and let her know that, I had got in touch with Kopoe, and she would call Miss Louse and let her know, that Elsie just didn't leave her, she had to come to work, Elsie she said to me thank you David, I said anytime there was a game on tv.

After I had call Elsie and talk to her, I start watching the football game, I start thinking about Miss Jenson, what is her game why she want to think me, for what I do for others, she always say that her and Jim want to think me, for putting up the canopy now after the marathon, she are saying thanks she don't have to do that, because Elsie she put me on the sheet, for the marathon and she ask me to put up that canopy, she had already thank me, that was thanks enough.

David L. Marshall

You see I am no fool about what they are thinking about, some want me to go back as the president, of the tenant council. When I was in there, I tried to treat everybody the same, I walk around the complex all the time, when someone needed me I was there for them, I took my own money with Miss Russell and Miss Elizabeth, and cook out two times a month, to raise money for the council.

Now they Misst that but what they want from me, they was saying that I was stealing the money, what money how can I steal my own money, so I now keep to myself doing what I have to do, for myself and the ones that appreciate me, so when they had me they didn't appreciate me, now I am still doing what make me happy, and if you want to be happy make your own, I still love me and now you want to think me, why?

My other friend Marilyn she wanted to go to the store, that Sunday morning of the marathon, but she waited until that Monday morning, so on that day I took Marilyn to the store, and came back home I call Toney, that make up my T. shirt. And made an order for 30 more T. shirts for passing through, then Miss Annett she had to go to Wal*Mark, I did that for her she don't want to take the cat bus.

Now there is another lady that live in here, I want give her name. She and I was outside talking about, how peoples are especially the ladies, she was saying that they want talk to her, why. Then she said is it because she sits and talk to me, that she had told her daughter that she only had one friend in here, and that is David.

Then I said well don't let other get you down, be yourself because peoples are going to be peoples, and they are going to do what they need to do, no matter how or why they do it, just be your own self. What can you do about why peoples are the way they are, then she said even the lady that be in the office, every time she see her and me out talking, she give her a sour look why, I said don't worry about them.

Then I said that I hear what they are saying about Elsie and me, but they don't know me and it was not what, they are thinking in their mind, they are thinking about sex not about love only. Now to me I am a good friend of Elsie, if they think otherwise then God bless them, and me to smile.

On December the 14th 06 I wrote "a user" everyone is a user, God use Jesus, Jesus use me, I use you, the devil he is a user, and we all use someone or something. On the 15th we had our inspection, Doris she did it this time, man the peoples that live in here, the ones who didn't have their apartment together and clean, now you know the stove, top of the stove, dishwasher and refrigerator was Doris concern, if they was clean you pass, if not she was coming back to see if, you did it.

Now this is life the way I see this, a father he will drop any and everything, for his daughter. Now if she had a man in her life she should not, need your father the man in her life, he take over for the father she are her man responsible, he are the man who are sleeping with her, do all and everything for her not the father.

My daughter she needed me to help her to move something, she and her old man and his father, came but they needed the dolly they didn't need me, that was ok because Elsie she had her meeting for that day, and I didn't want to Misst that.

Now every 2nd Wednesday my check it get in the bank, I make sure that all of my bills was paid, on the 20th Doris they gave the tenant a Christmas dinner, Toni and the others tenants hope to cook the dinner, Doris and Frank gave the money for the dinner, they do that every holiday, now I didn't go to the thanksgiving dinner.

One thing I don't eat that much is one reason, now I see how some peoples are they, treat me as they don't like what I am doing, or what I want to do because, I am a person a man that want something in life. And jealous has sit into some of them, and I see that so I stray away and stay at home, and do what God and Jesus want me to do.

If a friend need me I will be there for them, Elsie she said that Doris ask about me, she wanted to know why didn't I come to the dinner, Elsie she said that she told Doris that I had another commitment, now she didn't lie I did. Now with the Christmas dinner, some ask me was I coming to the dinner, I said no I don't think so because I am so behind, with the second book of mind, and have a good time.

Later on while the dinner was still going on, Elsie she calls me and asks me why, I was not at the dinner with my family. I told Elsie that I was working, she said put it down and come on, that they was waiting on me, I said ok that I was on my way. So I close my computer and went to the lobby, for my family dinner.

After I got into the lobby, it don't take me to long to see or know, what I need to see or know, some was glade I came in some was not to thrill, I saw that when I came into the lobby, and took a short look in there, I went and look into Elsie office it was full, of peoples I wanted her to know that I was at home.

Then I start to mingle with those that was there, I saw Mr. Maze I have seen him for a long time, he and I embrace then I ask him, how was marry life. He said it was ok he would survive, then he ask me how was I doing, I said that I was bless then I said that, the computer man and I if you didn't hurry up and, come from Africa he and I was going to send for him, Maze he start laughing and went back to Elsie office, I went back mingle to the peoples that was eating.

Miss Blackwell she ask me did I want her to fix me a plate, I said no food then I said ok give me, a piece of that cake that was all I need, she gave me some cake, I start messing with Miss Bill, I told her that she had thrown me away, but I had another one to take her place, then peoples start laughing Miss Bill she said, that was ok that I would be back, I said you are right because I love her.

Then Theron he gave me a reward. Elsie she saw that and came to me, and said give that back to her, I gave it to her. Then Elsie said that, someone else was coming by, and she was waiting on him. She was waiting on the guy that was with the marathon, then Elsie she got a phone call that, he was on his way.

Sure enough the guy he came, then Elsie she did the reward the way it should be, then she gave it to me, and she had one for Toni and the guy with, the marathon. Mind read, Teamwork December 2006 to: David Marshall thank you for your support. From Louise shell senior apartment resident.

Now that made me feel so good, I told the resident that I will be there for them, anytime that they need me for anything, then Theron said that in that envelop they gave to me, it was a $1000,00 in it that he had to go to the airport. I said now if there was not a $1000, 00 in there that, Theron he better start walking to the airport, everybody start laughing, then we all sit around laughing and talking.

Later on that day I went to the lobby, I saw and heard some didn't like it because, I got a reward one said to another that, they didn't give her a reward after she had, work so hard for the Thanksgiving dinner, then one lady she ask me David, was it a $1000, 00 in that envelop, I said no Theron he was just funning, one said that David and Elsie was getting it on, that was why he got a reward.

Later on that day my cousin Joyce she call me, and she are a sweetheart she always, be trying to help me with a job, now I appreciate her for that but like, I told Joyce that I was trying to finish my second book, and if I go to work. It would set me back from what God and Jesus. I needed me to do for myself.

Then Joyce said that Roseland have her aunt here, that are living with her that she was, from Tennessee and that they want me to meet her, now I am the person who don't want to, break someone heart, or Missuses anyone. I said ok but I want make no promise to anyone, or for anything but I will meet her, because I already have someone in my heart, Joyce said that was ok just meet her, I said ok.

Now at 5:30pm. I walk around to exercise myself, and see if Elsie she needed me for anything. As I was walking by her office, she still had the guy from the marathon in her office, I said to myself that she was ok, I can go back and make myself useful, because anyone who know me and Elsie, would not Mistreat her but sometime, you have to stay up on the ones you love, and don't let no one Missuses them.

Miss Queen she call me late afternoon, she and I was talking she are just like my mom. Miss Queen sometime she think like, the others lady that live in here. Queen and I start talking about Elsie not bad, if it was true it would be good for me, how good and how big her heart and how smart she are, and how she try to help others, I am the same way.

Then I said that the peoples that live in here, they sure think that Elsie and I are going together, Elsie she have a soul. Peoples see that good soul through sex; I see it through her eyes and her smile. That is the only thing that I want for Elsie, I think that she are a friend of mind, I can't lose that just for sex, I can get sex from another woman and go back home. But a friend is hard to find.

Miss Queen and I talk for about an hour, Queen she still said that Elsie love me, and that one of these days that Elsie and I, was going to get marry. And that she was a woman and she know that, and that if she live long enough that she will see, I said ok Miss Queen if that happen, that I wanted her to give me away, she said well that she will see, then Queen said that, because David you love Elsie and she love you.

Then I said Miss Queen I only can speak for myself, yes I do love Elsie that is no secret. But I can't speak for Elsie, you have to get that from her but to me, Elsie she don't see me in that away, Queen said well you will see, that she was a woman and another woman, she knows talk to me later, but she was still going to give me to Elsie, I said ok good luck for you, and for me.

Now I had some ticket from the guy from the marathon, he gave them out for peoples that want them, for Santa village I had call my friend Coco, to see if they wanted them so that they could take the kids, to Santa village. Coco she said yes then she and I talk for a while; I said that I would bring them to her in the morning, after I took Miss Queen to take care of her business. I would be there then, Coco said ok see me then.

The next morning I took Queen to take care of her business, so I took Queen with me to take the tickets to Coco, I got there and gave Coco the tickets, I said that I could not stay because I had, someone with me and that I was going to, take her back home and do something in my book, Coco said how are your book doing, I said it was doing pretty good, now I have to finish the second one, and that I would talk to her later, she said ok then Queen and I left, and came back home.

Now Elsie she had someone in her office talking, it was a man and a woman, the man he was black and the woman she was white, I had come into the lobby Elsie she call me

David, I said yes, now Kopoe she was in the lobby also watching tv. she said David sit down, now I am a man the last time I look at me, I can make my own decision, I went into the office to see what Elsie wanted with me.

When I got into the office, Elsie she induced me to them, Elsie she said passing through ant you, writing a book about Louise Shell Senior apartment, I said yes I am this is the second one, then I explain about what my grandmother, had raise me from a child now I am a man. we talk for a little while" now I can't think of the man name right now" but what I could see of him he was ok. I was telling him about the t. shirts, that I make up about passing through, the guy he ask me did I have one of the book, I said yes that I do, he said that he want one, I said ok that I will be right back.

Now I went home and got a book and came back, and gave it to the guy he thumb through the book, and said that he had a tv and a radio show, that he want to have an interview with me, he ask me to take the book and highlight, in there and what pages it was, so that he would know what I wanted to talk about in the book, and he want have to read the whole book. I said ok when he wanted it, he ask Elsie she said that she would be as a manager. He said yes, Elsie she said that it would be ready on Tuesday.

Then I went home and got 4 t. shirts and gave them to the guy and the lady, he said that he could ware these at the gym when he go. I said ok that I would love that, then they had other things to talk about, Elsie she said to me get out now, they had work to do, then Elsie she said to me to meet her at 2:pm for a cigarette. I said ok then I said to the man and the lady, nice to meet them and said to Elsie, see her at 2: pm then I left out and went back home, and started doing what the man needed, from my book.

Now Elsie when she have anything, that the tenant should know she type it up, and post it on every door in every building, the exit doors. So that the tenant can read it, at 2: pm I went back to meet Elsie. The guy and the lady they was still in Elsie office, so I sit out there and waited on Elsie, smoking a cigarette I saw Miss Lee driving to the exit gate, I spoke to her and ask her how was my buddy Mr. Lee doing.

Miss Lee she said that she was on her way, to the hospital now that they had call her, to come right away they had call code blue. I was speechless all I could say was O no, then she drove off and left, I was still on the outside waiting on Elsie, and saying to myself I hope Mr. Lee will be ok.

Then Elsie and her peoples came out from the office, and came out Elsie she said, that it was a long time for 2:pm she was so sorry, I said that was ok then I told Elsie, what Miss Lee had said about Mr. Lee. Then the guy and I was standing on the side walk talking, about my book and some of the book two, how my life had change and how, I love to help peoples who appreciate it.

Then the guy said that he had to go because, he had a meeting to go to that they was, waiting on him. Then Elsie and the lady was sitting in the sitting area, they walk over to where he and I was standing, we all kept on talking the guy he said David, man he have to keep in touch with me, I said that when he need me let Elsie know.

Elsie and I was still out talking, she ask me was I coming to the Christmas party, I said what party that I didn't know about it, she said why didn't I know because Lorraine and she, had put up the notice on the doors about it, I said that I didn't read it because, I had already read the others and I didn't look, Elsie she said ok right you are coming to this party, then she was going back to her office, I said what time, she said at 5:pm and you be there, I look at her and smile and said ok mom.

Now it was almost 5:pm I was still sitting out there, I saw Miss Lee driving through the gate, she had her daughter driving they stop by me, I said how was my buddy, Miss Lee she said that Mr. Lee pass. I said that she and the family had my comedian. Miss Lee said thank you David, then I said that if anything she need me for, let me know. She said ok that she will then they pull off.

This was on December the 23rd. Mr. Lee pass on to a better life, I went inside of the lobby and, went to Lorraine apartment and ask Karen could, PL go to the store with me to get something, for the party because I don't want to go empty handing, then I said hi to Lorraine, Karen she said that it was ok for PL to go with me, and to bring some ice back because we didn't have any, I said ok PL and I went to the store.

After PL and I came back I had got a case of soda, and some potato chips I put the sodas, on ice I saw Elsie coming from her office smiling, I told Elsie what Miss Lee had said to me about, Mr. Lee had pass I didn't bell it out because, Elsie she is the manager so she went, to Miss Lee apartment if I had told all the others, the house would be full to me, right now

Miss Lee didn't need a house full, so I only let the manager know.

After the Christmas party had started they had all kind of food, we all was sitting standing around talking, laughing having some fun, I did tell some like Miss Bill and Miss Russell, that Mr. Lee had pass then Elsie she had come back, into the lobby she would let them know, if they ask, now Karen she went and got a CD player, she got it from Betty, now Betty and another so call friend of mind and Betty, they are friends also they had stop speaking to me, why, don't ask me because I don't know why.

But I do have my own opinion why. Karen she said that she didn't have any tapes, I said that I had some but they was blues tapes, she said that was ok she love some blues sometime, so I went home and got some tapes and came back, I said that, I want mess with that tape player, Karen said why she would use it, I said that the lady that own that player, she don't talk to me anymore, Karen said put the music on that, if anyone said anything talk to her, I put on my tapes.

While the music was playing, there is another guy that live in here, he use to box as he said that but, everyone else have their own opinion like mind, he only was a sprawling partner. Some reason now he don't like me, once before he and I would laugh, talk and sometime go to the casino, and come back until I put that book out, he start acting funny like I care, another lady ask me one day why don't John like me, I said that I don't know and really don't care.

Then she and I was still talking she said that John was jealous, she said that John he always walk around with those pitches, that he have showing them all the time, that she are tried looking at them. Then she said to John why don't he do, the same as David did put them into a book, then she said that John said to her, don't say anything to him about David, she said that she ask him why, was he jealous of David.

Now at the party I tried talking to him but, he was not interesting in what I had to say, I said forget him who are he nothing but a cripple boxer, now tonight was the night before Jesus birthday, and that I was going to have me some fun, Lorraine she had some rum I had me some rum and coke, later the music start sounding good, took me way back in my pass, another lady she was playing the music now, after she go there.

She put on a tape from the temptation and David Ruffen, my girl. There was young guys at the party also I start singing my girl, as I was singing the kids start backing me up, they was singing and dancing with me, everyone else was singing also with me, I was putting those words to only one, she know who we all had a good time, until it was over.

When I thought it was over I was going home about 8:30pm. I saw Karen and Elsie sitting out at the sitting area talking. I didn't bother them, I went on home.

The rest of the night after someone had pick me up, I had a good time, later on I got back home before I went to sleep, I said happy birthday to Jesus.

That morning I got up, and said again happy birthday Jesus, and talk to my father God. That before last night Betty and

Lorraine, they were not speaking to me. But God you are a forgiven God, I went up to them and hug them, and said merry Christmas. And I had talk to my play sister Bobby Jean in Chicago, to say merry Christmas to her then I let everyone else that, was at the party say marry Christmas to Bobby Jean, now to now I am ok and I am bless.

I thank God and Jesus everything he done for me. Weaken me up this morning, for me to see the sunlight and for me, to breathing the air that he put in here, thank you father for everything, then the phone ring I answer it was Elsie.

That Sunday, Elsie she had come to the office for a little while, she call to say to me that I was a party animal, I said good morning that I was just thinking about her, I felt some hasty, Elsie she said that she and Lorraine was just talking about, how much fun I had last night, I said O yes didn't we have fun! Elsie said O yes then she said that she was not, going to be here at work long, that she had something that she had to get out, and then she was leaving. Then she said you party animal, I said ok merry Christmas, she said back to me marry Christmas and, she and I hung up the phone.

In my mind I said that as long as she had fun, that was all to me matter. Because all of my fun came from her, she did that for me. Later on I was watching tv on the news, that James Brown Mr. Please, please singer had pass on to a better place. I said rest in peace James Brown.

I had talk to the friend of Elsie, when we were talking about the interview, of book passing through. I took all of the 25th working on that, so it would be ready for him, when he asks Elsie for it would be in her hand, to give it to him.

That Tuesday I had it ready to give it to Elsie, I found out that Elsie she was not at work, so I took the papers and the book back home, so if and when she come back, she would have it so I did the same things that I do, each and every day.

Then later on that day I saw Elsie, she had come by here I ask her, did she want the talk show work now, she had so much work she said, make her remember. I told her I saw that she had other things on her mind; she had work up to her neck she was busy, she told me how busy that she was, and that we can wait until after New Year. I said ok that it was ready for her, she said ok then she close the office door.

Sometime I will be at home talking to my God and Jesus, I am in school. And thinking from my heart and mind, I said that when I see someone who has pass, they lay them out in a suit, not me. I want to be laid out with one of my T. shirt, passing through on me because as you see me laying there, and you see that is all I am doing is passing through, don't cry smile because I am at home with my father.

On the 28th Miss Grand she was coming back, to re inspect some of the apartment, that was in violation before she had, already inspect before one was mind, a little dust was on the refrigerator mind was, some had grease on the hood over the stove, and refrigerator, that day Miss Grand didn't come, but I had wipe off my refrigerator if she came.

Now that night the wind was blowing so hard, I start thinking about the canopy that I had just put up, I know all about how the wind blew down the other two, I could not sleep because I was thinking about that canopy, will it stand while the wind was blowing so hard, until tomorrow I was going to tie it down, with some ropes I had in my truck, to stop the wind blowing it down.

Now I got up because the wind was blowing so hard, it was blowing so hard it sound like, dogs howling. I walk out to see about it was ok still standing, I went back home and went back to bed, now the last time before the lobby open, I had went back out there about 5:am. To take a look at it was still standing, I said it stood through all that wind howling, like a dog it was blowing hard, I said that I do be leave that it will still be standing, later on I went back home to bed, there was someone with me in my bed.

That morning I got up and my company had left, then I went back out to check on the canopy, it was about 9: am I saw that the canopy was blowing down, the wind had pick up some more, after I had saw that it was down I said O no, not this one also maybe that something, are trying to tell us something that, we don't need one out there.

Now I know that the canopy was made with, some soft material that cannot stand with that wind long, then I said well God gave it and God took it away, there was a lady that live in building two, she said to me did I see that tree in the back, had been blowing down, I said know I didn't see it how big was it, she said that it was pretty big size, then the lady she got her mail and left.

Then on my way to my apartment I went to the back, of building two and I saw the tree, it was kind of big I went on home. Later on I saw Toni on the outside, talking on her phone then I heard Toni said, do you want to talk to him. Then Toni she hand me the phone it was Elsie, she ask me could I get the tree out from the street, I said that I need a power saw to cut it up, also that I need some heavy gloves because, that tree had thorn on it, then Elsie said that maybe that Toni could, look into the storage maybe one is in there, I said ok that we would see.

Then Toni and I went into every closet that had, looking for a power saw we could not see one, then I said to Toni did she have any heavy gloves, that I think that I had a hack saw, in my truck that might do the job, then Toni she had some rubber gloves, I took them and went to my truck, to find the hack saw.

Then I found the saw and went to the tree, I tried to cut the tree I was not doing anything, I said man it would take me two weeks, to cut that tree up then I put my hack saw back, into my truck and said to myself, I tried to cut it up but with the saw, I had to work with it want do it, but I did try.

Now after all week the heart of mind, she was doing her job here and others place also, then on that Saturday the 30th she was here at work, then she call me that she need me, I said that I was on my way, I got there she needed me to put some desks, into her vehicle I told her about the tree, and the hack saw then I put the desks into her vehicle. She showed me some pictures of her niece and nephew, they was here in Vegas.

Now while I was looking at the pictures, she said that I can't see the pictures because I, didn't have my glasses on, then I said that I saw them, they look like some good kids, before she left I said happy New Year to her, she said happy New Year, then I went back home and fix myself some food to eat.

That New Year eve I was going down town, and celebrate New Year eve but I said, that the streets was going to be full, and that there was no place to park because, they had close off the streets and I will, have to walk so for far to get to the union palace, and peoples was going out to have a good time, the same as I was going to do celebrate, and have a good time and when that time, to say happy New Year to someone.

Now I start thinking then I said no that, I don't want to wave through that crowd, I desire to stay at home, and make my own New Year resolution. Because I was at home alone at 12: midnight, I made my resolution with God and Jesus, better myself this year.

Now in 07 I want to be the best, you know peoples I don't know but I, am going to give you my opinion that, when someone are trying to be a friend, to another person call them, talk to them, do for them and will do anything to help someone" but kill" I want do that for you, I didn't put that life of a person here, if I take it from them, I can't give it back to them, or their family. Anything else I want to do for you, it would because I want to do it, and ask for anything or nothing in return.

Now Miss Queen she let me read a black bible, I read about the Garden of Eden was in Africa, from Adam his bones and flesh after a woman came, from his bone and flesh, the serpent must deceitful creature that God made, woman pick the fruit in the midst of the garden, listen to the serpent.

Noah and the great flood, Noah had three sons, Shem, Ham and Japheth was responsible for the father of all nations, Japheth was traveled north, of the Mediterranean Sea he became the father of Caucasian race in Europe.

Shem and ham move southeast and southwest Babel area, Shem occupied Syria, Assyria, the Persian Gulf, and a large part of Arabia, he also the father of the Hebrews, all are black, / from the book of black biblical heritage. By Dr. John L. Johnson, published and distributed by: Lushena books 1804-06 West Irving Park Rd. Chicago, Ill. 60613.

This is a new year now it is 07. I was walking around the complex as I always do, every evening and sometime I will walk around, anytime of night now no matter what time it was, I saw Miss Lee about 6:pm she was with guess, of hers getting out from her vehicle. I ask Miss Lee what time and the day of Mr. Lee funeral, she said it was going to be on the 3rd at 10am. Then she told me where it was going to be, and then she asks me was I going to be there! I said yes I was going to be there, she said thank David.

So I left and kept on walking around then I went back home, and did everything that I needed for myself. The next day it was on the 2nd of January 07, after working on my book I, went outside I saw Jennet she, was sitting out there she and I was talking, she ask me where was Elsie, I said how do I know, then I saw Elsie coming in her vehicle, through the gate I said to Jennet here come Elsie now, if she need her.

Jennet said that she don't want her, then Elsie she slow down and said to me, David meet her by the tree, I said ok then I went to the back between building 2 and 3, where the tree had been blowing down, after I got there Elsie she said that she wanted, to get the tree so that peoples can drive by it, I said they had drove through before now, and that I had tried to cut it up but, a hack saw would not do if for me.

Then she had a wire cutter in her hand she, could not open it she ask me to open it, I said what was she going to do with that, she said that she was going to cut up this tree, I said not with that she want, then she start cutting on the tree, now think about you got a wire cutter, trying to cut up a tree. I said that I had some ropes in my truck that, I was going to tie the ropes around the tree, and my truck and pull it away to that corner, out of the street then I went and got my truck.

When I came back I tie the tree with the rope, and to my boat ball and said to Elsie, get back that I was going to start pulling, she did not get out of my way saying that, she was giving the tree a haircut, then I start pulling the tree the rope broke, I tried it three times the rope broke. Then I thought about the chain the Lucky had, now I have it so I went and got it, and came back and chain up the tree to my truck, while I was doing that, I saw Elsie stuck one of those thorn in her hand, I told her to move that the tree would stick her, she was hard headed I wanted to laugh, but if I did laugh down on that tree I was falling.

After I got back into my truck, I said to Elsie once more move that, I was going to start pulling on the tree, she said that she could be in her office, getting her rent money orders. I said go on that I will take care of this, she have a hard head like a goat, as the tree was moving while I was pulling it, Miss Elsie she was walking with the tree, saying that she was giving the tree a haircut, then I pull the tree to where I wanted and stop.

Then I got out of the truck and ask Elsie, was it far enough out from the street, she said yes that someone was coming tomorrow to cut it up, then she left saying thank David, I said no problem then I came back into my apartment, and put up that chain.

On the 3rd of January I got dress to go to Mr. Lee funeral, now the other day Miss Bill and I, was talking she ask me was I going to Miss Lee, husband funeral. I said yes is she going, she said yes, I said that I didn't know how to get to the Church; Miss Bill said that I could ride with her. So I went outside to wait on Miss Bill.

Then Miss Bill came I got in her vehicle with her, she said now where are Mr. And Miss Jenson, they want to follow her to the Church, they don't know how to get there, then I look back and saw Mr. Jenson vehicle, I said here they are now then we went to Mr. Lee funeral. Then we all went into the Church.

Now Mr. And Miss Jenson I am trying to figure this out, going in the Church I almost walk on her feet, she was like she was lost or she was afraid. The funeral started and after the all service was over, now it was time to view the body, they always take the viewing by the rows, it was our row now Miss Jenson, she just stood there taken her own time to move, I took the service form in my hand and just, push on her a little to let her know, if she was not going to view the body, then let us do it for our self.

After everything was over with and, the family was going out the Church, Miss Jenson she said David would I keep an eye on Jim, I said ok but for what he can walk by himself, so after going outside by the steps, I ask Jim could he get off the steps by himself, he said O yes he was ok he then, got some steps in his step, I said to Miss Bill the Jenson they was a Puzzle, for me he was ok then we got to Miss Bill vehicle, and got in.

Miss Bill she had to wait on the Jenson, to get into their vehicle to show them, how to get back home then Jenson they got into their vehicle, and we left.

Later on that day I had a bad feeling, now I was not sick but in my heart, it felt as my heart was jumping and jumping, it was jumping and jumping then it would slow down. I started talking to my father. That my heart something was wrong and, if he was ready for me take me, that I was ready to meet him.

Then I got ok and I said, God and Jesus want me to slow down, relax everything was going to be alright, God told me that my heart was jumping and skipping, that is what a son do when he ask his father for help, when I needed him his hand was bigger than mind are, so what I do is put it in father hand and leave it along.

The next day I had to take Annett to Wal*Mart, so I did that and came back home, and I didn't do too much the same as some days.

Now I had got a letter from my truck insurance, they wanted to just talk to me to see, if anything they could help me with, I saw a Mr. Alfonso Greer from the farmers insurance, so I went to the interview and found out, that my insurance had went up for $10.00 more a month, I got a raise from my social security with $31.00, my insurance now are going up, there are always ways to take it from you.

Now I don't know what it is about Elsie. For some reason I can't just walk away from her, every time she Mistreat me wrongful, I always say that I am not going to, do anything for her any more, but look like someway or somehow I always say that, I am not going to look out for her anymore, because she don't want me to, I find myself feeling so good when she call me, that she need me there I go. But I did make a promise to her son, what it is now that I am being tested, I am being tested by God and Jesus, I can't touch her in bed, or I can't walk away from her, and I know that she had already told me, that she don't love anybody.

The day I was sitting at home on that Saturday, just before the super bowl play off, thinking about life and how much money, that I was going to put on the bears, if they win the play off. Now I am a loner if you like me I love you, and if you don't like me that was ok also, now God and Jesus was lonely I know because I am a son.

And a son he is always lonely, some peoples that are around him, they don't know him. All I can say is that I am a son of God, and my big brother is Jesus now mess with me, but every time I think that I had a friend, to love them make them comfortable around me, let them know who I am no one to harm them, just to give love and looking for nothing in return.

And all I want is to love someone, and that love can come from the heart, to be given to you. love is an over flow from my heart of the blood, my father pump through the vain, that is high blood to much blood in the heart, to take it down to where it should be, love someone, help someone, smile, laughing put a smile on the face, let someone know that the soul was happy, with a smile.

That a friend is something that is so hard to find, like a family or a friend I love them, and charity them, a family member is someone that you can't get away from, that came from the blood he or she will be with you for life, now a friend come and they go. When you have a friend you better try, and do your best to keep that, when you lose that it may not be so easy, to get it back.

A lady ask me one day why was I, afraid to make love to her, I said that I was not afraid to fuck her, she said don't say fuck say love, I said that there was a deference, she ask me what was it. I said that if I fuck her all the time, and don't love her now who doing the fucking now. I can love her without fucking her.

A marriage is like maintenance, a carpenter, a bricklayer, electricity, etc. and it break down you have to fix it, you go and get what you need to fix it, make sure you have the right thing to make it right, no matter what ever you needed.

Now I think about my mother now, when she said that she was beating the devil, out from me I was bad as hell, now

I think about my son now, I should have did that to him what my mom, did for me. When I was bad but I didn't do that to my kids, why because I was on the move, passing through looking for what! To this day I still not found it but trouble all I found.

Now my son he is the same as I was, some say that the apple don't, fall to far from the tree, I disapprove of that like I said before, I never been in the system of man, but the system of God this is where I am, and I owe it all to my grandmother and my mother. If I my mother had not did what she did for me, I don't know where this body would be, thank you grandmother and my mother, thank you for everything.

Now Elsie she has been fool by someone, the only way those woman want to be around her is, because I started doing any and everything for her, that she ask me for, and not looking for anything.

Now those that want me in their bed, they don't know that, I don't have to have sex with Elsie, or you to. Because this world is just like a fish bowl, and all we are doing is just swimming around, waiting to get catch by someone or thing. I can get all of the sex I want or need, on the outside and come back home, no one else would know about it but me, and my partner. I can be empty of sex and it want be from you.

Elsie on the 11th of January call me that, she was going to be by herself before, she get off work, I said ok that I would be there for her, she said ok. Then I said to myself any other time, Lorraine, Betty or Glen would be there for her in her office, but all I am is a so call friend, when her friends are not around.

Now being the man I am, I got up and went and waited on a friend, until she got off from work, and make sure that she was inside of her vehicle, going through the gate going home or whatever, she was going after that she was on her own, I went back home and got dress and went out.

One morning I was in the lobby waiting, on the mailman to run it was cold that morning, Elsie she was going to another building, she didn't have on no coat, one of the lady that was in the lobby, said to Elsie you need a coat on that, it was cold and she might get sick, I said that is right then I would have something to say, Elsie said excuse me and what is that. I said that you should have a coat on, Elsie she said that she was grown, I said now I don't have anything to say.

About that I can't say another word keep my mouth close, on the 13th was the monthly management meeting; Elsie said that she needed me to set up the lobby, for her meeting. She knew that I would do that for her, so I did that, and after the meeting was over I took, the chairs back upstairs Elsie said thank you David, I said no problem and went back home, later Elsie and I was on the outside, she ask me how was the meeting, I said it was a good meeting, she said thank for sitting up the lobby, and taken the chairs back, I said your meeting was the only one I go to.

Then Elsie said that is right you only be at the tenant meeting, when she had the floor talking why! I said with you peoples can get answers from, how I can get answer from those who, can't tell me what I need to know.

On Martin Luther King Jr. day, I didn't do anything but work on my book, and lay around the apartment doing anything, on the 17th a buddy of mind name Kevin, his picture is on the back of my first book, now he had to move his things from, the apartment that now he have, I ask Kevin for the address he could not tell me, the address for me to get to where he was, otherwise I would be just riding around, burning gas.

All he could tell me was the street and how to get there, where the complex was at, I said what was the address and the complex name, that I need to have that, he said that there was only one complex there, I can't go with that and don't know where I am going, then I said for him to call me back, before he was ready to move and, leave the address and the name of the complex, if I was not at home leave it on my answer machine.

Now to this day I never got that address to move Kevin, that night God and Jesus came to me, to let me know that I was doing good, and keep it up sooner or later, he was going to let me go from my problem, and see what I was going to do with it, he was telling me that the school was over now, that now I have pass my test, the test of life.

The next day a guy that live here where I live, name or what they call him art, he was going to the store he spoke, I was sitting outside talking to Jennet, I said art are you going to the store, he said yes did he want to bring something back, I said no that I was going to go with him, so I did," now God he will show you thing".

Art and I got to the drug store CVS, I saw Elsie vehicle park I said hum, Elsie is in the store, then I saw her ducking behind a post, I said that I see her then Elsie, she start telling me that they didn't have, the kind of cigarette that she smoke, then she went back into the store, with Art and I she look over the counter and said see, they don't have her brand, I said if she had call me she would had have, the brand that I had a pack in the box for her, but you didn't call me, she said well.

Then I said that when I get back home, I would bring them to her, she said ok that she only had two, and one was broken then she showed it to me. After Art and I got what we went to get, and came back I went home and got a pick of cigarette, and took it into Elsie office, Lorraine she was sitting in there with Elsie, I spoke to Lorraine and hand the pack of cigarette, to Elsie, "she fuck up" by calling me another man name, she said thank you Art man thank you Art, in front of Lorraine trying to be funny, but to me it was not funny, I went outside and sit and lit a cigarette.

That Saturday late evening Marilyn call me, about on Sunday taken her to the store, I said if my buddy Popeye don't call me, to take him to the store I would call her early, and if he want to go I would call her, after I got back home. Marilyn said thank David, she hung up I was watching the Chicago Bulls on tv.

That Sunday morning I got up Popeye didn't call, I waited until I think that Marilyn she was up, I call her and said at 8:30am. Now it was almost 8: am—I would be out on the front by the lobby, to take her to the store, she said ok she would be there. So I took Marilyn to the store, she got what she was getting and we was going, to leave the store my friend name Kim, that work at the Albertson food store, she ask me David was I coming back later, I said no baby not to day that, the playoff game was coming on, Kim said ok have a good game, and see me later.

After I took Marilyn home with her grocers, and got it in her apartment she said thank you David, we all love you I said thank Marilyn, then I left and went home to watch the game, first I put something in the computer before the game start.

That was a good game the bears won, and was going to the Super bowl. To see who was going to play the bears, in the Super bowl. Then I said that Love Smith he is the only, black man to coach the Super bowl, this is History man this is great, now there was other black that coach a team, but not in the Super bowl, Art Shell he was the first black to coach a pro team, no Super bowl. And Doug William he was the first black, to QB. A pro team we are moving on up.

After the other game was over the Colts won, I said man o man this is more History, Toney Dungy black coach the Colts, going to the Super bowl and both coach, are friends and don't live to far away from each other, Chicago to Indianapolis.

On 01-23-07 we got another maintenance man, the other one we had name James he quit, the other one is name David also, Elsie she induce him to me then Elsie she said, David Marshall, we are going to have a cigarette, come and join us and have one, it was right at 12:noon. Now my soaps are on but I will never let Elsie down, for nothing. I said ok see them out there, I put on my shoes and went to where Elise, and David the maintenance man was at outside.

Elsie and David I didn't see after I got there, I went inside the lobby and ask Miss Russell, she was in there where was Miss Elsie, then we saw Elsie coming to her office, I didn't say anything just went on the sitting area, then David he came out he and I start talking, then Elsie she came out side, we all was talking then they got ready to go to work, I said to David that, if he need me call me, then Elsie she said that if she needed anything, then she pointed at me, she would call this man. they went to work I went back home to, my soaps and my book, Later on after 3: pm Jennet, Gloria and I was sitting out talking, Elsie and Lorraine came out to sit out for a little while, Elsie and Lorraine sit at the other table, Gloria said why don't they sit with us, Jennet said yes sit with us.

Elsie she showed me her own match, that she had her own fire that she, could light her own cigarette, Lorraine she laugh and said, now that she had her own she can get smart hum. I said that was right if she wanted to sit over there, be happy ant you happy Elsie, she said yes, I said then that is all it matter.

Elsie then she got up and left going to her office, Lorraine she was still sitting out there, Gloria then said to Lorraine come and sit with us, I said why not we are not going to bite her, Jennet she laugh Lorraine she said, if he bite her she might like it. I could not say a word sometime. You have to keep your mouth close.

Elsie she said something about the valentine day, they was having about what they was going to do, I said yes whatever

I do, nobody will know about it, Elsie said that is right then she look at me, I smile and said don't I know that, is why I don't go to bed with them, because they will tell all.

On 01-24-07 you see why I love Elsie, is because I know her. Just as I know my own self, of what I see when I look into her eyes, face impression, her laughing, and how her inter power, to help someone else, she have a big heart same as I do. Now the others are not for the eyes to see, but what I see I know that because, I am who I am. That is why I just love Elsie so much.

On the 1-28-07 I had a lonely day, watching the basketball game, sometime writing in my book, I know that I am being tested by my father and Jesus, they have given me two chances in my life, to get it right but I mess it up, now I ask them for a third chance to get it right, it is hard and lonely. You see life are like teethe in your mouth, God only gave you two sets of teethe, if you don't take care of them and lose them, the next set you have to pay for them.

Now I have my third chance in life, he gave it to me right in front of my face, and I can't touch it because I think that, I am been tested God answer half of my prayer, the rest of it is up to me. Sometime I do be leave that Elsie she is afraid of me. For some reason like last night, she asks me was I doing anything to night! I said no, she said about the black Historical Society party, that she had tickets for that.

And that they was paid for from Louise Shell, that the party was at the Nevada Partners, she ask me did I know where it was, I said yes it was up the street, she said now are you going, I said yes see her there. I went home to be ready about 6: pm. I got ready and got into my truck, and I was going to the gate, I saw Elsie vehicle trunk up and the front door, of the lobby was wide open, I saw Lorraine and Betty standing by the outside, in front of the hallway outside door talking, I pull in to park to see if Elsie was ok.

Then Lorraine she saw me parking, she start running to the lobby say Elsie, Elsie where are you are you ok, I look and saw Elsie coming I waited, she had a box to hold the door open, after she had lock the door she pick up the box, I saw it was heavy, so I took it from her and put it into the trunk, of her vehicle and close it.

Jackie she live in building two she wanted to get, into the lobby to get her mail Elsie, she said that she could not get back in, because she didn't have her key, then Elsie ask me to go and get Miss Bill, and let her know that we was ready to leave, and that we all could leave together, so I went to find Miss Bill and knock on her side door, she came out to see me, I said that we was waiting on her, Miss Bill said that Elsie had said about 6:pm, I said that we was ready now, she said ok that she was on her way.

Now when I got back to where my truck, I didn't see Elsie then Miss Bill she came, she said now where are Elsie, I said that I don't know may be she, are in Betty apartment. Miss Bill said that she should knock on Betty window, because Elsie said 6:pm we was leaving, then I saw killer coming then Elsie and Lorraine, they was coming also Elsie she ask Miss Bill, could she let killer ride with her and let David ride, with her and Lorraine. So that was what we did.

After we got to Nevada Partners and sign in, and found a table Elsie she said that it was hot in here, I said give me her sweater so I could take off, she said no with a sour look, I said give it to me I would help her, she said no with another sour look, I sit down and let it along. Miss Bill, killer and Lorraine was just looking at Elsie, then Elsie she said something to me I didn't respond, Miss Bill she said she don't blame you Mr. Marshall, all you was trying to do was been nice.

Later on we start getting out food, Miss Grand she came she are Elsie boss, Elsie she was taking picture with killer, Miss Bill and Lorraine, then she ask me to take a picture with her, and the rest, I did then Elsie she took one of mind, then she was trying to show it to me, I said that is ok but on my mind I was trying to see, why did she do that to me why, now all the party was going out from me.

Then Elsie said to Miss Bill to sit there, where I was and take a picture with David, so Bill and I took the picture, I started to get up and leave but I didn't have my truck, so I stayed then killer he found someone that he knew, a woman she was sitting in Elsie seat, Elsie she was standing beside me, I said do she want me to move over, and she would have a seat, Elsie said no that she was going to sit, by Lorraine and that was what she did, Miss Bill she just look and shook her head.

Now after Miss Grand she left and everyone else, was getting ready to leave I was sitting there, I ask Elsie was she ready to leave, she didn't say anything. Now I have to look out for myself, Miss Bill and killer was going out, I got up and went out also, I lit myself a cigarette I said to Miss Bill ok you all didn't let me know that you all, was ready to go what you all was going to leave me, I said that you can bet, that I want get catch like this anymore, I will have my truck with me.

Then Elsie and Lorraine came out like man and woman, and ask me are you ready to go, I said you can bet that I got into the vehicle, we left and came home, I was trying to get out of Elsie vehicle, Lorraine she didn't want to move to let me out, I said Lorraine let me out, she said o then she let me out, I got out and said to Elsie thank you, she said ok then I heard Lorraine said to Elsie, are you going to take her on the back, Elsie said o yes, then I got into my truck and went home, as I was parking I saw Elsie and Lorraine coming, I park and went into my apartment.

After I got in my house I had forgot a phone number, I went back to my truck there was Elsie, and Lorraine sitting talking I got my number, from my truck I saw Elsie coming, she blew her horn while she was leaving, I wave and went inside of my apartment, and made my phone call and wait on my ride.

Now I told my other friend that pick me up, what had happen, she said that woman is a fool, every woman she talk to want to know you, but you want give them the time of the day, even to her now this woman have a chance, with you and she don't want it, David leave that along because she have all the, love that I needed with her, I said that I love her but not that king of way, I could not Miss use her. She said why would I Miss use her, because I can't go to bed with her, she mite hate me later on, she said no way then she said ok, now she see what it was I love Elsie, so much until if I go to be with her, I feel as I was Miss using Elsie, I said right. She said that I can forget that is hard to, beat another woman, that I would be the best to come on and, lay with her, I said that I would keep her in mind, but don't be no fool after I did that.

Now I feel the same pain of the pain, that Jesus felt and still feeling, about how the peoples treated him, but after all Jesus he died for you, he gave up his only life to live again, for you.

Now Jesus is a better man then I. They spit on him, kick him, though rocks on and at him, all he was trying to do was be with you, but instead of leaving him along, and just let him love you, not with sex but just let you love me.

But what did you do other than nailing him to a cross," those was the K. K. K. peoples that hate" what about you, was you one of them.

Jesus he died for you hanging on that cross, now he still live you can't kill him again, his blood is the blood of God, and his blood flow into me, take me out from my house to lay me down, all Jesus do is move into a newer house, and keep on living I am a living sole, and don't you forget that, is the truth.

Now Jesus tried to do everything for you, but that was not enough you tried to kill him, he gave his life for you, and to this day you don't appreciate it. Like myself will do anything for you, now please don't do me the same as you did to Jesus, I will walk away from you, I don't have the time to die, my father told me it take a good man to walk away, keep on going God and Jesus will take care of you.

Now Elsie she always had try to give me a massage, but every time I saw it what did I do but, overlook it until she embarrass me, then I saw it but I am not mad you know, I am proud of her and her independent, she have something that every woman, should have that make Elsie to me, a dam good woman.

Now she had to do it that away in order, for me to see that she can do for her own self, now I respect that and her, but I will always be there for her, if she needed me I will be there, for her.

You know peoples are what God has given you to sit on, some don't know how to do anything for themselves, as soon as someone else are doing something, for themselves or talking about it to someone else, there will be someone you know, or think you know want a part of it, some kind of way but to me, no matter how you try to keep up on me, you can't do it the way I can, no one can do it the same as you do it, what every you are doing, no two peoples are the same.

You see I am talking about my life I live that and this, back on the 25th I was in the lobby waiting on the mailman, this woman she came up to Toni and ask her, did Toni have a picture of her that she wanted, to get one from Elsie and Toni and, put them on a website, when she said that I smile, that she was doing a thing about Louise Shell. Now you see I am writing my book base on now, me living in Louse Shell.

One day Miss Russell and I was talking I, told her what this woman had said to Toni, Miss Russell said Mr. Marshall don't you know, peoples that know you want to do the same, as you do for yourself because they don't know, how to do for themselves, they want to ride on your coat tale, "like touching my garment.

On Friday the 26th I took Miss Queen to her doctor appointment, it was to be for 1: pm when we got there, the doctor was going to be late until 2: pm. I told the nurse if the doctor was still at the hospital, you are saying now 3:pm then I said to Miss Queen, why don't we go on and go to the bank, and after that stop by Popeye chicken, and get all that done. Then we would have killed sometime before 2: pm. Then we come back, Queen said ok then she and I left, to take care of that.

At 1:30 Queen and I came back, and sit in the truck she ate something, then it was time to wait on the doctor, when the doctor got there and Queen, had seen him we came back home, saw Queen to her apartment then I came home.

The next day my friend girl Kopoe, wanted me to take a chair to the nursing home, for dad her dad, so she and I went to the nursing home and took the chair, when we got there dad he saw that chair, and said now he know that he want be going back home, I said hi, dad how was he doing! He said that he was doing ok until he saw that chair.

On the news on the 29th the horse that I had bet on, once before that broken his leg, and they was trying to save him, that was the race after the KY. Derby, now they had to put him down, his name was BarBaro I lost money on that race, if that horse had not broken his leg, maybe I might have won.

Later on that evening my, white brother Anthony DeVries call me, that he need my help and see if I can help him, I said that I don't know but what was it. Anthony said that at Rhodes Ranch where he lives, "I use to work there in security, until the chief and the others, with a black woman sit me up" there was so much drugs and break in, that they had broken into his vehicle.

Anthony ask me could I come back and work undercover, I said that would not work and, it would be so danger if you are trying to get, in between of drugs that is so powerful is danger, and that the break in come with the drugs, to get the drugs you need money, so what do you do if you don't have the money, you break into someone else house and, take what they have and sell that for the money, to get the drugs.

Anthony ask why don't I come back, and start back working in security that, he do be leave that the security is behind of the break in, I said that this could be true, that is why the chief wanted me out, he knew all about what I was trying to tell him, when I was working out there, I was trying to stop the wrong he didn't want me to, stop it because every time I would report to him, about a house was broken into and the drugs, that was flowing around it was funny to him, I always had said to him it was not funny.

Then I said to Anthony that the only way, I could do undercover work was that, I would have to live out there, he said why! I said now if the homeowners see me walking around, every night or every day and they don't know me, they are going to ask question like, do you live here, who are you what are you doing in here, how can I explain that because I don't have an address out there, Anthony said then come and start working with the security, that they don't know who I am, the other that was working with me before, they are all going, I said that it would be danger going under cover.

Anthony and I talk for a while until Joy, his wife and their son came, they have a new son I said to tell Joy hi for me, Anthony said that he would and that he and I, have to keep in touch with each other, I said that we will talk soon, then Anthony and I hung up the phone, now I have something on my mind, I want to help them but my life, would be in danger I said now what should I do.

The next morning on the 30th I stayed away from, everyone I stayed at home all that day thinking. I only talk to Miss Queen then I call my cousin Joyce, I explain what my white brother and I had talk about, Joyce said immediately no. one day I was on the outside talking, to some who talk to me I explain it to them about that, they said that they would not do it was to danger, I call my sisters they told me the same thing, so I will leave that along, because they had me before, now they need me again.

Now I need answer the only way to get it was, talk to my father God and Jesus. Because I don't know what to do, so that was what I did, I got my answer.

On the 31st on that Tuesday, I ask Miss Elsie that I was going to check my breaks, on my truck and if they need to be change, that I would do it, she ask me when? I said on Saturday or Monday, she said do it on Saturday that she would be here, I said O so that if the truck fall on me, she would be here. Elsie said you know how Sunday morning was, to me that had anything to do with that, frank I had ask him for a tool he start laughing, I shook my head I ask her the others don't, and not anything be did about it.

Elsie said don't talk my business out here; I said that was not business, that I was letting her know that I was going to do that, because I know how to do the right thing.

That Saturday I got up to see if frank was going to do, what I ask for him not to do it for nothing, I pay my way, I sit out waiting on frank I didn't see him, I didn't see Elsie she was not here then, I saw David lee the new maintenance man, I explain to him that I had already talk to Elsie, that I was going to check my breaks out there, and if they needed to be change I would do that, David said ok, so that was what I did but the shoes, on my truck didn't need changing, I put the wheel back on my truck, and said now that I know what was wrong, I have to put on that valve.

That Friday they had an old but goodie set in the lobby, I didn't go because at 4:30pm they was not in the lobby, it was to start at 4:pm so I went back home, about 7:30pm I was waiting on someone to come and pick me up, something look like told me to get up, put on my shoes on and go outside, I did that put on my shoes and got up, and sit right back down, and said no there was no one out there needed me, I took off my shoes and sit back down. After 9: pm. The peoples that I was looking for came we left.

Now after I had check my breaks and they was ok, I saw Elsie, David the maintenance man and frank, Elsie she call me David Marshall come here, I said yes she said sit down, when they got to me they told me about, what had happen last night. I said what why didn't Elsie she call me, she should have call me when someone treat her.

Then Elsie said that the maintenance man David was still here, I said what time was it, Elsie said it was about 7: or 7: 30pm. Then she said that this man, she was talking about frank, he walk right by her and said anything, then I said that, as long as David lee was there she was in good hand. Then I said that it was at 9:pm my friend and I, was going out the gate, Elsie said then why didn't I see those lights on, in the lobby they had to lock the door, after David and her had got Mr. Magee and his kids out, from the apartment. Then they kept on listen to the music.

You know with the promise that I made to Elsie son, if it was not for that I would not have anything to, say or have anything to do with Elsie, but now she have push me away, that she don't need me for anything, I will give that to her I respect that, but until she push me all the way back, she have to tell me with her own words, David L. Marshall that she don't need me in her live, or looking out for her no kind of way, then I will walk away because that is what she are asking for.

Chapter 10

You SEE I CAN'T WALK away from Elsie all the way, I can't because if she need me and call me, I will have to go to her, one day I was at home doing nothing, I start thinking about a woman, how they are now I don't know how they are but, as long they are happy they are ok, so to find out what I need, I call up my father God and my big brother Jesus, and search my soul about a woman, and how they treat me or why I let them do it. I got my answer that is love.

There is a lady that live in here, right now I don't know her name, she did tell me before but now, after 64 years old you know, anyway she have a daughter that come in here to, see her mother she sure has a beautiful smile, now when I say beautiful it is. Every time she comes in to see her mother almost, I see her she will always wave with that beautiful smile that put a smile on my face.

Now I don't know her name that she, had told me before just as her mother did, but now I can't think of it, I can't say anything bad about them because, they never Mistreated me, this lady she have two little girls, I love kids one day I told the mother of the smaller, girl that I was going to steel that baby, and bring her home with me, the mother said take her that, I would bring her back.

That she was so bad, I said no way look at this angel, the mother of the baby she said, that she want stay away long from her mother, I said then I would have to take the mother also, she smile then they left.

Man February the 4th it was the super bowl Sunday, I had already made my bet with the Chicago bears, on that Sunday Elsie said that she was going, to be at work and that I was to be there, to watch the super bowl on the big screen in the lobby, so I made a dish of hot dogs, cheese with beacon rap and took them because, I want go empty handed no way, this is me I pay my way.

When the game started we had all kind of food, and we was having fun when the bears, took that kick off and went all the way, for a touchdown that made me move then, I said yes, didn't I just tell you that the bears was going to do that, yes before I could get it out of my mouth there it was woo, then I said to Elsie she was in her office, didn't she here that the bears go bears go.

For a little while I had it my way the bears was winning, until the table turn for the cotes they kick the bears ass, that was what it was an ass kicking and my money going, and the mud that the coats and Elsie kick on my face, with some others that knew that I had bet, on the bears well I had to wash my face, and let Elsie swoop down on me, after all she are the lady from my heart, she can swoop down on my.

Now after that Friday night, I told Elsie and the other David that, every night etc. she get off work or here in this complex, that I will be out there for Elsie to make sure, that nobody mess with her that is my second promise, that I made with her son.

Every night about 6:30pm I take my walk around the complex, and when it was time for Elsie to get off, I wait no matter how long it take on her, I know that she appreciate it because, she tell me that after she are getting into her vehicle, and that is when she and I can talk, other time she are working or some woman, are watching her to see or hear, Elsie to say something bad about me, that is something that Elsie she don't know, but other times I still love Elsie, but I can't touch her.

Now as long as Elsie are here I am here for her, anytime she need me I want walk away from her. On Sunday and Monday Elsie is off on those days sometime, that Tuesday at 6:30pm. I was outside waiting on Elsie, she ask me did I want to wait on her, into the lobby. I said no that I will wait out here, Elsie she went back working Lorraine and Betty, was in the office Elsie she was ok, I will wait and smoke a cigarette out here, until she get off work and in her vehicle, and going through the gate going home or whatever, but as long as she are around to me, I am responsible for her if she need me, here or out there also if she call for me.

Now Elsie she has so much work to do, she was here late up to 8: pm. I was still out there until I saw big Chris the security guy, at one time Chris and I work together at Rhodes Ranch, Chris he came through the gate I spoke to him, Chris he spoke back and saw Elsie vehicle, and said is that Elsie car, I said yes. Then Chris made his rounds the complex, and came back now the other David he was going, and I can't leave Elsie.

The other David before he left, had already told Elsie that I was still out here, now after Chris came back I ask him, was he going to be here, he said yes that he was going to be here, I said ok that I was going home as long as Elsie, she was going to be ok, I left walking going home I heard Elsie, she said something all I could hear was thank you David, I was out of site.

Now I can't be sure that Lorraine or Betty can help Elsie, if someone messes with her like I can, but now that big Chris is here I am ok with that.

On Wednesday the 7th I was waiting on Elsie to get off work, with Lorraine, now one day Elsie she didn't tell me that, she didn't want me to help her because she, had already showed me how independent she are, but in some ways she would let me know, how independent she are because, she would let me know that, now I have to respect that.

Now that mess up my mind, I would say why! She know that I love her so much, and will do anything for her, anything why can't she just love me back, anyway that night Elsie she had a box, in the trunk of her vehicle she had to take it out, and put into her office, she said David come on, so I went with her to her vehicle, she open the trunk and showed me the box, now before she made a stink about, when I took a box from her and put it in her trunk, she showed me that she are not helpless.

Now it was the same box, I said what are she going to do with it, she said pick it up, I smile, and take it into her office, now when I started to pick up the box, instead of just letting me pick the box up, and take it to the office by myself, Elsie she just had to help she pull, the box up to the top of the trunk, I kept on saying that let me get it, she had to do something.

Then she hand the box to me, I said boy, boy, boy Elsie she didn't say anything, but she knew what I was saying and thinking, I took the box into the office and wait on her, to get off work, then I went home.

On the 8th I took Miss Queen to her doctor appointment, and came back then I went and got Annett, she had to go to Wall* Mart, she and I went to the store, Annett she got what she came for, she and I came back home what I did was, when I got home was watch my soaps, of what was left on tv and thinking about, on valentine day what and how I was going to do, for Elsie my wife from my heart, now Elsie in my heart she are the wife, that I should have had and now know how to love her.

As doing everything or anything for her to make her happy, and keep her happy should I get flowers, or chocolate then I said maybe both of them, then I said no that I might not get away, with that so I said the chocolate, if she said no thank to me then it would be ok, I can eat the candy because I could not give, it away to someone else that would be, a hand it down what woman would like that.

Elsie she don't want me to do anything for her, I want to do everything for her now, what do I do she are so sweet, in her own ways we all have our own ways, so I do to love her in so many ways.

That same night this lady that I know, she had ask me to do something for her before, I told her that to call me when she got ready, but last night she call me to let me know, that she had did it now, that someone else did it for her, I said as long that she got it did she was ok. Then she wanted to talk nasty with me that was right in my alley.

She caught me in the mood for that, after I told her all about love and sex together in bed, she said that between her legs had start tingling, and that she needed to be bothered with! I said bring it to me. She got quite. She could not say another word, I said now that she had go quite, after she ask for something and got grand it to her, now she don't have anything else to say, then I said that she can't handle this, she said o no that she was trying to see, if she can get here to me, she kept on thinking about it, I said that I was going to go out, and play some poker and that I would talk to her later, then we hung up the phone.

On the 9th Miss Mary that live in building 2, she call me I was working in my book, she said that she had a flat tire, I said ok where was she at, she said that over to where she always park, I ask her was she going anywhere right now, she said no. I said that I would be there after 3: pm. She wanted to know if I had a jack, I said that I would be there about 3: pm, she said ok. I kept on working on my book, and watch my soaps at the same time, until after 3: pm then I turn off the computer, and went to Mary vehicle.

When I got there Mary she was not by her vehicle, I went to her porch trying to get her, she didn't answer I walk back to the vehicle, and I saw Mary coming around to by the vehicles, I got her keys and open the trunk of her vehicle, and change the tire I put on one of those donut tire, she was going to get the other tire fix.

That night I was waiting on Elsie about 7:pm to get off work, Lorraine she was in the office as always do, Elsie she must have ask Lorraine to call me in, to sit until she was still working, Lorraine call me, I went and went inside to wait until, Elsie got off work Elsie she let Lorraine out, to her apartment then Elsie had to lock the side door, then Elsie she put on the alarm she and I went outside, the door lock Elsie as she was going to, get into her vehicle she and I was talking, Elsie she said something to me" I already knew that" peoples they tried to break us up, but they could not do it.

That was when I said to Elsie that, I knew that they tried it very hard to do it, and then I said that no one can break this up but her. Elsie said that is right and that she appreciate me, I said that there was so many ways, that I have to protect her, she said thank David then she pull off, and left I went back home thinking about, what Elsie and I was talking about, I didn't think that she saw what those woman, was trying to do.

Now on Wednesday the 14th it is valentine day, I was thinking about not getting anything for, valentine for Elsie I want to respect her wishes, then I said ok I will do it this time, so I saw Theron he took me with him to Wal*Mark, I got some candy for Elsie. On Saturday the 10th the other David the maintenance man, he was in the office with Elsie talking, I said excuse me then I gave the candy to Elsie, she said thank you David, I said that I was giving it to her early before the 14th. Because if I don't do it now, I want have time later on to give it to her, because Lorraine would be all over her.

Now on that Sunday all I did was lay around, and do anything but put something, that I had to put into the computer, and thinking with my heart and mind, with God and Jesus that I had made my second promise, and that I want to step back from Elsie, but it seem that every time that I say, that I was not going to do anything with or for Elsie, I find myself doing the same thing that I, said that I was not going to do the same thing.

Now I know what that is, it is the love of God and Jesus. Now I was going to go out on the outside and sit, and smoke myself a cigarette to see who was out there, I saw David the maintenance man, he was moping the hallway in my building where I live, he and I talk for a little while, then he went back to moping the floor, I went back inside of my apartment, then I call Miss Queen.

To see how she was doing, Queen she had ask me awhile back that one day, she needed her mattress change from one bed to the other bed, I said that I would do it on Monday morning, I said about 9:am. Queen she said let it be at 10: am she, would be up then. I said ok that I would be there and do it for her; she said well ok she would be up, and I told Queen that I would be at home, all day if she needed me.

Now I am always thinking back of my pass life, of what I had or have done or what I wish it should be, about how I can make it better for me, what can I do now to make my life better, I don't know but I am always trying, all I do is put it into God and Jesus hand, and leave it along for God to help me.

Now God and Jesus is in my heart, I have to think all the time about a better life for me, my family or whom are with me, the other day Jennet and I was outside talking, she said to me that she have never seen a man like me, I guess she are thinking about the day before, she ask me if I don't let Elsie know, that I want her someone else will get her, I said if it was that was ok, as long Elsie are happy I am happy for her.

Now I guess that is why she have never meet a man like me, one who don't anymore jump into bed with, every woman find I see, that is all I can see what Jennet are talking about, so I smile because I am me to this day, trying to be straight and loving.

Like on Friday the 9th they was having a dusty set, in the lobby I went and listen to the music, and talk to the lady folks one I wanted to talk to, I said Miss Dorothy if these women, don't give you the blues I would ask her, to have a cigarette with me, Dorothy she don't smoke she look around and said, come on she will go out there with me, so Dorothy and I went out to the sitting area, as soon she and I got out there every one, that was in the lobby came out there, I said man when or how can I have some private, whenever I am talking to a woman.

Then I saw the lady that was spending the music, she had pack up her things, and she was putting them into her vehicle, she said that she would see us later, then she pull off. Dorothy she got ready to go she left, I and the other lady we all went our own self ways, I went home to come back later, to see about Elsie if she was going to be ok, but she didn't come back I knew that she was ok, she know how to take care of herself.

Before I had told you that I do believe in ASTROCAST, my sign is GEMINI on the day of 02-12-07. It says Partners can bring you beneficial or insightful information. Amorous meetings might have to be suspended until the love of your life has completed a pressing project. Now I only know one project that is my book, about the talk show.

Now I had to take Miss Queen to the doctor at 10: am. Before then I got a call and answer it, no one said anything I kept saying hello, hello, hello, then I said if they had the time to call, they should have the time to say something, then they hung up, I went and got Queen and took her to her doctor appointment.

After I finish with Miss Queen and came back, and saw her into her apartment, and came back outside I saw little Joe, Rose, Frank, and Jenson out there, I spoke but I only heard Rose said hay you, I sit on the other table and smoke myself a cigarette, while they was on the other table talking, I was not going to try to see, what they was talking about.

Later on I went back outside after 3:pm as I always do, talking to anyone who want to talk to me, I will talk to anyone who talk with some sense, now if you don't talk with love, I don't want to hear anything else.

And when peoples are talking anything other than love, and being crazy I don't know how to take that, I will sit still keep my eyes, ears open and my mouth close, my mind and heart is still open, for those who want in.

If not then keep on doing what they love, is not what I love. So I keep to myself and I will help anyone, with respect.

You know in my pass I would see a woman, that I wanted and be with, I would do anything to get her in bed with me, and after I got her in bed and it was over, I found out that it was not for me, there I go to another woman telling her almost, the same thing that I just got out of bed with, that was not right.

Now to this day I in my older days, want do that anymore, I found respect for a woman after all, my grandmother, mother, sister and my daughters, are ladies now I am being tested. God put someone in front of me I love dearly, but I can't say the wrong thing to her, unless she wanted to hear it, I can't put my hand or arms on her but, I still love her anyway so much, from my pass to now yes I am being tested.

One day I was in the office with Elsie, David the maintenance man talking, I told Elsie in front of the maintenance man David, that in my pass Elsie, she would not have a chance, she would be my woman I would be all over Elsie, but now I found respect and felling for love, and sex that man get it and walk away from it, I have to give this to her she have felling the same as a man, then Elsie she said to me get out of her office, I said see that now she are putting me out, then I said see them later and left.

Now David the maintenance man and I was talking, later on as he was checking the grounds, of the complex and I was doing my walk around, he and I was just talking like peoples do, just to get to know something about each other, how his life to me is almost perfect, I see when he talk to me about his family, I like that is something that I want for me, because my life has been rack over the coals, with my love a fares so now all I can do is wish, look out for her make sure, as long as she are in here as the manager, of Louise Shell and she needed me I am coming.

So now if you don't like that I am sorry, because Elsie, God and Jesus only can stop this felling, about the friend ship that I have for Elsie, she can stop it other peoples can't do that, only she not me I love what God and Jesus, have put here in front of me. So I am going to look and treat her like a lady, I will use my heart and my mind, to get through this felling I have for Elsie.

One morning I was thinking about peoples old and young, David the maintenance man and I was standing in front of the lobby talking, we saw some kids climbing over the wall, that separate Louise Shell and the housing complex, on the other side they climb because, it would be shorter to get to where they was going, David the maintenance man he start telling them to not do this, they could get hurt climbing over that wall.

They just look at David and kept on going, I said man that is no good they don't hear you, David said that he wasted his time talking to those kids, I said that was right then I told David, that on the back wall I use to see those kids, look like they was 9 or 10 years old, climb on the top of that wall I saw them, and said you kids should not climb on that wall, that they could get hurt, one of them ask me who was

I, I said that I was a man who don't want them to get hurt, then I kept on walking, they don't hear you when you are, telling them something to help them.

Now the same kids that David the maintenance man, had talk to the other day, I saw the same kids climbing over the wall one, he was on our side of the wall standing, the other one he was almost over the wall coming down, I said how was they then I said, if one of them fall and hurt himself, that his parent would feel bad, and that his brother or his friend would feel bad, and that he can't go to school because he was hurt, and he will mess all of his friends at school, do he want that. One of them said no the other he just look at me, then they walk away going out from our gates, I hope they heard me I think they did, hear me I could see it in them, as they was walking away.

Now kids today they don't listen, and I can't hold that on them because, when I was that age I didn't listen but now, I have some ones who I better listen to, because they know the best for me. Later on that day I saw the same kids, doing the same thing climbing over that wall, they saw me and drop their head, and kept on walking I didn't say anything, I kept on walking also if they get hurt, then that was on them because they want listen, by not listening one day could cost them so much money, and I know that.

The next morning I got up at 9:30am, I had to take Annett and Marilyn to WAL. * Mart, I did that and came back home, I saw Miss Bill and Lorraine in the lobby, they was clean I said to Miss Bill, that she was looking so good that I wanted to bite her, then I look at Lorraine and spoke to her, Miss Bill she said Mr. Marshall don't bit her, with that smile as they was going out from the lobby, I went and spoke to Elsie and left.

Then I had to take my other half of my heart, over to CVS drug store, I did that and came back, now I am at home I started thinking about this lady, that Kopoe had induce me to the other night, she induce me to her as Pat man she, was so find that she took my breath away from me, the door of my heart start opening.

You know when God and Jesus has did and done, everything for a friend everything with love, now I don't have anything else to give but love, but in my pass I would have gave plenty, now my pass is my memories, how can I forget that I have live in my pass.

But now my life is deference, on valentine day I was going to the party, that was going on in the lobby, I went and sit down talking Shellar she, came up to me and ask me was I going to be, one of the deacon, I said what do she mean I thought this was a valentine party, she said o yes but they was having church, playing church, I said o no that I better leave because I don't play with God and Jesus.

Then I left out then Gloria she was there also, she was clean as I was going outside I saw Gloria, she ask me was I going to sit out? I said yes that I can't stay in the lobby, they was having church, Gloria she said that was what they told her also, and that she don't play with God, and that she would be to un comfortable, I said that I would be the same that I, was going back home, Gloria she went to the lobby, I went home.

After I got home and took off my shoes, Elsie she calls me that she was, going outside for a cigarette, I said ok let me put on my shoes, she said ok. I put on my shoes and went to Elsie, she and I was talking she ask me why was I, not in the lobby with the others, I said that I don't play with God and Jesus, they was talking about having church, Elsie said they are not having church, I said that Sheller told me that.

Was what they was having and they also told Gloria the same, Elsie said peoples don't know what they are talking about, she said go on and see, I said don't ask me to do that please, Elsie said no she are not telling you to go there, unless I wanted that so I turn around, then I said that now they will have something to talk about, she said how, I said now that I was outside with her, now I am going into the lobby while they are, playing with God playing church.

Now here Elsie and David coming, that they will bet that Elsie made David come, Elsie said that she come to work every day, and that she don't care what they say, then she showed me her office and said that, she would be in there, I went and menial with the others, I saw that pretty lady Pat I gave her a seat, Kopoe said who was the last one through the door, Pat she said that it was David, I said no it was Pat, Kopoe she had a present in her hand, for the last one came in, when she give it to them they have to open it, in front everybody.

Then I look at killer and said was I the last one, he hump up his shoulder and that he don't know, now he was looking right at me, so I took the present and in front of the others, I started opening it then I would look into Kopoe eyes, she was smiling and laughing I pull out some more paper, I start feeling to see what it was, it was not no woman draws, I kept on feeling then I said that I can't get it all out.

Then Kopoe she took it after I hand it to her, she took the rest of the paper out from over, it was toilet paper now I had it coming, I said ok Theron said David someone are trying to tell you something, I said that now I see then I look at Kopoe, and said ok you got me, you got me from the other night.

Then I was standing by Theron watching the show, Theron said David boy you are something, then one of the lady said that David he have a harem, Theron he look at me and said David she are talking about you, I said that don't I know that, you see how they talk about me, but I love them all then I went over, and talk to my other half of my heart, and rub on her shoulder.

What was did to me that was fun, now I can handle that because we are, to be able to use yourself for fun sometime, because there are a time for everything, now after they started to set the stage, for playing acting like a preacher and the church members, that was not one of my time for that, I tried to get into it but, what is funny to someone else, is not to me, so what I did was go over to my other part of my heart, and told her that this don't move me, so that I was going to go.

Now she had a valentine gift for me, I told her that I would get it in the morning, she said ok my love see me then, I said ok then I left and got home and call my friend, to let her know that I was waiting on her, after my friend came I took her to put an arrow, into her heart for valentine day, I said to her happy valentine day, she was so happy I said this was for her, sweetheart this is for you.

Then there was another friend of mind that live in here, in the complex she gave me a box of cookies, and a very good loving valentine card, that read Special Wishes For Valentine Day, on the front the middle read Happy Valentine Day to someone with a BIG heart, that really shows you are the best. This is the way I live.

One time it was in my pass that I, use to call Elsie all the sweet things that, a loving man could call his lady, I use to light her cigarette and do anything for her, Elsie said one day that they, wanted her to light her own cigarette and not David, so all the good things that I wanted and love, for my own self. The other women took that away from me, but one thing for sure, there was one thing I know they want stop, the love I have for Elsie.

There is another card I got from my other half of my heart, for valentine it read on the front," good friends are family by choice, inside say happy valentine day, the other half of my heart Norman.

Some peoples that was at the valentine show party, in the lobby they said to me that, they left out when the show started because, they was not comfortable playing with God, I said that I was the same way that is why I left.

Now I can see having fun about our own self, about the toilet paper I can smile and laugh, about that and that I had told Kopoe about, her friend Pat with her pretty self, and that she was breath taken to me, Kopoe she tried to change the conversation, I said to Kopoe that she know what I was talking about, Kopoe she got up and said to me, David you need help the she strutted away from me, I said ok we are still friends.

The next day Elsie and I was outside on her break, Kopoe came through the gate in her vehicle, and park and came to where Elsie and I was sitting, we all was talking about the party, how some had fun, I said to Kopoe that I know why she kept, that last present for me because what I said, to her about her find friend Pat with her find self, Kopoe look at me and said, David you is a player and that I need some help, then she said that was why I got a roll of toilet paper, that I was full of shit.

On the 16th Joannen and Jackie with her find self, they was painting a dresser and need me to, take it back in Joannen apartment after it dry, I said ok that I was taken my walk now, that they would still be out there when the dresser dry, then I would take my dolly and put it, back into Joannen apartment, Jackie said ok, then I said that it was good that Jackie, she paint that dresser because, Joannen she would have paint all over her.

After the dresser had dry I took it back into Joannen apartment, and I came back and stayed in my apartment, then someone knock on my door, I answer it was Joannen they wanted me to go, to the movie with them, but before I had already told Joannen that, I had company coming that I could not go, Joannen said that is right, then Joannen she went back to her apartment, I said to myself that I should have went, boy that Jackie is one find woman, I can't make no move with her, I can't do that to her.

On the Sunday of the all-star game here in Vegas, I was laying around doing nothing, but thinking that if Elsie she was my lady, I would treat her as she was my queen, a queen in my life because I know her, I only know two things about Elsie, and those two are all I needed to know about her, one is her big heart and the second is her mind, Elsie she are no dumbly she is smart, the rest to me all girls, woman or a lady don't have that, a big heart with a mind Elsie, to me she have it going on, the rest will only put me in hell, if I went to bed and have sex with them.

On the 15th I had to take Annett to the laundry, to put her cloth to be clean, and came back to go and get them back on Monday.

On the 16th I had to take Miss Queen to her doctor appointment, for 11:30am I did that and stop at the sub. Sandwich shop, and got Queen a sub. Sandwich, and took her back home, then I came back home.

On the 17th that Saturday, it was the tenant meeting I had though, that it was manager meeting, I had call Elsie to let her know, that I was going to set up the lobby, for her meeting I left a message on the machine at 10:am.

After I left my apartment and came out side, I was at the lobby I saw Karen, she was looking for her mother Lorraine, I said that I didn't see her this morning, Karen said that she was not at home, and she should be at home, that her mother told her to keep the car.

Then Karen she said that she had just came back, that she was out of town. I said maybe she had a hot date and still in bed, Karen said that she was not at home and it was after 10:am, I said she was doing her thing give her that, Karen said she should have had enough, from last night, I said but it was better in the morning time. Karen she said no her mother should be at home, I said well that is what love will do, for you.

Then Karen ask me to let go out and, have a cigarette with her that she, had something to tell me, Karen and I went outside to the sitting area, then Karen start telling me to don't let, no one run me away from pussy, and let those peoples say anything that they want. Then I had to let Karen know that, as I was telling Karen how it was, some other lady she was going through, she said hi to Karen then she look at me and said.

David you better be good now, I said don't worry Karen she are the same sign as I am, she and I know too much about our self, then the lady she left I explain to Karen that, her mother she had a bad temper, and I had to back up from Lorraine, if I didn't there was going to be a problem. Karen said that her mother would cuss one out, then she would walk away, her mother want fight that she would call Karen, she would take care of her problem, I said with that it would still be a problem.

And that I don't need no problem, then Karen she told me something that, I didn't know that Betty and her mother, they was not like they use to be, I didn't ask why it was their problem. Then I said that her mother and Betty, they stop talking to me before Christmas, and at Christmas time we all had some fun, after all it was Christmas.

Then I said to Karen that to this day, I still don't know why Lorraine and Betty, stop speaking to me, that one day Elsie she ask me what was wrong, I said to Elsie the same thing that, I just told Karen I don't even know, what happen but I have a good guess why. But like I said I don't know why.

Now the things that I have put into this book two, of passing through about Elsie, it is to me in the future of the way, I should have treated the women's in my pass life. I wish that this woman is mind; she is the woman that every man need in his life. The way I have taken her out from my heart, through my mind and put it on paper, all of that is true and not true, that is not true is my wish.

Now it is getting to me I better slow down and think, because I think that I am slipping away from Elsie, but I still love her so much not crazy love, just love her I am now at the cross road, God and Jesus will show me the best way to go.

Today I was outside talking to Miss Blackwell, she was making a hat, and Jennet the white lady that live next door to me, we all heard plenty polices siren going fast, I said man I am glad that it is not me they are looking for, Miss Blackwell said maybe a police in trouble, with all those polices, I said or someone else have a gun.

We was still sitting out there, then we saw a police vehicle coming through the gate, they ask us did anyone see anybody going over the wall, or came through here running, I we said not as long we was out here we didn't see anyone, the police ask how long we was out here, I said that I was out here about a half hour, the police said that was ok and thank, then they drove around the complex and went out.

On the 20th I had to take Annett to pick up her cloths at 10: am, I did that and came back home, and the rest of the day I didn't do anything. Until the next day, Miss Queen she wanted me to take her over to CVS drug store, she wanted to know how her medical care card work, I took her over there and came back, and took Queen back home and I went home, and sit around go outside smoke a cigarette, talk if someone was outside to talk to, if not that was ok because I can go home, that was what I did.

Now Miss Russell she had call me about 9: am, that Blessing my God daughter, her mother was in the hospital and that she was in a comer, I said that I was sorry that she was in the hospital, and that she was going to come out of that comer, that she was going to be ok God know the best, then I said to Miss Russell to keep me inform, about how she was doing, Russell said ok honey talk to me later.

On 2-22-07 I was at home thinking about, all the love that I put in front of Elsie, if it was another woman she would take it, because anytime a man love a woman, like I love Elsie. Until he would do anything for his woman, but kill someone I can't do that for her. I can't give another life back that I take away, now the man that love her, is me now what you have read is true from my heart.

Now Elsie she have taken that from me, all the love that I could give her, doing things for her now it is over that is what she want, there is not anything else I can do for her, I can't write anything that I want to write about, that is the way I love Elsie. Now after She have put a stop to me about, when she call me I call her sweet things, that is what she ate I believe, and the things that I use to do for Elsie, is over now I have to start all over again, there is someone out there want a good man, in their life.

Now all I can write about is how proud I am, and sad I am that Elsie is not the one that, God and Jesus had put in front of me, I thought she was but I was wrong. But I am so proud to know her, and sad because I am not the one for her, but if anytime that she need me, no matter where she are or who she is with, or who I am with if Elsie need me, all she have to do is pick up the phone, and call me I will be there.

One Saturday Elsie she call me, to come and have a cigarette with her, that she had to go to the store and get her some, I said no don't do that I had a pack for her, she was kind of surprise that I had a pack for her, as that she didn't want me to do that, then she said well ok, I start thinking about that very hard, I know that she don't love me, because she had already told me before.

Now I got the cigarettes and went outside to meet Elsie, I stop in the lobby to give the cigarette to Elsie, she was in her office on the phone, I didn't go in there was Toni and Lorraine, they was sitting at one of the tables in the lobby, I spoke to them and went back outside, to the sitting area a little while Elsie came out, I gave her the pack of cigarette, she could not sit and have one with me, she said that she was going to have one, on her way to where she had to go, I said ok see her later she got into her car, and I went back home to my apartment.

On 2-25-07 I was out talking to a lady, she like for me to talk nasty to her, she said to me to put something in my book, that will make some woman happy to read about, what a woman love other than me. Then I said maybe, but after I did get back home thinking about, what that find woman want me to do, I did that.

The body of a woman is a dream, like magic art of influencing events by controlling, nature of spirit of mind, it is not my magnetization this is real, of what I want to do with it, I want to use it sometime like a head set, so I can hear the sweet sound of her morn, as she sit, lay or stand in the bed room or where she want, to make her happy with sex.

And she enjoy the moment of the love I have for her, with the gate of heaven to her sole, all she have to do is let me in, God took my flesh and made her with that, so she and I can enjoy our moments, to me to get through to her soul he put an open, so I can get in to me I call it a patch of flower, I don't mine parting my way to the goodness.

Of my happiness to the sole with sex, some might say that sex is nasty but, was it nasty when I came out with it to the world, that was my first time I got my taste of love, now I am passing through in my life, sometime I try to go back to one like I came through, the same I came out head first.

But first I have to kiss on her four head, eyes, noses, ears, neck and work on the boobs, down to the navel, sometime I will have some wine from the navel, and work down through the thy leg to the foot, suck on the toes to the other foot. And do the same as the other going back up, licking my way back to the flower garden of love.

The legs will open up like the pebbles of a rose, it might be wet by then, I will use my towel to dry it up, the fluid of love. Now there is a little boy that in the boat, you have to satisfy. While I am satisfying him he will start crying, sweating with moisture, that is good to me and for her.

Now after the body is bonfire with the express of joy, like burning rubbish hot, sincerity good faith I can go in, with all the love I can give, and dance with her soul the soul that I love, you know I can say that because I know me, and I am talking about me and only, and I want all the female that I have had, and showed that to them. They know what I am talking about is true, about it and they like and loved it, because I still have the scars on me, or in my heart, will be with me until I am going.

Now the one I love so much now, I can't do that to her because if, she live after I have pass on, she will get pregnant and the baby will be me, I can't and I want say where my soul, are going to be planted after it leave this body, I don't know do you.

On Saturday the 24th I saw Betty, her car window want go up and down, she ask me would I take a look at it, and see what could I do with it for her, I said ok that on Monday I would do that for her, then I had to go with my daughter Larissa, somewhere I had forgot that, so I went to Betty porch and got in touch with her, to let her know what I had to do with my daughter, and to park her vehicle by my truck, so if I need some tools they are in my truck, she said ok then I went back to my apartment.

On that Monday Larissa call me to let her in through the gate, after she had got to my apartment, she came in and after she and I was leaving, Rose she was at the end apartment talking to the lady, that live there Rose look at Larissa and said, hay baby girl how are you, to Larissa said that she was doing find, then Larissa and I left going what we had to do, then Larissa brought me back home, Betty vehicle was park by my truck, I said to Larissa that I better take a look at Betty car, to see why the window want go up and down, Larissa said ok daddy, she had something to do also she left.

Then I went to use the bathroom, and went to see what was wrong with Betty vehicle, to see if I could help her some kind of away, I took the window control switch off the door, and look inside the panel, I could see why the window was falling down, but my hand was too big to get inside, and I don't have the tools, to take the panel off so I saw Glen, and ask him would he let Betty know to come out here, Glen said ok that was what he did for me, Betty daughter she was there she came out, I explain to her what was going on, and to let her mother know.

She said ok so I put the window switch back on, and pull the window all the way up, and put some tape on the window to hold it up, the Betty and her daughter came out, Betty ask me how much did she owe me, I said nothing because I could not help her.

On the 27th Elsie, the other maintenance man David, Miss Charette and I, was sitting out talking it was after 5:pm smoking a cigarette, it was cold out there after the cigarette was over, we went back as well sit and talk to David for a while, but I had to use the washroom, Elsie and Miss Charette was going down the hallway, to Charette apartment

David had a question for Elsie, I said Elsie David have a question for her, she said that she heard him, and she will be right back.

 inside David the maintenance man, he was looking into the maintenance book, I said that I might After Elsie came back, David asks her what he needed to ask Elsie, we was sitting there talking, Elsie she ask me a question. She said David what do I want? I said don't ask me that, I want a million dollars. Then I ask Elsie what she wants. She said to get the entire empty apartment with someone in there, I said that I will help her, if I know someone looking for an apartment, I will let them know to come here.

Now Elsie she went into her office, Kopoe she came to the lobby she are moving out, she spoke and start into me David, you are out all night and coming home at 3: to 4:pm. That I should be at home at that time of night, I said well if I had someone in my bed, to keep me there I would not be out there, I am single and a man have to do, what he have to do. By that time Elsie, she was coming out from her office, Kopoe she saw Elsie coming, Kopoe said to me say it again, say it again I was stun all I could say was, come on the side I will tell her, Kopoe she said no say it now right now.

Now she had heard it she was trying to be funny, so I said it again the same thing the same way. David he look at me then Kopoe she left, I said to David man you see that, she knew Elsie was coming that is why she did that, David said he know that then he shook his head, I said that it was my time to go home, and see what I was going to do.

March the first in the morning, I got a call from my cousin Elizabeth, she are the sister of my cousin Hattie Reaco, she had been sick for a long time and she, was in the hospital so sick, I would talk to Hattie sometime to see how, Elizabeth and my others cousin was doing, the ones that I don't know or never seen them.

Now Hattie she would ask me about the ones, that she didn't know or know them but don't, know how they were doing or where they are at. I would let Hattie know, she and I are two brothers kids, now my other cousin Cat that live in Francisco, Ca. she and I was talking the other night about Hattie and how she was doing, that she was so sick, but God and Jesus have the power, she will be alright.

Now when Elizabeth call me, she ask me was I sitting or standing, I said that I was standing, Elizabeth said sit down, I did that now my incentive rousing, then I knew it was bad news that would hurt me, or make me Jealous. Then she said that Hattie pass this morning, I said no, no, no please don't tell me that, now my cousin has going on home, she has did what I and everyone else have to do one day.

Hattie she made it home before I did, now all her ache, pains and worry is all over, and I am still here with mind yes I am Jealous, but God and Jesus know the best. Now all I can do now is go and see the body of Hattie, that her spirit use to live in and give Hattie, all of my respect Hattie pass on 03-01-07. Elizabeth said the time was 6: 42 am.

Now life is so short, I love Elsie too much to walk away from her, but I do think about her all the time, sometime I get so lonely, I say to myself that I was going to take my imagination, and my dreams and forget about someone I want have, and go on and find another that want it all, my love and sex.

But in my heart I am like a man that is marry, and he was trying to find a way to leave his wife, not for another woman, but because they don't belong together. But look like as soon I see Elsie or hear her voice, that loving feeling come right back into my heart, my mind with my feeling, that I have for Elsie is like I have come to my end, of the rainbow looking for that treasure, they said that I would find is not there.

On the 2nd I had to take Miss Queen to her doctor appointment, at 10: am I did that and stop and got a sandwich for Queen, and took her back home, I also had to take Annett to pay her phone bill, and she needed to stop and pick up some money, her son sent to her and stop by the post office, I did that and brought Annett back home.

After that I park my truck, and did the same as I do, when I don't have anything else to do, because Kopoe cousin had a washing machine to sell, and another lady friend of mind name Judy, a friend of Miss Russell want the washer machine, she want me to go and get it, and bring it to her house that Miss Russell, she had the key to get in, and Judy she left a $140.00 for me and to pay for the washing machine.

Judy said that Kopoe would go with me after 12: noon. To pick up the machine Judy she was at work, now I took Miss Queen and Annett to take care, of what they need me to do, it before 12:noon I wait on Kopoe and wait on her, I talk to Judy and Miss Russell that I, was going to give Kopoe until 6:pm, and if she want to go in the morning, I would go and get it then otherwise, I would give the money back to Judy, Miss Russell said that is right because Kopoe, she tell some big lies.

Miss Russell and I was still on the outside, about 4:pm another lady name Else, she ask me to take her some place, that it was not too far about a mile, I said ok so I went and got my truck, and took Else to where she need to go, and came back and park and sit, back in the sitting area no Kopoe, about 6:30pm I was walking around the complex, I saw Kopoe coming through the gate, ready to go I said no maybe in the morning.

I have waiting on her until 6: pm. I told Judy and Miss Russell, that I would wait on Kopoe until 6: pm, now it is 6:30pm and I have someone to do for myself, Kopoe said that she can't go in the morning, because she had things to do also. I said well I can't go now, then she saw the other David coming out to go home, I ask David was Elsie still in there by herself, he said yes she don't want no body in there, I said well then I was going to sit out until, she get off to make sure that she was going to be ok.

Then when I said that he said that, Lorraine was in there with her, I said that was ok as long as she had someone with her, then Kopoe ask David could she pay him, to pick up a washing machine, he said no that he can't put anything in his van, that anyway he had to go home to his kids, I said to David that I had this, because I told Judy that I was going to give her money back, that Miss Russell will have it the morning.

That Saturday morning I call Miss Russell, to let her know that I was going to give that money, back to her after the lobby open because I had to wash, she said ok. So after the lobby open and I had put my cloth in the washer, I went on the outside to sit and smoke a cigarette, Miss Russell she was out there I gave her that money.

Later on I saw Kopoe coming through the gate, to see Joannen I guess, she wave and kept on going I wave back, and kept on talking a little while Miss Russell, her cell phone ring she answer it, then Miss Russell she start laughing so hard, I said ok I know who that is Judy, then I heard Miss Russell said, Kopoe is doing nothing but telling a lie, then Miss Russell gave me the phone to here that lie, that Kopoe is telling.

Kopoe had put on the recording of Judy phone, that I didn't want to go and get the washer machine, and he didn't give her the money to get someone else, to go and get it and that it was not his money, and that I can't see at night, I said that I can't stand a lien woman, and that peoples has always said that Kopoe, she was a big liar and I didn't believe that.

Now Glen he was out there also to hear that, and I said that Kopoe she can't say anything, else to me about anything because it would be a lie, then I went and put my cloth in the dryer, and came back outside then Elsie, the other David came out side to the sitting area, I was telling Elsie and David what Kopoe had did, then I ask Miss Russell to tell them what Kopoe had said, now David he know what had happen, I wanted Elsie to hear it maybe she would believe it.

Then we start talking about the Nicole Smith story. What was they going to do about the body, then Elsie she ask me, David what did I want to be did with my body, after I die. I said after the doctors take everything, that they can use to help keep someone else living, take the rest and cremate it, and take some ceramic and mix it in, and make a hand or hands with it, so I will leave something forever, other than my book.

After I got back home, I check my message on my phone, it was Judy she said David Marshall, this is Judy guess what. Kopoe she call her and she said that she came, to see if David Marshall was going to go and get the washer, but he is like he don't want to do it, so get your money back and thank, hum Kopoe don't know I have already did that.

Now on the 4th Glen he wanted me to move a couch, for him and take it over to blue diamond, I ask him what time. He told me, when it was that time I went and got my truck, and went to the building where Glen live, and park and open my tail gate of the truck, and got Glen but I guess that something, must have happen he could not do it right then, I said ok let me know when he got ready.

Then I got back in my truck and came home, and got into my computer to do some work, then as I was going good writing in my book, Glen he knock on my porch window, I went to see what he want, now he want to go and take the couch over to blue diamond, I said about 4:30pm Glen said ok, then he left I tried to go back to work, but I could not because now I have something else on my mind.

So what I did was cut off my computer, and went to see if I could find Glen, to let him know that we can go now and take the couch, he was not at home I came back to my apartment, and wrote a note to call me when he came home.

Later on Glen he came and found me at home, now he was ready to take the couch, I got ready and took my truck, and Glen and I we put the couch on the truck, and took the couch over to blue diamond, I had to get back but his lady wanted us to stay, so Glen and I left and came back to where we live, he thank me paid me and I park my truck, and came back home, how I am lazy don't want to do anything.

On the 5th a Monday I had to go and get my ticket, to go to Lancaster ca. for the funeral of my cousin, Hattie Ricco. I didn't want to drive by myself so I ask Glen, would he take me to the bus station to get my ticket, he had to do something for someone else, that he could go after he came back, but I saw little Joe and he rode with me, I got my ticket and went to the jewel store, I had them to do something for me, I did that and came back Joe and I, and went home.

Now I was getting my and Miss Queen mail, and coming back home I saw Elsie in her vehicle, she wait so I could get across the street, I wave for her to go on lady first, then Elsie she park at the building by Miss Blackwell, and came out I spoke to her and came back home, the love I have for Elsie is fading.

On Tuesday at 9:30am my bus was leaving going to Lancaster ca. so I had ask Mary live in building two, to take me to the bus station she did that for me, I ask her how much did I owe her, she said nothing all the things that I do for them, so I said thank to Mary.

She ask me did I want her to pick me up when I came back, I said that I would have to call her, because I might not leave until on Wednesday, that I would call her if it was not too late, Mary said ok then I went inside of the bus station, to wait on the bus to come.

After the bus came and was ready to be loading, I got on the bus and took a seat, I said to myself that it have been a long time, that I have been on a bus traveling, as the bus was moving, you will find any and every one that is on the bus, there is one that have a problem, one guy that was on the bus he could not sit still, he start talking to his self-checking the seats, to see if the seat was broken, then he came and got a seat in front of me, looking around moving around talking to himself.

Then the bus had to stop at another station to pick up, we had 20 minute to stretch our legs, and get some food, I didn't want any food or anything to drink, so I saw a Lotto store, I said that I was going to go and play the Lotto, so I did that and went back to the bus and got on, after we got to the next stop we had 15 minute, I found another Lotto store and got 2 more tickets, there was $270, million in that Lotto, I could use if I could get it, but I can't get it unless I play, if you don't play you can't win.

After the bus got to Lancaster ca. station I was lost, lost because, I never been there before but I had my cousin phone number, I call Isabell to let her know that I was here, she said ok David she would tell her son Joseph, I said that

I had on a brown jacket and long hair, that is why Joseph would know me, I never seen them and they never saw me, from my father side they are all my cousin.

In a little while this vehicle pulls up and asks me, is you ready to go. I said o yes now I was lost now I am found, we really didn't need any induction we are cousin, all we have to do now is be around our self, we will learn about our self, we got to the house and went inside, Joseph he call Isabell, she are Joseph mother to see if she was sleep, she was woke and came out, we hug each other and said that we love each other, then we sit down on the couch and talk, until I told Joseph that I need to find a hotel close.

We had already got some beer he and I was drinking, then Joseph he took me to a hotel, there was 2 or 3 hotels over there, but witch one was for me to stay at, so I took the hotel 6, I went inside and got my room it was $106.98, number 225, I put my things in the room, then Joseph and I got some food to eat, after that Joseph he had something to do, we stop and I got some crown royal, Joseph said that he might be back in a hour, then he left, I went in my room and watch tv.

Now while I was waiting to see if Joseph, was coming back to night I meet this woman, remind me to Elsie she and I talk, I told her what I was doing here for, she told me, I said that I was at room 225 and if she want to come by, she would be Welcome. She said that her girlfriend was in 226 right under me; I said ok hope to see her again, she look at me and said real soon, I went back inside of my room.

Now the sooner or later was soon, she came up with some beer she ask me was it ok, I said o yes come on in, she did.

she and I was drinking crown royal and beer, I said to her that she remind me of a I guess, a friend of mine name Elsie in Vegas, she said o yes how are she, I said find looking at her, and that she have something that I need in my life, she ask me what was that! I explain to her about my book and that, I need someone to take it and market it for me, and if I make money and go to the top, she would be up there with me, she said ok if she don't like that or want it, that I should find someone else to help you, then she cross her legs, man what a site.

My dog side came out from me, she and I had a good time, then she said that she was going because, she had to work in the morning but, then she kiss me again and said tomorrow, I said that I had to go to the funeral at 1: pm, she gave me her phone number and said, now I didn't have no other excuse, then she left I went to bed.

That morning I got up and said that I better call, some back in Vegas to let them know, that I made it to Lancaster ca. ok, I call Miss Queen, Larissa my daughter and my other half of my heart Norman, that I was ok and that I would be back on Thursday, that the funeral was on Wednesday at 1:pm, that was the day I call them, Larissa she said daddy don't I need a ride, to get back home, I said that I don't know what time the bus, was going to get back in Vegas.

Larissa said then how was I going to get home, I said that I will take a bus or a cab and go home, because it might be too late after I get home, Larissa said daddy call her one way or the other, when I get home, I said that I would do that.

Then I call my cousin Isabell and Joseph, that when he gets here to pick me up, for the funeral that I would be ready.

Then my lady friend she call me, to see if she could see me after the funeral, later on about 11:pm I said why not, that I had one more day here, she said ok see me at 11:pm.

Then I said that I better take my shower now, because when Joseph get here I would be ready, I got in the shower and took my shower and came out, there was a knock on the door, it was Joseph he was ready to go he needed to stop, at a store and get himself a new suit, he did that the peoples in the store was so nice, after we left they knew how to get my book, on line.

After Joseph got his suit he was hunger, I don't eat that much so he stop and got himself a sandwich, then his cell phone ring it was another cousin, coming to the funeral of Hattie Ricco, from Los Angeles ca. all I wanted was a coffee I order one, then I ask the lady that waited on me, how much was the coffee cost, she look at me and said to me nothing.

Then my other cousin with his wife came, he induce himself to me and said that after the funeral, we was going to hook up, I said ok, he went in the store and got some food, for themselves, then we all went and pick up Isabell, and went to the funeral, after we got inside for the funeral and got seated, the singers start and the preaching start, after that I got up and said my say, how and when I meet Hattie Ricco my cousin.

It was in Brewton Alabama I was in Chicago, I came home to see my daughter Jackie, I went to Jackie mother house looking for Jackie, I look at that woman looking so much, like my sister Margieree in Chicago, I said how did my sister get here before I did, Jackie mother Brenda said David this is Hattie your first cousin, after that Hattie and I go close, I would call her and talk to her and her sister Isabell, before I hung up. Now Hattie as I said in my book, all we are doing are just passing through this world.

Now I didn't know that Hattie was going to be cremate, after the funeral was over it was a close casket, the peoples that do the cremate, they came and took the body away, we all went over to Aaron house for the after funeral dinner, Aaron he has a beautiful house and I was made Welcome, we ate talk drink crown royal, until the ones that live in California, they had to leave and go back but, now they know how to get in touch with me.

Now the rest of us that was still out there, we went to the liquor store and I got another crown, and we came back and drink that, I wanted to ask Joseph about that lady I meet, but I said no that was ok he might know them, or whatever so sometime you have to keep, your mouth close and do your thing, then Joseph he was ready to leave everyone else, was ready to go home or what, so Joseph he drop me back to the hotel.

After I got into my room I use the washroom, and went on the landing and stood looking, then I saw the lady that I meet, she had some smokes, beer and some crown royal she and I had a good time, I said to her that I was thinking about moving here, she smile and said o yes, I said yes if I had something to come back to, she said here she was, I said o yes, she said why not that I was what she think, that she want, and I could call her and she could call me, I could come and see her for a couple of days, and she could come and see me sometime, and when I get ready to move here in Lancaster ca. that I could stay with her, I said no that would not be right.

She ask me why did I say that she are single, I said that is not that, I am a man and a man should stand on his own two feet, and take care of his woman and make her happy, then she ask me did I have a woman in Vegas, I said no but there are one that I do love, but it don't mean anything to her, she ask me what kind of woman she are, I said she are sweet with a big heart, and she have something that I need, she took my hand and put it between her legs, and said is it this, I said no.

Then I told her about my book and I need, someone to market it for me, and if and when I pass on she would finish the last book, and all of my book passing through will be hers, she said that she do some marking, I said o yes then if I came back will she do it for me, and if I get on the top, she would be right there with me, she said that she was that woman for me, I said ok that I would give it a year to think about that, if I do then she and I have to make each other a commitment, to each other's.

Then it was getting kind of late, she and I left something to each other to all ways, think about until we see each other again, then she had to leave go home to go to work, in the morning, I got my things ready to check out at 12: noon tomorrow, then I went to bed and watch tv, until I went to sleep.

That morning I woke up and got out of bed, I took my shower and call Isabell, to let her know that if I don't see her, before my bus was to leave at 2:30pm. That I want her and the rest of my cousin, keep sweet and take care of themselves, until I see them again, then Isabell said you want see her before I leave, I said that my check out is 12: noon, and Joseph he have something to do at 1:pm, and my bus was to leave at 1:30pm.

Isabell said that Joseph he was there now, and did I want to talk to him. I said no just tell him that at 11:30, that I will check out from the hotel, and that I would be standing on the outside, by the office waiting.

So at that time came I took my things and, went to the hotel office and check out, and stood by the office waiting on Joseph to come, I wait, and waited it was at that time almost 12: noon, no Joseph. Now I had a couple of minute from my room, I went back and call Isabell to see if Joseph had forgot me, no answer I left a message that I was still waiting, then I went back and stood by the office waiting.

Everyone I saw and know that I was waiting on a ride, saw me and said that I was still waiting hum, I said o yes that my bus was leaving at 1:30pm, that I might have to call a cab, because life go on they maybe have something to do, they have things to do also for themselves, and a man he have to do what a man have to do.

So as I said it was getting closer to 1: pm, I said o no then I went inside of the office, and ask the desk person would she call a cab for me, she said sure then she ask where was I going, I said that I need to go to the bus station, that my bus was to leave at 1:30pm. So the desk person she call the cab for me, I ask her how much for calling the cab, she said not anything, I thank her and waited on the cab.

About 10 minute the cab came, I got in the cab as the cab was going to the bus station, I saw Joseph vehicle at the light, I told the cab driver to turn around that, I see my cousin sitting at the light coming to get me, the driver he had to go to the next light to turn around, I said don't worry about the fair I have to pay for that, then my cell phone ring, I answer it was Joseph, I said stay where he was at because the cab, and I was turning around coming back, he said a cab, I said it started getting late and I was standing, out here from 11:30pm to now I thought he had something to do.

So Joseph he got me to the bus station, I told him that I was going to call them, twice of a month to see if they was ok, and to let them know that I was ok, and when I am ready to move there, I would be there so they can look out for me, a house or an apartment I was going to give it a year, to stay or leave Vegas, and for him to take care until then, he said ok and they was going to call me also, Joseph he pull of I was waiting on the bus.

As I was waiting on the bus to come, there was a guy out there he live here in Lancaster, he start talking about how he was trying to get away from here, he was talking about those gangs in L.A. when the apartments, come to be condominium, and they can't afford one, all those kinds of peoples are coming to Lancaster, then he told me about the time he was in Vegas, and him and his woman was staying at the western hotel, and she wanted some ice, he went and got the ice it smell like bleach, and coming back to take the ice back, he had a run in on one of the security guys.

And what he was telling me, I don't know nothing but what he are talking about, he said that the security guy said that he was flashing a gangs sign, and bust his head now he got a lawyer, I said hay man that is what you are supposed to do, I gave him and another white guy, one of my card for my book, the white guy he said that he work for a whole year, and save his money for this day, now he are going to places to places seeing, everything that he can see in a year on the busses, then he look at my card and said that, is all he was doing is passing through, for one year then go back to work.

That was when I said that I was going to move here, the black guy he said here in Lancaster, I said that is right! He said what he had told me, is the reason why he want to leave here, I said well now that I have found my, other side of my family. I want to try and find out about them, to do that I will think about a year, to see if this is what I want. Then way later the bus came I got on disappointed, well I can't say that I was disappointed, I just didn't do what I tell others to do, read.

The bus was taken me back to Vegas to me, the long way but it was on my ticket, what can I say this is what the way of the bus company, all I had to do now was sit and ride, because the bus have their own rout, they will stop drop off and pick up and, that will give you a little time to straighten your legs, I rode that hard ride on my behind until we, got to Vegas I got off the bus and started walking, looking for a cab or to see if the M. L. King busses running, my cousin

Joyce had call me to see how I was going, to get back home, I said take a bus or a cab, she said that she think it stop running, that time of night. I said if not I would take a cab, she said to call her, I said ok it would be late.

Because the bus didn't get here until 1:pm, I was not going to call and wake up someone, to pick me up I am at home now, I found a ride right a main street station, I needed help to get home, and this guy was sitting there in his vehicle, he said cab that he would take me, to where I needed to go with a couple of dollars, then he said about $7.00, I said ok that I would give him $10.00, he said get in, I did then I told him to stop at a AMT machine, so I could get some money, so we stop at a service station on M. L. King Blvd. And Bonanza, and got $20.00 and gave the guy bringing me home $10.00, on the way to where I live, the guy he said that he was here from the storm, that was in Louisiana that could I give him another $3.00, I said that I only took out what I needed to, I need that $10.00 for myself he said ok, we got to my complex at the gate, I got out his vehicle he ask could he get an apartment in here, I said yes go to the office I point to it for him, but he have one problem, his wife is not 55 years old but he are.

Now at the funeral I didn't have me reading glass, I could not see the written on the Home going Services, of Hattie Ricco until I had my glass on then I read it, Hattie leave to celebrate her beautiful life and memories: one sister Isabell Lowe, one brother John H. Lowe Jr. (Evelyn) three nieces Diane Samuel (Walter), Pamela Cole and Cheryl Breaux; 3 nephews, Rev. Alonzo K. Jackson, Sr. (Sandra), Joseph Lowe and Charles Malone; great nieces Alonzo Jr. Sascha, Dajanae, Adrian, Akilah, and Jacquline; great nephews,

Alonzo Jr. Aaron, Gerard, Damon, Dalmar, David, Dwon and Christopher and a host of relatives, friends and church family. Now I know my other side of my family.

Now I had to take Miss Queen to, have some blood drawing for the doctor, I took her there and they draw the blood, then she and I came back home. Now my rest of the day was free, of me to do whatever, in my book I have catch up in my life, now I knew that 0n the next day Annett want to go to the Wal * mart, so what I did was stay at home and think about, what a fool I was to love someone, and they don't want me or love me, because they told me in many ways.

Now I was thinking about, how a man can be better then, as a woman has always said that, a man is nothing but a dog, if she train him or turn him around, she would have a good dog, because every woman need a good dog to respect. Now if you turn the spelling of dog around, you will see it spell God.

Now I use to be a five legs dog, all of them give me a problem, from the old Arthritis to the one that is the satisfaction of a lady, that one is ok. That one give me also a problem, the lady get it and act a fool, they want it all and get mad if anyone else, try to get it they want the others woman to stay back, but I love them all, because I have to love them all they are all loving creature, they are not to go and lay around bed with them.

Now still on this day thinking about my life, I made my decision for the love that I have for Elsie almost. About what I want and don't want in my life, and what I have already have writing about her, and what I thought it should be for me, now I have to back track and rewrite it, about why I have to walk away from that love, I have for Elsie. Not because I don't want her I love her, and she are no fool I know that, I still love her so much.

Now I can't explain it from my mouth, but from my heart I can, but if you read this you would understand it, and why I have to walk away from Elsie, that is because I have gave all the love to give anymore. There is not anything that I can do anymore, to show her that I love her so much, she don't want it. Now I will keep my memory I have gave to myself, and move on.

Maybe someone else may want love and sex together, because sex and love is so beautiful in bed. Now I am at a cross road and don't know what to do, now I can see in my future, that is now my wish to go and find love, and be with my other part of my family that I have found, in Lancaster ca. when I went to my cousin Hattie funeral, that is the path that I will follow, that is my wish.

On the 10th I got up and got Annett and took her, to take care of what she need to do, and took her back home and I went back home, with my bleeding heart.

The next day Marilyn she needed to go to the store, I told her that I would be on the outside, in front of the lobby at 9:am to take her to the store, I did that and Marilyn she got her grocer from the store, and I took her back home and I went home, lonely, sad and along by myself, then I got a call from my other half of my heart, (Norman) she said that Peat needed me, to meet him at Target on Craig and

Clayton, he had a canopy that was too large for his vehicle, he need to take it home for him, I said ok that I was on my way I left and found Peat, with the canopy and put it on my truck, and took it to Peat house then I went back home, and did nothing.

On the 14th Annett she wanted me to take her and her cat, to the vet, I did that and she needed to stop at Wal* mart, to get something we did that and came back home, to see if the vet was going to call her, to pick up the cat later. I went home and waited until after my soaps was over, I went on the outside at 3: pm Jennet she was out there, she and I was talking then my cell phone ring, it was Annett the cat was ready to come back home, I said ok then I went and got my truck, and pick up the cat with Annett, and stop she needed some poster stamps, and came back home.

On the 15th all I did was the same things that I always do, every day if no one needs me other then, getting the mail for Miss Queen, sitting out until I decide to do anything or not. And watch my soaps and go out again after 3:pm, Jennet the white lady that live next to me, she was out with me she had something for Miss Queen, I showed Jennet how to get to Miss Queen porch, she went over to the porch and talk to Miss Queen.

After she was finish talking to Miss Queen, and was coming back to the table where I was at, she fell there was another lady that was sitting out, she and I got up running to see if Jennet was ok, then the other lady and I pull Jennet up, she said that she was ok, I ask did she want me to call 911. she said no just get her up, we did that and came and sit back down, Jennet she had some bruise on her arm, from the fall,

I said when she get home clean it and put some peroxide on it, she said ok that she had some peroxide.

Now after I got home Elsie she call me, I was watching the basketball game, Elsie she wanted my social security statement, so she could copy it was time for me to renew my lease, I said ok, she said that it could be tomorrow or later, in joy the game then she hung up, I said wait then I call Elsie right back, and said that I was going to bring that statement now, then I said that I had another pack of cigarette in my refrigerator, if she want it because it been in the refrigerator to long, she said ok, I went to the office.

After I got there the office was close, I turn the tv to the game and waited on Elsie, to come back to what she had to do. Then she and I went to her office she said sit down, I did then I said that this was the last time, I was going to get her kind of cigarette, and keep them in my refrigerator that long, she didn't say anything but hum, hum, hum. I said that now I don't have anyone to help now, I was going to give one more year then, I was going to move to Lancaster ca. all she would say was hum, hum, hum, then I said it was not her fault it was mind, I should not had got to close to her.

After she had said that she know how to marketing, I didn't want to lose her I told her that before, and I would do any and everything to keep her, that was all I wanted from Elsie nothing else, if she wanted more she could get it, but I want do anything to upset her nothing but happiness, now I see that she don't want to help me, then do whatever make her happy because, all I am doing is passing through this world, looking for my happiness anyway I can find it, in a year that will make up my mind if I, want to stay or move.

After I made up my mind to leave, I am thinking about relocated to Lancaster ca. and if I decide to stay, I will find another apartment and move to it, now Elsie she have put me down for her girlfriend, and don't want anything to do with me, I feel that I have use her, because I did write something very good about her, what I saw and how I saw it from my heart, she want benefit or take the advantage of the profit, it will make it. I wrote this because everyone is a user. God use Jesus, Jesus use me, I use you . . . the devil is a user. We all use someone or something.

At a little after 7:pm I went out walking as I always do, I saw Mr. Jenson sitting at the sitting area, by himself I stop and had a cigarette and talk to him, Elsie and Lorraine was still in the office, then Killer he came out there we all was sitting talking, then Elsie she turn off the lights from the lobby, she was ready to get off work, after Elsie had lock to lobby door, going to her vehicle with Lorraine they stood talking, after Elsie pull off we didn't see Lorraine go to her apartment, Elsie she slowed around before, she went to the gate to go out, we saw Lorraine in Elsie vehicle.

Mr. Jenson he was messing with her, why didn't she come far enough so we could see, after she did come for Jenson to see, Lorraine we didn't see. I said Lorraine is hiding so no one can see her, then someone said yes it must be true, what some are saying out here about them, I said that I heard that also, then Elsie she wave to us and pull of, with her play thing, I said that I don't want me any of that, no way.

Chapter 11

On the 16th Miss Queen she had a doctor appointment at 10:am, I went and took her there for her appointment, and we came back home, after that all I did was sit outside, and someone else came out I would talk to them, I was trying to get Elsie off my mind, after all she had already said to me that, she didn't love anyone even to her son, but I went too far with her, trying to try to get her to marking my book, I was falling in love with her, I told her that but it was not her fault, that was on me.

There was the other lady that, was trying to get her hook in me before, name Judy, Miss Russell friend she is a nice lady but, she was pusher to get what she wanted from me, I don't want no woman to, try and push me to be with her, you can't push love and sex to soon, it want work.

Before the 17th Judy and I start back talking again, I didn't hate her for what she had did to me before, because a woman she see something on someone, she think that is what she want, until she get it, then she see that is not what she want, and all she are doing is hurting a good man. You see now, I can't put all of that on a woman shoulder, there are some good woman out there, they had been hurt badly about a man, and they want open up to another good man. I have seen and meet them, while I am passing through.

On the 17th I said that Judy and I was going to, spend some time together just as a friend, because after all we all get lonely sometime, and need a friend to hold or talk to, if not then you are not human, or you don't have any feeling.

That Sunday the 18th a friend of mind Annett, she found me and ask me would I, move something around her apartment for her, the day before she got another bed and I, put it up for her and she wanted to change, the other room around. So I told her, that I would move it for her, so I did that for her, she is a nice lady and I am able, and capable to help her, God and Jesus help me. So why can I help others.

Later on I saw Glen, he and I went over to where the other apartments that Frank was building on another site, Glen said that the other day he meet Elsie Husband.

That was when I said that, Elsie said that she had got her Divorce before she got here, Glen said well she must have remarry him because he meet him, that he came over here looking for her, and he said that he was her Husband, I said then why would she lie? Glen he said there was plenty lies Elsie had told, I said don't peoples know that, if they tell a lie it would catch up to them.

We got to the other site that frank was building on, Frank he was there, Glen he wanted to talk to him about Miss Grand, I said man Frank is busy, he don't need to hear about that bull shit, then we saw Steward sitting by one of the building model, I said hay Steward how are he doing, he said hay David how are you doing, I said man, I can't complain because no one want to hear it, they have their own complain, so what I do is give it to God and Jesus, and go on and do what I have to do.

Steward he showed me the model, Glen he said to Steward, man when are they going to finish his apartment, that he wanted them to get it ready now, that he want to move in now, Steward he told Glen that they would get it ready soon, Glen he showed me his apartment, but to me they was smaller, then the ones over where I live in Louise Shell, then Glen said that they would have, washer and dryer in their apartment, and they want have to pay no utility.

Now I am no fool and I know about business, and I know how it work, the rent was more over there on the other site, because the utility is include in the rent, over at Louise Shell we have to pay our own utility bills, so it all come together, paying it in the rent or paying it yourself, one thing about it, you have to pay for it.

Then Glen and I got ready to leave, Steward said David, I said what up! He said Kopoe move hum, I said yes, she told me that she was moving in Henderson, that she had apartment over there, Steward said that she was telling a lie, that Miss Grand wanted her/ Kopoe to move because of her mouth, and that if Kopoe would get down on her knees, and beg that she could stay where she was at, I said what! When you get on your knees, you are ready to eat, something to make the other person happy, Steward, Glen and I had a good laugh, then I said to Steward talk to him later, Glen and I left Frank he was still busy, we came back home.

Now I go to my bank, and get my rent money early before the 1st of the month, and pay my rent then for the next month, I do that because the rent have to be paid anyway, so why hold the money, that away I will had been paid my rent, and I will know, that I can stay for another month, and the rest of the money that I have left, I pay my utility bills and my Insurance bills, and the rest of the money, I can use it the way I want to use it, I want owe anyone anything.

On the 20th I change my business cards, the way that I had before, passing through—by author—David L. Marshal— book purchase on www. Trafford Com-T-shirts available by calling David business manager-(702) 633-7402, the change I made was putting my picture on my new cards.

A neighbor of mind name is Floyd, that live across the hall from me, he was on the outside with a man that was looking at his vehicle, to work on it, he and I was talking about moving soon, he said that he was thinking about moving back to Alabama, I said that after a year, I was thinking about moving to Lancaster, Ca. that I had a year to think about it, because there was some of the old lady, that live in Louise Shell depend on me, like Miss Queen, and some of others I had to consider about them, like Jesus I will never leave them or forsake them.

Later on that day a friend of mind Judy call me, she and I was talking, my foot was itching I ask Judy, what was it when your foot start itching, she said well David don't take it the wrong way, it need washing then she and I start laughing,

David L. Marshall

after she and I had hung up, I went to the washroom and wash them, and said that Judy, then I said my foot was clean and, I start laughing again.

Now my other neighbor that live next door to me, name Jennet the day before, she was talking to Miss Queen by her porch, after Jennet had left and was coming back, to the sitting area where I was sitting, Jennet she fell on the side walk, I saw her fall the first thing I did was, jump up and went to her and pick her up, there was another lady, that was sitting on the other table, she went over to help Jennet also, I ask Jennet was she ok or was she hurt, she was bleeding on her arm.

Jennet she said that, she think that she are ok, she and I went and sit back down, I said why don't she go into the office, and report that she had falling! Jennet she said that she was ok she think, I said when she get back home, clean up her arm and put some peroxide on it, she said that she would do that.

That same day I had appointed to go, to the office it was close time, for me to renew my lease, and I had to bring something with me, like my bank statement and last year social security statement, so when it was time for my appointed, I went to the office so that Miss Elsie, the manger to copy the statements for my file, I explain to Elsie what had happen to Jennet, how and when Jennet had falling, I told Elsie because if, I had not told her later she, would have got on me, why didn't tell her what had happen.

Now after I got back home, I ask Jennet did she go and explain the office, what had happen to her about she had falling, she said no not yet.

Later on I was looking at tv, my phone ring it was Elsie, she said David, that she had Miss Jennet in her office, and she was telling her what had happen, about she had falling on the side walk, I told her the same thing that I had told her(Elsie) in her office, Elsie said to me, that was ok and that she was not using me for no messenger, I said that it was not that away, Elsie said ok think she and I hung up.

Now on the 23rd Jennet she went to the doctor, after I saw her later on that day, she said that her daughter had taken her to the doctor, and found out that she had a broken toe also, when she fell, all I could say was wow.

On that same day I went to the casino, Jerry Nugget to place my bet for the sweet sixteen, basketball playoff for UNVL team that was playing, Miss Russell she went with me, I ask her did she want to go inside with me, she said no that she will stay in the truck, until I put my bet in and came back, so I went and place my bet for a hundred dollars, for to take the three points on UNLV to win and came back.

After I came back to my truck, and got inside and started the truck, I was telling Miss Russell about what Judy, and I was talking about when my foot was itching, and I ask Judy what was it, she said that my foot needed washing, Miss Russell she started laughing, and said that girl is so crazy, I said that Judy was a nice lady, but I wash my foot anyway just in case.

Then Miss Russell said that, she had heard that when your foot itch, that mean that your foot was going to be place in International soil, I said well that book of mind, might take me anywhere, I don't know then we got back home, Miss

Russell said that she was going and, go and fix her some food to eat, I said think to her for take that ride with me, she said that was her pleasure, then I went back home and watch my soaps.

On the 26th my other half of my heart, Norman she call me that she needed me, to take her to Albertson food store, to pick up a fruit tray to take it over to Do little, the next day for bingo, I said ok that I would pick her up on the back side, of the building two where she live, I put on my shoes got in my truck and pick her up, and was going to the store, she was telling me how to get to that Albertson store, like I didn't know all I did was smile and kept on driving.

After we got closer to the store, Norman she look at me and said, you know where you are going, I smile and said o yes that I do, then I said that there is almost of the lady, that work there I know them, after we got into the store, I saw one of the black lady that work there, I have seen her for a while, at this time of the night it was at 7:pm, she is a supervisor in the store on the shift, she look at me and said David where have you been, she and some of the girls was putting up some sodas.

After I said that I have been looking for her, and at this time of the evening I be kind of busy, then I gave her one of my card, she look at me as to say now David, he got his woman with him and talking so sweet to me, what is up to that.

After Norman got the fruit tray, the supervisor she was working on one of the cash register, I got in line where she was at, and start telling her that how beautiful she look, and how find she are, she was smiling and looking at Norman,

I said that I see my girl Kim sometime, she said yes if Kim was here that I would be in her line, I said yes Kim would not mind it I was in your line, the supervisor she said I don't know, Kim is your girl, I said and you are to, then she look at Norman and said, if you was with her you would not, talk about another woman like that, I said o this is my other half of my heart, she is just a good friend of mind, but I love you then Norman and I left out.

You know God put all of his creation, on his earth for a reason. Even to you and every life he put here, no matter it being big or small, walking, crawling or standing.

That is all life God our Father put here. Now I don't know what your reason, in my pass I didn't know then, but now I do. He showed me the reason for ground of motive; faculty of thinking; sensible of logical of viewing of loving others, he put me on my own path to walk, sometime on my way it get hard, but he will get me through.

Now I know, it is hard to do a job for God and Jesus, of what they want you or me to do, to open up my heart and let all the love, God put into me. And let it shine from my heart, all through into my face, with smiles, without a frown of how peoples think about you, my happiness and blessing come when, doing things for them to make them smile and happy, if they are down a picker upper, when some don't get that from others, all I want or need is, to tell someone how nice they look, or just say that I love them with the life, God our Father has given to me, for them.

Some take my goodness for a weakness, some don't but some want more from me, that the things that now I can't or, want do any more like I have did in my pass life, as jumping in and out of bed with single or a marry woman, with sex that use to be me not anymore, a wise man change but a fool will never will.

God put Jesus on earth for a reason, look at what they peoples did to him, but Jesus, he are a better man then I, now I will love you the same as God want me to do, but if you throw rocks at me, or spit on me I am sorry and Hope God forgive me.

On the 28th I had appointment in the office from Miss Elsie, for 1:30pm. To sign my new renter lease, I did that took care of my business and left out, I was sitting out on the sitting area smoking a cigarette, someone else was out there also, they ask me a Question.

They wanted to know what was wrong with Elsie, and I that we don't talk or be out anymore smoking a cigarette. Now I started to put them into their place, but they did touch my heart, and I could not insult them then, all I said was ask Elsie.

On the 31st they had a cook out in the center, where we all sit out no one said David, that they was going to have a cook out, and did I want to come because, I do so much for them that they wanted me to come, I would have went but, no one ask me so I stayed. Away, I don't go anyplace if I am no invited; I don't crash any one party.

After the first of April my new lease was sign, and I have another year to stay here in Louise Shell complex, I was thinking about after another year, moving to Lancaster Ca.

but now, I have so much of felling for some of the lady, that need me to help them, one way or the other, and I don't want to leave them, so what I am going to do now, is put it in God hand and let him decide my destiny, he know better than I do.

On the 2nd of April Miss Queen she had an appointment, to go and have some blood drawn, she had it to be done before that Friday of the 13th of April, for her next doctor appointment, so she had to be there at 9: am. I took her there and she got her blood drawn, and she and I came back home. The rest of my day was Norman.

On the next day I did some work in my computer, for my book now I have catch up, for June the 5th to close book 2 of passing through, after my retirement and my birthday party, I was going to give for the peoples that live in the complex, if they wanted to be with me on that day, they are welcome. I saw this woman that I didn't know, but I have seen her going to the store, and coming back to building number 4, on this day Jennet and I was sitting out, this same lady I can't forget those big breast, she was carrying around with her, she stop and spoke and sit down with Jennet and I, was sitting.

She started talking as she knew me, she said that her mother would not let her smoke, in the house or on the porch, then she had some whiskey in her purse, she open what she had left and drink it, and put the bottler in the garbage can, Jennet she kept on looking at me, I kept looking at those big breast that woman, was carrying around with her.

Then she said that her mother was mad with her, because she went out and didn't come back home, until 4:am and that all she do while she are here, was cook because her husband he was a truck driver, and she had cook a good dinner for him, that he had sugar and he have to eat, I ask where did they live other then while she was in Vegas, she said that she live in L. A. and that on Saturday he was to pick her up and going back home, she was saying that how good she was to her old man, cook, rub his feet, give him a bath. I said that is a kind of woman that I need.

Then she wanted to know what building did I live in, I told her, she said that sometime would it be ok, if she come by my apartment and sit and talk to me, if I didn't have a wife holding on to me, I said there was no wife, she said that sometime she see me walking around, the complex with my find self, I said o yes, I have to keep in shape, then her cell phone ring she answer it, then she said that it was her mother, wanted to know where was she, that her mother didn't want her to have anything, to do with the peoples live in here, then she said that she had to go, I said call me when she need someone to talk to, she said ok she had my card then she left, Jennet she kept looking at me smiling, I said what! She said you are something, I said well I am not married.

On April the 4th it was Judy my friend birthday, so I gave her some passion perfume, and one of my book passing through, of my life so she would learn about me, from my pass, so I know that I would not see Judy, on her birthday I gave it to Miss Russell. Now Miss Russell she had brought my book, and she said that she was enjoying reading it, I know that she would give the book to Judy.

On the 5th it was at about 4:30am in that morning, I had come home and could not sleep, so what I do when I can't sleep, I walk around the complex for my health, the lady that I was talking about with, those big Breast her name is Brenda, she was standing on the outside, in front of the building of where her mother stay, I spoke to her and kept on walking, she stop me and ask me? What building did I live in! I told her in building #3, she ask me what time would I be back by here, I said, after I walk to the end of the complex, that I would be back through here what up, she said that she would tell me after I came back, I went to the end of the complex by Lake Mead, by Art live.

After I came back to where Brenda was standing, she ask me would I let her stay with me, until day light that her mother and her sister had put her out, I said ok until day light, then I told her to take her luggage and wait, by my truck until I came back, she did, I started thinking about that but, I remember at one time someone had, to do the same thing for me in my pass, so I hope her take her things into my apartment.

Now I had made some coffee before I went outside, I ask Brenda did she want some coffee, she said please that she need some, then she started telling me what had happen, while her mother had her sister put her out, that she had cook that dinner, and later on she went out to have a drink, and she was having fun and it got late, and after she got back home her mother told Brenda, that she had to stay out, and her sister brought her things to the door for her, that her mother didn't want Brenda back in her apartment.

Then Brenda she said that, she like the way that I have my apartment, and that she could clean and cook for me, and make me feel good then she wanted to smoke a cigarette, she said that we had to go out to the sitting area, I ask why we can sit on my porch, she said that her mother said that we could not smoke on the porch, I said that her mother she didn't know what she was talking about, Brenda she said then her mother told her a lie, she and I went out on the porch and smoke a cigarette, then I gave her a pillow, and let her get some sleep on the couch, until about a two hours, then I woke her up to go and talk to her mother, and got her business straighten out with them.

That same day I had got some ox tail from the store, that I was going to make some ox tail stew, before Miss Queen, Robin and I was talking about it, I said that I was going to get some and cook it, Miss Queen she said that she had some, that her son CREIG had brought and that, I could use them, I said know that when I go to the store that, I would get some and we could all have some.

Then Robin she ask me David, could she have some of my ox tail, I said o yes that she could have some also, with my sexist voice, Robin she gave me her sexist smile, with her sexist self and said, thank you David! I said that she was welcome, Miss Queen smile and look at me, she have always said to me that, one day one of those Ladies was going to call my bluff.

Later on that Friday we all was sitting out, it was Joanne, Jackie and I was talking, and Elsie, the maintenance man David and another guy, was standing buy the guy truck he was ready to leave, Jackie she said that she had to work the next day, and she would not be here to get any ox tail, I said ok did she want to go to my apartment, and get some now, Jackie she said no go and get her some, then I said that is right those Ladies, would have a fit if they saw Jackie, going to my apartment.

That was when Jackie said come on she was not afraid, she got up with me and she and I, was going to my apartment, I look back and saw Elsie she had turn around.

She look as to say what was going on with this, so Jackie and I got to my apartment, and she fix some food and she and I went back, Joanne she said it didn't take that long, Jackie she said it don't take long then she smile, now, Jackie she have a big trunk on her, with a lots of junk in that trunk, every man would love to open up that trunk, and take a look inside to see what was in there, I know that it would be a pleaser for me to see.

That Saturday I gave some ox tail stew to those who wanted some, they know who they are, right Miss Elsie. That day some of the tenant they had a yard sale, I didn't take no part in that, I stood by Miss Queen porch and talk to her, and went and got Miss Blackwell son David, a cocktail because he gave me one once before, I had to return the favor.

That Sunday on the 8th my cousin Joyce husband Robert, he was in the hospital I went and spent some time with him, talking to see how he was doing, then his doctor came into and saw him, Robert he thought that he was going to have to go back, under the knife again and that he didn't want to, that was when I said that God is the only one know, and he is a good God so put it in his hand, and don't think about it because he are the only doctor, man they are only an instrument for God, they are not God. Then about after 1: pm I told Robert that, I had to go and that, I would

David L. Marshall

come back to see him later, if he was still here, Robert said ok then I left.

You know life is precious, it is of great value, highly valued, affected, over refined like sugar and all of those sweetish things in life of love. In my life time, I am not all proud of, but in time a wise man will change, but a fool will never change, I am now a wise man, I have change my life for the better.

Now after I meet Elsie, I guess she showed me that I cannot have, everything in life that I see and want, at one time I was so in love with her, without jumping in and out of bed, because temptation sometime will fool you, let it go. I never would thought that, I would give my whole life and love to one woman, (she was a lady name Elsie) a lady that I would do and give her everything, if I had it, because I loved her that much.

Now after Lorraine and the other ladies that live in the complex where I live didn't want to see us together even to be as a friend. They tried everything they could, to block and stop that happens, why! Because I don't or didn't want them the way I love Elsie, they thought I was trying to get into Elsie pants, but if it was she wanted, it came with love. But all I wanted was to have someone, that if I needed to have talk to it, I had a way to better market my book, now that Elsie don't have anything else, to do with me or talk to me anymore, other than about my lease on my apartment, those ladies they still can't get me into their bed, because I don't want that. Like I said before, I don't want them auguring about me, because I went to bed with one of them.

You see even if it was Elsie, that went to bed with me, I would have to make a commitment to her to love and honor her, but she would have to do the same for me also, and have trust in me the same as I have in her, otherwise she would be the same as those ladies, stay away from her man, but she would have to do it in another way, she would wait until she and I was along, then I would catch hell because in bed, I don't play fair I love to win.

Now I want know because Elsie she told me that, she don't love anyone and that she don't need anyone help, especially me so I got her message. After that I have move on after all I am just passing through, I will find another one to love and give her, all the love that God gave me to give to another.

On the 9th I was at home along doing anything, two of my school buddy, I went to school with and played football with call me, they was Otis Redmond and Len Mcconnice, they wanted to let me know that, one of our teacher Miss Fisher she was going, to be 85 years older on her birthday, and that they was going to have something in Brewton, Alabama, for her on the 4th of July 07, and they wanted to see if I would come and be there, but like I told them right now, I can't say yes or not because, I had right now some other commitment, and I might not can get away from it, but I would let them know before the 4th of July, Otis he said is this the same David Lee Marshall, that we went to school with, I said that is he, Otis said was we that bad when we was coming up, I said o yes that I left out some of it, those are skeleton in our closes.

On the 10th Annett the lady that I look out for, when she have to go any place to, take care of her business she, needed me to take her to the cleaner, to take her cloths to have them clean, I did that and came back home about 9:30am. Because on the 12th Miss Queen, she had a doctor appointment for that day, and when I put it on my calendar for a date, that date is for her or them, now Queen she had a doctor appointment for, the 12th and the Friday the 13th but, on the 13th I could not take her.

Because she had to fill out some papers that I could not do for her, her daughter in law, Creig, Queen son wife she had to take her, to fill out the papers for her, but on the 12th I took Queen to the doctor appointment, and brought her back home. After Queen and I got back home, I went to get the mail from the lobby, I saw Jennet and some of the other tenants, sitting in the lobby I spoke to them, then I look at the window from Elsie office, there was some numbers on a paper, for the apartment numbers to call the office before 5: pm, Jennet said to me that my apartment was on it, I had saw that.

Then I said thanks that, I know what it was for because my rent was paid, all it could be was that they want to clean my carpet, and she wanted to give me appointment to do it, so I got Queen and my mail and took Queen mail to her, and I went back home.

After I got back home I call the office, but Elsie she was not in the office, so I left a message that I was calling to see, what she wanted that my apartment number was on the list, and that I would call her back, so later on I went to the lobby to wait on Elsie, Toni she and Jenson wife was in the lobby, I spoke to them and ask Toni, how was her father doing, because he was sick and he was in a nursing home now, that he could not take care of himself now, Toni she said that her dad was doing good now, then she ask me did I hear what had happen, I said no what? I knew but peoples will say anything, Toni said that her sister Kopoe, was trying to tell the peoples at the home, how to do their job. I said what! She said yes now they don't want Kopoe, to come and see dad now he are ok, I said good tell him that I ask about him.

Then I ask Toni was Elsie coming back to day, it was after 5: pm. She said yes that she was coming back, I waited and waited then I went back home, I knew then that Toni had told a lie, so what is new.

One day I was at home and the phone ring, I answer it was my play sister Bobby, from Chicago, there was one of the ladies that I use to go with, I was in love with her name is Candy, sweet Candy she and Bobby was on the phone, on the three way call, we talk for a while then Candy she said that, on the 14th she was going to see me, I said what are she coming to Vegas, Candy said that was right that, her mother, sister and some others peoples was coming on the 14th April. I said did she know how long that, I have seen her. Candy said too long, then Bobby she said boy she would love to be, a fly on the wall of that hotel room, that night when we saw each other, Candy said on that night.

Then I said that night was going to be very special, Candy she said that I took it right out of her mouth, then Bobby she said David, what are you and Candy going to do, Candy she said to Bobby, whatever David and she was going to do in bed, that was our thing, Then I ask Candy, did she still have that trophy of the memorial of, the victory of the loving that I put on her in the pass, Bobby she started to laughing and said, Candy what trophy David are talking about.

Candy said that she had to hide that picture, Bobby said laughing David, what picture Candy are talking about, I said that before Candy and I broke up, I took all of my cloth off naked, my big boy was so hard, I took my Polaroid Camera and took a picture of him, and call Candy to meet me, she did, we went to the hotel and made love, I gave Candy that picture and said that, as long I am in her heart keep this picture that, she have a trophy of me to remind her, of all those nights that she and I made love, together.

Then Candy said that on the 14th when she get here to Vegas, and call me to come to where she are, then she and I was going to rekindle that fire, I said that was a date and that I can't wait, she said ok see me on the 14th, we hung up.

On the 14th that day came, I had to work on my truck breaks before Candy plane arrival, so she and I could rekindle the love that she and I, use to enjoy, after I had fix the breaks on my truck, and came inside and clean myself up, the phone ring I answer it was Miss Elsie, she said that she had got both message that, I had left and that all she wanted to do was, to let me know that it was time for them to, clean my carpet and what day was my best day, for the man to clean it, I said any day is ok for me.

Then Elsie she said that, she was going to put a day and time sheet in my door, if I was not going to be at home, to let me know what day and time, the carpet man was coming, I said ok thank and she and I, hung up.

Later on there was a knock on my door, I open the door it was David the maintenance man, he hand me the cleaning notice, I said thank David then, I look around in the hall I saw Elsie, she wave and smile, I look at the maintenance man he was not smiling, I put a little smile on my face, as to say what is this, then they left and I close my door.

Now, I guess you are waiting to read about Candy and I rekindle, of our long lasting lover affair, will when someone are marry now, something have to be kept in the closet, keep that thing you eat with close, after all tongue and teeth fall out sometime, teeth will bite tongue, if it talk too much.

On that same day early I was in the office, you see I am the kind of a person that, I respect other peoples where as they don't respect them self, at one time like I said before, about Miss Elsie, I had and still have all the love and respect for her, no matter what she think about me, that morning there was the mailman, putting in mail into the box, and tenants was waiting to the mailman finish, putting the mail into the box, I spoke out loud to everybody, because some of the tenants they can't hear so good, and if they don't hear me, they will say what is wrong with David Marshall, so I made sure they heard me.

Then Elsie she call me David, I answer her, she said come here, I went to see what she wanted, there was David the maintenance man in the office also, I spoke to him and Elsie she was telling me, that Miss Grand had got my right date, for my lease and put it back to April the 1st, I said that was ok because, I was not going to lose the back days, that I was not staying here, I was still staying on Cheyenne and

David L. Marshall

M.L. King Blvd. I got my apartment key from Louise Shell, on April the first.

Elsie said now my lease was from April the first, I said thank and was going to leave out from her office, Elsie she call me back, I went back to see now what, she said why don't she get those hellos like, she use to get them, I said that was what she wanted ant it, she said that I say hello to the others with pride, I said that she didn't want to have anything else, to do with me and that I had to respect her wish, then she said that she wanted it back, I said you have to be careful about what you ask for, then she said that her wish now is that, for me to speak with her again with pride, I said to the maintenance man David, do you hear that, he said yep, then I said that whenever now, that I see Elsie again, she will have all of my attention of hello Miss Elsie, she said thank.

That Monday morning I waited on the carpet man, to clean my carpet I was in the lobby, talking to Toni about how was her dad doing, Toni said that dad was doing find, I said tell him that he and I, have to go and find a young lady, Toni said that she would tell him, then I saw the carpet man coming through the gate, he came to my apartment and clean my carpet, and left, I went to my bank and got my rent money order, fill it out and put it into the slot of the office door, got Queen and myself mail, took Queen her mail and then I went back home, and watch my soaps.

Now my cousin Joyce she still have not fill out my tax, and I had sent my rent rebate off with the tax, I said that it was now the last day for filling now, so I will lose that so I call Joyce, and told her that I have sent my rent rebate off now, so don't fill those tax out now that, it is now the 17th of April and it was too late, Joyce said that she was going to fill it out, I said that was ok now it was too late, I sent out the rent rebate.

Now this prejudice radio star Don IMUS, he said that he was not prejudice, sure that was what he said until he got catch, about those girl basketball team about their nappy hair, now he wish that he never had said that, now his ass is nappy and in trouble.

Now Miss Queen birthday is on the 20th of April, I said that on the 21st that Saturday, I was going to have a cook out for her, and secret tell some what I was going to do, so I did that and on the 19th Jenson he wanted me to go and get, a dresser that his wife had already paid for, I said ok when did he want to go and get it, he said that my time was his, I said ok how about Friday, he said ok.

Now on that same day Elsie she wanted to talk, so she and I went into her office and talk, I still love Elsie, and I always will but, if someone don't want me, I give then there space, after Elsie wanted to have a cigarette, I said ok it was about 5:pm Jenson wife, she was coming to the lobby I guess, she saw Elsie and I was going to smoke a cigarette, she came over to where we was at, we all was talking I start thinking that was when, I ask Jenson wife to call him to see if he wanted to go, and pick up what he needed for tomorrow, she said that she didn't have a phone, I gave her my phone to use.

She ask me to call him, I said no she call him that is her Husband so she did, and gave me the phone he said ok that we can go now, I said that when I go and get my truck, that I would meet him on the back side, of the building one where he live, I told Elsie that see her later that, I was going to do that for Jenson today, because tomorrow I might be busy, she said ok then I left, and got my truck and got Jim.

On the way to the store to pick up the dresser for, his wife he was piss off about, when he had stop in the cross walk, to talk to me about picking up the dresser, Elsie made him move he didn't like that, he said that one day he was going to move away, and go back to where he came from in Caroline, I said it would not have taken long to ask me that, he said that his wife said get over it, now they don't have no money if they did, they would not be over in her with these black peoples, I don't care if you read this and say that, I am wrong, I have seen the prejudice in him and his wife, and others has saw it also they told me about it, I said that was not news, I saw it before but he better not go too far with it, because black peoples don't take that anymore, not from anybody.

Now I got to the store and pick up the dresser and came back, I had to go and get my hand truck to move the dresser, to Jim apartment because he is no good, he can't pick up anything he is a cripple, I went to my apartment and got my dolly, and took the dresser to Jim apartment, he paid me what I ask for my truck, sometime I want charge for my labor, but I can't speech for my truck, I get $25.00 for it.

Chapter 12

Now ELSIE SHE HAD A meeting in the lobby, it was to be about when there is a fire alarm, going off in the building come out from your apartment, and go onto the center and wait, until a fireman or the manger say that, it was ok to go back into their apartment, don't let your neighbor tell you that, the alarm don't mean anything because, it was not from your apartment, who know, your neighbor might not like you hum, now don't take your neighbor word, about your safety get out until, it was safety to go back.

Now Miss Queen I had walk her over, to the lobby for the meeting with Miss EVELYN and Miss Louse, was there also, after the meeting was over and we left, Miss Queen she said David that she had to sit down for a while, she and I sit and Miss EVELYN and Miss Louse walk on, I had told other that Miss Queen she, didn't know about her birthday party, now peoples I don't know is they, stupid or be trying to be funny, now there is another woman that live in here, she saw Queen and I sitting she, ask me right in front of Queen, David what time is the party tomorrow, that stun me, I said some peoples should keep their dam mouth close, Queen she are no fool.

She act like she didn't hear that, so Queen she got up and walk on to her apartment, I went back home to start getting things ready for the party, the next day.

That Saturday morning I got up about 6:am, and took the meat from my apartment, and put it on my porch with the cooler and all the things, that I needed to work with by the grill, so that I would not have to keep on running back and forth, from my apartment to the barbecue area, because the night before I clean out the grill, and sit it up with the Charcoal, ready to be lighted to burn off the gas from the coal, and put the meat on to be cook, because I wanted all the meat ready before 12: noon.

Because before 12: I wanted to have all the meet cook and ready, with the other food that the others peoples was bringing, and I wanted to have my shower, and clean up so that I could have me some fun, so I did all of that with 15 minute to spare. Queen she said David you had 30 minute before 12: noon, and you went and have a shower clean up, and, I said and I smell good smell me, and I still have 15 minute to spare.

And after 12: noon that day, I did have myself some fun, all of mind and Miss Queen friends was there, and the ones who was not our friend, they know who they are. I was moving from one table to another, talking to those ladies trying to make them all happy, you see I love all females no matter their color, or their sizes I am not prejudice, a female can carry and bring life into this world, I know that because one carry and brought me here, that was my mother, almost every woman is a mother.

Now my friend Marilyn she was at the party also, she said that on Sunday morning that, she had to go to the store, and was I going to be busy, I said about or before 9: am, Marilyn she said ok sees me then because, now she was going to have herself some fun.

And she said David the food is so good, and she wanted to know who was the birthday lady, that she had a present for her, I induce Marilyn to Miss Queen, they talk then my other mom Ruth she came out, and said David who are the lady that the birthday is for, I induce Queen to mom Ruth they knew each other, they had a reunion.

That Sunday morning I got up and took Marilyn to the store, she got her grocers and I took her back home, and there is another lady that live in here, she have paint on her vehicle tires, after David the maintenance man had panted the curves, in here the lady she got to close to the curves, and got paint on the tires, I said that, I was going to change them over for her, that you can't see the paint, after I got back, I got in touch with her to help her, I took one of the tire off and made a call, but my buddy boss was there and I, had to put the tire back on the vehicle, and told her that I could not rotate the tires, for her because my buddy boss was at work, he could not brake the tires for me.

On the 24th I got a call from my cousin Joyce, she said that I could come and get my tax papers, the she have finish them, I said ok that if she was not going to be at home, leave the papers on the outside some place, that I could find them and I would get them, she ask me what time was I going to get over there, I said that it would be after 3:pm. Joyce said at that time Mike her son would be at home, and she would leave the papers on her desk, I said ok and hung up.

After I had talk to Joyce and hung up, Miss Queen was talking about going to go to the store, that now that she are feeling better now, you see Miss Queen she are about 84 years old, and she have been sick but now she are doing find, I keep a watchful eye on her, that is a promise I made to her son, Creag that I would do for him and Queen also, I said ok if that is what she wanted to do, then she and I would go, she said that she wanted to do something for herself, things that Creag want have to do, because he work so much and he be tried sometime, I said ok then call me and let me know, she said well ok.

Then something look like said to me, call Joyce and let her that, I was coming over now and get those tax papers, because I might have something to do later on, that I had talk to Miss Queen and, I might have to take her to the store later before 3:pm, she said ok that she would be at home for a little while, I said that, I was going to get little Joe and bring him with me, and that I was on my way, I found Joe and he and I went over to Joyce house, and got the papers, I thought that Robert Joyce Husband, was still in the Hospital, I ask how was Robert doing, she said that Robert was doing find, that he was out in the streets, I said what in the streets, she said yes he was out of the Hospital.

Then Joyce said that my birthday was June the 5th. And that she had a present for me she went and got it, she gave me a pair Jim shoes black and white, from Wilson. I said thanks then, I told her what, I was thinking about doing for my birthday, and that I would let her know, so she could invite some of her girlfriends if she wanted, Joyce said ok let her know, then she saw Joe in my truck she wave to him, then I said tell Robert hi for me, she said that she would do that, then she said that Robert had lost so much weight, I said o yes that is a good thing, she said hum, hum it is that he was down small like me, I said like me, she said hum, hum, I said tell Robert to keep it up, then Joe and I left.

On the way back I took a look at the tax papers refund, it was dated for April the 24th I, said Joe like I said she must have lost those tax forms, because it was not like my cousin to, have me waiting on her to do my tax return, she do them all the time she must have Misplace them, because they are dated for today date, she Just did them now, I have to send a copy of them off, to catch up with the rent rebate, so I did that.

Now I didn't get a call from Miss Queen that day, to take her to the store. The next day Queen she call me, to let me know that she was not going to, take a chance to walk around the store, that she didn't think that she was strong enough, I said ok she know more about herself, then I or anyone else know, so when she get ready she know that I will be with her, she said that she know that, I was in the computer, she said ok that she would see me or talk to me later, I said ok that, later I will be outside, she said ok.

Now before Miss Elizabeth Johnson, my other friend Lady she had ask me, that one day she had something to take over to her son house, and go over to another place and bring something back, to her house and that she would give me some gas money, I said to her to let me know, she said ok. Now on that Friday the 27th she wanted to move the things, to her son house and bring something back to her house, she gave me the gas money then she said, about 6:pm her son was coming to help me, I said to her just call me.

At 6:pm Elizabeth didn't call, but later on she call me that her son he was ready, I said ok on my way I, got my dolly and went to the building where she live, I had already park my truck there early, she was at the door to let me in, I meet her son and he and I got the entertainment center, and put it on the truck I tied it down on the truck, so it would not fall of and took it over to his house, and went about four to five more blocks, and pick up another entertainment center, and brought it back to Elizabeth apartment, and took it in there for her, after it all was inside I move my truck back to, where I park and went and took the dolly back in my apartment, and watch tv until I got sleepy.

On April the 30th was the last day, to send off for your rent rebate, so I hope that they get my tax return, with the rebate form. Later that evening after 7:pm. Miss Queen, my neighbor Joanne and I was sitting outside talking, then Theron he was coming through the gate, Miss Queen she said David who is that, I said it was Theron then I started messing with him, like he and I do when we see each other, it don't mean anything but in fun, about my other half of my heart, he was taking her someplace, I said to Theron what was he trying to do, take my woman from me he and I start laughing, and he left.

Then I was thinking about Jackie, I ask Joanne, what was wrong with Jackie, Joanne ask what! I said that she don't come out and sit anymore, Joanne she said first that it was a woman thing, then she said that, she don't know maybe someone mite, have something else to do, I said to Joanne that, Jackie she haven't been to me, the same after I had cook those ox tail, and gave her some, Joanne said while looking over to Jackie apartment, she don't know. Queen she start talking about something else as to say, David leave it along peoples are funny, and you are the same all the time.

May the first it was almost the time for me, to go on Medicare after I get 65 years old, that is June the 5th they will take out from my Social Security, $93.50 a month, Joyce she sell insurance she was telling me about, a plain about any, any, any that I, want have to pay out that $93.50 from my Social Security, and about 30 days before my birthday, she could sign me up for that, I said ok that would be find because, a person work all his life and when he, get older to retire they take almost all his Social Security, for Medicare with other insurance, and that some they don't get that much Social Security money, what can a poor person do, Joyce said when it was time, she was going to sign me up.

Now when it was time for me to sign up for any, any, any plain, something happen they cut it out Joyce told me, that they had a problem with that plain, she didn't tell me what the problem was, I said to myself that the government had something to, do with that because they was losing to much money, from the Social Security money from the poor peoples, they don't have anything as it is, so now the government are going to take that $93.50, from my check every month, I don't have any other chose.

After the government sent me a letter and my Medicare card, and how much money they was taken out from my check, each month I had to sign up with another insurance co. call

David L. Marshall

Senior Dimensions along with Medicare, on May the 1ˢᵗ I call and made my appointment for, Senior Dimensions to sign up with them, I had an appointment for 11: am that Tuesday morning on the 2ⁿᵈ. Now that Thursday before, I had taken 2 pairs of shoes to the shop, to be repair and I had to pick them up, on that Tuesday morning now do I wait.

Until after my appointment was over for the, Senior Dimensions or go early and pick up my shoes at 9:am, when they open and come back, so I said that let me go now and get my shoes and come back, so that was what I did and came back home, as soon as I got back into my apartment, I got a phone call it was a representative for Senior Dimensions, her name was Tina she want to know, that she was early, and would it be ok if she could come now for the appointment, I said that it would be ok come on now, she said that she was ten minute away from me, at about ten minute she came.

She call me from the gate, I told her how to get to me then I, open the gate for her to come in to get to my apartment, I was on my porch looking out for her, then I saw her coming I wave to let her see me, she park her vehicle David the maintenance man, he was in the outside parking lot by me, he said that he would open the security door and let her in, I said thank David then I went to my apartment door, and wait for her to get to my apartment, she came in and induce herself she said that she was Tina, I said hello and that I was David Marshall, she took my hand and said nice to meet me, I look at Tina and said it was nice to meet her also, she came in I said have a seat, she did.

After she had explain the insurance to me, and I had sign it, I gave her one of my T. shirt of passing through, she look

- 526 -

at me and said thank that it was a nice shirt, then I showed her my book then she left out, and went to her vehicle and left.

After Tina left I went and got Queen and my mail, and took Queen her mail to her, then I went back home to wait on my soaps to come on, just about 12: noon my phone ring I answer it, it was Norman my other half of my heart, she needed me to take her to the post office, now I can't refuse her so I went and pick her up, and took her to the post office. After she came out from the post office, she needed to go to the store, I said now! She said yes what I have something to do, I said yes I was going to put something into the computer, she said ok then we don't have to go, I said no we was going to go now, she and I went round and around but I won, I took her to the store.

After I told her that now my whole day was shot, that she had put a damper on what I had to do, then I explain to her that, if I had something to do early, my mind was on that only and I could relate to that, but if I don't have anything else to do, the rest of that day was for me to do what every I needed to do, for myself.

So I took Norman over to the food 4 less on Las Vegas Blvd. When we got there we saw the parking lot, full with polices they had 2 Mexican guy in hand cuff, when we got into the store, one of the store worker said that, those crazy guys was trying to stick up the store, so Norman and I got what we came for and left out, and came back home.

On May the 2nd Annett call me that she wanted me to, take her to the cleaner, to put her clothes in the cleaner, so she and I did that and Annett she, wanted me to take her over to Wal* Mart before we, got back home so we did that, and she got what she needed, and we came back home. After I got back home, I got the mail for Queen and myself.

After I got back home, I took a look at my answer machine, to see if I had any messages it was not any, so I said ok that no one else need me that, I will go into the computer and work on my book, as I was working on my book, I was watching the news also, about the Mexican demonstration about their rights, to be in America what I saw was, how the polices shot rubber bullets at them, when almost it was like they did the blacks, when we was demonstration for our rights, in Alabama and other parts of the county, that didn't want the black peoples there, it was to me just a flash back in the pass.

On the 3rd Queen she had another appointment, to go and have her blood drawing, it was to be at 9:30am I took her there and came back home. After I got back and went into the apartment, I got a call it was from Annett, she was letting me know that her cloths was ready, I ask her when was she ready to go and get them, she said in the morning, I said ok at 9:am, she said yes that she would be ready.

That next day I got up and got Annett, and took her to pick up her clothes after that, she needed something from the store, I said that she can get what she needed from, the Mexican store right next door, so I waited in the truck to watch her clothes, that was on the back of the truck until she came back, after she got what she went into the store to get, and came back to my truck we came back home, I took her things into her apartment, and I took my truck and myself back home.

Now I was talking about getting myself some, diamond ear rings and putting them into my ears, I saw Miss Lee grandson Jason and I, was talking to him about it, he said that he could get some for me, I said ok then I said to Jason when he get them let me know, he said ok. Awhile later Jason call me that, he had the ear rings form me, I ask him how much did they cost, he told me and brought them to me, I paid him they was some nice diamond ear rings, I showed them to Joanne and Elsie, they said that they was pretty ear rings, then I said now that, I have to find a jewel store and put them in.

The night before the 4th Joanne she told me that she, know where to take me and put the ear rings in my ear, I said ok and after that she and I could stop, and have some breakfast, she said ok and that she had a ticket from, Arizona Charlie casino for $8.00 to play with and, $5.00 off on breakfast, I said ok at 9: am we could go, Joanne she said ok.

On the 4th of May at 9:am I got Joanne and she and I, went to mall and shopping center and, when they open first I, was kind of afraid Joanne she ask me laughing, David Marshall did she have to hold my hand, I ask the girl that was piercing my ears was it going to hurt, she kind of smile and said not too much, then she did my ears I said see Joanne it didn't hurt, Joanne laugh and said right but you thought it was going to, while she was looking at the other jewels, then we left and went to Arizona Charlie casino, for breakfast.

David L. Marshall

After Joanne and I got back home she look at me, and said David those diamond ear rings, man they look good on you and don't forget to, put the ear care antiseptic to your ears, three times a day and turn them around and around, to help keep the hole open, I said that I want for get it then I went into my apartment, after I got inside my phone ring it was my cousin Joyce, she said David open the gate, I said ok are she coming to my apartment or, she are going to stop by the lobby, Joyce said that she was coming to my apartment, I open the gate, I saw Joyce and another lady with her, I look at the lady and said man that is a good looking woman.

After Joyce and the lady got to the security door I open it, for them my eyes was on that lady, Joyce induce her to me, Joyce said David this is her coworker MYRANH, then Joyce said MYRANH this is David her cousin, I look in her eyes and said nice to meet her, then I said come on in they came into my apartment, I said have a seat they did then Joyce, said that she had to go over to building #4, to see the guy that just move there, then Joyce told me his name and ask me have I saw him, I said was he is a Mexican, that I saw the other David the maintenance man, with a new guy taken him to building #4, Joyce said that it was him then she said that, I had a problem with a Mexican, I said no they are ok with me, because no one is not ok with me if, they are not right no matter what color they are, then she wanted my phone number, to give to the guy he might needed to move something later, I gave one of my cards to give to him with my number on it.

Then I gave MYRANH one of my card for her, if one day she might want to call the number she could, it was about 12: noon when Joyce and MYRANH came, then Joyce

said that she was going to go and see her client, she left
MYRANH she was still there with me talking, I was telling
her the work that I was doing, with my book and etc. and
got one of the book and showed it to her, she look as she
was excite cause to feel interesting, because of what I was
doing, then I ask her what size of T. shirt she ware, she told
me it was a large, I gave her all three T. shirts that I have put
out, she said thank and I do believe that she love them, I
didn't give her one of my book.

After Joyce came back and I let her back in, I was in smile
and she saw it, she look at me and I said don't say anything,
she knew that I like MYRANH, I gave Joyce another shirt
with I am—just a messenger, with on it and I gave one
to give to Mike also. Then they got ready to leave, I told
MYRANH to not let it be the last time, that I see her now,
she said that it want be, then they was going out in the
hallway to the back door, I was still looking at MYRANH
with a smile on my face, she look back at me with a pretty
smile, as she was going through the door, I said o yes a
Chicago girl man she are find.

Later on in that day that find lady she was still on my mind,
then Joyce call me and said o yes that, I like her girlfriend
don't I, I said o yes that I do, she look like as she are a good
woman, but time would tell if I see her again, Joyce said
who know she might call one day, I said that I hope she do,
then Joyce had to hang up she had another call.

On may the 5th was the day of the Kentucky Derby, I was
looking to see what horses was running in the Derby, so I
could make my bet, after I found out and look at the horses
running, I checked two off to bet that day but, I was so busy

that day, I could not get to the sport book to make my bet, after the race was over I didn't win or lose any money, the horses I was going to bet, they are still running.

On the 6th I went over to Joyce house to meet some other cousin, when I was there we all was talking Robert he, was there out from the hospital, he look so good now that he has lost that weigh, he said that now he has got down to me, I said not yet but he was looking good, with what he has lost, then I had to go later on that day, I told all of them that I had to go but, that I would see them later on then I left, and went back home.

It is almost the time for my birthday party and my retirement celebration, for June the 2nd. Now Jenson and Elizabeth Johnson, they ask me, that his birthday was in May, and that he might as well join in with mind, I said that was ok, and Elizabeth she said that after June the 7th she was, going to get her husband retirement, and that she was not going to work anymore, and that would it be ok if she, celebration with me and Jenson, I said why not that before that day, we would have a meeting to see, what we was going to do and how much money, that we was going to spent for the party, they was in agreement with that, and the meeting was on may the 7th that was on a Monday, before the mailman run they was in agreement with that also, that date was lock up.

On that Monday the 7th I, was sitting out in the sitting area waiting, then Elizabeth she came outside with me, she and I was talking waiting on Jenson, later on we saw Jenson going through the exit gate, going someplace he wave and said anything else, now my mind don't fool me, I had told Joanne the day she was with me, going to put my ear rings in my ears, that his wife was going to tell him, not to have anything with us(they are white), Joanne she said well David wait until after Monday. Now Elizabeth she are white also, but she are so sweet and, she are like I am don't see color, only what are in a person heart, so she and I talk about what we was going to do, and that is what it was going to be.

After I had got Queen and my mail, I took Queen mail to her and went back home, after I got into my apartment my phone ring, it was my buddy Popeye he needed me to take him to the store, he has been sick. I said ok what time he wanted to go, he said now, I said ok that I would pull the truck by the lobby; Popeye said ok I hung up and went and started up my truck, and got him and took him to the store. After Popeye got the things that he went to get, from the store, we got back home and got his things, into his apartment I came back home, and start looking at tv.

Every night while it is so hot outside, in the daytime some can't sit out in the sitting area, because it is so hot but I, sit out there sometime because the heat help my Arthritis, some don't know it because I don't complaint about, what hurt me because what can they do to help me, they are hurting themselves because, they are always complaint, what I do is give it to God and Jesus and keep on going, with those pain. After 6:30pm Queen, Miss Blackwell, Joanne, Mr. White another man that live in here, and I with some of others sometime, they sit out with us while it get cooler, until after 8:30pm they get sleepy like, Queen and Miss Blackwell they are ready to go home, I try to keep them out with me, as long as I can, Queen she say that David is a night owl, all he do at night is chase a woman, now I could not say anything but one, was that I was not marry, if I was that I would be at home with her, other than chase another one.

Now it is time for Medicare, and have to have another insurance, to make it work and they said that I, would have to have a Primary care physicians, on the other insurance, now the sales person showed me in the book, she said that he was a good doctor to call him, I did that call the doctor on the 8th, a doctor Clark Edward, I talk to his receptionist she said that, the doctor was not taken on anymore new client, later on that day my play sister Bobby she call me, now this friend lady of mind name is Candy, she had put in for another job with the Air Port, I said that she would get it just, put it in the hand of God and Jesus, and the job was hers, Bobby she call me that Candy she had got the job, I was so glad for Candy, I said to Bobby didn't I tell you that, Candy would get that job, Bobby and I talk for a little while, then we hung up.

The next day Joanne she was fixing Norman hair, and that she didn't have enough to finish it, so Joanne she ask me would I go in the morning, and get some more hair to finish, my other half of my heart head, I said yes what time, Joanne said that she would call me, then I said about 9: am Joanne said that would be ok. Later on Annett she call me and she wanted me, to take her to the Western union, that her son had sent her some money, and she need to pick it up, I said about 3:pm that I would pick her up, Annett said that she would walk over to the sitting area about 3:pm.

Now at 3:pm my soaps was over, I went to the center and park in front of the lobby, then I saw Annett she was sitting waiting on me, she got in the truck and I took her to the Western union, while she was to get her money I got some gas.

Because the Western union was at the gas station, after Annett took care of her business, I took her back home. Later on that Evening I was on the outside, with Blackwell, Miss Lee, Queen, and Miss Russell with a couples of the others, talking Elsie she came out on her break, to smoke a cigarette, Elsie came up and spoke to everyone, and walk up to me and ask me to move over on the other table, with her, she know that I still love her and I would still, do anything for her, so I move over on the other table with Elsie.

She and I was talking about my birthday party, about what I and Miss Elizabeth was going to do, and about putting on one of our picture on the flyer, and that Mr. Jenson he had ask me, could he join in with me with my birthday party, because his was sometime in May, then I said that he didn't come to the meeting that, Elizabeth and I was talking about what, and how we was going to do for the party, and he never gave us a picture to go on the flyer, Elsie said but David he might don't have any picture, I said to my love Elsie, yes he do because I have seen one, and if any man older as he, and he don't have a picture of himself, he and his wife is a poor person not to take one.

Then I said that Elizabeth and I have set up, what we was going to do and I, we was not going to let anyone stop or slow it down, we don't well I don't need Jenson, because he don't revolve around me, Elsie said that I was right, now I listen to Elsie and I do believe, that if she ask me for advice she would hear me, no matter if she don't like or love me, that to me don't matter, only what matter to me is, what I think about her and that is the love, that I have for Elsie.

Now on the 10th, I had to go to the store and get something for myself, so what I did was call Annett, before she wanted to get herself some mangos, from the store and they didn't have any looking to good, so I told her that, I had to go and get something for myself, and did she want to go with me, Annett she said yes what time, I said about 9:am, she said that she would be ready and thanks, I said ok see her in the morning.

That next morning I got up and waited on 8:30am, then I got into my truck, and went over to Annett apartment and knock on the window, to let her know that I was on the outside, she came out, then she and I went over to the food 4 less, and got what she and I needed to get, then we came back home, I took her things into her apartment, then my truck and I came home, I went after that and got Queen and my mail, and went back home to put something into my computer, for my book passing through ll.

Now on the Saturday of the 12th, the ladies was getting ready to have a mother day dinner, and a fashion show. Before they had said to me that they need, some man to model because they need them, then they ask me to model, I said that, I would but there was something that I needed to do. On that Friday the 11th, they was sitting up the lobby for the dinner and the show, I was standing by queen porch talking to her.

EVELYN PULLUM my home girl, that went to school with me, and Miss Blackwell they was getting some chairs, from Blackwell porch, my home girl she was trying to close one of the chairs, she was having a hard time closing the chair, I was looking at her trying to close the chair, and I was still talking to Queen, then I heard Miss Blackwell she said, if EVELYN can't close the chair, then I said let me show her how to close it, then I did and said that, there was not anything a woman can do with put a man, not anything if it was then show it to me! Then I ask do they need me to take them, to the lobby for them, my home girl laugh and said that would be nice David, then I took the chairs to the lobby for them, and put them into the lobby, there was others ladies sitting in there.

After I was leaving out from the lobby, I made the same statement that I made to, Miss Blackwell and my home girl, that there was not anything a woman can do, without a man if it was then show it to me, then Miss Blackwell and EVELYN was coming to the lobby, they heard the same thing again, Miss Blackwell she said that she was walking, I said not on her own power, then I went back to where Miss Queen was at, I was telling her that there was others ladies, in the lobby why didn't they help take the chairs, Queen she look at me and laugh and said, David you are something else, I said that, I know it.

On the 12th I went over to my cousin Joyce house, and sit and talk to the other cousins, now I had something that, I need Joyce to do for me about my book account on line, and to put two pictures on the flyer for my birthday party, so Joyce she went into my account, to see how my book was doing, after that she took the pictures that I needed, to put on my birthday flyer, every time she tried to put Elizabeth picture with mind, on the flyer it was one or the other would not come out right, it would be Elizabeth was to dark and mind was to light, or mind was to dark and hers was to light, so Joyce had to make two separate flyer, to get the flyer right.

After Joyce finish with what I needed, she said to me, that my publisher was not pushing my book, after all that money I paid to publisher that book, and that I should change publishers, then she ask me could I change publisher, I said yes whenever I want to change because, it was self-publisher. Then Joyce said that there was a lady go to her church, had a publisher company, and that she was going to talk to her, I said ok give her my phone number, Joyce said that she would see the lady, on Sunday in church, I said ok, then I sit and talk for another little while, and came back home.

After I got back home and park the truck, and went into my apartment, in a little while I went on the outside, and went and talk to Queen, she was telling me about the mother day, and the fashion show, that she didn't see to many peoples going into the lobby, that live in here going to the dinner and show, I said to Miss Queen because they had to pay $5.00, peoples that live in here want something for nothing, Queen said not her! I said that, I was not talking about her but I do know, those who are like that, because if it was free, the lobby would be full of them, then I said that, I was going to go sit and smoke myself a cigarette, and go back home and put something into my computer, Queen said ok that she would see me later, I went to the sitting area.

There was a few others sitting out there, I spoke to them and sit and lit a cigarette, then I saw my still to me sweet heart

Elsie, she was coming on the outside from the lobby, she came to the sitting area on the other table, she said David sit over there where she was at, I went over to the table where she was at, she was telling me how nice the dinner, and the fashion show was, and the fun that they had, then she said that she could not stand around with them, because she had work to do, I said that is right because some would call Miss Grand, just to have something to tell, then she said that I had things to do for myself, then I told her that, I was over to my cousin house, I explain what I was doing, because to me sometime she do like me, because sometime I hear her, and I inform her of what I am doing, checking in.

On that Sunday morning about 7:am my buddy Popeye call me, that he needed to go to the grocery store, I said ok that I would be in front of the lobby, about 10 minute, Popeye said ok. Then I needed to get something from the 99cent store, while I was out to get some water, so I went and got Popeye he and I went to Albertson food store, I said now that I will see my other friend Kim, the checker she is a nice lady, I wish that she was in my life, other than just a friend I see, other than at Albertson food store.

After Popeye got what he needed from the store, and Kim had check him out from the register, Kim said thank David then Kim hug me, and kiss me close in between my mouth and the jaw, I said that, I would see Kim later then Popeye and I left out the store, I put his grocery on the truck and before, going home the 99cent store was still not open, it was too early for opening so I took Popeye home, and put his grocery into his apartment, then I look at my watch it was 8:am, I said that the 99cent store now is open so, I went back to the store and got my water and etc. and came back home.

Now, that Saturday before, I had call my sister DeLoise in Chicago, to say happy mother day, she was not at home I left a message for her, then I call my play sister Bobby Jean in Chicago, to say happy mother day to her also, she and I talk for a little while, she had something to do we hung up until later. Now after I got back home from getting my water, I was going to call my older sister in Chicago, Margieree Smith every time I tried to get through, the phone line was busy I tried 4 times, then my phone ring it was my niece Becky Wagner, she said his uncle David, I said how is my niece Becky doing, she said find, I said that, I had been trying to call her mother, that is my sister to say happy mother day to her, Becky said what happen, I said that the line was busy.

Then Becky said that she had something to do now but, after 3: pm in Chicago time all of them would, be over to mother house even with her kids also, and that I could talk to everybody then, I said ok that, I love her and that after 3: pm I would call back, she said ok uncle David she would talk to me then, she and I hung up.

On the 14th I call the doctor to cancel the appointment that, I had made to go and see the doctor for the 16th, one reason was that, I don't know why he needed me, to come and visit his office for appointment, he don't need to give me no checkup, there is not anything wrong with me, now I don't need him right now, the only way I need him is when, I have to go to a hospital, then the hospital would call him, to let him know that, one of his client is in the hospital, and what to do until the doctor can see me, if he check me who know what he might find, I don't want to know. so stay out from me, until I need him to see me in a hospital, if it come to that otherwise, I don't need but two doctors, they are God and Jesus that I believe in.

After I had call the doctor office and cancel the appointment, I was over to Queen talking to her, by her porch waiting on the mail to run, I saw David the maintenance man he was taking those chairs, from the lobby back to Miss Blackwell porch, the chairs was falling off the dolly, he was picking them up and putting them back on the dolly, I said to him David that, they use the chairs and left them, for you to have to bring them back, he smile and said, well David Marshall that he don't mind, he will give her hand that she was good to him, then Queen she said that was his job, I said no it was not.

Queen said he work for the boss lady, (talking about Miss Grand) then David he said that he work for Frank Hawking, and that Miss Grand she was over him, I said that was the truth, Queen she said well, then I started telling David, what I had to tell them about, a woman can't do anything about a man, he start laughing and said David Marshall man, you are right you tell it like it is, that one day them women are going to run me ragged, I said for what because of the truth, David said well David Marshall, some peoples can't handle the truth, Queen she said that one day, some woman was going to be behind me, and I can't stop to open the gate, they was going to get me, I said that, all I have to do is jump over her porch, and sit right beside of her, she laugh and said that I would see. Then I said well mom Queen you, she would protect me, she said yep you will see.

On the 15th Joyce cousin had a bed that they got from Ross, they needed me to take it to the new house, that they just got and they was waiting on the keys, before taken the bed over there, Joyce she call me to be over to her house, after 3:pm that they would be there, I said ok that I would be there, after 3:pm I was going over to Joyce house, she call me on my cell that they was waiting on me, I said that, I was about two blocks from her house, and that I was in heavy traffic, that I would be there, she said ok, I didn't know why did I have to, go all the way to Joyce house other then, going over to Ross house and wait until, the rest of the help get there, I got to Joyce house and park.

There was two helpers was out there, then my little cousin Mike he came out to greet me, I ask where was Joyce, he said that she was at Ross house, then Robert he came out and said hi David, I said what happen Robert and how was he doing, he said that now he has got down with me, he was ok. I said after he lost that weigh he is looking good, but not as I am then he and I start laughing, then the other lady cousin she came out from the house, and said hi David, then I said hello then I hug her, Robert he look at me and said David, I was just like a brother to him, but something keep my arms away from, we just smile and was ready to go and move the bed.

The lady and the man cousin they, got in Robert truck with him, I got in the vehicle with the other guy name Curtis Rodgers, because I was thinking that the bed was going on Robert truck, as Joyce had said before, and that they was going to bring me back to my truck, then Robert said that I need to take my truck, I got out of Curtis vehicle and got into my truck, we went over to Ross house.

After we go to Ross house I back into her drive way, and we load the bed and tv stand with the mattress on my truck, and took it over to Long mountain and Lourdes, across Decatur where they had brought a new home, it was and is so nice up in there, right at a golf course, it is so beautiful we unload the truck and put, everything into the house and sit around talking shit, Joyce she call from my Medicate book, to find a doctor for my Health plan, they all was not taken any new client, Joyce look in the front of the book and said, don't worry about it that, if I had to go into a hospital they would call, one of the Health Medical Associates, then we was ready to leave.

Because Joyce she had to go and teach her class, I said that when they leave that I was, going to follow them back because, I will get lost. So we left going out from the complex, I was following them then after we got to a red light, Joyce and Robert was beside of me, then I said that now I know where I am, then Joyce said happy birth day to her, I said happy birth day talk to her on tomorrow, then the red light change we went our separately ways, I came home and when I saw, some of my lady friends they wanted to know, where have I been all day, I said been with my cousins all evening, then they said welcome back home, I said thank you that, I didn't know that I was Miss, one of them look at me, and ask me was I crazy, that when they don't see me, they Miss me and don't for me to forget that, I said that I want.

Now Queen she needed to go to the bank, before going to her doctor appointment, to get her money to pay her rent, for the next month. So what I did was, taken Queen to the bank first and after she, taken care of her business at the bank, I took her over to Martin Luther King Blvd. Behind the bank of America for her doctor appointment, after she had finish seen the doctor, I took her back home she went into her apartment, I took her keys and went to the lobby, and got her mail and mind, took her mail to her and I went back home, and did some work in my book.

On the 17th I didn't have anything to do, all I did was watch my soaps and sit around until, after 3: pm like I always do is go outside, and sit at the area where we sit and have a cigarette, and if any other come out and sit, we talk then when one of us have something, that we have to do then they leave, and take care of their business.

Now I saw Miss William, from building #5 she was riding with another lady, Miss William she ask the lady to ask me, don't I have a truck. I said yes that I do, she wanted me to pick up something for her, from Lowe hardware, I said when, the lady said now if I could, (I was tried) I said not to day that, I was waiting on someone right now, that I could do it tomorrow, the lady ask me what time! I said about 9: am that I would be park, by her building waiting for her, she said ok then they drove through the gate.

Later on that evening I was sitting outside, at the sitting area I saw Miss William, she was in another vehicle a van, with someone else was driving, the lady who was driving said that, Miss William wanted to let me know that, she had gotten what she needed to pick up, someone else did it for her, I said that was ok then they drove through the gate, because I had things to do for myself, my doctor appointment was on the 18th.

Now the next day of the 18th after 9: am I call the doctor office and cancel the doctor and the appointment, because I don't trust doctors prognosis trying to observation of symptoms that they think, that I have.

Later on that evening Miss Blackwell, Queen and I was, sitting on the sitting area Miss Bill, she came through the gate and spoke, then she said to Miss Blackwell that, don't forget about in the morning at 10:am, Miss Blackwell she said ok, then after Miss Bill pull off, Miss Blackwell she had forgot about what Bill was talking about, because Miss Queen ask Blackwell what was that, Blackwell said she don't know, then she said o yes now she know, it was about early voting, then I said that it was for Ricki Barlow, and that I might as well go to with them, Blackwell she said why not.

Now that Saturday morning I got up, and went outside at 9:30am to wait on the bus, to take us to the early voting poll to vote, now it was also the tenant meeting that Saturday, I was not going to it anyway, it was so hot outside to wait on the bus, so Killer and I was in the lobby waiting on the bus, peoples was coming to the tenant meeting, and some was waiting on the bus to go voting, it was about 9:45am I went on the sitting area, to have a smoke another lady came out with me, them Miss Bill she came to the area.

Now I had already said to the lady, that if the bus had not got here about 15: minute after 10:am, that I was going back home and go into my computer, and forget about voting to day, she said that the bus was late, then Miss Bill said that the lady with the bus, had call her and said that the bus was on the way, that they was running kind of late, I said way late then I went back home, as soon as I got in the house, one of the guys that live down the hall, from me he knock on my door, and said that the bus was here, I said ok then I went back and got on the bus.

After the bus had taken us to vote, they was going to take us to breakfast, Joanne she ask me did I know that we was, going to have breakfast, I said no that I don't know, Bill she said no because she didn't tell me, anyway after the bus had taken us all over Vegas, we went to the wild fire Restaurant for breakfast, after we was seated the waiter gave us a menu, Joanne she said to me David didn't I take, them over here before, I said yes that I did then I said, that I didn't need no menu, I know what I want because, I come here when I go to breakfast, I order what I wanted Miss Bill said, that she was ordering what I was going to have, so she did, after then I start fluting with the waiter, her name was, is Rosemara I had her going, I gave her my card to call me, Bill, Rose, and Blackwell they didn't like it, what could they do about it, I am my own man single.

Popeye, I am a friend to him but life, well it is one sided everyone have one, God gave it to them to live it or love it, with someone else to share it with them, he might not care about me but it don't mater, it is what I think about him, before he got sick and he needed to go, to some place he needed to go, he would call me I would take him, even to this day he call me I have to take him, whenever he call me.

After Popeye got some better from being sick, he call me to take him to the store that, he feel better to walk around the store now, I took him you see he don't call me, unless he need me, I would call him to see how he was doing, so on this Sunday Popeye he didn't call me, like he used to call about 7:am to take him to the store, and my other friend Marilyn she needed me, to take her to the store, look like something said, tell Marilyn that I would call her, to see what my buddy was going to do, because if Popeye needed to go, I would take him and come back, and call Marilyn to see if she was ready to go.

About 8:30am I was ready to call Marilyn to see, if she was ready to go to the store, my phone ring it was Popeye wanted to go, and get some grocer I said ok pick him up, in front of the lobby, then I call Marilyn and told her that, after I came back taken my buddy to the store, that I would call her, Marilyn she said ok. So I went and pick Popeye up and took him to the store, after he got what he came to get, I told my girlfriend that work at Albertson that, I would see her within a half hour, that I have to bring my other lady friend back, Kim she said ok.

After I had got Popeye back home, and took his grocer into his apartment, and told him that I would talk to him later, that I had to take my other lady friend to the store now, but Marilyn she live upstairs in building two, so I went up and knock on her door, and let her know that I, would be outside waiting on her, Marilyn she said ok that she was coming, I went back and waited in my truck, Marilyn she came out, she and I went to the store, she went to get what she needed to get, I played the slots until she finish with her grocer, Kim my friend said David thank for bringing them to Albertson, and was I coming back, I said no not to day but later on in the week, I was going to bring her a flyer to her, about my birthday party, Kim she kiss me and said ok, then Marilyn and I left out and came back home, I took her grocer into her apartment, and came back home.

Now queen she had ask me to get her some change, when I
go back to the store so, I call Queen and let her know that,
I was coming over and get her money to get, the change
that she need, she said ok that she was on the porch, I got
there and got a hundred dollar bill, that Queen need change
for then I went to Wal * Mart, so I got some of the meats
that, I needed for my and Elizabeth party, and came back
and gave Queen her money, she said David you have been
going, and going all morning, I said o yes that I have but,
after I put the meat into my box, that I was going to lay
back and relax, Queen said that if I didn't have room in my
box, to put all the meat in bring the other and put it into
hers, I said ok then I went back home, and got all the meat
into my box.

On the 22nd I need to go back to Wal* Mart and get
something, I didn't want to go by myself, and Marilyn she
had said that, she needed to pick up some things else also,
so what I did was call Marilyn and ask her, did she want to
ride with me, she said yes what time, I told her that we can
leave at 9:am, she said ok that she would be ready, so I got
ready and went and pick up Marilyn, I needed to get some
gas Marilyn she wanted to give me $5.00, I said no, she said
that my truck cannot run on air.

That was when I said that, I know that but, I invited her
and to put her money back into her pocket, she said ok that
she would buy herself something sweet, when we got to the
gas station they was out of gas, I said ok that we can get
the gas on Lake Mead, going to Wal* Mart at that station
so that is what I did, we got to the store and got what we
needed, I finish before she did and waited on her, after she
finish we put our things on my truck, and came back home

she don't like me to pick up, too much things that is heavy she said David no, give her some of that, I said no go on that I got it, and that she don't want me to fuss at her, Marilyn she said no that is not what she want, she and I got her things in to her apartment, and I came back home and took mind inside, of my apartment.

Now on the 23rd I needed to go and get some cigarette, and Miss Queen she need some 2 cents stamps, because the 39 cent stamps went up to 41 cent, she need 23 more stamps to go with the 22 others 39 cent she have, now she owe me one 2 cent stamp I let her have before, so I went to the post office and got the stamps, and went to the smoke shop and got a carton of cigarette, I smoke first one full flavor and came back home. Now Queen she had said that the peoples was coming, and bring her a scooter they was with her, when I took her stamps, I said that she was busy, and that I would see her later on, she said ok, then I went back home.

Later on that day about 4:pm my baby Elsie call me, to smoke a cigarette, I said ok let me put on some shoes, then someone must have come into Elsie office, she said make it about 15 minute someone came in, I said ok that I would meet her out there, when it was time for me to meet Elsie, outside I did later Elsie came out, we all need someone to talk to, she was telling me about how peoples was, and how they talk about thing that they don't know, I said honey don't let that worry her, peoples don't have any other thing in their vocalist, to talk about and that she don't need the stress, don't worry about them, Elsie said ok then she and I went back, she went back to her office, and I went back home, with her on my mind of how much I love her, and I can't get her out of my mind as long, as I see her and sit and talk to her, how can I get her out of mi mind, man.

After 6:30pm I was going out from the hallway, going outside when I open the door, the door hit something on the other side of the door, it was my other neighbor Rose on her scooter, I look at her she didn't have anything on other a blouse, and it was not fasten all the way, and the bottom she was naked as a jay bird, after I was on the outside one of the other tenant, live in building two her porch is in view of the door, she was on her porch I ask her, did she see that, she said that she saw Rose on her scooter, I said but she was naked, then I shook my head and went on outside to the sitting area.

After I got to the sitting area Jennet she saw there, some of the things that she say, it get on my nerve but what can I say, after all she live here and she have her rights, to sit out there in the sitting area, I didn't tell her anything about what I saw, about Rose.

Later Miss Queen, and Joanne came outside, I said to Joanne what I saw about Rose, Joanne said that Rose she came to her apartment, and ask her did she have some shorts for her to put on, and she didn't have any cloths on she was naked, Queen she said sure enough, I said that is no lie when I saw her she was naked, then Lorraine she came out and sit by me talking, and looking back to the office, I guess she was waiting on Elsie, then Miss Blackwell she came out and sit, on the other side of me we all was talking, Elsie she still had not came out, Lorraine look back and said where was Elsie, I was still talking to Miss Blackwell, then I look over to the office, I saw Elsie coming outside then I saw Mr. White he was coming on his scooter, Elsie she walk over to me and said.

Come on and move over to the other table, to smoke a cigarette, she knows that I will do almost anything for her, so I move over with her.

After I move over to the table Lorraine she move over also, and ask for a cigarette, and she don't smoke, she wanted one of my cigarette I got up, mind was on the other table, I got her one Elsie said to Lorraine, that she don't smoke, I gave it to her and she was grown, then I gave Lorraine a light also.

Now that was the night was the America idol was on tv, and I don't watch it Joanne and Lorraine, they wanted me to go into the lobby and watch it, but they knew I was going to say no, so Elsie she through those eyes on me, with that sexy voice and said David, why don't you want to watch it with us, for some reason I said that, I don't watch it and look into Elsie eyes, and said ok I will watch it with her, she said yes, yes, yes come on, so I got my cigarette and went with them, and stayed until it was over and Elsie, had lock the door and was into her vehicle, and left then Joanne and I came home? She went to her apartment, and I went to mind and did whatever.

Miss Queen she is a sweet lady, to me she is like my grandmother, my mother, my sister or just a friend; I will do anything to help her. After she got her scooter she was not use to it, she tore up a dresser, she call me and explain it to me what had happen, and wanted me to fix it for her, and move something around so she could drive the scooter, in and out without tearing things up, I said that before getting the mail that, I will be over there, she said ok, so I finish with what I was doing, and went to look at the dresser.

After I got over to Miss Queen apartment, I look at the dresser she had taps all over the floor, Queen she ask me could I fix it, I said yes that what I was going do was, go back to my apartment and get what I needed to fix it, so I went back home and got some little nails, and came back and fix the dresser, then I put all the tapes back inside, and move back the table so that she could move around, without running over things, then I went and got the mail, and gave Queen hers she ask me how much that she owe me, I said for what! She said for fixing the dresser, I said that she don't have that kind of money to pay me, she smile and said ok, then I said that, I was going home and get busy, she said ok now David for me to be good, I said that I was going to be good, then I left and went back home, it was almost time for my soaps.

After 6:30pm as we always do, that evening sitting out in the sitting area, was Queen, Blackwell, Killer, Mr. White, Jennet, Mary Ann, Lorraine and I was talking, to me it seem that Lorraine she, are trying to get back on my good side, but I am the kind of a guy that, when someone is or was trying to stand in my way, to get what I want or need, and after they see that they was wrong for doing that, then they slide back under me again, as it was still ok, I don't think so.

While we all was talking Lorraine she, would start to answer or want to say something, she would look at me or touch me on my arm, as that I am going to go along with, what she was trying to say, or when I say that, later on that I was going out and have a good time, Lorraine would ask me with who or where was I going, I just look at her without saying anything, she would say that it was not her business, I would say that was right, you see I don't have to give in a count to her, where I go or do.

Then we started talking about passing through life and after death, I said that, I do believe in life after death that, one day the same life that, left the body that God put it into, now to be laid back to earth to rest, that the sole don't die it go back to God, and to me I do believe when a baby is born God, he place that sole or another sole into a newborn.

The same he did as Jesus to Mary, but instead direct to a woman he place the seed, into man to transact his seed into a woman that, she would bring the sole his creation back into the world, the only way you would know is that, a baby has been born, another life that God have place back into his world.

Then I said that life don't die it carry on because, life is God. Before I start telling my belief Miss Lee she had walk out with us, she had no commit but some they, still don't have belief in what I had said, but that is their opinion we all have one.

Every Saturday or every other Saturday it depend, I do my washing but on the 26th was a Saturday, that I was so busy trying to pre pair, for my birthday party that I didn't have the time, but that was ok and on the 28th I still had things to get, now my neighbor Rose she was in the hospital, so later on I got a call from the hospital, looking for information that I could not give, because I didn't know or had any to give to them, and there is another neighbor that just move in here, right next door to me, she told me that her name was Highland, and what I see with her, she are ok, I don't have a problem with her.

On the 29th Joanne, Mr. White, Killer, Queen, Miss Blackwell, my mother in law, Miss Louise and I was outside talking, Miss Queen her nephew they came to see her, they induce themselves to all until, one came to Jennet and tried to induce himself to her, she I guess was too good to meet or say anything to the guy, because he had extend his hand to her, she didn't want it all he said was whatever, then he sit and talk to myself and the others, Queen she had taken one of her nephew to her apartment, he had something for her, then Theron he came through the gate and park, he start talking he sell safari hats, he sold two of them to the guys, then Queen and the other nephew came back, then they was ready to leave, one had a birthday party to go to.

Then Queen she said that, her nephew had brought her some fish from Oklahoma, that they gave her a big bag of fish, and that she was going to give me some of it, I said ok, then Miss Blackwell and my mother in law they, was ready to leave and go home they left, the rest they was still out there, then Mr. White said that he wanted to give me $5.00, to help on the food for my birthday party, he went home and got $6.00 and gave it to me, I thank him, then everyone was ready to leave, so Jennet, Joanne and I came home, we live in the same building #3, we went into our own apartment.

Now I had already cook the pinto beans, with smoke ham hocks and smoke neck bones in it, and the next day I had to get some others things, so Joanne she said that, she was going to go with me, I said ok and that, before I go to bed on that Thursday night, that I was going to clean the grill, and sit it up for that Friday morning about 6:am, that I was going to start the fire to burn off the racks, so I could clean them before putting the meat on it, then I start looking at tv until going to bed, another friend of mind name Judy, she let me use her large umbrella to shade the sun, Miss Russell went with me to get the umbrella from, Judy garage they been knowing each other, for a long time.

That Thursday morning about 9:am Joanne and I, went to Wal*mart and got the rest of the things, that I needed for the party and came back, I had already taken out the chicken and, the rest of the meat from my freezer, to be thawed out and be clean and wash before, that Friday morning, so later on that Thursday night I, clean and wash the chicken and put them into, two heavy bags and put it into the refrigerator, and then I went to bed.

On that Friday of the first of June, I got up about 5:am to put the party meats on my truck, to take it to the barbecue area, so I could not have to go back and forth, from my apartment to get what I needed, hum I got up in time, so I lay in bed.

Trying to get my composer to get out of bed, to do what I needed to do that day, but I went back to sleep for a little while, then I jump up and got dress and put my truck, by the porch and got everything that I need to work with, for the barbecue.

Now I knew that it was going to be hot as hell that day, that was why I was starting cooking early, so I could finish before the hot part of the day, I put some ice on the chicken in the bag to, keep it cool until I was ready for it, I got the fire going and sit up the umbrella, and put some chicken on both grills, everybody came through the gate coming and going, wanted to know when the food was going to be ready, one ask me why was I cooking for my own birthday party, things like that.

Now it started getting hotter and hotter, but I had to do what I had to do then mom Queen, she came out and sit around with me under the umbrella, then little Joe he came out, now I had told Miss Blackwell before that, her son name is David also, his birthday was just a couples of days before of mind, that he might as well come and party with me, on my birthday and he and I could party together, she said that, she would tell him, but every time I saw her son coming over to see his mother, I would speak to him but, he never said that he got my message or not, what he was going to do.

Until I was almost finish cooking, Miss Blackwell son he came and saw me on the grill, he came to me that he was going to go, and get some ribs for me to put on the grill, but first he had to take his mother, to take care of some business and that he would be back, I said that it was going to take longer to cook ribs, other than chicken that it was too hot out there, that is why I didn't get any ribs, but he said that he was still going to get some, but that was on him he know how to barbecue, but I was almost finish.

Now after I had thought that, I was finish cooking all the hot links, hamburger, smoke sausages, hot dogs and chicken I was finish until I, was going to throughout the ice from the bag, to give the bags to the maintenance man David, he had come out there I found some more smoke sausages, I said to David the maintenance man and little Joe, man look at this I thought that, I was finish cooking now I got to put these sausages, on the grill as I was putting them on, now man it want take that long to cook them.

As the sausages was almost finish cooking, Miss Blackwell son David came back, I had start taken the umbrella up to be ready, to take them back to Judy house where I got them from, I took everything off the grill and put, everything else on my truck with the umbrella, and food ready to take it to my apartment, to later on put the barbecue sauce on the meat, to only have to warm it up the day of the party, so I could have a good time on my birthday party, I gave the ribs and the grill to Miss Blackwell son, to take care of his own I was finish, then I went back to my apartment, and put everything up so I could now relax for a little while, to take the umbrella with Miss Russell to go with me, to take them back to where they belong to, Judy house.

Later on after I had finish cutting up the chicken, and putting on the barbecue sauce to the meat that, I was going to put the sauce on because, some peoples don't like sauce on their meat, after I had finish with all I had to do, I call Elsie to see if she was hunger, and if she was that she could come and get some food, or she could send the maintenance man David, because he might want some also, she said ok that she would tell David.

Later on David he call me, and said that Elsie told him to come to my apartment, I said come on and get a plate, he said ok, then he came right away because it was almost, the

David L. Marshall

time to get off work, he fix a plate and he and I talk for a little while, because his lady she was in his van and it was hot, in the van.

That was when I said that tomorrow, we all was going to have a good time, that is why I did today what I did cook early, for tomorrow because I was going to have myself, a good time on my birthday, then David he was ready to leave after he got his plate, I said that later on, that I was going outside for a little while, he said ok and that he would see me tomorrow, because that Elsie she was going to be off, I said ok see him then.

Later after I was getting ready to go outside, the phone ring I answer it was Elsie, she said that she was coming over to my apartment, I said ok then she hung up the phone, I waited on her to get here. After she got to my apartment, I said to her with that big smile of mind, come on in, she came to get herself a plate, I said to her get whatever she want, and how much she want, then she said that she was off on Saturday, for my birthday and at 12noon that day, she was going to heat up the food and get ready for, my birthday party to start so she could party with me, with in her heart. I said that she would be with me, as she are all the time in my heart, then she was ready to leave because, it was almost the time for her get off work, I wanted to say how much that, I love her but she already know that, then she left and I went outside, I saw her when she left.

After I had Joyce to make up the flayer for Elizabeth and my party, it read like this, A birthday and retirement celebration for, David L. Marshall, the Author of "Passing Through" and the retirement for Elizabeth Johnson, come and celebrate with us, Saturday June the 2nd 2007 at 12: noon, that the party is outside in the picnic area, come eat all you want, dance all you can, have as much fun as life allows.

Now every time I or someone else, have something with food or etc. peoples, they would just come to get a plate and take it back home, with them without sitting and eat have fun, with the others that be there, so what I did was to stop that was, Joyce put on footnote on the bottom of the flayer, A $3.00 donation is required for carry out only, that means fix a plate and go back home. I had Joyce to put a picture of Elizabeth and I on the flayer, to see what she and I look like.

On that Saturday morning I got up, took the food and put it into the oven to be heated up, then I took my shower, after all the food was heated up, I took it to the lobby and put it in one of the office, with the maintenance man David and I, then I came back home to relax until, I got dress and went back, and found David, his last name is my middle name," Lee" David Lee, he and I put the food on the table, with the help of Miss Russell and the others, that fix the side dish that they fix and brought, after the man that wanted to take pictures, for the party we was waiting on Elizabeth to come, down stairs she was late coming down, there is another lady live up stairs by Elizabeth.

Her name is Mary Ann I said to her, what is Elizabeth doing up stairs putting on a gown, we are not getting marry, Mary Ann ask me did I want her to go up and see, I said yes that the man are going to take the picture, we are waiting on her the time now is 12:30pm, we was to start at 12: noon she are late, so Mary Ann went up to see, what was keeping Miss Elizabeth, I said to the man to take the pictures, she will be here soon.

Later on Mary Ann came back and said, that is what she are doing putting on a gown, then she said that Elizabeth was coming but, the picture taker guy has left, then Elizabeth she came down she was looking good, I said that the man was going to take our picture, he has left then he came back, then Elizabeth and I pose for our picture, then I said to our guess that now we can fix some food, and eat and have some fun that is what we all did, I know that was what I did have myself some fun.

Now my God daughter Blessing she was there also, and I was entertaining my guess, Joanne my little sister she was playing the music, mom Queen, mom Evelyn, and a host of friends was there, another lady name Mary I was talking to her, she had her arm around me just talking, Blessing she came up to where Mary and I was, and took Mary hand off me, now Blessing she is not two years old yet, she told Mary to take her hand off her God father, Mary she look at Blessing and said that she was sorry, Blessing said to Mary and everyone else, who put there arm, hand or dance with me, that her God father belong to her, now I was kind of shock but that is the way, a daughter are about their father, they are if they love him protected to him, then another lady that just move in building 2, a white lady name is also Mary Ann, she and I went outside to smoke a cigarette.

Then a vehicle came to the gate, the driver said daddy open the gate I, look and look it was my other daughter Larissa, she said daddy open the gate that, she said that I look as,

I don't know who she was, then I recognize her, I went to and open the gate and said that, it been so long that I have seen her, then I ask Larissa where was the kids, she said they was at home that she had just left work, now in here she are no stranger.

When she got inside and park, we went into the lobby the ones that she know, I induce her to them like the new ones, like David the maintenance man and others, but the rest that remember when Larissa had, work here as the manager know her, she saw how Blessing was doing, Larissa look at Blessing and said to her, don't you know our father by now, then she said no not yet that she are to young but, one day Blessing will find out that our father is and always will be, a lady man that she better get used to that, I smile because it was true, but when I get the one, that I want it will stop, she know who she are and my daughter Larissa, she know also.

Later on Larissa said dad that she had to go back to work, that she left to come to my birthday party, she told her job that her dad was having a birthday party, and she was going to it for a little while, I said why didn't she bring them with her, Larissa she said that, she ask some of them did they wanted to come, then she said her good byes and went back to work, we was still dancing and singing, just having fun then my cousin Joyce, Robert and Mike they came, and gave me a card as lots of my guess did, mom Queen she had a good time, receiving my birthday cards and present as they came in.

At one time I was looking for my little sister Joanne, to put on a tape with a song, that I wanted to dance with a lady, Joanne she was going and it was almost 5:pm, because at 5:

David he get off work, and from 12: noon to 5:pm is long enough to have a party, so I with David and others start cleaning up the lobby, I told them to take some food home with them for later, David he was putting on a plate a little food, I said come on David put some food on that plate, he smile and said he did, I said what about his lady put some more, food for her I laugh and said, do he want me to put it on a plate for her, he smile and said that he would, I said that is lesser that I don't have to take back home.

Then Theron his radio talk was over, it is on from 1: pm to 2: pm on klav 1230am station, I had seen Sheller fixing a plate to go, I didn't know who it was for, I told Theron to don't forget to fix himself some food, and get as much he want, he said that someone had did that for him, I said who? He said someone had taken care of him, I look at Sheller, she nodded her head to me, I said ok as lone he got what he wanted.

Then after I had got the rest of the food inside, of my apartment and put on the table, I said that I was going back on the outside, and sit have a cigarette and laugh and talk with the others, that was going to sit outside, so I went outside everyone I saw.

They was telling me how good the food was, and the music was sounding good and, all the fun that they had, that made me feel so good inside because, I had fun with Miss Bill that, I can talk and have fun with her without, she are looking for something else, "you know what I am talking about" and there are some others like Miss Bill, and there are some that I can't talk to, like Miss Bill and the others, they want the beef.

Every time I see the ones that came to my birthday party, they are still talking about, the good time that they had and how good the food was, on the 3rd that Sunday morning I got up, and got ready and took my dolly, and went to the lobby to finishing cleaning up, because we didn't finish cleaning up the lobby, after the party, I told the maintenance man David, that in the morning I would be over and finish, a man is only good when he stand by his word, after we finish cleaning up the lobby, and taken the chairs back upstairs, I took my dolly back home, because I had told David Lee, smile, that I would come back and sit and talk, for a little while and smoke a cigarette, so I did that and came back home, and the rest of that day all I did was, lay around and relax.

Now another woman she are not, truthful for her word, she had wanted me to tell my guess that, on that Sunday she was going to have something, in the lobby for someone else, and that she wanted all of us to come, now she have told so many lies, to me in the pass that, I can't put no trust in her, I told her my truth, that was no I can't do that she, have told me one lie to much.

Now like I said that, all that day all I did was lay around and relax until, after 6:30pm it was so hot outside all day, after 6:30 it start to kind of cooling off some, so Jennet, Miss Queen, Miss Blackwell, Miss Lee, mom William sometime, Killer, Mr. White, Glen he come out later on, Joanne and I we all sit around talking and one of us, bring out and put some goody on the table, so we all can snack on, we alternate bringing some goody out to snack on, don't have one do it all the time, sometime when some leave and go inside, I with some others stay out until later, before going home.

On the 4th I had to take Annett to Wal* Mart to the bank to, take care of some business, then after she finish with what she had to do, I took her back home and I went back home, and got the mail as I do every day for mom Queen and I, and go back home and work on my book of my life.

Now my friend Reba with her find self, she is almost as find as my other lady friend Elsie, I had invited Reba to my birthday party, she didn't come because she had to work, and Joanne she said to me that Reba she, had to get me a present for my birthday, I said that she don't have to do that because, she already have it and all she have to do is unwrap it, Joanne said woo David Marshall, she was going to tell Reba then Joanne start laughing, Miss Queen she was looking at me smiling, as to say what are David talking about, Joanne she said that she know what I was talking about, I said that is right.

On June the 5th of my birthday, now I am 65 years older and I feel the same, as I was 64 or younger almost as the same day I was born, the only thing about me is that my body has change, that is all those days that my, our father have let me stay and live, on his earth and in his world I am bless, and I know that and I thank him for everything, that he have done for me in Passing Through his world, breathing his air, seen the sun light that he provide for me, after he had woke me up in every morning and kept me every day, that was not promise to me I thank him for that,(do you?) and he keep me safe for every second, of that day that he gave to me, some was happy some was not happy, some was with good surprising and some was not good, but that is all about life full of surprise. And I thank him for the wisdom that he gave to Jesus, and put all of him and his wisdom into me, to let it shine through me, to let others see and feel it what God has done for me, all the love that he fill my heart with, to show to others and that love is God and Jesus, and how he gave me the strength to, have to help those who can't help themselves, thank to you Jesus the son of God, the same as I.

There is so much I have to thank God and Jesus for, is for this day, when he planted me my seed into my daddy, and how he put it into my mother, and let it grow and she carry me, until it was time for me to come into God world, for me to place my feet on God soil, to walk and use what God had gave to me, to use for me, and to this day I thank to God for that, for everything that he have did for me, I am his star.

And also how my grandmother how she took me, after I was born and kept me with her, and she kept me safe and she showed me how, and she gave me the tool to take care of myself, my grandmother she showed me everything almost, that she know and gave it to me, to take care of myself, how to tilt the earth and plant and grow my food, and how to keep it from the weather not to spoil, and how to work with what God have gave to me, my grandmother taught me until, God he got ready to take her from me for himself, before she left to join God and Jesus, she put me into God and Jesus hand, and to this day they still have their arm around me, yes, I have all trust and belief in God and Jesus, they are real and Jesus is still here, he never left look close to others, and yourself.

Chapter 13

WHILE I WAS WRITING BOOK #1 I was going to call it, once a child and now a man, before I came to Vegas from Chicago, I had written 1500 pages of my book, and after I start working for Rhodes Ranch after four years, the chief of Security thought that I wanted his job, but that was not true he was insecure of his own job, because I teach him about what he didn't know, because I had been there before, he tried to set me up with a white girl but that didn't work, so he hired a loud mouth black girl to do the job for him, instead of getting read of her from the day shift, because he told me that she stayed in and out, of others peoples business, he put her on my shift, I was her Captain she lied on me as sex advance, that was a lie I told the Chief, that I didn't want what I had, now what do I need with a woman like her, they let me go, they did me a favor but later on I, found out that the Chief and the others was going also, I had things to do someone else could not do, I got read of the 1500 pages I had, and went with what I knew from my heart.

After God and Jesus gave to me something else, to write Passing Through I, change once a child to a man to Passing Through. I start writing about what my grandmother had told me, before she pass how to hunt, fish, plant into the earth for food to keep me going, living. There was something that in my pass, that I would change and some I won't change, as shooting at my brother that was wrong and, not going to school getting everything that I could, and not playing hooker now I know better, and playing with the females heart and their emotion that was wrong, I broke hearts and got mind broken also, but that was because of the things that I brought on myself.

To this day, I confess for all the Girls, woman and Ladies that I, have broken their heart to day, I want to say that I am sorry, so sorry about what I have did in my pass, to you that should not have been to you, that I did to you now, those that have broken my heart, and what they have did to me in my pass, they have to one day confess for their sin, like I said above some things I would change, and some I want, because a man or a woman.

In life you need someone or things that was good to you or for them, at that time they didn't know it until, it was gone then they wanted it back but, they can't get it back because, every time you throw something or someone away, it became someone else Treasure.

Now I know that after I found God and Jesus in my life, all my life on my birthday, if there was a party I had to do it for myself, or it would not have been done who care it was no oversight, peoples who knew it they didn't care, not even from a card, on my birthday June the 5th 07, I had my own 65th birthday party, I receive peasants and 20 birthday cards, I am putting them in for my Memories, as my little sister Joanne told me one day, that whereas I know it or not, that I was love for so many peoples old and young. I want to share my cards to you, with my Memories.

From my Insurance Company Farmers Al Greer, LUTCF—it's your birthday—the one day of the year you really can have your cake and eat it, too!

Another one from Charlotte live where I live—David has a blessed Happy Birthday, Charlotte. And there was another say, Happy, Happy, Happy Birthday Wishing you non-stop fun on your special day—from Mary Joe. There is this one say Happy Birthday—May this day be filled with all the things you enjoy most! Happy Birthday! Wishing you all the happiness in the world you deserve it, pray and love to you for many, many more Birthdays, mom Ruthie.

Another one said have a beautiful day—I hope this day brings you everything you hope for, happy birthday—Evelyn Hamilton. This one say especially for you—to son-in-law wishing you happiness the whole year through, Love Mom-in-law, smile have a happy one David. Here is another one, it show some present say shop, happy and a pair of lips with lip stick 21am-up, a diamond ring, flowers birthday a hand with a bracelet say pamper, and some more cake say indulge—dear David Best Wishes for an Absolutely Fabulous day, have a great day God bless you with love, Florence Blackwell.

This one say Celebrating your Retirement—your retirement is a perfect time to do your favorite things, remember great accomplishments and all the pride they bring—dear David it's a time for friends and family to celebrate with you and honor this achievement, you have been looking forward to.

Congratulations and may God continue to bless you, Betty lucky. This one say have a Happy Birthday—May your birthday be filled with everything that make you happy, May every day hold something wonderful for you! Happy Birthday God blesses you Dorothy.

This one say Birthday wishes for you—with many good wishes for your Birthday, and every day throughout the coming year. To David from Jennet next door—this one say also A Birthday Wish—for today, tomorrow and always happy birthday Evelyn Hamilton,—another one say Having another birthday? Well remember one thing—go on. Try to remember ONE thing, anything! You can't do it, can you? Geez, you are old! Happy Birthday from Sam and Dorothy, neighbor and friend, now this one is from my cousin, it is a champagne glass with a bottle of champagne, Congratulations, congratulations, congratulations, congratulations—It's time to celebrate your 65th birthday, from Joyce, Robert and Mike.

This one I love and know it say, with a teddy bear Happy Birthday, because you are so special—inside she wrote wishing you all that life can give not only on this day, but for the rest of your life, the other half of your heart.

This one in my life, for you, Dad my Guard Father—you have taught so much simply by the way you live your life, you have encouraged—influenced—inspired—all just by being the man, and the dad, you are. Happy birthday may God bless you and keep you always, with our love your Guard Daughter and Miss Russell.

This one is a Special Birthday Wishes, Walter There will always be warm greetings and special Wishes, too, as long as there are birthdays and peoples nice as you, happy birthday from Ed. DI Poto. This one say to a terrific friend on your birthday—dearest David please take these few words to heart—Friends are keepers of secrets and each other's heart", God bless you—your friendship is good for my heart and soul. Have your best birthday yet, from Annette L. Castro. Now this one I have to smile with, Here's a little something to help you have a good time on your birthday! It has a watch with the time 2:53pm and on the watch ban it read, time for a drink, time for drink—inside it say may all your hours be happy hours, from my sweetheart Evelyn Beals.

Now this one is from my mom, it read my birthday Wishes for you—because it is your birthday, I did like to make some very special wishes just for you, I wish you the happiness of special times spent with people you really care about—I also wish you the kinds of things we sometime take for granted-good health, peace of mind, and time to relax and enjoy life—and most of all, I wish you the special kind of happiness that comes from being loved. Happy birthday love Queen.

As I had said above in my book that I, after my birthday and I was going to be 65 years older, I went on social security at 62 early, so now that I am 65 my retirement is now effective, now I am retired, I had said that, I was going to close Passing through book number Two then, and that I was going to start book three of Passing through, now after I start book three, I might not live long enough to finish that one, because in the future we don't know, God let me finish two of books about my life, and another one is not promise if yes, it will be the grace of God, if not the one who know about me, or with me they will write the end of book three, and if I pass on this is what I want them to do for me, my last will and testament my final word, cremate my body, take my ash and put it into ceramics, and make two hands with it, why? Just do it / my father day card / because you are special / a day of relaxation, reflection, and easy contentment / you deserve all that and so much more. Happy Father's day from the other half of your heart (smile) Norman Contrell that is why, and let me be around forever in Memories, of my hand my heart and my word, from my book Passing Through this world. Close out June the 21st 07, to start book three later on.

David Lee Marshall Author,

A foot note from me to you, with the word of God and Jesus, Parent of God and Jesus Children, love your young as lone they are living, they want get younger all they are going to do is, get older and older and the Children of God and Jesus, respect your elders as I said, you want get younger, one day if you live, you are going to get old and want you, want respect also give the same to your neighbor, as you want it, D. L. M.

When you think that you have finish of what you are doing, when there was things to do, look into your heart and you will see that, there are one more thing that you have to do, listen to your heart and you will find it, on this day of June the 27th I was going to proof read, my second book but as the other things that I write about, I can't rest until God give me the go ahead, that it was finish. When now this is my opinion, someone who always trying to tell or show you, something that they have done and it didn't work with them, and they tell you that is wrong, who are they to say it was wrong, who are they to judge you, what don't work with them it might work with you, only God know you not them.

And when you hear someone always talking about religion, the system of faith and worshiping for you, watch them. Because they in there pass have did everything under the sun, now they want to tell you what to do, because they are using you to forgive their sin, that they have did to themselves, other than trusting God and Jesus they are, you should be trying to get right with not man, trust in your heart and let the light of the love, that God have put into your heart shine, when you do that others will see that light shining, from your heart where God and Jesus live, you don't have to every time you see man or woman, you see that you love them show them they will know, because you can make your mouth say anything that you want, but that don't make it be the truth.

And when God and Jesus have something, for another to tell or show you listen to them, other than trying to tell them that you don't know about, God didn't give it to you to tell or spread it, he gave it to the messenger he wanted to give, to give to you all you have to do is listen to the word, otherwise you will be lost. Keep your mouth close your mind and your heart open, in order to receive the word of God. I had to put that in my book now because, that is what God wanted me to do.

Mary you are my unforgotten love, before you pass on you said, love dies, memories live forever, I have never forgotten that, every time I see and read your valentine card, that you had given to me before you pass on, read that, I am so glad

I (she) found you (me) that if I (she) had my (her) life to live over again, next time I (she) did find you (me) sooner so I (she) could love you (me) longer, that is still in my memories today. Now Mary if today I find someone like you, and want the same thing that says those same words to me, their love will never be unforgotten, I still love you Mary.

My greater memories of love, is the pass life that I have love and not been loved, because today I found out that, the love of life is the fruit of life from God, of living.

Sometime life not all the time is sweet, kind, loving, understanding, to be desire to be love, given or receive love, with passion to be honor, with respect of others and yourself, I know everyone need one or all of those above, I know myself today need all of them, after my pass life the life that I have left behind me, I want have it no other way if I, can't have all not one, two are three above, I have to seller for all of them or leave the rest along, because I don't need the head ache, that come with part of it.

Once in my life I can say this, that I thought all of the above, it had come into my life in 05, but on 8-23-07 something happen that I see that made me think, I had to think very, very hard about it because, it was something that was going to hurt me dearly, breaking a promise, my word that I had given, the word of God and Jesus.

When God and Jesus put you on a path to trivial, you do your best to honor stay on that path, because there is a blessing on it somewhere sooner or later, stay there it is coming otherwise, if you don't stay you can Miss it, your blessing.

When someone as it be a boy or a man child, put his mother hand, heart, feeling of her life, into another man hand, to trust in him to see that his mother will be alright, while he was away that is trust and the love that he have, for his mother and another man.

There was a young man that I meet in 05, that I thought that I kind of knew his mother, he and I was talking one day after a dinner that, I had fix for him, he and I was smoking a cigarette outside, the lobby he saw where his mother was going to be working, he turn to me now I had not knew him long just meet him, he said to me man David he don't think that, he want his mother to be working in here, (I guess he saw something wrong) I then turn to him and I said.

Mike don't worry about your mother, that I will take care of her and look out for her, that made him know that he had my word, now after Mike taken my word to look out for his mother, that made me have to be marry to his mother, from my heart that he had trust me with his heart, (his mother) not on paper my word that he trust from God and Jesus.

Now I am a man and a man or a woman, should honor their word that is all they have, the word from God, if you loss that you have anything left, I gave my word a promise.

This woman that I made that promise to her son, I took her for my wife in the heart, I treated her better than some treat their wife, I loved her (not sex) treated her with respect, do and did everything to make her happy, now to this day 8-28-07 there are not anything forever, every road have to end somewhere, someplace, sometime, it didn't end because of me my word is still with me, she didn't want me doing anything else for her, I respect her word that she have someone else, to do things for her where as it be a man or a woman, long as she are happy.

You see I tried everything that I thought, that she needed or if she would say in my present, introduce formally: show: point or aim: I would try and do or get it for her, until those she devils stood in my way, and came into her life maybe it was for the best, the best for me because I had starting having strong feeling for her, I was falling in love with her, I could not walk away because of my promise, I gave my word.

Those she devils is those women that, you see I use to be that man in my pass, that would go to bed with any or every woman, that I saw now as I got older a wise man will change, a fool will never will change, they think that what is between their legs is everything, but I am looking for more than that, I am sorry.

Some don't know that there is a deference from, the love of God from the love of sex in bed, those devils that want both of them I stay away, now they know that I would do any and everything for that woman, they don't like it because it is not them, so what those devils did was they got closer to the woman, that I would do anything for her, and spoil her from me to change to their ways, the power from one woman to another woman, they can't have me why can the other woman, have it all.

David L. Marshall

Hum all my life I have wander what, could two women do together in bed, other than rubbing on each other and sucking on each other's, now if you get the right man in bed a woman, you could have it all with the beef, you see what I am talking about.

The woman that was sitting and standing beside me before, that I thought was with me carry weight, the devils tilt the scale shift away from me, it change me to another position to where, they wanted the other woman wanted they wanted her to slide, to leave me along some had said before that, they saw that the woman and I was to close that, they was going to break that up, I ask break up what!

Now after the other woman have change with me, and what she did to me the devils have won, I have move on not because I wanted to, now I can't do anything but break my promise, not me she did that for me that promise I made to her son, that was her choice not mind, so before I took it, I took it to God and Jesus, that it was not my choice it was hers, after all I am just passing through, looking for another that will love to have what the other woman above had, well now I am all along but not along, I have God and Jesus that is all I need, but thank you for reading what was in my pass life, book number one and two of passing through, book three is coming soon I hope, thank you from my heart good night or a good day. David L. Marshall.

PASSING THROUGH BOOK 2 OF TESTIMONY.
ANTOBIOGRAPHY LIFE OF DAVID L. MARSHALL

PASSING THROUGH THE MIST INTO THE FUTURE
THE EDITED BY DENEEN WAGNER

DAVID L.
MARSHALL JR.
3-31-1962
TO
OCT. 19TH 1983

UNIVERSITY OF ILL.
STEELWORKER GRIEVANCE ETC. SCHOOL CLASS. IN SPRINGFIELD ILL. LOCAL 1719

FIND ME DAVID L. MARSHALL
PRESIDENT OF LOCAL 1719 STEELWORKER
1973

UNIVERSITY OF ILL.
STELLWORKER GRIEVANCE ETC. SCHOOL CLASS. IN SPRINGFIELD, ILL. LOCAL 1719

FIND ME DAVID L. MARSHALL

PRESIDENT OF LOCAL 1719 STELLWORKER
1972

ANN THERESA MOORE=EDDIE JOE CROSBY — WANDER HILL
DAVID L. MARSHALL. MY FAMILY

HATTIE RICCO
MY COUSIN—7-14-23—3-07

DELOISE HILL   THERESA MOORE
MY SISTER   FRIEND
          DAVID
          L
    MARSHALL

RICKY   MY NEPHEW —EDDIE BROTHER

MY SISTER IN THE MIDDLER MARGET SMITH + FRIENDS | UNICE CROSBY - EDDIE CROSBY

THERESA SMITH, MY NIECE THAT PASS

MARGEITA ANN SMITH LUTER - MY NIECE THAT PASS

DAVID L. MARSHALL

MARIC CROSBY - MY BROTHER

DENNICE CROSBY - MY BROTHER

(CROSBY) EDDIE CROSBY KIDS. MY NEPHEW, AND NIECE

JOHN MARSHALL

JOHN MARSHALL +HIS FRIEND

BRIANT, MY
GRANDDAUGHTER
JOHN, CHILD.

JACKIE DAUGHTER - IN LAW AND
ONE BABY I
HAVE SEEN.
?

BRIANT/ MARSHALL

ROBINA. MARSHALL - JA'NYAA MARSHALL -
JOHN W. MARSHALL - MY GREAT GRANDKIDS
JOHN W. MARSHALL II KIDS.

MY NIECE ADDIE

AGNESS BRY

P.L.- JOHN- JACKIE - DAVID
MARSHALL- FRANK -

PRETTY PAT- PATS SISTER &
DAVID L. MARSHALL.

DAVID BROWNLEE.
KEE KEE MY DAUGHTER
EDDIE BROWNLEE, DAVID
DAD, LEASER MY FRIEND

DAVID L. MARSHALL AT
GIL'S LOUNGE 91ST AND
ASHLAND.

BEN, DRINKING ON GIL'S BAR, COW BOYS.

LOOKING OVER THE WATER, THINKING
DAVID MARSHALL

AT ONE OF MY BIRTHDAY PARTY, AT SNEAK PEAT LOUNGE.
NEXT TO GIL'S LOUNGE 9½ ASHLAND, CHICAGO, ILL.

MY BROTHER DENNICE CROSBY — PASS ON.

JACKIE CHILDS— DAVID L. MARSHALL
MY WIFE.

ANNIE AND DAVID L. MARSHALL

DAVID — JACKIE CHILDS — AMANDA

CUSSING PAT —   DAVID L. MARSHALL

ELSIE --   DAVID L MARSHALL

LITTLE JOHNNIE MARSHALL — DAVID MARSHALL III
GRAND SON OF OHIO

DAVID AND A FRIEND OF MIND

GLENDA — LARISSA — MY DAUGHTER —

DONNIA RAY PASS ON

MY GRANDSONS — JACKIE MY
DAUGHTER SONS

COCO MY FRIEND DAUGHTER AND HER KIDS

MY BROTHER CHARLES RUSSELL JR.

NATE BAND THAT PLAY BE HIND ME ON STAGE, WHEN I WAS SINGING..."HUMP" I WROTE IT.

FRED JACKIE BROTHER,

MY GRANDDAUGHTER

BLACK MAGGIE AND CANDY

DEANO AND HIS MOTHER, FROM BRENTON, ALA.

LEN McCONNICE - SCHOOL FRIEND

DEANO DAUGHTER

SOME OF MY FAMILY

NUNNIE - JACKIE SISTER SMILING

C.B. MY COUSIN - CHARLES SMITH

SUTT   –NICK– ARUGE–

BAY RUTH – BRENTON, ALA.   SMOOTH – BRENTON, ALA.

PAUL AND A FRIEND OF HIS

PEE WEE AND BETTY ANN ~ MY COUSINS

AMBUS J. HARVEY MY COUSIN AND HIS SON.
PENSACOLA, FL.

MR. CHARLES CASS ON, FROM
CHICAGO TO VEGAS.

RAC SMITH, WENT TO SCHOOL WITH ME.

PEARL AND CLIFFORD BENNETT — MY BROTHER
IN TEXAS.

DAVID, SALLY,
NICOLE, 4/21/05 CHRISSY.

I WISH SHE WAS MINE — SMILE — FROM
BREWTON, ALA.

Looking Back

Looking Back

Looking BACK

Cousins of mine from my Dad side.

Looking Back....

DAVID L. MARSHALL AT LOUISE SNELL SENIOR APARTMENTS, ON THE B.B.Q GRILL, WHAT I LOVE TO DO IS COOKING, PEOPLES HAVING FUN EVEN IF I DONT EAT, BUT I SPENT MY MONEY, HAVE FUN DONT WORRY ABOUT ME,

ELIZABETH JOHNSON AND DAVID L. MARSHALL, AT OUR BIRTHDAY PARTY — 6-5-07 — I MADE 65 YEARS OLD.

The Westside in 1942

LAS VEGAS, NV